2011 SUPPLEMENT

CASES AND MATERIALS

MW01489484

SECURITIES REGULATION

ELEVENTH EDITION

by

JOHN C. COFFEE, JR.
Adolf A. Berle Professor of Law
Columbia University School of Law

HILLARY A. SALE
Walter B. Coles Professor of Law
Washington University in Saint Louis

FOUNDATION PRESS

NEW YORK, NEW YORK

2011

© 2003, 2004 FOUNDATION PRESS
© 2005, 2007–2010 THOMSON REUTERS/FOUNDATION PRESS
© 2011 By THOMSON REUTERS/FOUNDATION PRESS
   1 New York Plaza, 34th Floor
   New York, NY 10004
   Phone Toll Free 1–877–888–1330
   Fax 646–424–5201
   foundation-press.com
Printed in the United States of America

ISBN 978–1–60930–041–8

Mat #41177318

PREFACE

In 2010, the"Dodd-Frank Wall Street Reform and Consumer Protection Act" was passed chiefly to address the problem of systemic risk and the "too-big-to-fail" financial institution. In 2011, the Act has begun to be implemented, but progress has been slow. Although the Act was often sweeping in its language, the regulatory steps to implement it have been generally modest, halting and equivocal. Both the SEC and the CFTC are behind schedule in seeking to meet the one-year-after-passage deadline on implementing regulations, and this delay is attributable in some measure to industry resistance and footdragging. In addition, some rules that have been adopted – such as SEC's rule on "proxy access" – have been challenged in court, and a decision from the D.C. Circuit on proxy access is pending.

This Supplement opens with the Conference Report to the Dodd-Frank legislation in order to provide a brief overview of the Act's intended scope. Thereafter, a brief memorandum summarizes some of the securities-related provisions, including (1) its litigation provisions; (2) its corporate governance provisions (such as "access to the proxy statement" and "say on pay"); and (3) its approach to executive compensation. Recent SEC rulemaking in this area is discussed.

The last two years have also seen the Supreme Court take an enhanced interest in securities regulation. In 2010, in <u>Free Enterprise Fund v. PCAOB</u>, it largely upheld the constitutionality of the Public Company Accounting Oversight Board (PCAOB). Plaintiffs had asserted that the statute infringed the constitutional authority of the President, because it permitted the PCAOB's commissioners to be removed only by the SEC and only "for cause." This decision proved to be largely a non-event for securities lawyers, as the Court both rejected plaintiffs' primary challenge under the Appointments Clause and granted only modest relief with respect to the constitutional violation that it did find under the removal provisions relating to the PCAOB's commissioners. Although the Court found that the "double for cause" limitation under which the President can only remove the SEC's Commissioners "for cause" and the SEC in turn can only remove the PCAOB's Commissioners "for good cause shown" effectively placed executive officers beyond the President's ability to monitor or control them, the net result was only that the Court made the PCAOB's Commissioners subject to "at will" removal (i.e., for any reason at any time) by the SEC, instead of "for cause" removal. Given the SEC's already strong controlling position over the PCAOB's budget and appointments, this change is likely to matter little. In any event, plaintiffs' attempts to enjoin the PCAOB or, more broadly, to hold Sarbanes-Oxley unconstitutional failed utterly. As a result, we have only excerpted a brief portion of that decision that explains the outcome and largely omits the full constitutional analysis.

The recent decision with the greatest practical impact is almost certainly Morrison v. National Australia Bank, in which the Supreme Court significantly redefined the exraterritorial application of the federal securities laws and largely discarded the "conduct" test developed decades ago by Second Circuit Judge Henry Friendly. (The Dodd-Frank Act spares the SEC from the impact of this decision by giving it extraterritorial jurisdiction whenever there is substantial conduct in the United States that furthered the violation – exactly the result that Morrison rejected for private litigants). In the year since that decision, a torrent of lower court case law has addressed such issues as the location of a sale and whether securities listed on U.S. exchanges are automatically covered, even if the sale occurs abroad (with all decisions to date saying no).

Similarly adopting a sweeping "bright line" test by a 5-4 margin in Janus Capital Group v. First Derivative Traders, the Court defined the "maker of a statement" for purposes of Rule 10b-5 to be "the person or entity with ultimate authority over the statement" – in effect, a "control" test that spares from liability those who may actually draft or prepare the statement.

Although Morrison and Janus Capital have sparked controversy, two Supreme Court decisions in 2011 affirmed traditional principles. In Matrixx Initiatives Inc. v. Siracusano, the Court returned (for the first time in over 20 years) to the linchpin issue of materiality and largely reaffirmed its decision in Basic, Inc. v. Levinson. In Erica P. John Fund, Inc. v. Halliburton Co., the Court resolved a conflict among the Circuits, ruling that plaintiffs did not need to demonstrate loss causation at the class certification stage.

Other recent decisions have addressed very specialized contexts. In Jones v. Harris Associates, the Court reconsidered the standard of liability under Section 36 of the Investment Company Act (but ultimately made no significant change). In Merck & Co. v. Reynolds, it clarified the running of the statute of limitations under Rule 10b-5 in a manner that significantly advantages plaintiffs (indeed, this may be the most pro-plaintiff securities law decision in recent years). We also have included the much-noted 2010 decision by U.S. District Judge Jed Rakoff that rejected the SEC's proposed settlement of its enforcement action against Bank of America, because (although a revised settlement was later approved), the decision triggered an important national debate over the effectiveness of SEC enforcement.

JOHN C. COFFEE, JR.
HILLARY A. SALE

June 17, 2011

TABLE OF CONTENTS

[The page number at which the new material appears in this Supplement is indicated in the right column; the page number of the Casebook at which we suggest the new material should be considered appears in the left column. Many of the footnotes to the cases have been omitted; those retained have not been renumbered. Parallel citations to cases and statutes have also been omitted without so indicating.]

A. Statute of Limitations

Chapter 18

Civil Liability

Chapter 20

Chapter 22

APPENDICES

App.

CASES AND MATERIALS

SECURITIES REGULATION

. . . .

Title I – Financial Stability

Title I, which establishes a specific framework for ensuring financial stability, consists of three subtitles. Subtitle A establishes a Financial Stability Oversight Council to monitor potential threats to the financial system and provide for more stringent regulation of nonbank financial companies and financial activities that the Council determines, based on consideration of risk-related factors, pose risks to financial stability. Subtitle B establishes an Office of Financial Research that supports the Council by collecting information, conducting research, and analyzing data. Subtitle C provides a specific, more stringent supervisory framework for regulating large, interconnected bank holding companies, nonbank financial companies that the Council subjects to more stringent regulation, and activities and practices that the Council determines may pose systemic threats.

Title II – Orderly Liquidation Authority

Title II establishes an orderly liquidation authority that may be used only if the Secretary of the Treasury (in consultation with the President), based on the written recommendation of two other federal regulators, agrees that doing so is necessary to mitigate serious adverse effects on financial stability in the United States. When the authority is used, the FDIC is appointed receiver and must liquidate the company in a manner that mitigates significant risks to financial stability and minimizes moral hazard. All costs of an orderly liquidation under this title are borne first by shareholders and unsecured creditors, and, if necessary, by risk-based assessments on large financial companies. Taxpayers specifically are protected from losses associated with use of this authority.

Title III – Transfer of Powers to the Comptroller of the Currency, the Corporation, and the Board of Governors

Prudential Regulator Restructuring

Title III of the conference report transfers the functions of the Office of Thrift Supervision to the Office of the Comptroller of the Currency, which will now supervise federal thrifts, to the Federal Deposit Insurance Corporation ("FDIC"), which will supervise state-chartered thrifts, and to the Federal Reserve Board, which will supervise thrift holding companies.

The conference report also protects employees affected by the regulatory streamlining by preserving pay and benefits, and protecting them from involuntary separation or relocation for a period of time. Title III requires comprehensive coordination of the integration of the agencies, and reporting to the House Financial

Services Committee and Senate Banking Committee regarding the implementation of the merger.

Federal Deposit Insurance Reforms

The title revises the FDIC's assessment base for deposit insurance, maintaining the risk-based nature of the assessment structure but transitioning to a broader assessment base for bank premiums based on total assets (minus tangible equity). The conference report also includes additional reforms that will enhance FDIC's ability to manage the Deposit Insurance Fund.

The title makes permanent the increase in deposit insurance to $250,000, and makes the increase retroactive to January 1, 2008. Full insurance of noninterest-bearing transaction accounts is also extended for an additional two years and a comparable program is authorized for credit unions.

Office of Minority and Women Inclusion

The title requires the establishment of offices of Minority and Women Inclusion by the Treasury Department, and the financial regulators, to coordinate technical assistance to minority-owned and women-owned businesses and to promote diversity in the workforce of the regulators.

Title IV: Regulation of Advisers to Hedge Funds and Others

The conference report eliminates the "private adviser" exemption in the Investment Advisers Act of 1940 ("IAA") thus registering advisers to private funds with the U.S. Securities and Exchange Commission ("SEC"). It expands the advisers' reporting requirements to the SEC as necessary or appropriate in the public interest and for the protection of investors or for the assessment of risk by the Financial Stability Oversight Council. The SEC is authorized to take into account the size, governance, and investment strategy of an adviser to the fund to determine if the fund poses a systemic risk. The conference report also amends the IAA to allow the SEC to require investment advisers to disclose the identity, investments, or affairs of their clients for purposes of systemic risk.

The report includes exemptions for certain private fund advisers. It provides an exemption from registration requirements for advisers of private funds, each with less than $150 million in assets under management, while maintaining reporting requirements as directed by the SEC; an SEC reporting requirement for advisers to venture capital funds, as defined by the SEC and otherwise exempt from the framework; and an exemption for Family Offices. The conference report raises the assets threshold for federal regulation of investment advisers from $30 million to $100 million. Those advisers who qualify to register with their home state must register with the SEC should the adviser operate in more than 15 states.

Finally, the report clarifies the SEC's authority to make rules necessary for the exercise of the powers conferred upon the SEC by the IAA. The SEC must adjust for the effects of inflation any dollar amount measures used in making determinations of the qualified client standard.

Advisers must comply with the new provisions within one year of enactment of the conference report, though the report allows advisers to register earlier with the SEC.

Title V-Insurance

Subtitle A, the Federal Insurance Office Act of 2010, creates a Federal Insurance Office (FIO) in the Treasury Department to provide the Executive Branch and the Congress with a source of information on the national insurance marketplace. FIO is not a federal regulator or supervisor of insurance. Rather, its functions include collecting information about the insurance industry; monitoring for systemic risk in the insurance industry, including serving in an advisory capacity to the Financial Stability Oversight Council; and administering the Terrorism Risk Insurance Program. Further, FIO will consult with the states regarding insurance matters of national importance and prudential insurance matters of international importance. FIO will also coordinate federal efforts and develop federal policy on prudential aspects of international insurance matters, including representing the United States in international insurance fora, and assisting the Treasury Secretary in negotiations of international insurance agreements with respect to the business of insurance or reinsurance. FIO will have a narrow and limited preemption power over state insurance measures that are inconsistent with such international insurance agreements.

The Federal Insurance Office Act of 2010 expressly provides the Secretary of the Treasury, jointly with the USTR, the authority to negotiate and enter into international insurance agreements. To assure uniform, national application of prudential measures such as reinsurance collateral requirements, the Federal Insurance Office Act provides the Director with the authority to identify and narrowly preempt state insurance measures inconsistent with a defined category of international insurance agreements.

Subtitle B, the Nonadmitted and Reinsurance Reform Act of 2010, will reform and modernize two important sectors of the commercial insurance marketplace, nonadmitted insurance (also known as 'surplus lines' insurance) and reinsurance. Specifically, the Nonadmitted and Reinsurance Reform Act of 2010 creates a uniform system for nonadmitted insurance premium tax payments based upon the home state of the policyholder, encourages the states to develop a compact or other procedural mechanism for uniform tax allocation, and establishes regulatory deference for the home state of the insured. The Act adopts uniform eligibility requirements for nonadmitted insurers as developed and promulgated by the National Association of Insurance Commissioners (NAIC) in the Nonadmitted Insurance Model Act. The Nonadmitted and Reinsurance Reform Act of 2010 will allow direct access to the nonadmitted insurance markets for certain sophisticated commercial purchasers. The Nonadmitted and Reinsurance Reform Act also streamlines the regulation of reinsurance by applying single state regulation for financial solvency and credit for reinsurance. Credit for reinsurance determinations will be controlled by the state of domicile of the ceding insurer. Reinsurance solvency regulation will be controlled by the state of domicile of the reinsurer provided such state is NAIC-accredited or has financial solvency requirements substantially similar to the requirements necessary for NAIC accreditation. Under the Act, non-domiciliary states are specifically prohibited from applying their reinsurance laws in an extra-territorial manner.

Title VI-Improvements to Regulation of Bank and Savings Association Holding Companies and Depository Institutions

Title VI improves prudential regulation of banks, saving associations, and their holding companies. The improvements include significant limitations on proprietary trading and sponsoring or investing in hedge funds or private equity funds by banking entities through the Volcker rule, better supervision of nonbank subsidiaries of holding companies, enhanced restrictions on transactions with affiliates, limits on derivatives and securities lending credit exposure, and a requirement that any company that controls an insured depository institution serve as a source of financial strength to the institution.

Title VII-Wall Street Transparency and Accountability

The conference report establishes a new regulatory framework to cover a broad range of participants and institutions in the over-the-counter derivatives market. The Commodity Futures Trading Commission ("CFTC") and the Securities and Exchange Commission ("SEC") are authorized to write rules for the swaps and security-based swaps markets, respectively. The Commissions shall consult and coordinate on rules and include the prudential regulators, to the extent possible, to assure regulatory consistency and comparability. The Commissions will register participants in the market including dealers, major participants, clearing agencies and organizations, exchanges, swap execution facilities, and trade repositories. Exemptions and exclusions from registration will apply as outlined in the report or at the discretion of the regulators. The Commissions will have enforcement authority in their jurisdictions while the prudential regulators maintain exclusive authority to enforce provisions for capital and margin for banks and branches or agencies of foreign banks.

The report provides definitions for terms used in the Commodity Exchange Act and Securities Exchange Act of 1934. The regulatory framework outlines provisions for:

- Mandatory clearing of swaps and security-based swaps for those trades that are eligible for clearing as determined by both the clearing houses and the regulators;
- Mandatory trading on an exchange or swap (or security based swap) execution facility should the transactions be cleared and a facility will accept it for trading;
- Public trade reporting of all cleared and uncleared swaps and security-based swaps;
- Regulators have authority to impose capital on dealers and major swap participants;
- Regulators have authority to impose margin requirements only on dealers and major participants for uncleared swaps, adding safeguards to the system by ensuring dealers and major swap participants have adequate financial resources to meet obligations;
- Position limits on swaps contracts that perform or affect a significant price discovery function and requirements to aggregate limits across markets; and
- Prohibitions against market manipulation.

The report includes a prohibition of federal assistance to swaps and security- based swap entities, including federal deposit insurance, access to the Federal Reserve discount window or Federal Reserve credit facility, to swaps entities in connection with their trading in swaps or securities-based swaps.

The report establishes a code of conduct for all registered swap dealers and major swap participants requiring them to disclose to the swap entity the material risks and characteristics of a swap and any conflicts of interest or material incentives. When acting as counterparties to a pension fund, endowment fund, or state or local government, dealers are to have a reasonable basis to believe that the fund or governmental entity has an independent representative advising them.

The report requires a number of studies, including studies on international swap regulation, the regulation of carbon markets, stable value contracts, and the effect of position limits on exchanges.

Title VIII – Payment, Clearing, and Settlement Supervision

Title VIII establishes a specific framework for promoting uniform risk-management standards for systemically important financial market utilities (FMUs) and systemically important payment, clearing, and settlement (PCS) activities conducted by financial institutions. The Board of Governors of the Federal Reserve System (Board), the Securities and Exchange Commission (SEC), or the Commodity Futures Trading Commission (CFTC), as appropriate, is primarily responsible for establishing and enforcing risk-management standards for FMUs and PCS activities that the Council identifies as systemically important. If the Board determines that the standards imposed by the SEC or the CFTC or the enforcement actions of such agencies are insufficient, then the Council can require the SEC or CFTC to impose additional standards or take additional enforcement actions.

Title IX-Investor Protections and Improvements to the Regulation of Securities

Subtitle A-Increasing Investor Protection establishes mechanisms to assist investors in their dealings with the SEC by creating an Office of Investor Advocate and an Ombudsman. It also creates an Investor Advisory Committee at the SEC, and clarifies the authority of the SEC to engage in investor testing. Subtitle A directs the SEC to study the standards of care applicable to broker-dealers and investment advisers giving investment advice to retail customers, and it authorizes the SEC to promulgate rules imposing a fiduciary duty on broker-dealers and investment advisers to protect retail customers. In addition, the subtitle streamlines filing procedures for self-regulatory organizations. Subtitle A also clarifies the authority of the SEC to require investor disclosures before purchase of investment products and services. Finally, the subtitle requires studies on the enhancement of investment adviser examinations, financial literacy, mutual fund advertising, conflicts of interest, improved investor access to information on investment advisers and broker-dealers, and financial planners and the use of financial designations.

Subtitle B-Increasing Regulatory Enforcement and Remedies strengthens the SEC's authority to conduct investigations, impose liability on control persons, and assess penalties for violations of the securities laws. It also makes clear that the intent standard in SEC enforcement actions for aiding and abetting is recklessness, and it requires a study regarding the issue of aiding and abetting liability in private actions. Under subtitle B, the SEC has the authority to restrict pre-dispute mandatory arbitration. The subtitle further enhances incentives and protections for whistleblowers providing information leading to successful SEC enforcement actions. Awards to whistleblowers will range from 10 percent to 30 percent of the amounts collected by the SEC in actions where the SEC obtained monetary sanctions exceeding $1 million. The subtitle also works to protect the confidentiality of whistleblowers.

The subtitle further enhances the ability of the SEC to ban violators from all parts of the securities industry, disqualifies felons and other bad actors from using the Regulation D offering exemption, and provides for the equal treatment of self-regulatory organization (SRO) rules. It streamlines SRO rule filing procedures by requiring the SEC to complete the process of reviewing and taking action on proposed SRO rules within specified time frames. The subtitle enhances the ability of the SEC to issue subpoenas, bring cases against individuals, and share information with other authorities. It also updates the law governing the Securities Investor Protection Corporation (SIPC). These reforms include increasing the minimum assessments on SIPC members; raising penalties for fraud; and establishing civil and criminal penalties against any person who misrepresents membership in SIPC. Subtitle B gives the SEC authority to enhance public reporting of aggregate information on short selling, prohibits manipulative short sales, and requires notification to customers that they may choose not to allow their securities to be used in connection with short sales. The subtitle further establishes procedures to notify investors about missing securities, and it requires the SEC to complete investigations and examinations within certain time frames, subject to exceptions for complex cases. Finally, the subtitle requires a study regarding the issue of aiding and abetting liability in private actions for securities fraud.

Subtitle C- Improvement to the Regulation of Credit Rating Agencies gives broader powers to the SEC to regulate nationally recognized statistical rating organizations ("NRSROs"). A new Office of Credit Ratings ("Office") is required to examine NRSROs at least once a year and make key findings public. The Office will write new rules, including requiring NRSROs to (1) set up internal controls over the process for determining credit ratings; (2) establish an independent board of directors; (3) make greater disclosures to the public and investors; and (4) develop universal ratings across asset classes and types of issuer. The report also gives the Office the authority to deregister an NRSRO for providing bad ratings over time. New professional standards are established that require ratings analysts to pass qualifying exams and have continuing education.

The report includes provisions to address conflicts of interest. It prohibits compliance officers from working on ratings, methodologies, or sales and prevents other employees from both marketing ratings services and performing the ratings of securities. The subtitle includes on additional conflict of interest mitigation including a new requirement for NRSROs to conduct a one-year look-back review when an NRSRO employee goes to work for an obligor or underwriter of a security or money market instrument subject to a rating by that NRSRO; and report to the SEC when certain employees of the NRSRO go to work for an entity that the NRSRO has rated in the previous twelve months. The SEC shall make such reports publicly available.

To reduce the reliance on ratings, the report amends several statutes to remove references to credit ratings, credit rating agencies and NRSROs. The subtitle includes a requirement that all Federal agencies review their regulations, policies and practices that reference credit ratings, credit rating agencies, and NRSROs. After identifying where the agency relies on or makes these references, the agencies shall modify their regulations by striking these references and substituting a standard of creditworthiness to be established by the agencies.

New provisions address information gathering. NRSROs must consider information in their ratings that comes to their attention from a source other than the organizations being rated, if they find it credible. In addition, the subtitle includes an elimination of the credit rating agency exemption from Regulation Fair Disclosure, commonly known as Reg FD.

The report also addresses liability measures for the NRSRO. The report allows investors to bring private rights of action against credit rating agencies for a knowing or reckless failure to conduct a reasonable investigation of the facts or to obtain analysis from an independent source. The report also nullifies Rule 436(g) which provides an exemption for credit ratings provided by NRSROs from being considered a part of the registration statement prepared or certified by a person under the "expert liability" regime of Section 7 and Section 11 of the Securities Act of 1933. The subtitle requires all references to "furnish" be replaced with the word "file" in existing law. Information that is "furnished" to the SEC is subject to a lower standard of accuracy and liability than information "filed" with the SEC.

The report also directs the SEC to establish a system that prohibits issuers of structured finance from selecting the NRSRO that will provide the initial credit rating. The system would mandate that initial rating assignments for structured finance securities be made on a random or semi-random basis, unless the SEC determines, after study, that an alternative system of assigning ratings would better protect investors and serve the public interest.

Subtitle D-Improvements to Asset-Backed Securitization Process requires securitizers to retain an economic interest in a material portion of the credit risk for any asset that securitizers transfer, sell, or convey to a third party. Risk retention requirements and exemptions will be determined by regulators, which will include setting risk retention requirements for different asset classes that are securitized and allocating risk retention obligations between securitizers and originators. An exemption is provided for qualified residential mortgages, as defined by the regulators, but which can be no broader than the definition of qualified mortgage in Title XIV. Regulators may tailor risk retention requirements as appropriate to the structure of collateralized debt obligations and other complex asset-backed securities. Subtitle D also requires enhanced disclosure by issuers of asset-backed securities, including data related to the underlying loans or assets. Express exemptions are provided for the Farm Credit System and any residential, multi-family, or health care facility mortgage loan asset or securitization which is insured or guaranteed by the United States or an agency of the United States. Regulators also are required to issue total or partial exemptions from risk retention and disclosure requirements for municipal securities and for securitizations of assets issued or guaranteed by federal agencies, as long as the exemption is in the public interest and for the protection of investors.

Subtitle E: Accountability and Executive Compensation is designed to address shareholder rights and executive compensation practices. In this subtitle, Congress provides shareholders in a public company with a vote on executive compensation and additional disclosures involving compensation practices. Under the conference report, at least every three years shareholders can cast an advisory vote to approve the compensation of executives and, where appropriate, golden parachutes for executives. Also under this subtitle, (i) board committees that set compensation policy will consist only of directors who are independent; (ii) companies will tell shareholders about the relationship between the executive compensation the company paid and the company's financial performance; (iii) companies will be required to have a policy to recover money erroneously paid to executives based on financials that later have to be restated due to an accounting error; and (iv) companies will be required to disclose in the annual proxy statement whether employees or members of the board may hedge or offset any decrease in the market value of equity securities granted. This subtitle also requires federal financial regulators to monitor incentive-based payment arrangements of federally regulated financial institutions larger than $1 billion and prohibit incentive-based payment arrangements that the regulators determine jointly could threaten financial institutions' safety and soundness or could have serious adverse effects on economic conditions or financial stability. Finally, subtitle E prohibits brokers who are not beneficial owners of a security from voting through company proxies unless the beneficial owner has instructed the broker to vote on the owner's behalf.

Subtitle F- Improvements to the Management of the Securities and Exchange Commission requires several reports designed to assess SEC performance and provide recommendations for improvements. These involve assessment of the management of the SEC related to internal supervisory controls, personnel management, financial controls, and oversight of national securities associations. Subtitle F also creates a suggestion program for SEC employees and requires the Divisions of Trading and Markets and Investment Management to have examiners on their staffs. It requires the SEC to hire a consultant to study the SEC's operations and determine whether there is a need for comprehensive reform. Finally, Subtitle F requires the GAO to study issues surrounding employees who leave the SEC to work in the securities industry.

Subtitle G- Strengthening Corporate Governance authorizes the SEC to write rules allowing shareholders to nominate candidates for an issuer's board of directors, and to have such candidates listed on the issuer's own proxy materials. In writing such rules, the SEC must consider the burden on small issuers, and may issue exemptions from proxy access rules. Issuers must also disclose why the issuer has chosen to have a single person, or different individuals, serve as CEO and Chairman of the board of the company.

Subtitle H- Municipal Securities requires the registration of municipal financial advisors and subjects them to rules to be promulgated by the Municipal Securities

Rulemaking Board (MSRB), which will be enforced by the SEC. An Office of Municipal Securities is created within the SEC. The MSRB will be reconstituted, so that a majority of members are independent of the municipal securities industry. Municipal advisors will have a fiduciary duty to municipal entities. Subtitle H calls for studies of municipal securities markets, and ways to increase disclosure to investors. It also provides a certain source of funding for the Government Accounting Standards Board.

Subtitle I-Public Company Accounting Oversight Board, Portfolio Margining, and Other Matters subtitle I allows the Public Company Accounting Oversight Board (PCAOB) to examine the auditors of broker-dealers. It further authorizes the PCAOB to share information with foreign authorities. The conference report also authorizes portfolio margining for accounts that hold both securities and futures. In response to problems related to securities borrowing and lending, the conference report requires more transparency. It also raises the dollar threshold that triggers a full "material loss review" by federal banking regulators' inspectors general. Subtitle I improves the coordination, activities, flexibility, and accountability of inspectors general at Federal financial agencies. Subtitle I also exempts small issuers (those with less than $75,000,000 in market capitalization) from the external audit of internal controls requirements of Sarbanes-Oxley Section 404(b), and requires studies on the impact of such an exemption and the exemption for mid-sized companies. The subtitle also creates an exemption for certain annuities from federal securities regulation. Further, it makes numerous technical and conforming changes to Federal securities laws.

Subtitle J: Securities and Exchange Commission Match Funding maintains the role of the Appropriations Committees in setting the Securities and Exchange Commission's annual budgets on and after FY2012. Transaction fee receipts would be treated as offsetting collections equal to the amount of the appropriation. Any excess collections would go to the Treasury as general revenue and not offset any current or future appropriations. Subtitle J sets annual registration fee targets that will produce $5 billion of revenues over ten years that will go to the Treasury general fund. It also requires SEC's budget to be submitted to Congress concurrent with the earliest submission to the Office of Management and Budget and submitted unaltered by the President; builds in flexibility for multi-year budget authority and unanticipated needs; and authorizes graduated funding level increases for the SEC for FYs 2011-2015.

Title X-Bureau of Consumer Financial Protection

Title X establishes the Bureau of Consumer Financial Protection (Bureau), which will be an independent bureau within the Federal Reserve System. It will be run by a Director who is Presidentially appointed and Senate confirmed. The Bureau will have the authority and accountability to ensure that existing consumer protection laws and regulations are comprehensive, fair, and vigorously enforced.

The Bureau will have authority to issue rules applicable to all financial institutions, including depository institutions that offer financial products and services to consumers. It will also have authority to issue rules under existing consumer banking statutes, including the Truth in Lending Act, the Equal Credit Opportunity Act, and the Real Estate Settlement Procedures Act. Furthermore, the Bureau will have authority to regulate unfair, deceptive and abusive practices and consumer products that it identifies (UDAP authority). The Bureau also may issue regulations relating to disclosures about consumer financial products and services.

Title X also establishes the Bureau as the federal agency with examination and enforcement authority over very large banks and nonbank financial institutions for compliance with the consumer protection laws. The prudential regulators will retain this authority for insured depository institutions and credit unions with assets of $10 billion or less. Exclusions from supervision and enforcement are provided for nonfinancial companies, including merchants, retailers, attorneys, accountants, and real estate brokers, that finance the purchase of their non-financial consumer products and services under certain conditions and where the nonfinancial company is not significantly engaged in such financing. There is also an exclusion from the authority of the Bureau for automobile dealers, for which the Federal Reserve Board will continue to write regulations under the enumerated federal consumer laws, to be enforced by the Federal Trade Commission (FTC). The FTC will also be able to write rules proscribing unfair or deceptive acts or practices with regard to auto dealers under the procedures set out under the Administrative Procedures Act.

The conference report also revises the standard the OCC will use to preempt state consumer protection laws. It codifies the standard in the 1996 Supreme Court case *Barnett Bank of Marion County, N.A. v. Nelson* to allow for the preemption of State consumer financial laws that prevent or significantly interfere with national banks' exercise of their powers. State Attorneys General also are given authority to enforce the UDAP and other authorities of the Bureau against banks and savings associations.

To address consumer protection and fair lending matters, Title X establishes the Office of Fair Lending and Equal Opportunity within the Bureau. This Office will oversee the enforcement of federal laws intended to ensure fair, equitable and nondiscriminatory access to credit for individuals and communities, including the Equal Credit Opportunity Act (ECOA) and Home Mortgage Disclosure Act (HMDA). The Office will promote coordination of fair lending enforcement efforts with other federal agencies and State regulators, as appropriate, to provide consistent, efficient and effective enforcement of federal fair lending laws.

Note on Litigation, Corporate Governance and Executive Compensation Provisions of Dodd-Frank

(a) <u>Litigation and Enforcement</u>: The SEC gains several new powers under the Dodd-Frank Act: First, Section 20(c) of the Securities Exchange Act is amended so that the SEC can sue aiders and abetters of securities law violations based on a "recklessness" standard (rather than a higher "knowing" standard). In addition, the Commission is empowered to similarly sue aiders and abetters under the Securities Act of 1933 and the Investment Company Act. Next, the SEC's authority to bring "cease and desist" proceedings and impose monetary penalties was expanded by provisions that enable the Commission to impose monetary penalties on any person who violates any provision, rule or regulation under the federal securities laws and who was a "cause of the violation" (whereas previously this "cease and desist" authority was limited to registered entities). Perhaps more importantly, in light of the Supreme Court's decision in <u>Morrison v. National Australia Bank</u>, the Commission's extraterritorial jurisdiction was clarified by provisions amending Section 22 of the Securities Act, Section 27 of the Securities Exchange Act, and Section 214 of the Investment Advisers Act, in each case to expressly authorize the SEC or the "United States" (i.e., the Department of Justice in criminal cases), but not private litigants, to bring an action where the violation involved:

"(1) conduct within the United States that constitutes significant steps in furtherance of the violation, even if the securities transaction occurs outside the United States and involves only foreign investors; or

"(2) conduct occurring outside the United States that has a foreseeable substantial effect with in the United States.".

As a further means of discovering securities law violations, Section 922 of the Dodd Frank Act added a new Section 21F to the Securities Exchange Act to protect and incentivize whistleblowers, including by mandating bounties to be paid to them of between 10% and 30% (as the SEC determines) of the monetary damages in any successful enforcement action brought by the SEC based on information they "voluntarily" supply. This 10% minimum could often result in payments well in excess of $10 million or more based on the scale of recent SEC enforcement settlements and may produce much more active assistance (or at least many more allegations) from whistleblowers. The SEC has already adopted new rules to implement the provisions of new Section 21F. See Securities Exchange Act Release No. 34-64545 (May 10, 2011). Under these rules, the Commission must generally pay awards to eligible whistleblowers who "voluntarily" provide original information to the Commission that leads to a successful SEC enforcement action (or certain related actions). The most controversial issue in promulgating these rules was whether the whistleblower should be required to first provide the information to the corporation's internal compliance staff. In the final rule, the SEC declined to mandate such prior internal reporting (which arguably might expose the whistleblower to retaliation), but did try to encourage internal reporting by indicating that larger bounties would be presumptively awarded where such prior internal reporting occurred.

As an additional deterrent to executive misconduct, the Dodd-Frank Act adds a new Section 10D ("Recovery of Erroneously Awarded Compensation Policy") to the Securities Exchange Act, which requires mandatory "clawbacks" of executive compensation in the event of "an accounting restatement due to the material noncompliance of the issuer with any financial reporting requirement under the securities laws." In such event, the issuer is to recover from any current or former "executive officer" who received incentive-based compensation during the 3-year period preceding "the date on which the issuer is required to prepare an accounting restatement." Thus, if the issuer announces a restatement reducing its earnings from $10 per share to $4 per share, it must determine

what incentive compensation it would have paid for the lesser $4 per share earnings and recover the

excess. This provision is far broader than an earlier provision in the Sarbanes-Oxley Act because it

applies to all current and former executive officers, has a three-year window, and does not require

any finding of "misconduct" (as Sarbanes-Oxley did). Still, no new procedural mechanism has been

created to enforce it.

The ability of private litigants to bring suit under the securities laws was enhanced by one

potentially significant provision that will govern suits against credit rating agencies. Section 933(a)

("State of Mind in Private Actions") of the Dodd-Frank Act amended Section 15E(m) of the

Securities Exchange Act to read as follows:

"(m) ACCOUNTABILITY.—

"(1) IN GENERAL.—The enforcement and penalty provisions of this title shall apply to statements made by a credit rating agency in the same manner and to the same extent as such provisions apply to statements made by a registered public accounting firm or a securities analyst under the securities laws, and such statements shall not be deemed forward-looking statements for the purposes of section 21E.

"(2) RULEMAKING.—The Commission shall issue such rules as may be necessary to carry out this subsection.".

Then, Section 933(b) of the Act amended Section 21D(b)(2) of the Securities Exchange Act to

provide the following in the case of actions brought against credit rating agencies:

"(B) EXCEPTION.—In the case of an action for money damages brought against a credit rating agency or a controlling person under this title, it shall be sufficient, for purposes of pleading any required state of mind in relation to such action, that the complaint state with particularity facts giving rise to a strong inference that the credit rating agency knowingly or recklessly failed—

"(i) to conduct a reasonable investigation of the rated security with respect to the factual elements relied upon by its own methodology for evaluating credit risk; or "(ii) to obtain reasonable verification of such factual elements (which verification may be based on a sampling technique that does not amount to an audit) from other sources that the credit rating agency considered to be competent and that were independent of the issuer and underwriter.".

The combined impact of these two provisions is to change the pleading rule on a motion to dismiss an action against a rating agency, but not to change the liability standard under Rule 10b-5, either at trial or on a motion for summary judgment. Thus, at these later stages, evidence of scienter will still be required, but the plaintiff can survive the motion to dismiss (and thus obtain discovery under the PSLRA) if it can allege with particularity the failure to conduct adequate factual verification. The intent of this provision was less to impose high liability on the rating agencies than to create a strong incentive for rating agencies to conduct due diligence or require the receipt of a due diligence report from competent and independent third parties.

(b) Corporate Governance Provisions: The Dodd-Frank Act also addresses a number of long-standing corporate governance issues. First, Section 971 ("Proxy Access") adds a new Section 14(a)(2) to the Securities Exchange Act that authorizes the SEC to adopt rules permitting shareholders under certain conditions to make nominations for director on the corporation's own proxy statement. In Securities Act Release No. 33-9136 (September 16, 2010), the SEC adopted Rule 14a-11, which requires that holders of not less than 3% of the corporation's voting power (who must also have each held their shares for not less than three years) join in the nomination. As contemplated, the rule would enable a low cost procedure for the nomination of directors, but the SEC's rules will only authorize its use for a small number of minority directors (and never for a full scale control contest). In addition, the 3% nomination limitation may as a practical matter exempt the largest Fortune 500 companies, and the three year holding period may preclude hedge funds (who could potentially acquire 3% of many companies) from making nominations. In any event, the rule has been stayed pending the outcome of litigation brought by The Business Roundtable (and others) in the D.C. Circuit to invalidate the rule, on the ground that the SEC failed to adequately balance the costs and benefits of its proposed rule.

The Dodd-Frank Act also adopted a limited "say on pay" provision which will give shareholders an advisory, non-binding vote on executive compensation. A new Section 14A is added to the Securities Exchange Act to provide for such a shareholder vote (which is modeled after a similar British procedure). However, under a last minute compromise, this vote must occur not less than every third year (depending on whether shareholders vote to require the vote to be held on a 1, 2, or 3 year basis). Given the high number of "say on pay" votes in 2011, the role of the proxy advisor is becoming increasingly important, as few institutional investors are prepared to make hundreds of voting decisions on an individualzed basis and so defer to the advice of their proxy advisor.

The Act also displaces state corporate law by adding a new Section 10C to the Securities Exchange Act that mandates "independence" on the part of both (1) members of the compensation committees of listed companies, and (2) any compensation consultants hired by them. The committee is also given special federal powers to hire and fire such consultants, but the board remains free to make its own judgments about, and disregard the committee's views on, executive compensation. The term "independence" is delegated to the stock exchanges to define, within parameters set by Section 10C.

(c) Executive Compensation: The Dodd-Frank Act did not stop with governance reforms in attempting to curb excessive executive compensation. Section 956 of Dodd-Frank requires a "covered financial institution" to disclose to its respective regulator "the structure of all incentive-based compensation" paid to officers, directors and employees in order to enable the regulator to prohibit excessive incentive-based compensation "that could lead to material financial loss to the covered financial institution." The obvious challenge posed by Section 956's broad language was how to identify those persons whose behavior could inflict "material financial loss" on their institutions.

The principal financial regulators (including the SEC) responded in unison to this challenge in April, 2011 with a joint set of rules. See Securities Exchange Act Release No. 34-64140 (April 14, 2011). In the case of "covered financial institutions" (meaning basically any financial institution with total consolidated assets of $1 billion or more), these rules require an annual report that "describes the structure of the covered financial institution's incentive based compensation arrangements . . . that is sufficient to allow an assessment of whether the structure or features of those arrangements provide or are likely to provide covered persons with excessive compensation, fees, or benefits to covered persons or could lead to material financial loss to the covered financial person." This language is rather general and abstract, and no specific data was required. For example, it might have been useful to know how many employees at a firm received bonuses of over $1 million in the prior year (even if none were identified by name). Instead, the required general description of "structure" may largely produce only boilerplate from securities lawyers skilled at covering the waterfront in opaque prose.

In the case of financial institutions with over $50 billion in total consolidated assets, more was required by the joint rules. In the case of such "too big to fail" institutions, the same regulation requires a description of "incentive-based compensation policies and procedures" for two categories of persons: (1) executive officers, and (2) such "other covered persons who the board of directors, or a committee thereof, of the covered financial institution has identified and determined . . .

individually have the ability to expose the covered financial institution to possible losses that are

substantial in relation to the covered institution's size, capital or overall risk tolerance."

Even in these cases, however, the rules still delegate to each covered financial institution the

determination of who (beyond executive officers) could expose it to "substantial" loss. This

delegation is significant because only the covered persons so identified (and executive officers)

become subject to additional substantive requirements. In the case of the executive officers of these

financial institutions, the proposed rules require deferral of at least 50% of the annual incentive-

based compensation awarded for a period of not less than three years. See Proposed Section

248.205(b)(3). However, in the case of those other persons specifically identified by the board (or

committee) of the covered financial institution as being capable of exposing the institution to

"substantial loss," no deferral was required; instead, the board or committee must only approve the

incentive-based compensation arrangements for such persons and further determine "that the

arrangement . . . effectively balances the financial rewards to the covered person and the range and

time horizon of risks associated with the covered persons activities, employing appropriate methods

for ensuring risk sensitivity, such as deferral of payments . . ." In short, the only requirement for

even those persons identified by the firm as being capable of causing it "substantial losses" is that

the board or committee think seriously about deferral or some other means of ensuring "risk

sensitivity."

Why have financial regulators, in common, pulled their punches by (1) requiring little

specific data, (2) allowing the firms to alone decide who can cause them significant loss, and (3) not

even requiring deferral of bonuses by the persons so identified? The most logical answer is that regulators knew that a more sweeping rule might provoke significant employee defections, as "star" traders moved from investment banks to less regulated trading firms. Realistically, the non-executive officer most likely to be able to cause a substantial loss to a "covered financial institution" is a trader who is authorized to trade on a large position basis. Such traders have in recent memory caused staggering losses to some financial institutions (including Barings and Societe Generale). Although it is likely that most covered firms will report some employees who can cause it substantial losses, the number so reported may be far below the number that would be disclosed if more objective criteria were used. Underreporting the number of such persons both makes the firm appear safer in general and spares the board (or committee) the obligation to engage in a specific assessment of whether adequate risk sensitivity has been structured into the identified person's incentive compensation.

Special disclosures are also required in the proxy statement about executive pay and its relationship to the corporation's stock performance, as is disclosure about why the corporation does or does not separate the offices of the CEO and board chairman.

(d) Miscellaneous. Finally, the SEC is instructed to study and potentially adopt rules with respect to several topics, the most important of which are: (1) the validity of mandatory pre-dispute arbitration provisions in brokerage agreements (the SEC could bar such provisions or, more likely, revise existing arbitration procedures with the goal of creating a fairer remedy for customers); and (2) a common fiduciary duty standard for brokers and investment advisers (brokers today are not generally subject to such a fiduciary standard, while investment advisers are). No action has yet been taken by the SEC on these latter provisions.

Free Enterprise Fund v. Public Company Accounting Oversight Board

Supreme Court of the United States (2010)

130 S. Ct. 3138, 177 L. Ed. 2d 706

■ CHIEF JUSTICE ROBERTS delivered the opinion of the Court.

Our Constitution divided the "powers of the new Federal Government into three defined categories, Legislative, Executive, and Judicial." *INS v. Chadha, 462 U.S. 919, 951 (1983).* Article II vests "[t]he executive Power . . . in a President of the United States of America," who must "take Care that the Laws be faithfully executed." Art. II, § 1, cl. 1; *id.,* § 3. In light of "[t]he impossibility that one man should be able to perform all the great business of the State," the Constitution provides for executive officers to "assist the supreme Magistrate in discharging the duties of his trust." 30 Writings of George Washington 334 (J. Fitzpatrick ed. 1939).

Since 1789, the Constitution has been understood to empower the President to keep these officers accountable -- by removing them from office, if necessary. See generally *Myers v. United States, 272 U.S. 52 (1926).* This Court has determined, however, that this authority is not without limit. In *Humphrey's Executor v. United States, 295 U.S. 602 (1935),* we held that Congress can, under certain circumstances, create independent agencies run by principal officers appointed by the President, whom the President may not remove at will but only for good cause. Likewise, in *United States v. Perkins, 116 U.S. 483 (1886),* and *Morrison v. Olson, 487 U.S. 654 (1988),* the Court sustained similar restrictions on the power of principal executive officers -- themselves responsible to the President -- to remove their own inferiors. The parties do not ask us to reexamine any of these precedents, and we do not do so.

We are asked, however, to consider a new situation not yet encountered by the Court. The question is whether these separate layers of protection may be combined. May the President be restricted in his ability to remove a principal officer, who is in turn restricted in his ability to remove an inferior officer, even though that inferior officer determines the policy and enforces the laws of the United States?

We hold that such multilevel protection from removal is contrary to Article II's vesting of the executive power in the President. The President cannot "take Care that the Laws be faithfully executed" if he cannot oversee the faithfulness of the officers who execute them. Here the President cannot remove an officer who enjoys more than one level of good-cause protection, even if the President determines that the officer is neglecting his duties or discharging them improperly. That judgment is instead committed to another officer, who may or may not agree with the President's determination, and whom the President cannot remove simply because that officer disagrees with him. This contravenes the President's "constitutional obligation to ensure the faithful execution of the laws." *Id., at 693.*

I

A

After a series of celebrated accounting debacles, Congress enacted the Sarbanes-Oxley Act of 2002 (or Act), 116 Stat. 745. Among other measures, the Act introduced tighter regulation of the accounting industry under a new Public Company Accounting Oversight Board. The Board is composed of five members, appointed to staggered 5-year terms by the Securities and Exchange Commission. It was modeled on private self-regulatory organizations in the securities industry -- such as the New York Stock Exchange -- that investigate and discipline their own members subject to Commission oversight. Congress created the Board as a private "nonprofit corporation," and Board members and employees are not considered Government "officer[s] or employee[s]" for statutory purposes. *15 U.S.C. §§ 7211(a), (b)*. The Board can thus recruit its members and employees from the private sector by paying salaries far above the standard Government pay scale. See *§§ 7211(f)(4), 7219*.[1]

Unlike the self-regulatory organizations, however, the Board is a Government-created, Government-appointed entity, with expansive powers to govern an entire industry. Every accounting firm -- both foreign and domestic -- that participates in auditing public companies under the securities laws must register with the Board, pay it an annual fee, and comply with its rules and oversight. *§§ 7211(a), 7212(a), (f), 7213, 7216(a)(1)*. The Board is charged with enforcing the Sarbanes-Oxley Act, the securities laws, the Commission's rules, its own rules, and professional accounting standards. *§§ 7215(b)(1), (c)(4)*. To this end, the Board may regulate every detail of an accounting firm's practice, including hiring and professional development, promotion, supervision of audit work, the acceptance of new business and the continuation of old, internal inspection procedures, professional ethics rules, and "such other requirements as the Board may prescribe." *§ 7213(a)(2)(B)*.

The Board promulgates auditing and ethics standards, performs routine inspections of all accounting firms, demands documents and testimony, and initiates formal investigations and disciplinary proceedings. §§ 7213-7215 (2006 ed. and Supp. II). The willful violation of any Board rule is treated as a willful violation of the Securities Exchange Act of 1934, 48 Stat. 881, *15 U.S.C. § 78a et seq.* -- a federal crime punishable by up to 20 years' imprisonment or $ 25 million in fines ($ 5 million for a natural person). *§§ 78ff(a), 7202(b)(1)* (2006 ed.). And the Board itself can issue severe sanctions in its disciplinary proceedings, up to and including the permanent revocation of a firm's registration, a permanent ban on a person's associating with any registered firm, and money penalties of $ 15 million ($ 750,000 for a natural person). *§ 7215(c)(4)*. Despite the provisions specifying that Board members are not Government officials for statutory purposes, the parties agree that the Board is "part of the Government" for constitutional purposes, *Lebron v. National Railroad Passenger Corporation, 513 U.S. 374, 397 (1995)*, and that its members are "'Officers of the United States'" who "exercis[e] significant authority pursuant to the laws of the United States," *Buckley v. Valeo, 424 U.S. 1, 125-126 (1976) (per curiam)* (quoting Art. II, § 2, cl. 2); cf. Brief for Petitioners 9, n. 1; Brief for United States 29, n. 8.

---

[1] The current salary for the Chairman is $ 673,000. Other Board members receive $ 547,000. Brief for Petitioners 3.

The Act places the Board under the SEC's oversight, particularly with respect to the issuance of rules or the imposition of sanctions (both of which are subject to Commission approval and alteration). *§§ 7217(b)-(c)*. But the individual members of the Board -- like the officers and directors of the self-regulatory organizations -- are substantially insulated from the Commission's control. The Commission cannot remove Board members at will, but only "for good cause shown," "in accordance with" certain procedures. *§ 7211(e)(6)*.

Those procedures require a Commission finding, "on the record" and "after notice and opportunity for a hearing," that the Board member

> "(A) has willfully violated any provision of th[e] Act, the rules of the Board, or the securities laws;

> "(B) has willfully abused the authority of that member; or

> "(C) without reasonable justification or excuse, has failed to enforce compliance with any such provision or rule, or any professional standard by any registered public accounting firm or any associated person thereof." *§ 7217(d)(3)*.

Removal of a Board member requires a formal Commission order and is subject to judicial review. See *5 U.S.C. §§ 554(a), 556(a), 557(a), (c)(B)*; *15 U.S.C. § 78y(a)(1)*. Similar procedures govern the Commission's removal of officers and directors of the private self-regulatory organizations. See *§ 78s(h)(4)*. The parties agree that the Commissioners cannot themselves be removed by the President except under the *Humphrey's Executor* standard of "inefficiency, neglect of duty, or malfeasance in office," *295 U.S., at 620* (internal quotation marks omitted); see Brief for Petitioners 31; Brief for United States 43; Brief for Respondent Public Company Accounting Oversight Board 31 (hereinafter PCAOB Brief); Tr. of Oral Arg. 47, and we decide the case with that understanding.

. . . .

IV

Petitioners' complaint argued that the Board's "freedom from Presidential oversight and control" rendered it "and all power and authority exercised by it" in violation of the Constitution. App. 46. We reject such a broad holding. Instead, we agree with the Government that the unconstitutional tenure provisions are severable from the remainder of the statute.

"Generally speaking, when confronting a constitutional flaw in a statute, we try to limit the solution to the problem," severing any "problematic portions while leaving the remainder intact." *Ayotte v. Planned Parenthood of Northern New Eng., 546 U.S. 320, 328-329 (2006)*. Because "[t]he unconstitutionality of a part of an Act does not necessarily defeat or affect the validity of its remaining provisions," *Champlin Refining Co. v. Corporation Comm'n of Okla., 286 U.S. 210, 234 (1932)*, the "normal rule" is "that partial, rather than facial, invalidation is the required course," *Brockett v. Spokane Arcades, Inc., 472 U.S. 491, 504 (1985)*. Putting to one side petitioners' *Appointments Clause* challenges (addressed below), the existence of the Board does not violate the separation of powers, but the substantive removal restrictions imposed by §§ 7211(e)(6) and 7217(d)(3) do. Under the traditional default rule, removal is incident to the power of appointment. See, *e.g.*, *Sampson v. Murray, 415 U.S. 61, 70, n. 17 (1974)*; *Myers, 272 U.S., at 119*; *Ex parte Hennen*, 13 Pet., at 259-260. Concluding that the removal restrictions are invalid leaves the Board removable by the Commission at will, and leaves the President separated from Board members by only a single level of good-cause tenure. The Commission is then fully responsible for the Board's actions, which are no less subject than the Commission's own functions to Presidential oversight.

The Sarbanes-Oxley Act remains "'fully operative as a law'" with these tenure restrictions excised. *New York, 505 U.S., at 186* (quoting *Alaska Airlines, Inc. v. Brock, 480 U.S. 678, 684 (1987))*. We therefore must sustain its remaining provisions "[u]nless it is evident that the Legislature would not have enacted those provisions . . . independently of that which is [invalid]." *Ibid.* (internal quotation marks omitted). Though this inquiry can sometimes be "elusive," *Chadha, 462 U.S., at 932*, the answer here seems clear: The remaining provisions are not "incapable of functioning independently," *Alaska Airlines, 480 U.S., at 684*, and nothing in the statute's text or historical context makes it "evident" that Congress, faced with the limitations imposed by the Constitution, would have preferred no Board at all to a Board whose members are removable at will. *Ibid.*; see also *Ayotte, supra, at 330*.

It is true that the language providing for good-cause removal is only one of a number of statutory provisions that, working together, produce a constitutional violation. In theory, perhaps, the Court might blue-pencil a sufficient number of the Board's responsibilities so that its members would no longer be "Officers of the United States." Or we could restrict the Board's enforcement powers, so that it would be a purely recommendatory panel. Or the Board members could in future be made removable by the President, for good cause or at will. But such editorial freedom -- far more extensive than our holding today -- belongs to the Legislature, not the Judiciary. Congress of course remains free to pursue any of these options going forward.

V

Petitioners raise three more challenges to the Board under the *Appointments Clause*. None has merit.

First, petitioners argue that Board members are principal officers requiring Presidential appointment with the Senate's advice and consent. We held in *Edmond v. United States, 520 U.S. 651, 662-663 (1997)*, that "[w]hether one is an 'inferior' officer depends on whether he has a superior," and that "'inferior officers' are officers whose work is directed and supervised at some level" by other officers appointed by the President with the Senate's consent. In particular, we noted that "[t]he power to remove officers" at will and without cause "is a powerful tool for control" of an inferior. *Id., at 664*. As explained above, the statutory restrictions on the Commission's power to remove Board members are unconstitutional and void. Given that the Commission is properly viewed, under the Constitution, as possessing the power to remove Board members at will, and given the Commission's other oversight authority, we have no hesitation in concluding that under *Edmond* the Board members are inferior officers whose appointment Congress may permissibly vest in a "Hea[d] of Departmen[t]."

But, petitioners argue, the Commission is not a "Departmen[t]" like the "Executive departments" (*e.g.,* State, Treasury, Defense) listed in *5 U.S.C. § 101.* In *Freytag, 501 U.S., at 887, n. 4,* we specifically reserved the question whether a "principal agenc[y], such as . . . the Securities and Exchange Commission," is a "Departmen[t]" under the *Appointments Clause.* Four Justices, however, would have concluded that the Commission is indeed such a "Departmen[t]," see *id., at 918* (SCALIA, J., concurring in part and concurring in judgment), because it is a "free-standing, self-contained entity in the Executive Branch," *id., at 915.*

Respondents urge us to adopt this reasoning as to those entities not addressed by our opinion in *Freytag,* see Brief for United States 37-39; PCAOB Brief 30-33, and we do. Respondents' reading of the *Appointments Clause* is consistent with the common, near-contemporary definition of a "department" as a "separate allotment or part of business; a distinct province, in which a class of duties are allotted to a particular person." 1 N. Webster, American Dictionary of the English Language (1828) (def. 2) (1995 facsimile ed.). It is also consistent with the early practice of Congress, which in 1792 authorized the Postmaster General to appoint "an assistant, and deputy postmasters, at all places where such shall be found necessary," § 3, 1 Stat. 234 -- thus treating him as the "Hea[d] of [a] Departmen[t]" without the title of Secretary or any role in the President's Cabinet. And it is consistent with our prior cases, which have never invalidated an appointment made by the head of such an establishment. See *Freytag, supra, at 917*; cf. *Burnap v. United States, 252 U.S. 512, 515 (1920); United States v. Germaine, 99 U.S. 508, 511 (1879).* Because the Commission is a freestanding component of the Executive Branch, not subordinate to or contained within any other such component, it constitutes a "Departmen[t]" for the purposes of the *Appointments Clause.*

But petitioners are not done yet. They argue that the full Commission cannot constitutionally appoint Board members, because only the Chairman of the Commission is the Commission's "Hea[d]." The Commission's powers, however, are generally vested in the Commissioners jointly, not the Chairman alone. See, *e.g., 15 U.S.C. §§ 77s, 77t, 78u, 78w.* The Commissioners do not report to the Chairman, who exercises administrative and executive functions subject to the full Commission's policies. See Reorg. Plan No. 10 of 1950, § 1(b)(1), 64 Stat. 1265. The Chairman is also appointed from among the Commissioners by the President alone, *id.,* § 3, at 1266, which means that he cannot be regarded as "the head of an agency" for purposes of the Reorganization Act. See *5 U.S.C. § 904.* (The Commission as a whole, on the other hand, does meet the requirements of the Act, including its provision that "the head of an agency [may] be an individual or a commission or board with more than one member.")

As a constitutional matter, we see no reason why a multimember body may not be the "Hea[d]" of a "Departmen[t]" that it governs. The *Appointments Clause* necessarily contemplates collective appointments by the "Courts of Law," Art. II, § 2, cl. 2, and each House of Congress, too, appoints its officers collectively, see Art. I, § 2, cl. 5; *id.,* § 3, cl. 5. Petitioners argue that the Framers vested the nomination of principal officers in the President to avoid the perceived evils of collective appointments, but they reveal no similar concern with respect to inferior officers, whose appointments may be vested elsewhere, including in multimember bodies. Practice has also sanctioned the appointment of inferior officers by multimember agencies. See *Freytag, supra, at 918* (SCALIA, J., concurring in part and concurring in judgment); see also Classification Act of 1923, ch. 265, § 2, 42 Stat. 1488 (defining "the head of the department" to mean "the officer *or group of officers* . . . who are not subordinate or responsible to any other officer of the department" (emphasis added)); *37 Op. Atty. Gen. 227, 231 (1933)* (endorsing collective appointment by the Civil Service Commission). We conclude that the Board members have been validly appointed by the full Commission.

In light of the foregoing, petitioners are not entitled to broad injunctive relief against the Board's continued operations. But they are entitled to declaratory relief sufficient to ensure that the reporting requirements and auditing standards to which they are subject will be enforced only by a constitutional agency accountable to the Executive. See *Bowsher, 478 U.S., at 727, n. 5* (concluding that a separation of powers violation may create a "here-and-now" injury that can be remedied by a court (internal quotation marks omitted)).

* * *

The Constitution that makes the President accountable to the people for executing the laws also gives him the power to do so. That power includes, as a general matter, the authority to remove those who assist him in carrying out his duties. Without such power, the President could not be held fully accountable for discharging his own responsibilities; the buck would stop somewhere else. Such diffusion of authority "would greatly diminish the intended and necessary responsibility of the chief magistrate himself." The Federalist No. 70, at 478.

While we have sustained in certain cases limits on the President's removal power, the Act before us imposes a new type of restriction -- two levels of protection from removal for those who nonetheless exercise significant executive power. Congress cannot limit the President's authority in this way.

The judgment of the United States Court of Appeals for the District of Columbia Circuit is affirmed in part and reversed in part, and the case is remanded for further proceedings consistent with this opinion.

It is so ordered.

Matrixx Initiatives, Inc. v. Siracusano

Supreme Court of the United States, 2011

131 S. Ct. 1309, 179 L. Ed. 2d 398

■ JUSTICE SOTOMAYOR delivered the opinion of the Court.

This case presents the question whether a plaintiff can state a claim for securities fraud under § 10(b) of the Securities Exchange Act of 1934, and Securities and Exchange Commission (SEC) *Rule 10b-5*, based on a pharmaceutical company's failure to disclose reports of adverse events associated with a product if the reports do not disclose a statistically significant number of adverse events. Respondents, plaintiffs in a securities fraud class action, allege that petitioners, Matrixx Initiatives, Inc., and three of its executives (collectively Matrixx), failed to disclose reports of a possible link between its leading product, a cold remedy, and loss of smell, rendering statements made by Matrixx misleading. Matrixx contends that respondents' complaint does not adequately allege that Matrixx made a material representation or omission or that it acted with scienter because the complaint does not allege that Matrixx knew of a statistically significant number of adverse events requiring disclosure. We conclude that the materiality of adverse event reports cannot be reduced to a bright-line rule. Although in many cases reasonable investors would not consider reports of adverse events to be material information, respondents have alleged facts plausibly suggesting that reasonable investors would have viewed these particular reports as material. Respondents have also alleged facts "giving rise to a strong inference" that Matrixx "acted with the required state of mind." *15 U.S.C. A. § 78u-4(b)(2)(A)*. We therefore hold, in agreement with the Court of Appeals for the Ninth Circuit, that respondents have stated a claim under *§ 10(b)* and *Rule 10b-5*.

I

A

Through a wholly owned subsidiary, Matrixx develops, manufactures, and markets over-the-counter pharmaceutical products. Its core brand of products is called Zicam. All of the products sold under the name Zicam are used to treat the common cold and associated symptoms. At the time of the events in question, one of Matrixx's products was Zicam Cold Remedy, which came in several forms including nasal spray and gel. The active ingredient in Zicam Cold Remedy was zinc gluconate. Respondents allege that Zicam Cold Remedy accounted for approximately 70 percent of Matrixx's sales.

Respondents initiated this securities fraud class action against Matrixx on behalf of individuals who purchased Matrixx securities between October 22, 2003, and February 6, 2004. The action principally arises out of statements that Matrixx made during the class period relating to revenues and product safety. Respondents claim that Matrixx's statements were misleading in light of reports that Matrixx had received, but did not disclose, about consumers who had lost their sense of smell (a condition called anosmia) after using Zicam Cold Remedy. Respondents' consolidated amended complaint alleges the following facts, which the courts below properly assumed to be true. See *Ashcroft v. Iqbal, 556 U.S. ___, ___, 129 S. Ct. 1937, 173 L. Ed. 2d 868 (2009)* (slip op., at 14).

In 1999, Dr. Alan Hirsch, neurological director of the Smell & Taste Treatment and Research Foundation, Ltd., called Matrixx's customer service line after discovering a possible link between Zicam nasal gel and a loss of smell "in a cluster of his patients." App. 67a-68a. Dr. Hirsch told a Matrixx employee that "previous studies had demonstrated that intranasal application of zinc could be problematic." *Id.*, at 68a. He also told the employee about at least one of his patients who did not have a cold and who developed anosmia after using Zicam.

In September 2002, Timothy Clarot, Matrixx's vice president for research and development, called Miriam Linschoten, Ph.D., at the University of Colorado Health Sciences Center after receiving a complaint from a person Linschoten was treating who had lost her sense of smell after using Zicam. Clarot informed Linschoten that Matrixx had received similar complaints from other customers. Linschoten drew Clarot's attention to "previous studies linking zinc sulfate to loss of smell." *Ibid.* Clarot gave her the impression that he had not heard of the studies. She asked Clarot whether Matrixx had done any studies of its own; he responded that it had not but that it had hired a consultant to review the product. Soon thereafter, Linschoten sent Clarot abstracts of the studies she had mentioned. Research from the 1930's and 1980's had confirmed "[z]inc's toxicity." *Id.*, at 69a. Clarot called Linschoten to ask whether she would be willing to participate in animal studies that Matrixx was planning, but she declined because her focus was human research.

By September 2003, one of Linschoten's colleagues at the University of Colorado, Dr. Bruce Jafek, had observed 10 patients suffering from anosmia after Zicam use. Linschoten and Jafek planned to present their findings at a meeting of the American Rhinologic Society in a poster presentation entitled "Zicam tm Induced Anosmia." *Ibid.* (internal quotation marks omitted). The American Rhinologic Society posted their abstract in advance of the meeting. The presentation described in detail a 55-year-old man with previously normal taste and smell who experienced severe burning in his nose, followed immediately by a loss of smell, after using Zicam. It also reported 10 other Zicam users with similar symptoms.

Matrixx learned of the doctors' planned presentation. Clarot sent a letter to Dr. Jafek warning him that he did not have permission to use Matrixx's name or the names of its products. Dr. Jafek deleted the references to Zicam in the poster before presenting it to the American Rhinologic Society.

The following month, two plaintiffs commenced a product liability lawsuit against Matrixx alleging that Zicam had damaged their sense of smell. By the end of the class period on February 6, 2004, nine plaintiffs had filed four lawsuits.

Respondents allege that Matrixx made a series of public statements that were misleading in light of the foregoing information. In October 2003, after they had learned of Dr. Jafek's study and after Dr. Jafek had presented his findings to the American Rhinologic Society, Matrixx stated that Zicam was "'poised for growth in the upcoming cough and cold season'" and that the company had "'very strong momentum.'" *Id.*, at 72a-74a. Matrixx further expressed its expectation that revenues would "'be up in excess of 50% and that earnings, per share for the full year [would] be in the 25 to 30 cent range.'" *Id.*, at 74a. In January 2004, Matrixx raised its revenue guidance, predicting an increase in revenues of 80 percent and earnings per share in the 33-to-38-cent range.

In its Form 10-Q filed with the SEC in November 2003, Zicam warned of the potential "'material adverse effect'" that could result from product liability claims, "'whether or not proven to be valid.'" *Id.*, at 75a-76a. It stated that product liability actions could materially affect Matrixx's "'product branding and goodwill,'" leading to reduced customer acceptance. *Id.*, at 76a. It did not disclose, however, that two plaintiffs had already sued Matrixx for allegedly causing them to lose their sense of smell.

On January 30, 2004, Dow Jones Newswires reported that the Food and Drug Administration (FDA) was "'looking into complaints that an over-the-counter common-cold medicine manufactured by a unit of Matrixx Initiatives, Inc. (MTXX) may be causing some users to lose their sense of smell'" in light of at least three product liability lawsuits. *Id.*, at 79a-80a. Matrixx's stock fell from $ 13.55 to $ 11.97 per share after the report. In response, on February 2, Matrixx issued a press release that stated:

> "All Zicam products are manufactured and marketed according to FDA guidelines for homeopathic medicine. Our primary concern is the health and safety of our customers and the distribution of factual information about our products. Matrixx believes statements alleging that intranasal Zicam products caused anosmia (loss of smell) are completely unfounded and misleading.
>
> "In no clinical trial of intranasal zinc gluconate gel products has there been a single report of lost or diminished olfactory function (sense of smell). Rather, the safety and efficacy of zinc gluconate for the treatment of symptoms related to the common cold have been well established in two double-blind, placebo-controlled, randomized clinical trials. In fact, in neither study were there any reports of anosmia related to the use of this compound. The overall incidence of adverse events associated with zinc gluconate was extremely low, with no statistically significant difference between the adverse event rates for the treated and placebo subsets.
>
> "A multitude of environmental and biologic influences are known to affect the sense of smell. Chief among them is the common cold. As a result, the population most likely to use cold remedy products is already at increased risk of developing anosmia. Other common causes of olfactory dysfunction include age, nasal and sinus infections, head trauma, anatomical obstructions, and environmental irritants." *Id.*, at 77a-78a (internal quotation marks omitted).

The day after Matrixx issued this press release, its stock price bounced back to $ 13.40 per share.

On February 6, 2004, the end of the class period, Good Morning America, a nationally broadcast morning news program, highlighted Dr. Jafek's findings. (The complaint does not allege that Matrixx learned of the news story before its broadcast.) The program reported that Dr. Jafek had discovered more than a dozen patients suffering from anosmia after using Zicam. It also noted that four lawsuits had been filed against Matrixx. The price of Matrixx stock plummeted to $ 9.94 per share that same day. Zicam again issued a press release largely repeating its February 2 statement.

On February 19, 2004, Matrixx filed a Form 8-K with the SEC stating that it had "'convened a two-day meeting of physicians and scientists to review current information on smell disorders'" in response to Dr. Jafek's presentation. *Id.*, at 82a. According to the Form 8-K, "'In the opinion of the panel, there is insufficient scientific evidence at this time to determine if zinc gluconate, when used as recommended, affects a person's ability to smell.'" *Ibid.* A few weeks later, a reporter quoted Matrixx as stating that it would begin conducting "'animal and human studies to further characterize these post-marketing complaints.'" *Id.*, at 84a.

On the basis of these allegations, respondents claimed that Matrixx violated *§ 10(b)* of the Securities Ex change Act and SEC *Rule 10b-5* by making untrue statements of fact and failing to disclose material facts necessary to make the statements not misleading in an effort to maintain artificially high prices for Matrixx securities.

B

Matrixx moved to dismiss respondents' complaint, arguing that they had failed to plead the elements of a material misstatement or omission and scienter. The District Court granted the motion to dismiss. Relying on *In re Carter-Wallace, Inc., Securities Litigation, 220 F.3d 36 (CA2 2000)*, it held that respondents had not alleged a "statistically significant correlation between the use of Zicam and anosmia so as to make failure to public[ly] disclose complaints and the University of Colorado study a material omission." App. to Pet. for Cert. 50a. The District Court similarly agreed that respondents had not stated with particularity facts giving rise to a strong inference of scienter. See *15 U.S.C. A. § 78u-4(b)(2)(A) (Feb. 2011 Supp.)*. It noted that the complaint failed to allege that Matrixx disbelieved its statements about Zicam's safety or that any of the defendants profited or attempted to profit from Matrixx's public statements. App. to Pet. for Cert. 52a.

The Court of Appeals reversed. *585 F.3d 1167 (CA9 2009)*. Noting that "'[t]he determination [of materiality] requires delicate assessments of the inferences a "reasonable shareholder" would draw from a given set of facts and the significance of those inferences to him,'" *id., at 1178* (quoting *Basic Inc. v. Levinson, 485 U.S. 224, 236, 108 S. Ct. 978, 99 L. Ed. 2d 194 (1988)*; some internal quotation marks omitted; alterations in original), the Court of Appeals held that the District Court had erred in requiring an allegation of statistical significance to establish materiality. It concluded, to the contrary, that the complaint adequately alleged "information regarding the possible link between Zicam and anosmia" that would have been significant to a reasonable investor. *585 F.3d at 1179, 1180*. Turning to scienter, the Court of Appeals concluded that "[w]ithholding reports of adverse effects of and lawsuits concerning the product responsible for the company's remarkable sales increase is 'an extreme departure from the standards of ordinary care,'" giving rise to a strong inference of scienter. *Id., at 1183*.

We granted certiorari, *560 U.S. ___, 130 S. Ct. 3411, 177 L. Ed. 2d 323 (2010)*, and we now affirm.

II

Section 10(b) of the Securities Exchange Act makes it unlawful for any person to "use or employ, in connection with the purchase or sale of any security . . . any manipulative or deceptive device or contrivance in contravention of such rules and regulations as the Commission may prescribe as necessary or appropriate in the public interest or for the protection of investors." *15 U.S.C. § 78j(b)*. SEC *Rule 10b-5* implements this provision by making it unlawful to, among other things, "make any untrue statement of a material fact or to omit to state a material fact necessary in order to make the statements made, in the light of the circumstances under which they were made, not misleading." *17 CFR § 240.10b-5(b)*. We have implied a private cause of action from the text and purpose of *§ 10(b)*. See *Tellabs, Inc. v. Makor Issues & Rights, Ltd., 551 U.S. 308, 318, 127 S. Ct. 2499, 168 L. Ed. 2d 179 (2007)*.

To prevail on their claim that Matrixx made material misrepresentations or omissions in violation of *§ 10(b)* and *Rule 10b-5*, respondents must prove "(1) a material misrepresentation or omission by the defendant; (2) scienter; (3) a connection between the misrepresentation or omission and the purchase or sale of a security; (4) reliance upon the misrepresentation or omission; (5) economic loss; and (6) loss causation." *Stoneridge Investment Partners, LLC v. Scientific-Atlanta, Inc., 552 U.S. 148, 157 (2008)*. Matrixx contends that respondents have failed to plead both the element of a material misrepresentation or omission and the element of scienter because they have not alleged that the reports received by Matrixx reflected statistically significant evidence that Zicam caused anosmia. We disagree.

A

We first consider Matrixx's argument that "adverse event reports that do not reveal a statistically significant increased risk of adverse events from product use are not material information." Brief for Petitioners 17 (capitalization omitted).

1

To prevail on a § 10(b) claim, a plaintiff must show that the defendant made a statement that was "*misleading* as to a *material* fact." *Basic, 485 U.S., at 238*. In *Basic*, we held that this materiality requirement is satisfied when there is "'a substantial likelihood that the disclosure of the omitted fact would have been viewed by the reasonable investor as having significantly altered the "total mix" of information made available.'" *Id., at 231-232* (quoting *TSC Industries, Inc. v. Northway, Inc., 426 U.S. 438, 449 (1976))*. We were "careful not to set too low a standard of materiality," for fear that management would "'bury the shareholders in an avalanche of trivial information.'" *485 U.S., at 231* (quoting *TSC Industries, 426 U.S., at 448-449*).

Basic involved a claim that the defendant had made misleading statements denying that it was engaged in merger negotiations when it was, in fact, conducting preliminary negotiations. See *485 U.S., at 227-229*. The defendant urged a bright-line rule that preliminary merger negotiations are material only once the parties to the negotiations reach an agreement in principle. *Id., at 232-233*. We observed that "[a]ny approach that designates a single fact or occurrence as always determinative of an inherently fact-specific finding such as materiality, must necessarily be overinclusive or underinclusive." *Id., at 236*. We thus rejected the defendant's proposed rule, explaining that it would "artificially exclud[e] from the definition of materiality information concerning merger discussions, which would otherwise be considered significant to the trading decision of a reasonable investor." *Ibid.*

Like the defendant in *Basic*, Matrixx urges us to adopt a bright-line rule that reports of adverse events associated with a pharmaceutical company's products cannot be material absent a sufficient number of such reports to establish a statistically significant risk that the product is in fact causing the events. Absent statistical significance, Matrixx argues, adverse event reports provide only "anecdotal" evidence that "the user of a drug experienced an adverse event at some point during or following the use of that drug." Brief for Petitioners 17. Accordingly, it contends, reasonable investors would not consider such reports relevant unless they are statistically significant because only then do they "reflect a scientifically reliable basis for inferring a potential causal link between product use and the adverse event." *Id.*, at 32.

As in *Basic*, Matrixx's categorical rule would "artificially exclud[e]" information that "would otherwise be considered significant to the trading decision of a reasonable investor." *485 U.S., at 236, 108 S. Ct. 978, 99 L. Ed. 2d 194*. Matrixx's argument rests on the premise that statistical significance is the only reliable indication of causation. This premise is flawed: As the SEC points out, "medical researchers . . . consider multiple factors in assessing causation." Brief for United States as *Amicus Curiae* 12. Statistically significant data are not always available. For example, when an adverse event is subtle or rare, "an inability to obtain a data set of appropriate quality or quantity may preclude a finding of statistical significance." *Id.*, at 15; see also Brief for Medical Researchers as *Amici Curiae* 11. Moreover, ethical considerations may prohibit researchers from conducting randomized clinical trials to confirm a suspected causal link for the purpose of obtaining statistically significant data. See *id.*, at 10-11.

A lack of statistically significant data does not mean that medical experts have no reliable basis for inferring a causal link between a drug and adverse events. As Matrixx itself concedes, medical experts rely on other evidence to establish an inference of causation. See Brief for Petitioners 44-45, n. 22. We note that courts frequently permit expert testimony on causation based on evidence other than statistical significance. See, *e.g., Best v. Lowe's Home Centers, Inc., 563 F.3d 171, 178 (CA6 2009)*; *Westberry v. Gislaved Gummi AB, 178 F.3d 257, 263-264 (CA4 1999)* (citing cases); *Wells v. Ortho Pharmaceutical Corp., 788 F.2d 741, 744-745 (CA11 1986)*. We need not consider whether the expert testimony was properly admitted in those cases, and we do not attempt to define here what constitutes reliable evidence of causation. It suffices to note that, as these courts have recognized, "medical professionals and researchers do not limit the data they consider to the results of randomized clinical trials or to statistically significant evidence." Brief for Medical Researchers as *Amici Curiae* 31.

The FDA similarly does not limit the evidence it considers for purposes of assessing causation and taking regulatory action to statistically significant data. In assessing the safety risk posed by a product, the FDA considers factors such as "strength of the association," "temporal relationship of product use and the event," "consistency of findings across available data sources," "evidence of a dose-response for the effect," "biologic plausibility," "seriousness of the event relative to the disease being treated," "potential to mitigate the risk in the population," "feasibility of further study using observational or controlled clinical study designs," and "degree of benefit the product provides, including availability of other therapies." FDA, Guidance for Industry: Good Pharmacovigilance Practices and Pharmacoepidemiologic Assessment 18 (2005) (capitalization omitted), http://www.fda.gov/downloads/ RegulatingInformation/Guidances/UCM126834.pdf (all Internet materials as visited Mar. 17,

2011, and available in Clerk of Court's case file); see also Brief for United States as *Amicus Curiae* 19-20 (same); FDA, The Clinical Impact of Adverse Event Reporting 6 (1996) (similar), http://www.fda.gov/downloads/safety/MedWatch/UCM168505.pdf. It "does not apply any single metric for determining when additional inquiry or action is necessary, and it certainly does not insist upon 'statistical significance.'" Brief for United States as *Amicus Curiae* 19.

Not only does the FDA rely on a wide range of evidence of causation, it sometimes acts on the basis of evidence that suggests, but does not prove, causation. For example, the FDA requires manufacturers of over-the-counter drugs to revise their labeling "to include a warning as soon as there is reasonable evidence of an association of a serious hazard with a drug; a causal relationship need not have been proved." *21 CFR § 201.80(e)*. More generally, the FDA may make regulatory decisions against drugs based on postmarketing evidence that gives rise to only a suspicion of causation. See FDA, The Clinical Impact of Adverse Event Reporting, *supra*, at 7 ("[A]chieving certain proof of causality through postmarketing surveillance is unusual. Attaining a prominent degree of suspicion is much more likely, and may be considered a sufficient basis for regulatory decisions" (footnote omitted)).

This case proves the point. In 2009, the FDA issued a warning letter to Matrixx stating that "[a] significant and growing body of evidence substantiates that the Zicam Cold Remedy intranasal products may pose a serious risk to consumers who use them." App. 270a. The letter cited as evidence 130 reports of anosmia the FDA had received, the fact that the FDA had received few reports of anosmia associated with other intranasal cold remedies, and "evidence in the published scientific literature that various salts of zinc can damage olfactory function in animals and humans." *Ibid.* It did not cite statistically significant data.

Given that medical professionals and regulators act on the basis of evidence of causation that is not statistically significant, it stands to reason that in certain cases reasonable investors would as well. As Matrixx acknowledges, adverse event reports "appear in many forms, including direct complaints by users to manufacturers, reports by doctors about reported or observed patient reactions, more detailed case reports published by doctors in medical journals, or larger scale published clinical studies." Brief for Petitioners 17. As a result, assessing the materiality of adverse event reports is a "fact-specific" inquiry, *Basic, 485 U.S., at 236*, that requires consideration of the source, content, and context of the reports. This is not to say that statistical significance (or the lack thereof) is irrelevant -- only that it is not dispositive of every case.

Application of *Basic*'s "total mix" standard does not mean that pharmaceutical manufacturers must disclose all reports of adverse events. Adverse event reports are daily events in the pharmaceutical industry; in 2009, the FDA entered nearly 500,000 such reports into its reporting system, see FDA, Reports Received and Reports Entered in AERS by Year (as of Mar. 31, 2010), http://www.fda.gov/Drugs/GuidanceComplianceRegulatoryInformation /Surveillance/ AdverseDrugEffects/ ucm070434. htm. The fact that a user of a drug has suffered an adverse event, standing alone, does not mean that the drug caused that event. See FDA, Annual Adverse Drug Experience Report: 1996, p. 2 (1997). The question remains whether a *reasonable* investor would have viewed the nondisclosed information "'as having *significantly* altered the "total mix" of information made available.'" *Basic, 485 U.S., at 232* (quoting *TSC Industries, 426 U.S., at 449*; emphasis added). For the reasons just stated, the mere existence of reports of adverse events -- which says nothing in and of itself about whether the drug is causing the adverse events -- will not satisfy this standard. Something more is needed, but that something more is not limited to statistical significance and can come from "the source, content, and context of the reports," *supra*, at 15. This contextual inquiry may reveal in some cases that reasonable investors would have viewed reports of adverse events as material even though the reports did not provide statistically significant evidence of a causal link.

Moreover, it bears emphasis that *§ 10(b)* and *Rule 10b-5(b)* do not create an affirmative duty to disclose any and all material information. Disclosure is required under these provisions only when necessary "to make . . . statements made, in the light of the circumstances under which they were made, not misleading. *17 CFR § 240.10b-5(b)*; see also *Basic, 485 U.S., at 239, n. 17, 108 S. Ct. 978, 99 L. Ed. 2d 194* ("Silence, absent a duty to disclose, is not misleading under *Rule 10b-5*"). Even with respect to information that a reasonable investor might consider material, companies can control what they have to disclose under these provisions by controlling what they say to the market.

2

Applying *Basic*'s "total mix" standard in this case, we conclude that respondents have adequately pleaded materiality. This is not a case about a handful of anecdotal reports, as Matrixx suggests. Assuming the complaint's allegations to be true, as we must, Matrixx received information that plausibly indicated a reliable causal link between Zicam and anosmia. That information included reports from three medical professionals and researchers about more than 10 patients who had lost their sense of smell after using Zicam. Clarot told Linschoten that Matrixx had received additional reports of anosmia. (In addition, during the class period, nine plaintiffs commenced four product liability lawsuits against Matrixx alleging a causal link between Zicam use and anosmia.) Further, Matrixx knew that Linschoten and Dr. Jafek had presented their findings about a causal link between Zicam and anosmia to a national medical conference devoted to treatment of diseases of the nose. Their presentation described a patient who experienced severe burning in his nose, followed immediately by a loss of smell, after using Zicam -- suggesting a temporal relationship between Zicam use and anosmia.

Critically, both Dr. Hirsch and Linschoten had also drawn Matrixx's attention to previous studies that had demonstrated a biological causal link between intranasal application of zinc and anosmia. Before his conversation with Linschoten, Clarot, Matrixx's vice president of research and development, was seemingly unaware of these studies, and the complaint suggests that, as of the class period, Matrixx had not conducted any research of its own relating to anosmia. See, *e.g.*, App. 84a (referencing a press report, issued after the end of the class period, noting that Matrixx said it would begin conducting "'animal and human studies to further characterize these post-marketing complaints'"). Accordingly, it can reasonably be inferred from the complaint that Matrixx had no basis for rejecting Dr. Jafek's findings out of hand.

We believe that these allegations suffice to "raise a reasonable expectation that discovery will reveal evidence" satisfying the materiality requirement, *Bell Atlantic Corp. v. Twombly, 550 U.S. 544, 556 (2007)*, and to "allo[w] the court to draw the reasonable inference that the defendant is liable for the misconduct alleged," *Iqbal, 556 U.S., at ___*. The information provided to Matrixx by medical experts revealed a plausible causal relationship between Zicam Cold Remedy and anosmia. Consumers likely would have viewed the risk associated with Zicam (possible loss of smell) as substantially outweighing the benefit of using the product (alleviating cold symptoms), particularly in light of the existence of many alternative products on the market. Importantly, Zicam Cold Remedy allegedly accounted for 70 percent of Matrixx's sales. Viewing the allegations of the complaint as a whole, the complaint alleges facts suggesting a significant risk to the commercial viability of Matrixx's leading product.

It is substantially likely that a reasonable investor would have viewed this information "'as having significantly altered the "total mix" of information made available.'" *Basic, 485 U.S., at 232* (quoting *TSC Industries, 426 U.S., at 449*). Matrixx told the market that revenues were going to rise 50 and then 80 percent. Assuming the complaint's allegations to be true, however, Matrixx had information indicating a significant risk to its leading revenue-generating product. Matrixx also stated that reports indicating that Zicam caused anosmia were "'completely unfounded and misleading'" and that "'the safety and efficacy of zinc gluconate for the treatment of symptoms related to the common cold have been well established.'" App. 77a-78a. Importantly, however, Matrixx had evidence of a biological link between Zicam's key ingredient and anosmia, and it had not conducted any studies of its own to disprove that link. In fact, as Matrixx later revealed, the scientific evidence at that time was "'insufficient . . . to determine if zinc gluconate, when used as recommended, affects a person's ability to smell.'" *Id.*, at 82a.

Assuming the facts to be true, these were material facts "necessary in order to make the statements made, in the light of the circumstances under which they were made, not misleading." *17 CFR § 240.10b-5(b)*. We therefore affirm the Court of Appeals' holding that respondents adequately pleaded the element of a material misrepresentation or omission.

B

Matrixx also argues that respondents failed to allege facts plausibly suggesting that it acted with the required level of scienter. "To establish liability under *§ 10(b)* and *Rule 10b-5*, a private plaintiff must prove that the defendant acted with scienter, 'a mental state embracing intent to deceive, manipulate, or defraud.'" *Tellabs, 551 U.S., at 319* (quoting *Ernst & Ernst v. Hochfelder, 425 U.S. 185, 193-194, and n. 12 (1976))*. We have not decided whether recklessness suffices to fulfill the scienter requirement. See *Tellabs, 551 U.S., at 319, n. 3*. Because Matrixx does not challenge the Court of Appeals' holding that the scienter requirement may be satisfied by a showing of "deliberate recklessness," see *585 F.3d at 1180* (internal quotation marks omitted), we assume, without deciding, that the standard applied by the Court of Appeals is sufficient to establish scienter.

Under the PSLRA, a plaintiff must "state with particularity facts giving rise to a strong inference that the defendant acted with the required state of mind." *15 U.S.C.A. § 78u-4(b)(2)(A) (Feb. 2011 Supp.)*. This standard requires courts to take into account "plausible opposing inferences." *Tellabs, 551 U.S., at 323, 127 S. Ct. 2499, 168 L. Ed. 2d 179*. A complaint adequately pleads scienter under the PSLRA "only if a reasonable person would deem the inference of scienter cogent and at least as compelling as any opposing inference one could draw from the facts alleged." *Id.*, at 324. In making this determination, the court must review "all the allegations holistically." *Id.*, at 326. The absence of a motive allegation, though relevant, is not dispositive. *Id.*, at 325.

Matrixx argues, in summary fashion, that because respondents do not allege that it knew of statistically significant evidence of causation, there is no basis to consider the inference that it acted recklessly or knowingly to be at least as compelling as the alternative inferences. "Rather," it argues, "the most obvious inference is that petitioners did not disclose the [reports] simply because petitioners believed they were far too few . . . to indicate anything meaningful about adverse reactions to use of Zicam." Brief for Petitioners 49. Matrixx's proposed bright-line rule requiring an allegation of statistical significance to establish a strong inference of scienter is just as flawed as its approach to materiality.

The inference that Matrixx acted recklessly (or intentionally, for that matter) is at least as compelling, if not more compelling, than the inference that it simply thought the reports did not indicate anything meaningful about adverse reactions. According to the complaint, Matrixx was sufficiently concerned about the information it received that it informed Linschoten that it had hired a consultant to review the product, asked Linschoten to participate in animal studies, and convened a panel of physicians and scientists in response to Dr. Jafek's presentation. It successfully prevented Dr. Jafek from using Zicam's name in his presentation on the ground that he needed Matrixx's permission to do so. Most significantly, Matrixx issued a press release that suggested that studies had confirmed that Zicam does not cause anosmia when, in fact, it had not conducted any studies relating to anosmia and the scientific evidence at that time, according to the panel of scientists, was insufficient to determine whether Zicam did or did not cause anosmia.[15]

These allegations, "taken collectively," give rise to a "cogent and compelling" inference that Matrixx elected not to disclose the reports of adverse events not because it believed they were meaningless but because it understood their likely effect on the market. *Tellabs, 551 U.S., at 323, 324*. "[A] reasonable person" would deem the inference that Matrixx acted with deliberate recklessness (or even intent) "at least as compelling as any opposing inference one could draw from the facts alleged." *Id., at 324*. We conclude, in agreement with the Court of Appeals, that respondents have adequately pleaded scienter. Whether respondents can ultimately prove their allegations and establish scienter is an altogether different question.

* * *

For the reasons stated, the judgment of the Court of Appeals for the Ninth Circuit is

Affirmed.

---

[15] One of Matrixx's *amici* argues that "the most cogent inference regarding Matrixx's state of mind is that it delayed releasing information regarding anosmia complaints in order to provide itself an opportunity to carefully review all evidence regarding any link between Zicam and anosmia." Brief for Washington Legal Foundation as *Amicus Curiae* 26. We do not doubt that this may be the most cogent inference in some cases. Here, however, the misleading nature of Matrixx's press release is sufficient to render the inference of scienter at least as compelling as the inference suggested by *amicus*.

Erica P. John Fund, Inc. v. Halliburton Co.

Supreme Court of the United States, 2011

131 S. Ct. __, 2011 U.S. LEXIS 4181 (June 6, 2011)

■ CHIEF JUSTICE ROBERTS delivered the opinion of the Court.

To prevail on the merits in a private securities fraud action, investors must demonstrate that the defendant's deceptive conduct caused their claimed economic loss. This requirement is commonly referred to as "loss causation." The question presented in this case is whether securities fraud plaintiffs must also prove loss causation in order to obtain class certification. We hold that they need not.

I

Petitioner Erica P. John Fund, Inc. (EPJ Fund), is the lead plaintiff in a putative securities fraud class action filed against Halliburton Co. and one of its executives (collectively Halliburton). The suit was brought on behalf of all investors who purchased Halliburton common stock between June 3, 1999, and December 7, 2001.

EPJ Fund alleges that Halliburton made various misrepresentations designed to inflate its stock price, in violation of *§ 10(b)* of the Securities Exchange Act of 1934 and Securities and Exchange Commission *Rule 10b-5*. The complaint asserts that Halliburton deliberately made false statements about (1) the scope of its potential liability in asbestos litigation, (2) its expected revenue from certain construction contracts, and (3) the benefits of its merger with another company. EPJ Fund contends that Halliburton later made a number of corrective disclosures that caused its stock price to drop and, consequently, investors to lose money.

After defeating a motion to dismiss, EPJ Fund sought to have its proposed class certified pursuant to *Federal Rule of Civil Procedure 23*. The parties agreed, and the District Court held, that EPJ Fund satisfied the general requirements for class actions set out in *Rule 23(a)*: The class was sufficiently numerous, there were common questions of law or fact, the claims of the representative parties were typical, and the representative parties would fairly and adequately protect the interests of the class. See App. to Pet. for Cert. 3a.

The District Court also found that the action could proceed as a class action under *Rule 23(b)(3)*, but for one problem: Circuit precedent required securities fraud plaintiffs to prove "loss causation" in order to obtain class certification. *Id.*, at 4a, and n. 2 (citing *Oscar Private Equity Invs. v. Allegiance Telecom, Inc., 487 F.3d 261, 269 (CA5 2007)*). As the District Court explained, loss causation is the "'causal connection between the material misrepresentation and the [economic] loss'" suffered by investors. App. to Pet. for Cert. 5a, and n. 3 (quoting *Dura Pharms., Inc. v. Broudo, 544 U.S. 336, 342 (2005)*). After reviewing the alleged misrepresentations and corrective disclosures, the District Court concluded that it could not certify the class in this case because EPJ Fund had "failed to establish loss causation with respect to any" of its claims. App. to Pet. for Cert. 54a. The court made clear, however, that absent "this stringent loss causation requirement," it would have granted the Fund's certification request. *Ibid.*

The Court of Appeals affirmed the denial of class certification. See *597 F.3d 330 (CA5 2010)*. It confirmed that, "[i]n order to obtain class certification on its claims, [EPJ Fund] was required to prove loss causation, i.e., that the corrected truth of the former falsehoods actually caused the stock price to fall and resulted in the losses." *Id., at 334*. Like the District Court, the Court of Appeals concluded that EPJ Fund had failed to meet the "requirements for proving loss causation at the class certification stage." *Id., at 344*.

We granted the Fund's petition for certiorari, *562 U.S. ___ (2011)*, to resolve a conflict among the Circuits as to whether securities fraud plaintiffs must prove loss causation in order to obtain class certification. Compare *597 F.3d at 334* (case below), with *In re Salomon Analyst Metromedia Litigation, 544 F.3d 474, 483 (CA2 2008)* (not requiring investors to prove loss causation at class certification stage); *Schleicher v. Wendt, 618 F.3d 679, 687 (CA7 2010)* (same); *In re DVI, Inc. Secs. Litig., 2011 U.S. App. LEXIS 6302, No. 08-8033 etc., 2011 WL 1125926, *7 (CA3, Mar. 29, 2011)* (same; decided after certiorari was granted).

II

EPJ Fund contends that the Court of Appeals erred by requiring proof of loss causation for class certification. We agree.

A

As noted, the sole dispute here is whether EPJ Fund satisfied the prerequisites of *Rule 23(b)(3)*. In order to certify a class under that Rule, a court must find "that the questions of law or fact common to class members predominate over any questions affecting only individual members, and that a class action is superior to other available methods for fairly and efficiently adjudicating the controversy." *Fed. Rule Civ. Proc. 23(b)(3)*. Considering whether "questions of law or fact common to class members predominate" begins, of course, with the elements of the underlying cause of action. The elements of a private securities fraud claim based on violations of *§ 10(b)* and *Rule 10b-5* are: "'(1) a material misrepresentation or omission by the defendant; (2) scienter; (3) a connection between the misrepresentation or omission and the purchase or sale of a security; (4) reliance upon the misrepresentation or omission; (5) economic loss; and (6) loss causation.'" *Matrixx Initiatives, Inc. v. Siracusano, 563 U.S. ___, ___, 131 S. Ct. 1309 (2011)* (quoting *Stoneridge Investment Partners, LLC v. Scientific-Atlanta, Inc., 552 U.S. 148, 157 (2008))*.

Whether common questions of law or fact predominate in a securities fraud action often turns on the element of reliance. The courts below determined that EPJ Fund had to prove the separate element of loss causation in order to establish that reliance was capable of resolution on a common, classwide basis.

"Reliance by the plaintiff upon the defendant's deceptive acts is an essential element of the *§ 10(b)* private cause of action." *Stoneridge, supra, at 159*. This is because proof of reliance ensures that there is a proper "connection between a defendant's misrepresentation and a plaintiff's injury." *Basic Inc. v. Levinson, 485 U.S. 224, 243 (1988)*. The traditional (and most direct) way a plaintiff can demonstrate reliance is by showing that he was aware of a company's statement and engaged in a relevant transaction -- *e.g.*, purchasing common stock -- based on that specific misrepresentation. In that situation, the plaintiff plainly would have relied on the company's deceptive conduct. A plaintiff unaware of the relevant statement, on the other hand, could not establish reliance on that basis.

We recognized in *Basic*, however, that limiting proof of reliance in such a way "would place an unnecessarily unrealistic evidentiary burden on the *Rule 10b-5* plaintiff who has traded on an impersonal market." *Id., at 245, 108 S. Ct. 978, 99 L. Ed. 2d 194.* We also observed that "[r]equiring proof of individualized reliance from each member of the proposed plaintiff class effectively would" prevent such plaintiffs "from proceeding with a class action, since individual issues" would "overwhelm[ ] the common ones." *Id., at 242.*

The Court in *Basic* sought to alleviate those related concerns by permitting plaintiffs to invoke a rebuttable presumption of reliance based on what is known as the "fraud-on-the-market" theory. According to that theory, "the market price of shares traded on well-developed markets reflects all publicly available information, and, hence, any material misrepresentations." *Id., at 246.* Because the market "transmits information to the investor in the processed form of a market price," we can assume, the Court explained, that an investor relies on public misstatements whenever he "buys or sells stock at the price set by the market." *Id., at 244, 247* (internal quotation marks omitted); see also *Stoneridge, supra, at 159*; *Dura Pharmaceuticals, 544 U.S., at 341-342.* The Court also made clear that the presumption was just that, and could be rebutted by appropriate evidence. See *Basic, supra, at 248.*

B

It is undisputed that securities fraud plaintiffs must prove certain things in order to invoke *Basic*'s rebuttable presumption of reliance. It is common ground, for example, that plaintiffs must demonstrate that the alleged misrepresentations were publicly known (else how would the market take them into account?), that the stock traded in an efficient market, and that the relevant transaction took place "between the time the misrepresentations were made and the time the truth was revealed." *Basic, 485 U.S., at 248, n. 27*; *id., at 241-247*; see also *Stoneridge, supra, at 159.*

According to the Court of Appeals, EPJ Fund also had to establish loss causation at the certification stage to "trigger the fraud-on-the-market presumption." *597 F.3d at 335* (internal quotation marks omitted); see *ibid.* (EPJ Fund must "establish a causal link between the alleged falsehoods and its losses in order to invoke the fraud-on-the-market presumption"). The court determined that, in order to invoke a rebuttable presumption of reliance, EPJ Fund needed to prove that the decline in Halliburton's stock was "because of the correction to a prior misleading statement" and "that the subsequent loss could not otherwise be explained by some additional factors revealed then to the market." *Id., at 336* (emphasis deleted). This is the loss causation requirement as we have described it. See *Dura Pharmaceuticals, supra, at 342*; see also *15 U.S.C. § 78u-4(b)(4).*

The Court of Appeals' requirement is not justified by *Basic* or its logic. To begin, we have never before mentioned loss causation as a precondition for invoking *Basic*'s rebuttable presumption of reliance. The term "loss causation" does not even appear in our *Basic* opinion. And for good reason: Loss causation addresses a matter different from whether an investor relied on a misrepresentation, presumptively or otherwise, when buying or selling a stock.

We have referred to the element of reliance in a private *Rule 10b-5* action as "transaction causation," not loss causation. *Dura Pharmaceuticals, supra, at 341-342* (citing *Basic, supra, at 248-249*). Consistent with that description, when considering whether a plaintiff has relied on a misrepresentation, we have typically focused on facts surrounding the investor's decision to engage in the transaction. See *Dura Pharmaceuticals, supra, at 342.* Under *Basic*'s fraud-on-the-market doctrine, an investor presumptively relies on a defendant's misrepresentation if that "information is reflected in [the] market price" of the stock at the time of the relevant transaction. See *Basic, 485 U.S., at 247.*

Loss causation, by contrast, requires a plaintiff to show that a misrepresentation that affected the integrity of the market price *also* caused a subsequent economic loss. As we made clear in *Dura Pharmaceuticals*, the fact that a stock's "price on the date of purchase was inflated because of [a] misrepresentation" does not necessarily mean that the misstatement is the cause of a later decline in value. *544 U.S., at 342* (emphasis deleted; internal quotation marks omitted). We observed that the drop could instead be the result of other intervening causes, such as "changed economic circumstances, changed investor expectations, new industry-specific or firm-specific facts, conditions, or other events." *Id., at 342-343.* If one of those factors were responsible for the loss or part of it, a plaintiff would not be able to prove loss causation to that extent. This is true even if the investor purchased the stock at a distorted price, and thereby presumptively relied on the misrepresentation reflected in that price.

According to the Court of Appeals, however, an inability to prove loss causation would prevent a plaintiff from invoking the rebuttable presumption of reliance. Such a rule contravenes *Basic's* fundamental premise -- that an investor presumptively relies on a misrepresentation so long as it was reflected in the market price at the time of his transaction. The fact that a subsequent loss may have been caused by factors other than the revelation of a misrepresentation has nothing to do with whether an investor relied on the misrepresentation in the first place, either directly or presumptively through the fraud-on-the-market theory. Loss causation has no logical connection to the facts necessary to establish the efficient market predicate to the fraud-on-the-market theory.

The Court of Appeals erred by requiring EPJ Fund to show loss causation as a condition of obtaining class certification.

C

Halliburton concedes that securities fraud plaintiffs should not be required to prove loss causation in order to invoke *Basic*'s presumption of reliance or otherwise achieve class certification. See Tr. of Oral Arg. 26-29. Halliburton nonetheless defends the judgment below on the ground that the Court of Appeals did not actually require plaintiffs to prove "loss causation" as we have used that term. See *id.*, at 27 ("it's not loss causation as this Court knows it in *Dura*"). According to Halliburton, "loss causation" was merely "shorthand" for a different analysis. Brief for Respondents 18. The lower court's actual inquiry, Halliburton insists, was whether EPJ Fund had demonstrated "price impact" -- that is, whether the alleged misrepresentations affected the market price in the first place. See, *e.g., id.*, at 16-19, 24-27, 50-51; see also Tr. of Oral Arg. 27

(stating that the Court of Appeals' "test is simply price impact" and that EPJ Fund's "only burden under the Fifth Circuit case law was to show price impact").

"Price impact" simply refers to the effect of a misrepresentation on a stock price. Halliburton's theory is that if a misrepresentation does not affect market price, an investor cannot be said to have relied on the misrepresentation merely because he purchased stock at that price. If the price is unaffected by the fraud, the price does not reflect the fraud.

We do not accept Halliburton's wishful interpretation of the Court of Appeals' opinion. As we have explained, loss causation is a familiar and distinct concept in securities law; it is not price impact. While the opinion below may include some language consistent with a "price impact" approach, see, e.g., 597 F.3d at 336, we simply cannot ignore the Court of Appeals' repeated and explicit references to "loss causation," see id., at 334 (three times), 334 n. 2, 335, 335 n. 10 (twice), 335 n. 11, 336, 336 n. 19, 336 n. 20, 337, 338, 341 (twice), 341 n. 46, 342 n. 47, 343, 344 (three times).

Whatever Halliburton thinks the Court of Appeals meant to say, what it said was loss causation: "[EPJ Fund] was required to prove loss causation, i.e., that the corrected truth of the former falsehoods actually caused the stock price to fall and resulted in the losses." 597 F.3d at 334; see id., at 335 ("we require plaintiffs to establish loss causation in order to trigger the fraud-on-the-market presumption" (internal quotation marks omitted)). We take the Court of Appeals at its word. Based on those words, the decision below cannot stand.

* * *

Because we conclude the Court of Appeals erred by requiring EPJ Fund to prove loss causation at the certification stage, we need not, and do not, address any other question about *Basic*, its presumption, or how and when it may be rebutted. To the extent Halliburton has preserved any further arguments against class certification, they may be addressed in the first instance by the Court of Appeals on remand.

The judgment of the Court of Appeals is vacated, and the case is remanded for further proceedings consistent with this opinion.

It is so ordered.

Query: Basic, Inc. v. Levinson said that the fraud on the market presumption was rebuttable. But when can defendants seeks to rebut the presumption? Under Halliburton, the most likely answer is at the summary judgment stage, but the possibility remains open that rebuttal could occur earlier at the motion to dismiss stage if there were no factual issues.

C. Who Is The Maker Of a Statement?

Janus Capital Group, Inc. v. First Derivative Traders

Supreme Court of the United States, 2011

131 S. Ct. __, 2011 U.S. LEXIS 4380 (June 13, 2011)

■ JUSTICE THOMAS delivered the opinion of the Court.

This case requires us to determine whether Janus Capital Management LLC (JCM), a mutual fund investment adviser, can be held liable in a private action under Securities and Exchange Commission (SEC) *Rule 10b-5* for false statements included in its client mutual funds' prospectuses. *Rule 10b-5* prohibits "mak[ing] any untrue statement of a material fact" in connection with the purchase or sale of securities. We conclude that JCM cannot be held liable because it did not make the statements in the prospectuses.

I

Janus Capital Group, Inc. (JCG), is a publicly traded company that created the Janus family of mutual funds. These mutual funds are organized in a Massachusetts business trust, the Janus Investment Fund. Janus Investment Fund retained JCG's wholly owned subsidiary, JCM, to be its investment adviser and administrator. JCG and JCM are the petitioners here.

Although JCG created Janus Investment Fund, Janus Investment Fund is a separate legal entity owned entirely by mutual fund investors. Janus Investment Fund has no assets apart from those owned by the investors. JCM provides Janus Investment Fund with investment advisory services, which include "the management and administrative services necessary for the operation of [Janus] Fun[d]," App. 225a, but the two entities maintain legal independence. At all times relevant to this case, all of the officers of Janus Investment Fund were also officers of JCM, but only one member of Janus Investment Fund's board of trustees was associated with JCM. This is more independence than is required: By statute, up to 60 percent of the board of a mutual fund may be composed of "interested persons." See 54 Stat. 806, as amended, *15 U.S.C. § 80a-10(a)*; see also *15 U.S.C. A. § 80a-2(a)(19) (2009 ed. and Feb. 2011 Supp.)* (defining "interested person").

As the securities laws require, Janus Investment Fund issued prospectuses describing the investment strategy and operations of its mutual funds to investors. See *15 U.S.C. §§ 77b(a)(10), 77e(b)(2), 80a-8(b), 80a-2(a)(31), 80a-29(a)-(b)*. The prospectuses for several funds represented that the funds were not suitable for market timing and can be read to suggest that JCM would implement policies to curb the practice. For example, the Janus Mercury Fund prospectus dated February 25, 2002, stated that the fund was "not intended for market timing or excessive trading" and represented that it "may reject any purchase request . . . if it believes that any combination of trading activity is attributable to market timing or is otherwise excessive or potentially disruptive to the Fund." App. 141a. Although market timing is legal, it harms other investors in the mutual fund.

In September 2003, the Attorney General of the State of New York filed a complaint against JCG and JCM alleging that JCG entered into secret arrangements to permit market timing in several funds run by JCM. After the complaint's allegations became public, investors withdrew significant amounts of money from the Janus Investment Fund mutual funds. Because Janus Investment Fund compensated JCM based on the total value of the funds and JCM's management fees comprised a significant percentage of JCG's income, Janus Investment Fund's loss of value affected JCG's value as well. JCG's stock price fell nearly 25 percent, from $ 17.68 on September 2 to $ 13.50 on September 26.

Respondent First Derivative Traders (First Derivative) represents a class of plaintiffs who owned JCG stock as of September 3, 2003. Its complaint asserts claims against JCG and JCM for violations of *Rule 10b-5* and *§ 10(b)* of the Securities Exchange Act of 1934. First Derivative alleges that JCG and JCM "caused mutual fund prospectuses to be issued for Janus mutual funds and made them available to the investing public, which created the misleading impression that [JCG and JCM] would implement measures to curb market timing in the Janus [mutual funds]." App. to Pet. for Cert. 60a. "Had the truth been known, Janus [mutual funds] would have been less attractive to investors, and consequently, [JCG] would have realized lower revenues, so [JCG's] stock would have traded at lower prices." *Id.*, at 72a.

First Derivative contends that JCG and JCM "materially misled the investing public" and that class members relied "upon the integrity of the market price of [JCG] securities and market information relating to [JCG and JCM]." *Id.*, at 109a. The complaint also alleges that JCG should be held liable for the acts of JCM as a "controlling person" under *15 U.S.C. A. § 78t(a)* (Feb. 2011 Supp.) (*§ 20(a)* of the Act).

The District Court dismissed the complaint for failure to state a claim. *In re Mutual Funds Inv. Litigation, 487 F. Supp. 2d 618, 620 (D Md. 2007)*. The Court of Appeals for the Fourth Circuit reversed, holding that First Derivative had sufficiently alleged that "JCG and JCM, by participating in the writing and dissemination of the prospectuses, *made* the misleading statements contained in the documents." *In re Mutual Funds Inv. Litigation, 566 F.3d 111, 121 (2009)* (emphasis in original). With respect to the element of reliance, the court found that investors would infer that JCM "played a role in preparing or approving the content of the Janus fund prospectuses," *id., at 127*, but that investors would not infer the same about JCG, which could be liable only as a "control person" of JCM under *§ 20(a). Id., at 128, 129-130*.

II

We granted certiorari to address whether JCM can be held liable in a private action under *Rule 10b-5* for false statements included in Janus Investment Fund's pro-spectuses. *561 U.S. ___, 130 S. Ct. 3499 (2010)*. Under *Rule 10b-5*, it is unlawful for "any person, directly or indirectly, . . . [t]o make any untrue statement of a material fact" in connection with the purchase or sale of securities. *17 CFR § 240.10b-5(b)*. To be liable, therefore, JCM must have "made" the material misstatements in the prospectuses. We hold that it did not.[5]

---

[5] Although First Derivative argued below that JCG violated *Rule 10b-5* by making the statements in the prospectuses, it now seeks to hold JCG liable solely as a control person of JCM

A

The SEC promulgated *Rule 10b-5* pursuant to authority granted under *§ 10(b)* of the Securities Exchange Act of 1934, *15 U.S.C. § 78j(b)*. Although neither *Rule 10b-5* nor *§ 10(b)* expressly creates a private right of action, this Court has held that "a private right of action is implied under *§ 10(b).*" *Superintendent of Ins. of N. Y. v. Bankers Life & Casualty Co., 404 U.S. 6, 13, n. 9 (1971)*. That holding "remains the law," *Stoneridge Investment Partners, LLC v. Scientific-Atlanta, Inc., 552 U.S. 148, 165 (2008)*, but "[c]oncerns with the judicial creation of a private cause of action caution against its expansion," *ibid*. Thus, in analyzing whether JCM "made" the statements for purposes of *Rule 10b-5*, we are mindful that we must give "narrow dimensions . . . to a right of action Congress did not authorize when it first enacted the statute and did not expand when it revisited the law." *552 U.S., at 167*.

1

One "makes" a statement by stating it. When "make" is paired with a noun expressing the action of a verb, the resulting phrase is "approximately equivalent in sense" to that verb. 6 Oxford English Dictionary 66 (def. 59) (1933) (hereinafter OED); accord, Webster's New International Dictionary 1485 (def. 43) (2d ed. 1934) ("*Make* followed by a noun with the indefinite article is often nearly equivalent to the verb intransitive corresponding to that noun"). For instance, "to make a proclamation" is the approximate equivalent of "to proclaim," and "to make a promise" approximates "to promise." See 6 OED 66 (def. 59). The phrase at issue in *Rule 10b-5*, "[t]o make any . . . statement," is thus the approximate equivalent of "to state."

For purposes of *Rule 10b-5*, the maker of a statement is the person or entity with ultimate authority over the statement, including its content and whether and how to communicate it. Without control, a person or entity can merely suggest what to say, not "make" a statement in its own right. One who prepares or publishes a statement on behalf of another is not its maker. And in the ordinary case, attribution within a statement or implicit from surrounding circumstances is strong evidence that a statement was made by -- and only by -- the party to whom it is attributed. This rule might best be exemplified by the relationship between a speechwriter and a speaker. Even when a speechwriter drafts a speech, the content is entirely within the control of the person who delivers it. And it is the speaker who takes credit -- or blame -- for what is ultimately said.

This rule follows from *Central Bank of Denver, N. A. v. First Interstate Bank of Denver, N. A., 511 U.S. 164 (1994)*, in which we held that *Rule 10b-5*'s private right of action does not include suits against aiders and abettors. See *511 U.S., at 180*. Such suits -- against entities that contribute "substantial assistance" to the making of a statement but do not actually make it -- may be brought by the SEC, see *15 U.S.C. A. § 78t(e)*, but not by private parties. A broader reading of "make," including persons or entities without ultimate control over the content of a statement, would substantially undermine *Central Bank*. If persons or entities without control

---

under *§ 20(a)*. The only question we must answer, therefore, is whether JCM made the misstatements. Whether First Derivative has stated a claim against JCG as a control person depends on whether it has stated a claim against JCM.

over the content of a statement could be considered primary violators who "made" the statement, then aiders and abettors would be almost nonexistent.[6]

This interpretation is further supported by our recent decision in *Stoneridge*. There, investors sued "entities who, acting both as customers and suppliers, agreed to arrangements that allowed the investors' company to mislead its auditor and issue a misleading financial statement." *552 U.S., at 152-153*. We held that dismissal of the complaint was proper because the public could not have relied on the entities' undisclosed deceptive acts. *552 U.S., at 166-167*. Significantly, in reaching that conclusion we emphasized that "nothing [the defendants] did made it necessary or inevitable for [the company] to record the transactions as it did." *552 U.S., at 161*. This emphasis suggests the rule we adopt today: that the maker of a statement is the entity with authority over the content of the statement and whether and how to communicate it. Without such authority, it is not "necessary or inevitable" that any falsehood will be contained in the statement.

Our holding also accords with the narrow scope that we must give the implied private right of action. *552 U.S., at 167*. Although the existence of the private right is now settled, we will not expand liability beyond the person or entity that ultimately has authority over a false statement.

2

The Government contends that "make" should be defined as "create." Brief for United States as *Amicus Curiae* 14-15 (citing Webster's New International Dictionary 1485 (2d ed. 1958) (defining "make" as "[t]o cause to exist, appear, or occur")). This definition, although perhaps appropriate when "make" is directed at an object unassociated with a verb (*e.g.*, "to make a chair"), fails to capture its meaning when directed at an object expressing the action of a verb.

Adopting the Government's definition of "make" would also lead to results inconsistent with our precedent. The Government's definition would permit private plaintiffs to sue a person who "provides the false or misleading information that another person then puts into the statement." Brief for United States as *Amicus Curiae* 13.[8] But in *Stoneridge*, we rejected a private *Rule 10b-5*

---

[6] The dissent correctly notes that *Central Bank* involved secondary, not primary, liability. *Post*, at 4 (opinion of BREYER, J.). But for *Central Bank* to have any meaning, there must be some distinction between those who are primarily liable (and thus may be pursued in private suits) and those who are secondarily liable (and thus may not be pursued in private suits).

We draw a clean line between the two -- the maker is the person or entity with ultimate authority over a statement and others are not. In contrast, the dissent's only limit on primary liability is not much of a limit at all. It would allow for primary liability whenever "[t]he specific relationships alleged . . . warrant [that] conclusion" -- whatever that may mean. *Post*, at 11.

[8] Because we do not find the meaning of "make" in *Rule 10b-5* to be ambiguous, we need not consider the Government's assertion that we should defer to the SEC's interpretation of the word elsewhere. Brief for United States as *Amicus Curiae* 13 (citing Brief for SEC as *Amicus Curiae* in *Pacific Inv. Mgmt. Co. LLC v. Mayer Brown LLP, 603 F.3d 144*); see *Christensen v. Harris County, 529 U.S. 576, 588, 120 S. Ct. 1655, 146 L. Ed. 2d 621 (2000)*. We note, however, that we have previously expressed skepticism over the degree to which the SEC should receive deference regarding the private right of action. See *Piper v. Chris-Craft Industries, Inc., 430 U.S.*

suit against companies involved in deceptive transactions, even when information about those transactions was later incorporated into false public statements. *552 U.S., at 161.* We see no reason to treat participating in the drafting of a false statement differently from engaging in deceptive transactions, when each is merely an undisclosed act preceding the decision of an independent entity to make a public statement.

For its part, First Derivative suggests that the "well-recognized and uniquely close relationship between a mutual fund and its investment adviser" should inform our decision. Brief for Respondent 21. It suggests that an investment adviser should generally be understood to be the "maker" of statements by its client mutual fund, like a playwright whose lines are delivered by an actor. We decline this invitation to disregard the corporate form. Although First Derivative and its *amici* persuasively argue that investment advisers exercise significant influence over their client funds, see *Jones v. Harris Associates L. P., 559 U.S. ___, ___, 130 S. Ct. 1418 (2010) (slip op., at 1-2)*, it is undisputed that the corporate formalities were observed here. JCM and Janus Investment Fund remain legally separate entities, and Janus Investment Fund's board of trustees was more independent than the statute requires. *15 U.S.C. § 80a-10.* Any reapportionment of liability in the securities industry in light of the close relationship between investment advisers and mutual funds is properly the responsibility of Congress and not the courts. Moreover, just as with the Government's theory, First Derivative's rule would create the broad liability that we rejected in *Stoneridge.*

Congress also has established liability in *§ 20(a)* for "[e]very person who, directly or indirectly, controls any person liable" for violations of the securities laws. *15 U.S.C. A. § 78t(a).* First Derivative's theory of liability based on a relationship of influence resembles the liability imposed by Congress for control. To adopt First Derivative's theory would read into *Rule 10b-5* a theory of liability similar to -- but broader in application than, see *post*, at 9 -- what Congress has already created expressly elsewhere.[10] We decline to do so.

B

Under this rule, JCM did not "make" any of the statements in the Janus Investment Fund prospectuses; Janus Investment Fund did. Only Janus Investment Fund -- not JCM -- bears the statutory obligation to file the prospectuses with the SEC. *15 U.S.C. §§ 77e(b)(2), 80a-8(b), 80a-29(a)-(b)*; see also *17 CFR § 230.497* (imposing requirements on "investment companies"). The SEC has recorded that Janus Investment Fund filed the prospectuses. There is no allegation that

---

1, 41, n. 27 (1977) (noting that the SEC's presumed expertise "is of limited value" when analyzing "whether a cause of action should be implied by judicial interpretation in favor of a particular class of litigants"). This also is not the first time this Court has disagreed with the SEC's broad view of *§ 10(b)* or *Rule 10b-5*. See, *e.g., Central Bank of Denver, N. A. v. First Interstate Bank of Denver, N. A., 511 U.S. 164, 188-191 (1994)*; *Dirks v. SEC, 463 U.S. 646, 666, n. 27 (1983)*; *Ernst & Ernst v. Hochfelder, 425 U.S. 185, 207 (1976)*; *Blue Chip Stamps v. Manor Drug Stores, 421 U.S. 723, 746, n. 10 (1975)*.

[10] We do not address whether Congress created liability for entities that act through innocent intermediaries in *15 U.S.C. A. § 78t(b)*. See Tr. of Oral Arg. 6, 61.

JCM in fact filed the prospectuses and falsely attributed them to Janus Investment Fund. Nor did anything on the face of the prospectuses indicate that any statements therein came from JCM rather than Janus Investment Fund -- a legally independent entity with its own board of trustees.

First Derivative suggests that both JCM and Janus Investment Fund might have "made" the misleading statements within the meaning of *Rule 10b-5* because JCM was significantly involved in preparing the prospectuses. But this assistance, subject to the ultimate control of Janus Investment Fund, does not mean that JCM "made" any statements in the prospectuses. Although JCM, like a speechwriter, may have assisted Janus Investment Fund with crafting what Janus Investment Fund said in the prospectuses, JCM itself did not "make" those statements for purposes of *Rule 10b-5*.

The statements in the Janus Investment Fund prospectuses were made by Janus Investment Fund, not by JCM. Accordingly, First Derivative has not stated a claim against JCM under *Rule 10b-5*. The judgment of the United States Court of Appeals for the Fourth Circuit is reversed.

It is so ordered.

DISSENT

JUSTICE BREYER, with whom JUSTICE GINSBURG, JUSTICE SOTOMAYOR, and JUSTICE KAGAN join, dissenting.

This case involves a private Securities and Exchange Commission (SEC) *Rule 10b-5* action brought by a group of investors against Janus Capital Group, Inc., and Janus Capital Management LLC (Janus Management), a firm that acted as an investment adviser to a family of mutual funds (collectively, the Janus Fund or Fund). The investors claim that Janus Management knowingly made materially false or misleading statements that appeared in prospectuses issued by the Janus Fund. They say that they relied upon those statements, and that they suffered resulting economic harm.

Janus Management and the Janus Fund are closely related. Each of the Fund's officers is a Janus Management employee. Janus Management, acting through those employees (and other of its employees), manages the purchase, sale, redemption, and distribution of the Fund's investments. Janus Management prepares, modifies, and implements the Janus Fund's long-term strategies. And Janus Management, acting through those employees, carries out the Fund's daily activities.

Rule 10b-5 says in relevant part that it is unlawful for "any person, directly or indirectly . . . *[t]o make* any untrue statement of a material fact" in connection with the purchase or sale of securities. *17 CFR § 240.10b-5(b) (2010)* (emphasis added). The specific legal question before us is whether Janus Management can be held responsible under the Rule for having "ma[d]e" certain false statements about the Janus Fund's activities. The statements in question appear in the Janus Fund's prospectuses.

The Court holds that only the Janus Fund, not Janus Management, could have "ma[d]e" those statements. The majority points out that the Janus Fund's board of trustees has "ultimate authority" over the content of the statements in a Fund prospectus. And in the majority's view, only "the person or entity with ultimate authority over the statement, including its content and whether and how to communicate it" can "make" a statement within the terms of *Rule 10b-5*. *Ante*, at 6.

In my view, however, the majority has incorrectly interpreted the Rule's word "make." Neither common English nor this Court's earlier cases limit the scope of that word to those with "ultimate authority" over a statement's content. To the contrary, both language and case law indicate that, depending upon the circumstances, a management company, a board of trustees, individual company officers, or others, separately or together, might "make" statements contained in a firm's prospectus -- even if a board of directors has ultimate content-related responsibility. And the circumstances here are such that a court could find that Janus Management made the statements in question.

I

Respondent's complaint sets forth the basic elements of a typical *Rule 10b-5* "fraud on the market" claim. It alleges that Janus Management made statements that "created the misleading impression that" it "would implement measures to curb" a trading strategy called "market timing." Second Amended Complaint P6 (hereinafter Complaint), App. to Pet. for Cert. 60a. The complaint adds that Janus Management knew that these "market timing" statements were false; that the statements were material; that the market, in pricing securities (including related securities) relied upon the statements; that as a result, when the truth came out (that Janus Management indeed permitted "market timing" in the Janus Fund), the price of relevant shares fell; and the false statements thereby caused respondent significant economic losses. Complaint PP4-10, *id.*, at 60a-63a. Cf. *Stoneridge Investment Partners, LLC v. Scientific-Atlanta, Inc., 552 U.S. 148, 157 (2008)* (identi-fying the elements of "a typical § 10(b) private action").

The majority finds the complaint fatally flawed, however, because (1) *Rule 10b-5* says that no "person" shall "directly or indirectly . . . *make* any untrue statement of a material fact," (2) the statements at issue appeared in the *Janus Fund's* prospectuses, and (3) only "the person or entity with ultimate authority over the statement, including its content and whether and how to communicate it" can "make" a false statement. *Ante*, at 2-3, 5-6.

But where can the majority find legal support for the rule that it enunciates? The English language does not impose upon the word "make" boundaries of the kind the majority finds determinative. Every day, hosts of corporate officials make statements with content that more senior officials or the board of directors have "ultimate authority" to control. So do cabinet officials make statements about matters that the Constitution places within the ultimate authority of the President. So do thousands, perhaps millions, of other employees make statements that, as to content, form, or timing, are subject to the control of another.

Nothing in the English language prevents one from saying that several different individuals, separately or together, "make" a statement that each has a hand in producing. For example, as a matter of English, one can say that a national political party has made a statement even if the only written communication consists of uniform press releases issued in the name of local party branches; one can say that one foreign nation has made a statement even when the officials of a different nation (subject to its influence) speak about the matter; and one can say that the President has made a statement even if his press officer issues a communication, sometimes in the press officer's own name. Practical matters related to context, including control, participation, and relevant audience, help determine who "makes" a statement and to whom that statement may properly be "attributed," see *ante*, at 11, n. 11 -- at least as far as ordinary English is concerned.

Neither can the majority find support in any relevant precedent. The majority says that its rule "follows from *Central Bank of Denver, N. A. v. First Interstate Bank of Denver, N. A., 511 U.S. 164 (1994),*" in which the Court "held that *Rule 10b-5*'s private right of action does not include suits against aiders and abettors." *Ante*, at 7. But *Central Bank* concerns a different matter. And it no more requires the majority's rule than free air travel for small children requires free air travel for adults.

Central Bank is a case about *secondary* liability, liability attaching, not to an individual making a false statement, but to an individual helping *someone else* do so. *Central Bank* involved a bond issuer accused of having made materially false statements, which overstated the values of property that backed the bonds. *Central Bank* also involved a defendant that was a bank, serving as indenture trustee, which was supposed to check the bond issuer's valuations. The plaintiffs claimed that the bank delayed its valuation checks and thereby *helped* the issuer make its false statements credible. The question before the Court concerned the bank's liability -- a *secondary* liability for "aiding and abetting" the bond issuer, who (on the theory set forth) was primarily liable.

The Court made this clear. The question presented was "whether private civil liability under § 10(b) extends . . . to those *who do not engage in the manipulative or deceptive practice*, but who aid and abet the violation." *511 U.S., at 167* (emphasis added). The Court wrote that "aiding and abetting liability reaches persons *who do not engage in the proscribed activities at all*, but who give a degree of aid to those who do." *511 U.S. at 176* (emphasis added). The Court described civil law "aiding and abetting" as "'know[ing] that *the other's conduct constitutes a breach of duty* and giv[ing] substantial assistance or encouragement to the other . . . .'" *511 U.S., at 181* (quoting *Restatement (Second) of Torts § 876(b)* (1977); emphasis added). And it reviewed a Court of Appeals decision that had defined the elements of aiding and abetting as "(1) *a primary violation* of *§ 10(b)*; (2) recklessness by the aider and abettor as to the existence of the primary violation; and (3) *substantial assistance given to the primary violator* by the aider and abettor." *511 U.S., at 168* (emphasis added). Faced with this question, the Court answered that *§ 10(b)* and *Rule 10b-5* do not provide for this kind of "aiding and abetting" liability in private suits.

By way of contrast, the present case is about *primary* liability -- about individuals who allegedly themselves "make" materially false statements, not about those who help *others* to do so. The question is whether Janus Management is *primarily* liable for violating the Act, not whether it simply helped others violate the Act. The *Central Bank* defendant concededly did *not* make the false statements in question (others did), while here the defendants allegedly *did* make those statements. And a rule (the majority's rule) absolving those who allegedly *did* make false statements does not "follow from" a rule (*Central Bank*'s rule) absolving those who concededly did *not* do so.

The majority adds that to interpret the word "make" as including those "without ultimate control over the content of a statement" would "substantially undermine" *Central Bank*'s holding. *Ante*, at 7. Would it? The Court in *Central Bank* specifically wrote that its holding did

> "not mean that secondary actors in the securities markets are always free from liability under the securities Acts. *Any person or entity, including a lawyer, accountant, or bank, who* employs a manipulative device or *makes a material misstatement* (or omission) on which a purchaser or seller of securities relies *may be liable as a primary violator under 10b-5*, assuming *all* of the requirements for primary liability under *Rule 10b-5* are met." *511 U.S., at 191* (some emphasis added).

Thus, as far as *Central Bank* is concerned, depending upon the circumstances, board members, senior firm officials, officials tasked to develop a marketing document, large investors, or others (taken together or separately) all might "make" materially false statements subjecting themselves to primary liability. The majority's rule does not protect, it *extends*, *Central Bank*'s holding of no-liability into new territory that *Central Bank* explicitly placed outside that holding. And by ignoring the language in which *Central Bank* did so, the majority's rule itself undermines *Central Bank*. Where is the legal support for the majority's "draw[ing] a clean line," *ante*, at 7, n. 6, that so seriously conflicts with *Central Bank?* Indeed, where is the legal support for the majority's suggestion that plaintiffs must show some kind of "attribution" of a statement to a defendant, *ante*, at 11, n. 11 -- if it means plaintiffs must show, not only that the defendant "ma[d]e" the statement, but something more?

The majority also refers to *Stoneridge,* but that case offers it no help. In *Stoneridge*, firms that supplied electronic equipment to a cable television company agreed with the cable television company to enter into a series of fraudulent sales and purchases, for example, a sale at an unusually high price, thereby providing funds which the suppliers would use to buy advertising from the cable television company. These arrangements enabled the cable television company to fool its accountants (and ultimately the public) into believing that it had more revenue (for example, advertising revenue) than it really had. As part of the agreement, the companies exchanged letters and backdated contracts to conceal the fraud. Investors subsequently sued the cable television company, some of its officers, its auditors, and the equipment suppliers, as well, claiming that all of them had engaged in a scheme to defraud securities purchasers. In respect to most of the defendants, investors identified allegedly materially false statements contained in the cable television company's financial statements or similar docu- ments. But in respect to the equipment suppliers, in-vestors claimed that the relevant deceptive conduct was in the letters, backdated contracts, and related oral conversations about the scheme. The investors argued that the equipment suppliers, "by participating in the transactions," violated *§ 10(b)* and *Rule 10b-5. Stoneridge, 552 U.S., at 155*.

The Court held that the equipment suppliers could not be found liable for securities fraud in a private suit under *§ 10(b)*. But in doing so, it did not deny that the equipment suppliers *had made* the false statements contained in the letters, contracts, and conversations. See *552 U.S., at 158-*

159. Rather, the Court said the issue in the case was whether "any deceptive statement or act respondents made was not actionable because it did not have the requisite *proximate relation* to the investors' harm." *Ibid.* (emphasis added). And it held that these deceptive statements or actions could not provide a basis for liability because the investors could not prove sufficient *reliance* upon the particular false statements that the equipment suppliers had made.

The Court pointed out that the equipment suppliers "had no duty to disclose; and their deceptive acts were not communicated to the public." *552 U.S., at 159*. And the Court went on to say that "as a result," the investors "cannot show reliance upon any" of the equipment suppliers' actions, "except in an indirect chain that we find too remote for liability." *Ibid.* The Court concluded,

> "[the equipment suppliers'] deceptive acts, which were not disclosed to the investing public, are too remote to satisfy the requirement of reliance. It was [the cable company], not [the equipment suppliers], that misled its auditor and filed fraudulent financial statements; nothing [the equipment suppliers] did made it necessary or inevitable for [the cable company] to record the transactions as it did." *552 U.S., at 161*.

Insofar as the equipment suppliers' conduct was at issue, the fraudulent "arrangement . . . took place in the marketplace for goods and services, not in the investment sphere." *552 U.S., at 166*.

It is difficult for me to see how *Stoneridge* "support[s]" the majority's rule. *Ante*, at 7. No one in *Stoneridge* disputed the *making* of the relevant statements, the fraudulent contracts and the like. And no one in *Stoneridge* contended that the equipment suppliers were, in fact, the *makers* of the cable company's misstatements. Rather, *Stoneridge* was concerned with whether the equipment suppliers' *separate* statements were sufficiently disclosed in the securities marketplace so as to be the basis for investor reliance. They were not. But this is a different inquiry than whether statements acknowledged to have been disclosed in the securities marketplace and ripe for reliance can be said to have been "ma[d]e" by one or another actor. How then does *Stoneridge* support the majority's new rule?

The majority adds that its rule is necessary to avoid "a theory of liability similar to -- but broader in application than" -- *§ 20(a)*'s liability, for "'[e]very person who, directly or indirectly, controls any person liable'" for violations of the securities laws. *Ante*, at 10 (quoting *15 U.S.C. A. § 78t(a)* (Feb. 2011 Supp.)). But that is not so. This Court has explained that the possibility of an express remedy under the securities laws does not preclude a claim under *§ 10(b)*. *Herman & MacLean v. Huddleston, 459 U.S. 375, 388 (1983)*.

More importantly, a person who is liable under *§ 20(a)* controls another *"person" who is "liable"* for a securities violation. *Morrison v. National Australia Bank Ltd., 561 U.S. ___, ___, n. 2 (2010)* ("Liability under *§ 20(a)* is obviously derivative of liability under some other provision of the Exchange Act"). We here examine whether a person is primarily liable whether they do, or they do not, control another person *who is liable*. That is to say, here, the liability of some "other person" is not at issue.

And there is at least one significant category of cases that *§ 10(b)* may address that derivative forms of liability, such as under *§ 20(a)*, cannot, namely, cases in which one actor exploits another as an innocent intermediary for its misstatements. Here, it may well be that the Fund's board of trustees knew nothing about the falsity of the prospectuses. See, *e.g., In re Lammert,* Release No. 348, 93 S. E. C. Docket 5676, 5700, 2008 SEC LEXIS 937 (2008) (Janus Management was aware of market timing in the Janus Fund no later than 2002, but "[t]his knowledge was never shared with the Board"). And if so, *§ 20(a)* would not apply.

The possibility of guilty management and innocent board is the 13th stroke of the new rule's clock. What is to happen when guilty management writes a prospectus (for the board) containing materially false statements and fools both board and public into believing they are true? Apparently under the majority's rule, in such circumstances *no one* could be found to have "ma[d]e" a materially false statement -- even though under the common law the managers would likely have been guilty or liable (in analogous circumstances) for doing so as *principals* (and not as aiders and abettors). See, *e.g.,* 2 W. LaFave, Substantive Criminal Law § 13.1(a) (2d ed. 2003); 1 M. Hale, Pleas of the Crown 617 (1736); Perkins, Parties to Crime, 89 U. Pa. L. Rev. 581, 583 (1941) (one is guilty as a principal when one uses an innocent third party to commit a crime); *Restatement (Second) of Torts § 533* (1976). Cf. *United States v. Giles, 300 U.S. 41, 48-49 (1937).*

Indeed, under the majority's rule it seems unlikely that the SEC itself in such circumstances could exercise the authority Congress has granted it to pursue primary violators who "make" false statements or the authority that Congress has specifically provided to prosecute aiders and abettors to securities violations. See § 104, 109 Stat. 757 (codified at *15 U.S.C. A. § 78t(e)* (Feb. 2011 Supp.)) (granting SEC authority to prosecute aiders and abettors). That is because the managers, not having "ma[d]e" the statement, would not be liable as principals and there would be no other primary violator they might have tried to "aid" or "abet." *Ibid.; SEC v. DiBella, 587 F.3d 553, 566 (CA2 2009)* (prosecution for aiding and abetting requires primary violation to which offender gave "substantial assistance" (internal quotation marks omitted)).

If the majority believes, as its footnote hints, that *§ 20(b)* could provide a basis for liability in this case, *ante,* at 10, n. 10, then it should remand the case for possible amendment of the complaint. "There is a dearth of authority construing *Section 20(b),*" which has been thought largely "superfluous in 10b-5 cases." 5B A. Jacobs, Disclosure and Remedies Under the Securities Law § 11-8, p. 11-72 (2011). Hence respondent, who reasonably thought that it referred to the proper securities law provision, is faultless for failing to mention *§ 20(b)* as well.

In sum, I can find nothing in *§ 10(b)* or in *Rule 10b-5,* its language, its history, or in precedent suggesting that Congress, in enacting the securities laws, intended a loophole of the kind that the majority's rule may well create.

II

Rejecting the majority's rule, of course, does not decide the question before us. We must still determine whether, in light of the complaint's allegations, Janus Management could have "ma[d]e" the false statements in the prospectuses at issue. In my view, the answer to this question is "Yes." The specific relationships alleged among Janus Management, the Janus Fund, and the prospectus statements warrant the conclusion that Janus Management did "make" those statements.

In part, my conclusion reflects the fact that this Court and lower courts have made clear that at least *sometimes* corporate officials and others can be held liable under *Rule 10b-5* for having "ma[d]e" a materially false statement even when that statement appears in a document (or is made by a third person) that the officials do not legally control. In *Herman & MacLean*, for example, this Court pointed out that "certain individuals who play a part in preparing the registration statement," including corporate officers, lawyers, and accountants, may be primarily liable even where "they are not named as having prepared or certified" the registration statement. *459 U.S., at 386, n. 22*. And as I have already pointed out, this Court wrote in *Central Bank* that a "lawyer, accountant, or bank, who . . . makes a material misstatement (or omission) on which a purchaser or seller of securities relies *may be liable as a primary violator under 10b-5*, assuming *all* of the requirements for primary liability under *Rule 10b-5* are met." *511 U.S., at 191* (some emphasis added).

Given the statements in our opinions, it is not surprising that lower courts have found primary liability for actors without "ultimate authority" over issued statements. One court, for example, concluded that an accountant could be primarily liable for having "ma[d]e" false statements, where he issued fraudulent opinion and certification letters reproduced in prospectuses, annual reports, and other corporate materials for which he was not ultimately responsible. *Anixter v. Home-Stake Production Co., 77 F.3d 1215, 1225-1227 (CA10 1996)*. In a later case postdating *Stoneridge*, that court reaffirmed that an outside consultant could be primarily liable for having "ma[d]e" false statements, where he drafted fraudulent quarterly and annual filing statements later reviewed and certified by the firm's auditor, officers, and counsel. *SEC v. Wolfson, 539 F.3d 1249, 1261 (CA10 2008)*. And another court found that a corporation's chief financial officer could be held primarily liable as having "ma[d]e" misstatements that appeared in a form 10-K that she prepared but did not sign or file. *McConville v. SEC, 465 F.3d 780, 787 (CA7 2006)*.

One can also easily find lower court cases explaining that corporate officials may be liable for having "ma[d]e" false statements where those officials use innocent persons as conduits through which the false statements reach the public (without necessarily attributing the false statements to the officials). See, *e.g., In re Navarre Corp. Securities Litigation, 299 F.3d 735, 743 (CA8 2002)* (liability may be premised on use of analysts as a conduit to communicate false statements to market); *In re Cabletron Systems, Inc., 311 F.3d 11, 38 (CA1 2002)* (rejecting a test requiring legal "control" over third parties making statements as giving "company officials too much leeway to commit fraud on the market by using analysts as their mouthpieces" (internal quotation marks omitted)); *Novak v. Kasaks, 216 F.3d 300, 314-315 (CA2 2000)*; *Cooper v. Pickett, 137 F.3d 616, 624 (CA9 1997)*; *Freeland v. Iridium World Communications, Ltd., 545 F. Supp. 2d 59, 75-76 (DC 2008)*.

My conclusion also reflects the particular circumstances that the complaint alleges. The complaint states that "Janus Management, as investment advisor to the funds, is responsible for the day-to-day management of its investment portfolio and other business affairs of the funds. Janus Management furnishes advice and recom-mendations concerning the funds' investments, as well as administrative, compliance and accounting services for the funds." Complaint P18,

App. to Pet. for Cert. 65a. Each of the Fund's 17 officers was a vice president of Janus Management. App. 250a-258a. The Fund has "no assets separate and apart from those they hold for shareholders." *In re Mutual Funds Inv. Litigation, 384 F. Supp. 2d 845, 853, n. 3 (Md. 2005)*. Janus Management disseminated the fund prospectuses through its parent company's Web site. Complaint P38, App. to Pet. for Cert. 72a. Janus Management employees drafted and reviewed the Fund prospectuses, including language about "market timing." Complaint P31, *id.*, at 69a; *In re Mutual Funds Inv. Litigation, 590 F. Supp. 2d 741, 747 (Md. 2008)*. And Janus Management may well have kept the trustees in the dark about the true "market timing" facts. Complaint P51, App. to Pet. for Cert. 80a; *In re Lammert*, 93 S. E. C. Docket, at 5700, 2008 SEC LEXIS 937.

Given these circumstances, as long as some managers, sometimes, can be held to have "ma[d]e" a materially false statement, Janus Management can be held to have done so on the facts alleged here. The relationship between Janus Management and the Fund could hardly have been closer. Janus Management's involvement in preparing and writing the relevant statements could hardly have been greater. And there is a serious suggestion that the board itself knew little or nothing about the falsity of what was said. See *supra*, at 9, 13. Unless we adopt a formal rule (as the majority here has done) that would arbitrarily exclude from the scope of the word "make" those who manage a firm -- even when those managers perpetrate a fraud through an unknowing intermediary -- the management company at issue here falls within that scope. We should hold the allegations in the complaint in this respect legally sufficient.

With respect, I dissent.

---

1. Impact. The outcome in *Janus Capital* underlines the importance of, and limits on, "controlling person liability" under Section 20(a) of the Securities Exchange Act. That section makes a "controlling person" (as defined) liable "to the same extent as [the] controlled person is liable." But if the Janus Investment Fund lacked scienter (which is entirely possible because investment advisers seldom disclose fraud or misconduct to the fund's board), then none of Janus Investment Fund, JCM or JCG could be held liable under Rule 10b-5 under this language where the controlled person was not liable. In a strongly worded editorial immediately after the decision, the New York Times asked in its caption: "So No One's Responsible?" (N.Y. Times, June 15, 2011 at A-26). Note, however, that in footnote 10 of the majority decision, the majority reserved decision on whether "Congress created liability for entities that act through innocent intermediaries" (but the majority did not remand for further consideration of this issue).

Merck & Co., Inc., et al., v. Reynolds, et al.

Supreme Court of the United States, 2010

130 S. Ct. 1784, 176 L. Ed. 2d 582

■ JUSTICE BREYER delivered the opinion of the Court.

This case concerns the timeliness of a complaint filed in a private securities fraud action. The complaint was timely if filed no more than two years after the plaintiffs "discover[ed] the facts constituting the violation." *28 U.S.C. § 1658(b)(1).* Construing this limitations statute for the first time, we hold that a cause of action accrues (1) when the plaintiff did in fact discover, or (2) when a reasonably diligent plaintiff would have discovered, "the facts constituting the violation" -- whichever comes first. We also hold that the "facts constituting the violation" include the fact of scienter, "a mental state embracing intent to deceive, manipulate, or defraud," *Ernst & Ernst v. Hochfelder, 425 U.S. 185, 194, n. 12 (1976).* Applying this standard, we affirm the Court of Appeals' determination that the complaint filed here was timely.

I

The action before us involves a claim by a group of investors (the plaintiffs, respondents here) that Merck & Co. and others (the petitioners here, hereinafter Merck) knowingly misrepresented the risks of heart attacks accompanying the use of Merck's pain-killing drug, Vioxx (leading to economic losses when the risks later became apparent). The plaintiffs brought an action for securities fraud under *§ 10(b)* of the Securities Exchange Act of 1934. . . .

The applicable statute of limitations provides that a "private right of action" that, like the present action, "involves a claim of fraud, deceit, manipulation, or contrivance in contravention of a regulatory requirement concerning the securities laws . . . may be brought not later than the earlier of --

"(1) 2 years after the discovery of the facts constituting the violation; or

"(2) 5 years after such violation." *28 U.S.C. § 1658(b).*

The complaint in this case was filed on November 6, 2003, and no one doubts that it was filed within five years of the alleged violation. Therefore, the critical date for timeliness purposes is November 6, 2001 -- two years before this complaint was filed. Merck claims that before this date the plaintiffs had (or should have) discovered the "facts constituting the violation." If so, by the time the plaintiffs filed their complaint, the 2-year statutory period in *§ 1658(b)(1)* had run. The plaintiffs reply that they had not, and could not have, discovered by the critical date those "facts," particularly not the facts related to scienter, and that their complaint was therefore timely.

A

We first set out the relevant pre-November 2001 facts, as we have gleaned them from the briefs, the record, and the opinions below.

1. 1990's. In the mid-1990's Merck developed Vioxx. In 1999 the Food and Drug

Administration (FDA) approved it for prescription use. Vioxx suppresses pain by inhibiting the body's production of an enzyme called COX-2 (cyclooxygenase-2). COX-2 is associated with pain and inflammation. Unlike some other anti-inflammatory drugs in its class like aspirin, ibuprofen, and naproxen, Vioxx does not inhibit production of a second enzyme called COX-1 (cyclooxygenase-1). COX-1 plays a part in the functioning of the gastrointestinal tract and also platelet aggregation (associated with blood clots). App. 50-51.

2. March 2000. Merck announced the results of a study, called the "VIGOR" study. *Id.*, at 291-294. The study compared Vioxx with another painkiller, naproxen. The study showed that persons taking Vioxx suffered fewer gastrointestinal side effects (as Merck had hoped). But the study also revealed that approximately 4 out of every 1,000 participants who took Vioxx suffered heart attacks, compared to only 1 per 1,000 participants who took naproxen. *Id.*, at 296, 306; . . . .

Merck's press release acknowledged VIGOR's adverse cardiovascular data. But Merck said that these data were "consistent with naproxen's ability to block platelet aggregation." App. 291. Merck noted that, since "Vioxx, like all COX-2 selective medicines, does not block platelet aggregation[, it] would not be expected to have similar effects." *Ibid.* And Merck added that "safety data from all other completed and ongoing clinical trials . . . showed no indication of a difference in the incidence of thromboembolic events between Vioxx" and either a placebo or comparable drugs. *Id.*, at 293 (emphasis deleted).

This theory -- that VIGOR's troubling cardiovascular findings might be due to the absence of a benefit conferred by naproxen rather than due to a harm caused by Vioxx -- later became known as the "naproxen hypothesis." In advancing that hypothesis, Merck acknowledged that the naproxen benefit "had not been observed previously." *Id.*, at 291. Journalists and stock market analysts reported all of the above -- the positive gastrointestinal results, the troubling cardiovascular finding, the naproxen hypothesis, and the fact that the naproxen hypothesis was unproved. . . .

3. February 2001 to August 2001. Public debate about the naproxen hypothesis continued. In February 2001, the FDA's Arthritis Advisory Committee convened to consider Merck's request that the Vioxx label be changed to reflect VIGOR's positive gastrointestinal findings. The VIGOR cardiovascular findings were also discussed. *Id.*, at 392-395, 558-577. In May 2001, a group of plaintiffs filed a products-liability lawsuit against Merck, claiming that "Merck's own research" had demonstrated that "users of Vioxx were four times as likely to suffer heart attacks as compared to other less expensive, medications." *Id.*, at 869. In August 2001, the Journal of the American Medical Association wrote that the available data raised a "cautionary flag" and strongly urged that "a trial specifically assessing cardiovascular risk" be done. *Id.*, at 331-332; Mukherjee, Nissen, & Topol, Risk of Cardiovascular Events Associated with Selective Cox-2 Inhibitors, 286 JAMA 954 (2001). At about the same time, Bloomberg News quoted a Merck scientist who claimed that Merck had "additional data" that were "very, very reassuring," and Merck issued a press release stating that it stood "behind the overall and cardiovascular safety profile . . . of Vioxx." App. 434, 120 (emphasis deleted; internal quotation marks omitted).

4. September and October 2001. The FDA sent Merck a warning letter released to the public on September 21, 2001. It said that, in respect to cardiovascular risks, Merck's Vioxx marketing was "false, lacking in fair balance, or otherwise misleading." *Id.*, at 339. At the same time, the FDA acknowledged that the naproxen hypothesis was a "possible explanation" of the VIGOR results. *Id.*, at 340. But it found that Merck's "promotional campaign selectively present[ed]" that hypothesis without adequately acknowledging "another reasonable explanation," namely, "that Vioxx may have pro-thrombotic [*i.e.*, adverse cardiovascular] properties." *Ibid.* The FDA ordered Merck to send healthcare providers a corrective letter. *Id.*, at 353.

After the FDA letter was released, more products-liability lawsuits were filed. See *id.*, at 885-956. Merck's share price fell by 6.6% over several days. See *id.*, at 832. By October 1, the price rebounded. See *ibid.* On October 9, 2001, the New York Times said that Merck had reexamined its own data and "found no evidence that Vioxx increased the risk of heart attacks." App. 504. It quoted the president of Merck Research Laboratories as positing "'two possible interpretations'": "'Naproxen lowers the heart attack rate, or Vioxx raises it.'" *Ibid.* Stock analysts, while reporting the warning letter, also noted that the FDA had not denied that the naproxen hypothesis remained an unproven but possible explanation. See *id.*, at 614, 626, 628.

B

We next set forth three important events that occurred *after* the critical date.

1. October 2003. The Wall Street Journal published the results of a Merck-funded Vioxx study conducted at Boston's Brigham and Women's Hospital. After examining the medical records of more than 50,000 Medicare patients, researchers found that those given Vioxx for 30-to-90 days were 37% more likely to have suffered a heart attack than those given either a different painkiller or no painkiller at all. *Id.*, at 164-165. (That is to say, if patients given a different painkiller or given no painkiller at all suffered 10 heart attacks, then the same number of patients given Vioxx would suffer 13 or 14 heart attacks.) Merck defended Vioxx and pointed to the study's limitations. *Id.*, at 165-167.

2. September 30, 2004. Merck withdrew Vioxx from the market. It said that a new study had found "an increased risk of confirmed cardiovascular events beginning after 18 months of continuous therapy." *Id.*, at 182 (internal quotation marks omitted). A Merck representative publicly described the results as "totally unexpected." *Id.*, at 186. Merck's shares fell by 27% the same day. *Id.*, at 185, 856.

3. November 1, 2004. The Wall Street Journal published an article stating that "internal Merck e-mails and marketing materials as well as interviews with outside scientists show that the company fought forcefully for years to keep safety concerns from destroying the drug's commercial prospects." *Id.*, at 189-190. The article said that an early e-mail from Merck's head of research had said that the VIGOR "results showed that the cardiovascular events 'are clearly there,'" that it was "'a shame but . . . a low incidence,'" and that it "'is mechanism based as we worried it was.'" *Id.*, at 192. It also said that Merck had given its salespeople instructions to "'DODGE'" questions about Vioxx's cardiovascular effects. *Id.*, at 193.

C

The plaintiffs filed their complaint on November 6, 2003. As subsequently amended, the complaint alleged that Merck had defrauded investors by promoting the naproxen hypothesis, knowing the hypothesis was false. It said, for example, that Merck "knew, at least as early as

1996, of the serious safety issues with Vioxx," and that a "1998 internal Merck clinical trial . . . revealed that . . . serious cardiovascular events . . . occurred six times more frequently in patients given Vioxx than in patients given a different arthritis drug or placebo." *Id.*, at 56, 58-59 (emphasis and capitalization deleted).

Merck, believing that the plaintiffs knew or should have known the "facts constituting the violation" at least two years earlier, moved to dismiss the complaint, saying it was filed too late. The District Court granted the motion. The court held that the (March 2001) VIGOR study, the (September 2001) FDA warning letter, and Merck's (October 2001) response should have alerted the plaintiffs to a *"possibility* that Merck had knowingly misrepresented material facts" no later than October 9, 2001, thus placing the plaintiffs on "inquiry notice" to look further. *In re Merck & Co. Securities, Derivative & "ERISA" Litigation, 483 F. Supp. 2d 407, 423 (NJ 2007)* (emphasis added). Finding that the plaintiffs had failed to "show that they exercised reasonable due diligence but nevertheless were unable to discover their injuries," the court took October 9, 2001, as the date that the limitations period began to run and therefore found the complaint untimely. *Id., at 424.*

The Court of Appeals for the Third Circuit reversed. A majority held that the pre-November 2001 events, while constituting "storm warnings," did not suggest much by way of scienter, and consequently did not put the plaintiffs on "inquiry notice," requiring them to investigate further. *In re Merck & Co. Securities, Derivative & "ERISA" Litigation, 543 F.3d 150, 172 (2008).* A dissenting judge considered the pre-November 2001 events sufficient to start the 2-year clock running. *Id., at 173* (opinion of Roth, J.).

Merck sought review in this Court, pointing to disagreements among the Courts of Appeals. Compare *Theoharous v. Fong, 256 F.3d 1219, 1228 (CA11 2001)* (limitations period begins to run when information puts plaintiffs on "inquiry notice" of the need for investigation), with *Shah v. Meeker, 435 F.3d 244, 249 (CA2 2006)* (same; but if plaintiff *does* investigate, period runs "from the date such inquiry should have revealed the fraud" (internal quotation marks omitted)), and *New England Health Care Employees Pension Fund v. Ernst & Young, LLP, 336 F.3d 495, 501 (CA6 2003)* (limitations period *always* begins to run only when a reasonably diligent plaintiff, after being put on "inquiry notice," should have discovered facts constituting violation (internal quotation marks omitted)). We granted Merck's petition.

II

Before turning to Merck's arguments, we consider a more basic matter. The parties and the Solicitor General agree that *§ 1658(b)(1)*'s word "discovery" refers not only to a plaintiff's *actual* discovery of certain facts, but also to the facts that a reasonably diligent plaintiff would have discovered. We agree. But because the statute's language does not make this interpretation obvious, and because we cannot answer the question presented without considering whether the parties are right about this matter, we set forth the reasons for our agreement in some detail.

We recognize that one might read the statutory words "after the discovery of the facts constituting the violation" as referring to the time a plaintiff *actually* discovered the relevant facts. But in the statute of limitations context, the word "discovery" is often used as a term of art in connection with the "discovery rule," a doctrine that delays accrual of a cause of action until the plaintiff has "discovered" it. The rule arose in fraud cases as an exception to the general limitations rule that a cause of action accrues once a plaintiff has a "complete and present cause of action," *Bay Area Laundry and Dry Cleaning Pension Trust Fund v. Ferbar Corp. of Cal., 522 U.S. 192, 201 (1997)* (citing *Clark v. Iowa City, 87 U.S. 583 (1875)*; internal quotation marks omitted). This Court long ago recognized that something different was needed in the case of fraud, where a defendant's deceptive conduct may prevent a plaintiff from even *knowing* that he or she has been defrauded. Otherwise, "the law which was designed to prevent fraud" could become "the means by which it is made successful and secure." *Bailey v. Glover, 88 U.S. 342 (1875)*. Accordingly, "where a plaintiff has been injured by fraud and remains in ignorance of it without any fault or want of diligence or care on his part, the bar of the statute does not begin to run until the fraud is *discovered*." *Holmberg v. Armbrecht, 327 U.S. 392, 397 (1946)* (internal quotation marks omitted; emphasis added). And for more than a century, courts have understood that "[f]raud is deemed to be discovered . . . when, in the exercise of reasonable diligence, it could have been discovered." 2 H. Wood, Limitation of Actions § 276b(11), p. 1402 (4th ed. 1916); see *id.,* at 1401-1403, and nn. 74-84 (collecting cases and statutes). . . .

More recently, both state and federal courts have applied forms of the "discovery rule" to claims other than fraud. See 2 C. Corman, Limitation of Actions §§ 11.1.2.1, 11.1.2.3, pp. 136-142, and nn. 6-13, 18-23 (1991 and 1993 Supp.) (hereinafter Corman) (collecting cases); see, *e.g., United States v. Kubrick, 444 U.S. 111 (1979)*. Legislatures have codified the discovery rule in various contexts. 2 Corman § 11.2, at 170-171, and nn. 1-9 (collecting statutes); see, *e.g., 28 U.S.C. § 2409a(g)* (actions to quiet title against the United States). In doing so, legislators have written the word "discovery" directly into the statute. And when they have done so, state and federal courts have typically interpreted the word to refer not only to actual discovery, but also to the hypothetical discovery of facts a reasonably diligent plaintiff would know. See, *e.g., Peacock v. Barnes, 142 N. C. 215, 217-220, 55 S. E. 99, 100 (1906)*. . . .

Thus, treatise writers now describe "the discovery rule" as allowing a claim "to accrue when the litigant first knows *or with due diligence should know* facts that will form the basis for an action." 2 Corman § 11.1.1, at 134 (emphasis added); see also *ibid.,* n. 1 (collecting cases); *37 Am. Jur. 2d, Fraud and Deceit § 347*, p. 354 (2001 and Supp. 2009) (noting that the various formulations of "discovery" all provide that "in addition to actual knowledge of the fraud, once a reasonably diligent party is in a position that they should have sufficient knowledge or information to have actually discovered the fraud, they are charged with discovery"); *id.,* at 354-355, and nn. 2-11 (collecting cases).

Like the parties, we believe that Congress intended courts to interpret the word "discovery" in *§ 1658(b)(1)* similarly. Before Congress enacted that statute, this Court, having found in the federal securities laws the existence of an implied private § 10(b) action, determined its governing limitations period by looking to other limitations periods in the federal securities laws. *Lampf, Pleva, Lipkind, Prupis & Petigrow v. Gilbertson, 501 U.S. 350 (1991)*. Noting the existence of various formulations "differ[ing] slightly in terminology," the Court chose the language in *15 U.S.C. § 78i(e)*, the statutory provision that governs securities price manipulation claims. *501 U.S., at 364, n. 9*. And in doing so, the Court said that private § 10(b) actions "must be commenced within one year *after the discovery of the facts constituting the violation* and within three years after such violation." *Id.,* at 364 (emphasis added). (The Court listed among the various formulations the one in *15 U.S.C. § 77m*, on which the concurrence relies. See *post,* at 2-4 (SCALIA, J., concurring in part and concurring in judgment); *Lampf, supra, at 360* and n. 7 (quoting *§ 77m*).)

Subsequently, every Court of Appeals to decide the matter held that "discovery of the facts constituting the violation" occurs not only once a plaintiff *actually* discovers the facts, but also when a hypothetical reasonably diligent plaintiff would have discovered them. See, *e.g., Law v. Medco Research, Inc., 113 F.3d 781, 785-786 (CA7 1997)*. . . . Some of those courts noted that other limitations provisions in the federal securities laws explicitly provide that the period begins to run "'after the discovery of the untrue statement . . . *or after such discovery should have been made by [the] exercise of reasonable diligence*,'" whereas the formulation adopted by the Court in *Lampf* from *15 U.S.C. § 78i(e)* does not. . . . But, courts reasoned, because the term "discovery" in respect to statutes of limitations for fraud has long been understood to include discoveries a reasonably diligent plaintiff would make, the omission of an explicit provision to that effect did not matter. . . .

In 2002, when Congress enacted the present limitations statute, it repeated *Lampf*'s critical language. The statute says that an action based on fraud "may be brought not later than the earlier of . . . 2 years *after the discovery of the facts constituting the violation*" (or "5 years after such violation"). § 804 of the Sarbanes-Oxley Act, 116 Stat. 801, codified at *28 U.S.C. § 1658(b)* (emphasis added). (This statutory provision does *not* make the linguistic distinction that the concurrence finds in a *different* statute, *§ 77m*, and upon which its argument rests. Cf. *29 U.S.C. § 1113(2)* (statute in which Congress provided that an action be brought "three years after the earliest date on which the plaintiff had *actual knowledge* of the breach or violation" (emphasis added)).) Not surprisingly, the Courts of Appeals unanimously have continued to interpret the word "discovery" in this statute as including not only facts a particular plaintiff knows, but also the facts any reasonably diligent plaintiff would know. See, *e.g., Staehr v. Hartford Financial Servs. Group, Inc., 547 F.3d 406, 411 (CA2 2008); Sudo Properties, Inc. v. Terrebonne Parish Consolidated Govt., 503 F.3d 371, 376 (CA5 2007).*

We normally assume that, when Congress enacts statutes, it is aware of relevant judicial precedent. See, *e.g., Edelman v. Lynchburg College, 535 U.S. 106, 116-117, and n. 13 (2002); Commissioner v. Keystone Consol. Industries, Inc., 508 U.S. 152, 159 (1993)*. Given the history and precedent surrounding the use of the word "discovery" in the limitations context generally as well as in this provision in particular, the reasons for making this assumption are particularly strong here. We consequently hold that "discovery" as used in this statute encompasses not only those facts the plaintiff actually knew, but also those facts a reasonably diligent plaintiff would have known. And we evaluate Merck's claims accordingly.

III

We turn now to Merck's arguments in favor of holding that petitioners' claims accrued before November 6, 2001. First, Merck argues that the statute does not require "discovery" of scienter-related "facts." See Brief for Petitioners 19-28. We cannot agree, however, that facts about scienter are unnecessary.

The statute says that the limitations period does not begin to run until "discovery of the *facts constituting the violation*." *28 U.S.C. § 1658(b)(1)* (emphasis added). Scienter is assuredly a "fact." In a § 10(b) action, scienter refers to "a mental state embracing intent to deceive, manipulate, or defraud." *Ernst & Ernst, 425 U.S., at 194, n. 12.* And the "'state of a man's mind is as much a fact as the state of his digestion.'" *Postal Service Bd. of Governors v. Aikens, 460 U.S. 711, 716 (1983)* (quoting *Edgington* v. *Fitzmaurice*, [1885] 29 Ch. Div. 459, 483).

And this "fact" of scienter "constitut[es]" an important and necessary element of a § 10(b) "violation." A plaintiff cannot recover without proving that a defendant made a material misstatement *with an intent to deceive* -- not merely innocently or negligently. See *Tellabs, Inc. v. Makor Issues & Rights, Ltd., 551 U.S. 308, 319 (2007)*; *Ernst & Ernst, supra.* Indeed, Congress has enacted special heightened pleading requirements for the scienter element of § 10(b) fraud cases. See *15 U.S.C. § 78u-4(b)(2)* (requiring plaintiffs to "state with particularity *facts* giving rise to a strong inference that the defendant acted with the required state of mind" (emphasis added)). As a result, unless a *§ 10(b)* plaintiff can set forth facts in the complaint showing that it is "at least as likely as" not that the defendant acted with the relevant knowledge or intent, the claim will fail. *Tellabs, supra, at 328.* (emphasis deleted). It would therefore frustrate the very purpose of the discovery rule in this provision -- which, after all, specifically applies only in cases "involv[ing] a claim of fraud, deceit, manipulation, or contrivance," *§ 1658(b)* -- if the limitations period began to run regardless of whether a plaintiff had discovered any facts suggesting scienter. So long as a defendant concealed for two years that he made a misstatement with an intent to deceive, the limitations period would expire before the plaintiff had actually "discover[ed]" the fraud.

We consequently hold that facts showing scienter are among those that "constitut[e] the violation." In so holding, we say nothing about other facts necessary to support a private § 10(b) action. Cf. Brief for United States as *Amicus Curiae* 12, n. 1 (suggesting that facts concerning a plaintiff's reliance, loss, and loss causation are not among those that constitute "the violation" and therefore need not be "discover[ed]" for a claim to accrue).

Second, Merck argues that, even if "discovery" requires facts related to scienter, facts that tend to show a materially false or misleading statement (or material omission) are ordinarily sufficient to show scienter as well. See Brief for Petitioners 22, 28-29. But we do not see how that is so. We recognize that certain statements are such that, to show them false is normally to show scienter as well. It is unlikely, for example, that someone would falsely say "I am not married" without being aware of the fact that his statement is false. Where *§ 10(b)* is at issue, however, the relation of factual falsity and state of mind is more context specific. An incorrect prediction about a firm's future earnings, by itself, does not automatically tell us whether the speaker deliberately lied or just made an innocent (and therefore nonactionable) error. Hence, the statute may require "discovery" of scienter-related facts beyond the facts that show a statement (or omission) to be materially false or misleading. Merck fears that this requirement will give life to stale claims or subject defendants to liability for acts taken long ago. But Congress' inclusion in the statute of an unqualified bar on actions instituted "5 years after such violation," *§ 1658(b)(2)*, giving defendants total repose after five years, should diminish that fear. Cf. *Lampf, 501 U.S., at 363* (holding comparable bar not subject to equitable tolling).

Third, Merck says that the limitations period began to run prior to November 2001 because by that point the plaintiffs were on "inquiry notice." Merck uses the term "inquiry notice" to refer to the point "at which a plaintiff possesses a quantum of information sufficiently suggestive of wrongdoing that he should conduct a further inquiry." Brief for Petitioners 20. And some, but not all, Courts of Appeals have used the term in roughly similar ways. See, *e.g., Franze v. Equitable Assurance, 296 F.3d 1250, 1254 (CA11 2002)* ("[I]nquiry notice [is] '"the term used for knowledge of facts that would lead a reasonable person to begin investigating the possibility that his legal rights had been infringed'"). Cf. *Dodds, 12 F.3d at 350* ("duty of inquiry" arises once "circumstances would suggest to an investor of ordinary intelligence the probability that she had been defrauded"); *Fujisawa Pharmaceutical Co. v. Kapoor, 115 F.3d 1332, 1335-1336 (CA7 1997)* ("The facts constituting [inquiry] notice must be sufficien[t] . . . to incite the victim to investigate" and "to enable him to tie up any loose ends and complete the investigation in time to file a timely suit"); *Great Rivers Cooperative of Southeastern Iowa v. Farmland Industries, Inc., 120 F.3d 893, 896 (CA8 1997)* ("Inquiry notice exists when the victim is aware of facts that would lead a reasonable person to investigate *and* consequently acquire actual knowledge of the defendant's misrepresentations" (emphasis added)).

If the term "inquiry notice" refers to the point where the facts would lead a reasonably diligent plaintiff to investigate further, that point is not necessarily the point at which the plaintiff would already have discovered facts showing scienter or other "facts constituting the violation." But the statute says that the plaintiff's claim accrues only after the "discovery" of those latter facts. Nothing in the text suggests that the limitations period can sometimes begin *before* "discovery" can take place. Merck points out that, as we have discussed, see *supra,* at 8-9, the court-created "discovery rule" exception to ordinary statutes of limitations is not generally available to plaintiffs who fail to pursue their claims with reasonable diligence. But we are dealing here with a statute, not a court-created exception to a statute. Because the statute contains no indication that the limitations period should occur at some earlier moment before "discovery," when a plaintiff would have *begun* investigating, we cannot accept Merck's argument.

As a fallback, Merck argues that even if the limitations period does generally begin at "discovery," it should nonetheless run from the point of "inquiry notice" in one particular situation, namely, where the actual plaintiff fails to undertake an investigation once placed on "inquiry notice." In such circumstances, Merck contends, the actual plaintiff is not diligent, and the law should not "effectively excuse a plaintiff's failure to conduct a further investigation" by placing that nondiligent plaintiff and a reasonably diligent plaintiff "in the same position." Brief for Petitioners 48.

We cannot accept this argument for essentially the same reason we reject "inquiry notice" as the standard generally: We cannot reconcile it with the statute, which simply provides that "discovery" is the event that triggers the 2-year limitations period -- for all plaintiffs. Cf. *United States v. Mack, 295 U.S. 480, 489* ("Laches within the term of the statute of limitations is no defense at law"). Furthermore, the statute does *not* place all plaintiffs "in the same position" no matter whether they investigate when investigation is warranted. The limitations period puts plaintiffs who fail to investigate once on "inquiry notice" at a disadvantage because it lapses two years after a reasonably diligent plaintiff would have discovered the necessary facts. A plaintiff who fails entirely to investigate or delays investigating may well not have discovered those facts by that time or, at least, may not have found sufficient facts by that time to be able to file a § 10(b) complaint that satisfies the applicable heightened pleading standards. Cf. *Young v. Lepone, 305 F.3d 1, 9 (CA1 2002)* ("[A] reasonably diligent investigation . . . may consume as little as a few days or as much as a few years to get to the bottom of the matter").

Merck further contends that its proposed "inquiry notice" standard is superior, because determining when a hypothetical reasonably diligent plaintiff would have "discover[ed]" the necessary facts is too complicated for judges to undertake. But courts applying the traditional discovery rule have long had to ask what a reasonably diligent plaintiff would have known and done in myriad circumstances. And courts in at least five Circuits already ask this kind of question in securities fraud cases. See, *e.g.*, *Rothman v. Gregor, 220 F.3d 81, 97 (CA2 2000)*; *New England Health Care, 336 F.3d at 501*; *Young, supra, at 1, 9-10*; *Sterlin v. Biomune Systems, 154 F.3d 1191, 1201 (CA10 1998)*; *Marks v. CDW Computer Centers, Inc., 122 F.3d 363, 367-368 (CA7 1997)*. Merck has not shown this precedent to be unworkable. We consequently find that the "discovery" of facts that put a plaintiff on "inquiry notice" does not automatically begin the running of the limitations period.

We conclude that the limitations period in *§ 1658(b)(1)* begins to run once the plaintiff did discover or a reasonably diligent plaintiff would have "discover[ed] the facts constituting the violation" -- whichever comes first. In determining the time at which "discovery" of those "facts" occurred, terms such as "inquiry notice" and "storm warnings" may be useful to the extent that they identify a time when the facts would have prompted a reasonably diligent plaintiff to begin investigating. But the limitations period does not begin to run until the plaintiff thereafter discovers or a reasonably diligent plaintiff would have discovered "the facts constituting the violation," including scienter -- irrespective of whether the actual plaintiff undertook a reasonably diligent investigation.

IV

Finally, Merck argues that, even if all its other legal arguments fail, the record still shows that, before November 6, 2001, the plaintiffs had discovered or should have discovered "the facts constituting the violation." In respect to scienter Merck primarily relies upon (1) the FDA's September 2001 warning letter, which said that Merck had "'minimized'" the VIGOR study's "'potentially serious cardiovascular findings'" and (2) pleadings filed in products-liability actions in September and October 2001 alleging that Merck had "'omitted, suppressed, or concealed material facts concerning the dangers and risks associated with Vioxx'" and "*purposefully* downplayed and/or understated the serious nature of the risks associated with Vioxx." Brief for Petitioners 36-37 (quoting App. 340, 893).

The FDA's warning letter, however, shows little or nothing about the here-relevant scienter, *i.e.*, whether Merck advanced the naproxen hypothesis with fraudulent intent. See Part I-A*(4)*, *supra*. The FDA itself described the pro-Vioxx naproxen hypothesis as a "possible explanation" for the VIGOR results, faulting Merck only for failing sufficiently to publicize the alternative less favorable to Merck, that Vioxx might be harmful. App. 340.

The products-liability complaints' statements about Merck's knowledge show little more. See Part I-A*(3)*, *supra*. Merck does not claim that these complaints contained any specific information suggesting the fraud alleged here, *i.e.*, that Merck knew the naproxen hypothesis was false even as it promoted it. And, without providing any reason to believe that the plaintiffs had special access to information about Merck's state of mind, the complaints alleged only in general terms that Merck had concealed information about Vioxx and "purposefully downplayed

-62-

and/or understated" the risks associated with Vioxx -- the same charge made in the FDA warning letter. App. 893.

In our view, neither these two circumstances nor any of the other pre-November 2001 circumstances that we have set forth in Part I-A, *supra,* whether viewed separately or together, reveal "facts" indicating scienter. Regardless of which, if any, of the events following November 6, 2001, constituted "discovery," we need only conclude that prior to November 6, 2001, the plaintiffs did not discover, and Merck has not shown that a reasonably diligent plaintiff would have discovered, "the facts constituting the violation." In light of our interpretation of the statute, our holdings in respect to scienter, and our application of those holdings to the circumstances of this case, we must, and we do, reach that conclusion. Thus, the plaintiffs' suit is timely. We need not -- and do not -- pass upon the Court of Appeals' suggestion that the November 2003 Brigham and Women's study might have triggered the statute of limitations. The judgment of the Court of Appeals is

Affirmed.

Jones v. Harris Associates L.P.

Supreme Court of the United States (2010)

130 S. Ct. 1418, 176 L. Ed. 2d 265

■ JUSTICE ALITO delivered the opinion of the Court.

We consider in this case what a mutual fund shareholder must prove in order to show that a mutual fund investment adviser breached the "fiduciary duty with respect to the receipt of compensation for services" that is imposed by § 36(b) of the Investment Company Act of 1940, *15 U.S.C. § 80a-35(b)* (hereinafter *§ 36(b)*).

I

A

The Investment Company Act of 1940 (Act), *15 U.S.C. § 80a-1 et seq.*, regulates investment companies, including mutual funds. "A mutual fund is a pool of assets, consisting primarily of [a] portfolio [of] securities, and belonging to the individual investors holding shares in the fund." *Burks v. Lasker, 441 U.S 471, 480 (1979)*. The following arrangements are typical. A separate entity called an investment adviser creates the mutual fund, which may have no employees of its own. See *Kamen v. Kemper Financial Services, Inc., 500 U.S. 90, 93 (1991)*; *Daily Income Fund, Inc. v. Fox, 464 U.S. 523, 536 (1984)*; *Burks, 441 U.S., at 480-481*. The adviser selects the fund's directors, manages the fund's investments, and provides other services. See *id., at 481*. Because of the relationship between a mutual fund and its investment adviser, the fund often "'cannot, as a practical matter sever its relationship with the adviser. Therefore, the forces of arm's-length bargaining do not work in the mutual fund industry in the same manner as they do in other sectors of the American economy.'" *Ibid.* (quoting S. Rep. No. 91-184, p. 5 (1969) (hereinafter S. Rep.)).

"Congress adopted the [Investment Company Act of 1940] because of its concern with the potential for abuse inherent in the structure of investment companies." *Daily Income Fund, 464 U.S., at 536* (internal quotation marks omitted). Recognizing that the relationship between a fund and its investment adviser was "fraught with potential conflicts of interest," the Act created protections for mutual fund shareholders. *Id., at 536-538* (internal quotation marks omitted); *Burks, supra, at 482-483*. Among other things, the Act required that no more than 60 percent of a fund's directors could be affiliated with the adviser and that fees for investment advisers be approved by the directors and the shareholders of the fund. See *§§ 10, 15(c)*.

The growth of mutual funds in the 1950's and 1960's prompted studies of the 1940 Act's effectiveness in protecting investors. See *Daily Income Fund, 464 U.S., at 537-538*. Studies commissioned or authored by the Securities and Exchange Commission (SEC or Commission) identified problems relating to the independence of investment company boards and the compensation received by investment advisers. See *ibid.* In response to such concerns, Congress amended the Act in 1970 and bolstered shareholder protection in two primary ways.

First, the amendments strengthened the "cornerstone" of the Act's efforts to check conflicts of interest, the independence of mutual fund boards of directors, which negotiate and scrutinize adviser compensation. *Burks, supra, at 482*. The amendments required that no more than 60 percent of a fund's directors be "persons who are interested persons," *e.g.*, that they have no interest in or affiliation with the investment adviser. *15 U. S. C. § 80a-10(a)*; *§ 80a-2(a)(19)*; see also *Daily Income Fund, supra, at 538*. These board members are given "a host of special responsibilities." *Burks, 441 U.S. at 482-483*. In particular, they must "review and approve the contracts of the investment adviser" annually, *id., at 483*, and a majority of these directors must approve an adviser's compensation, *15 U.S.C. § 80a-15(c)*. Second, § 36(b) of the Act imposed upon investment advisers a "fiduciary duty" with respect to compensation received from a mutual fund, *15 U.S.C. § 80a-35(b)*, and granted individual investors a private right of action for breach of that duty, *ibid*.

The "fiduciary duty" standard contained in *§ 36(b)* represented a delicate compromise. Prior to the adoption of the 1970 amendments, shareholders challenging investment adviser fees under state law were required to meet "common-law standards of corporate waste, under which an unreasonable or unfair fee might be approved unless the court deemed it 'unconscionable' or 'shocking,'" and "security holders challenging adviser fees under the [Investment Company Act] itself had been required to prove gross abuse of trust." *Daily Income Fund, 464 U.S., at 540, n. 12*. Aiming to give shareholders a stronger remedy, the SEC proposed a provision that would have empowered the Commission to bring actions to challenge a fee that was not "reasonable" and to intervene in any similar action brought by or on behalf of an investment company. *Id., at 538*. This approach was included in a bill that passed the House. H.R. 9510, 90th Cong., 1st Sess., § 8(d) (1967); see also S. 1659, 90th Cong., 1st Sess., § 8(d) (1967). Industry representatives, however, objected to this proposal, fearing that it "might in essence provide the Commission with ratemaking authority." *Daily Income Fund, 464 U.S., at 538*.

The provision that was ultimately enacted adopted "a different method of testing management compensation," *id., at 539* (quoting S. Rep., at 5 (internal quotation marks omitted)), that was more favorable to shareholders than the previously available remedies but that did not permit a compensation agreement to be reviewed in court for "reasonableness." This is the fiduciary duty standard in *§ 36(b)*.

B

Petitioners are shareholders in three different mutual funds managed by respondent Harris Associates L. P., an investment adviser. Petitioners filed this action in the Northern District of Illinois pursuant to *§ 36(b)* seeking damages, an injunction, and rescission of advisory agreements between Harris Associates and the mutual funds. The complaint alleged that Harris Associates had violated *§ 36(b)* by charging fees that were "disproportionate to the services rendered" and "not within the range of what would have been negotiated at arm's length in light of all the surrounding circumstances." App. 52.

The District Court granted summary judgment for Harris Associates. Applying the standard adopted in *Gartenberg v. Merrill Lynch Asset Management, Inc., 694 F.2d 923 (CA2 1982)*, the court concluded that petitioners had failed to raise a triable issue of fact as to "whether the fees charged . . . were so disproportionately large that they could not have been the result of arm's-length bargaining." App. to Pet. for Cert. 29a. The District Court assumed that it was relevant to compare the challenged fees with those that Harris Associates charged its other clients. *Id.,* at 30a. But in light of those comparisons as well as comparisons with fees charged by other investment advisers to similar mutual funds, the Court held that it could not reasonably be found that the challenged fees were outside the range that could have been the product of arm's-length bargaining. *Id.,* at 29a-32a.

A panel of the Seventh Circuit affirmed based on different reasoning, explicitly "disapprov[ing] the *Gartenberg* approach." *527 F.3d 627, 632 (2008).* Looking to trust law, the panel noted that, while a trustee "owes an obligation of candor in negotiation," a trustee, at the time of the creation of a trust, "may negotiate in his own interest and accept what the settlor or governance institution agrees to pay." *Ibid.* (citing *Restatement (Second) of Trusts § 242,* and *Comment f*)). The panel thus reasoned that "[a] fiduciary duty differs from rate regulation. A fiduciary must make full disclosure and play no tricks but is not subject to a cap on compensation." *527 F.3d at 632.* In the panel's view, the amount of an adviser's compensation would be relevant only if the compensation were "so unusual" as to give rise to an inference "that deceit must have occurred, or that the persons responsible for decision have abdicated." *Ibid.*

The panel argued that this understanding of *§ 36(b)* is consistent with the forces operating in the contemporary mutual fund market. Noting that "[t]oday thousands of mutual funds compete," the panel concluded that "sophisticated investors" shop for the funds that produce the best overall results, "mov[e] their money elsewhere" when fees are "excessive in relation to the results," and thus "create a competitive pressure" that generally keeps fees low. *Id.,* at 633-634. The panel faulted *Gartenberg* on the ground that it "relies too little on markets." *527 F.3d at 632.* And the panel firmly rejected a comparison between the fees that Harris Associates charged to the funds and the fees that Harris Associates charged other types of clients, observing that "[d]ifferent clients call for different commitments of time" and that costs, such as research, that may benefit several categories of clients "make it hard to draw inferences from fee levels." *Id.,* at *634.*

The Seventh Circuit denied rehearing en banc by an equally divided vote. *537 F.3d 728 (2008).* The dissent from the denial of rehearing argued that the panel's rejection of *Gartenberg* was based "mainly on an economic analysis that is ripe for reexamination." *537 F.3d, at 730* (opinion of Posner, J.). Among other things, the dissent expressed concern that Harris Associates charged "its captive funds more than twice what it charges independent funds," and the dissent questioned whether high adviser fees actually drive investors away. *Id., at 731.*

We granted certiorari to resolve a split among the Courts of Appeals over the proper standard under *§ 36(b)*

II

A

Since Congress amended the Investment Company Act in 1970, the mutual fund industry has experienced exponential growth. Assets under management increased from $ 38.2 billion in 1966 to over $ 9.6 trillion in 2008. The number of mutual fund investors grew from 3.5 million in 1965 to 92 million in 2008, and there are now more than 9,000 open- and closed-end funds.

During this time, the standard for an investment adviser's fiduciary duty has remained an open question in our Court, but, until the Seventh Circuit's decision below, something of a consensus had developed regarding the standard set forth over 25 years ago in *Gartenberg, supra.* The *Gartenberg* standard has been adopted by other federal courts, and "[t]he SEC's regulations have recognized, and formalized, *Gartenberg*-like factors." Brief for United States as *Amicus Curiae* 23. See 17 CFR § 240.14a-101, Sched. 14A, Item 22, para. (c)(11)(i) (2009); *69 Fed. Reg. 39801, n.3, 39807-39809 (2004).* In the present case, both petitioners and respondent generally endorse the *Gartenberg* approach, although they disagree in some respects about its meaning.

In *Gartenberg*, the Second Circuit noted that Congress had not defined what it meant by a "fiduciary duty" with respect to compensation but concluded that "the test is essentially whether the fee schedule represents a charge within the range of what would have been negotiated at arm's-length in the light of all of the surrounding circumstances." *694 F.2d, at 928.* The Second Circuit elaborated that, "[t]o be guilty of a violation of *§ 36(b),* . . . the adviser-manager must charge a fee that is so disproportionately large that it bears no reasonable relationship to the services rendered and could not have been the product of arm's-length bargaining." *Ibid.* "To make this determination," the Court stated, "all pertinent facts must be weighed," *id., at 929,* and the Court specifically mentioned "the adviser-manager's cost in providing the service, . . . the extent to which the adviser-manager realizes economies of scale as the fund grows larger, and the volume of orders which must be processed by the manager." *Id., at 930.* Observing that competition among advisers for the business of managing a fund may be "virtually non-existent," the Court rejected the suggestion that "the principal factor to be considered in evaluating a fee's fairness is the price charged by other similar advisers to funds managed by them," although the Court did not suggest that this factor could not be "taken into account." *Id., at 929.* The Court likewise rejected the "argument that the lower fees charged by investment advisers to large pension funds should be used as a criterion for determining fair advisory fees for money market funds," since a "pension fund does not face the myriad of daily purchases and redemptions throughout the nation which must be handled by [a money market fund]." *Id., at 930, n. 3.*

B

The meaning of *§ 36(b)*'s reference to "a fiduciary duty with respect to the receipt of compensation for services"[7] is hardly pellucid, but based on the terms of that provision and the role that a shareholder action for breach of that duty plays in the overall structure of the Act, we conclude that *Gartenberg* was correct in its basic formulation of what *§ 36(b)* requires: to face liability under *§ 36(b),* an investment adviser must charge a fee that is so disproportionately large that it bears no reasonable relationship to the services rendered and could not have been the product of arm's length bargaining.

---

[7] *Section 36 (b)* provides as follows:

"[T]he investment adviser of a registered investment company shall be deemed to have a fiduciary duty with respect to the receipt of compensation for services, or of payments of a material nature, paid by such registered investment company, or by the security holders thereof, to such investment adviser." 84 Stat. 1429 (codified at *15 U.S.C. § 80a-35(b)*).

1

We begin with the language of *§ 36(b)*. As noted, the Seventh Circuit panel thought that the phrase "fiduciary duty" incorporates a standard taken from the law of trusts. Petitioners agree but maintain that the panel identified the wrong trust-law standard. Instead of the standard that applies when a trustee and a settlor negotiate the trustee's fee at the time of the creation of a trust, petitioners invoke the standard that applies when a trustee seeks compensation after the trust is created. Brief for Petitioners 20-23, 35-37. A compensation agreement reached at that time, they point out, "'will not bind the beneficiary' if either 'the trustee failed to make a full disclosure of all circumstances affecting the agreement'" which he knew or should have known or if the agreement is unfair to the beneficiary. *Id.*, at 23 (quoting *Restatement (Second) of Trusts § 242, Comment i*). Respondent, on the other hand, contends that the term "fiduciary" is not exclusive to the law of trusts, that the phrase means different things in different contexts, and that there is no reason to believe that *§ 36(b)* incorporates the specific meaning of the term in the law of trusts. Brief for Respondent 34-36.

We find it unnecessary to take sides in this dispute. In *Pepper v. Litton, 308 U.S. 295*, we discussed the meaning of the concept of fiduciary duty in a context that is analogous to that presented here, and we also looked to trust law. At issue in *Pepper* was whether a bankruptcy court could disallow a dominant or controlling shareholder's claim for compensation against a bankrupt corporation. Dominant or controlling shareholders, we held, are "fiduciar[ies]" whose "powers are powers [held] in trust." *Id., at 306.* We then explained:

> "Their dealings with the corporation are subjected to rigorous scrutiny and where any of their contracts or engagements with the corporation is challenged the burden is on the director or stockholder not only to prove the good faith of the transaction but also to show its inherent fairness from the viewpoint of the corporation and those interested therein . . . . *The essence of the test is whether or not under all the circumstances the transaction carries the earmarks of an arm's length bargain.* If it does not, equity will set it aside." *Id., at 306-307* (emphasis added; footnote omitted); see also *Geddes v. Anaconda Copper Mining Co., 254 U.S. 590, 599 (1921)* (standard of fiduciary duty for interested directors).

We believe that this formulation expresses the meaning of the phrase "fiduciary duty" in *§ 36(b)*. The Investment Company Act modifies this duty in a significant way: it shifts the burden of proof from the fiduciary to the party claiming breach, *15 U.S.C. § 80a-35(b)(1)*, to show that the fee is outside the range that arm's-length bargaining would produce.

The *Gartenberg* approach fully incorporates this understanding of the fiduciary duty as set out in *Pepper* and reflects *§ 36(b)(1)*'s imposition of the burden on the plaintiff. As noted, *Gartenberg* insists that all relevant circumstances be taken into account, see *694 F.2d at 929*, as does *§ 36(b)(2), 84 Stat. 1429* ("[A]pproval by the board of directors . . . shall be given such consideration by the court as is deemed appropriate under *all the circumstances* " (emphasis added)). And *Gartenberg* uses the range of fees that might result from arm's-length bargaining as the benchmark for reviewing challenged fees.

2

Gartenberg's approach also reflects *§ 36(b)*'s place in the statutory scheme and, in particular, its relationship to the other protections that the Act affords investors.

Under the Act, scrutiny of investment adviser compensation by a fully informed mutual fund board is the "cornerstone of the . . . effort to control conflicts of interest within mutual funds." *Burks, 441 U.S., at 482*. The Act interposes disinterested directors as "independent watchdogs" of the relationship between a mutual fund and its adviser. *Id., at 484* (internal quotation marks omitted). To provide these directors with the information needed to judge whether an adviser's compensation is excessive, the Act requires advisers to furnish all information "reasonably . . . necessary to evaluate the terms" of the adviser's contract, *15 U.S.C § 80a-15(c)*, and gives the SEC the authority to enforce that requirement. See *§ 80a-41*. Board scrutiny of adviser compensation and shareholder suits under *§ 36(b), 84 Stat. 1429*, are mutually reinforcing but independent mechanisms for controlling conflicts. See *Daily Income Fund, 464 U.S., at 541* (Congress intended for *§ 36(b)* suits and directorial approval of adviser contracts to act as "independent checks on excessive fees"); *Kamen, 500 U.S., at 108* ("Congress added *§ 36(b)* to the [Act] in 1970 because it concluded that the shareholders should not have to rely solely on the fund's directors to assure reasonable adviser fees, notwithstanding the increased disinterestedness of the board" (internal quotation marks omitted)).

In recognition of the role of the disinterested directors, the Act instructs courts to give board approval of an adviser's compensation "such consideration . . . as is deemed appropriate under all the circumstances." *§ 80a-35(b)(2)*. Cf. *Burks, 441 U.S., at 485* ("[I]t would have been paradoxical for Congress to have been willing to rely largely upon [boards of directors as] 'watchdogs' to protect shareholder interests and yet, where the 'watchdogs' have done precisely that, require that they be totally muzzled").

From this formulation, two inferences may be drawn. First, a measure of deference to a board's judgment may be appropriate in some instances. Second, the appropriate measure of deference varies depending on the circumstances.

Gartenberg heeds these precepts. *Gartenberg* advises that "the expertise of the independent trustees of a fund, whether they are fully informed about all facts bearing on the [investment adviser's] service and fee, and the extent of care and conscientiousness with which they perform their duties are important factors to be considered in deciding whether they and the [investment adviser] are guilty of a breach of fiduciary duty in violation of *§ 36(b)*." *694 F.2d, at 930*.

III

While both parties in this case endorse the basic *Gartenberg* approach, they disagree on several important questions that warrant discussion.

The first concerns comparisons between the fees that an adviser charges a captive mutual fund and the fees that it charges its independent clients. As noted, the *Gartenberg* court rejected a comparison between the fees that the adviser in that case charged a money market fund and the fees that it charged a pension fund. *694 F.2d at 930, n. 3* (noting the "[t]he nature and extent of the services required by each type of fund differ sharply"). Petitioners contend that such a comparison is appropriate, Brief for Petitioners 30-31, but respondent disagrees. Brief for

Respondent 38-44. Since the Act requires consideration of all relevant factors, *15 U.S.C. § 80a-35(b)(2)*; see also *§ 80a-15(c)*, we do not think that there can be any categorical rule regarding the comparisons of the fees charged different types of clients. See *Daily Income Fund, supra, at 537* (discussing concern with investment advisers' practice of charging higher fees to mutual funds than to their other clients). Instead, courts may give such comparisons the weight that they merit in light of the similarities and differences between the services that the clients in question require, but courts must be wary of inapt comparisons. As the panel below noted, there may be significant differences between the services provided by an investment adviser to a mutual fund and those it provides to a pension fund which are attributable to the greater frequency of shareholder redemptions in a mutual fund, the higher turnover of mutual fund assets, the more burdensome regulatory and legal obligations, and higher marketing costs. *527 F.3d at 634* ("Different clients call for different commitments of time"). If the services rendered are sufficiently different that a comparison is not probative, then courts must reject such a comparison. Even if the services provided and fees charged to an independent fund are relevant, courts should be mindful that the Act does not necessarily ensure fee parity between mutual funds and institutional clients contrary to petitioners' contentions. See *id., at 631*. ("Plaintiffs maintain that a fiduciary may charge its controlled clients no more than its independent clients").[8]

By the same token, courts should not rely too heavily on comparisons with fees charged to mutual funds by other advisers. These comparisons are problematic because these fees, like those challenged, may not be the product of negotiations conducted at arm's length. See *537 F.3d at 731-732* (opinion dissenting from denial of rehearing en banc); *Gartenberg, supra, at 929* ("Competition between money market funds for shareholder business does not support an inference that competition must therefore also exist between [investment advisers] for fund business. The former may be vigorous even though the latter is virtually non-existent").

Finally, a court's evaluation of an investment adviser's fiduciary duty must take into account both procedure and substance. See *15 U.S.C. § 80a-35(b)(2)* (requiring deference to board's consideration "as is deemed appropriate under all the circumstances"); cf. *Daily Income Fund, 464 U.S., at 541* ("Congress intended security holder and SEC actions under *§ 36(b)*, on the one hand, and directorial approval of adviser contracts, on the other, to act as independent checks on excessive fees"). Where a board's process for negotiating and reviewing investment-adviser compensation is robust, a reviewing court should afford commensurate deference to the outcome of the bargaining process. See *Burks, 441 U.S., at 484* (unaffiliated directors serve as "independent watchdogs"). Thus, if the disinterested directors considered the relevant factors,

---

[8] Comparisons with fees charged to institutional clients, therefore, will not "doo[m] [a]ny [f]und to [t]rial." Brief for Respondent 49; see also *Strougo v. BEA Assocs., 188 F. Supp. 2d 373, 384 (SDNY 2002)* (suggesting that fee comparisons, where permitted, might produce a triable issue). First, plaintiffs bear the burden in showing that fees are beyond the range of arm's-length bargaining. *§ 80a-35(b)(1)*. Second, a showing of relevance requires courts to assess any disparity in fees in light of the different markets for advisory services. Only where plaintiffs have shown a large disparity in fees that cannot be explained by the different services in addition to other evidence that the fee is outside the arm's-length range will trial be appropriate. . . .

their decision to approve a particular fee agreement is entitled to considerable weight, even if a court might weigh the factors differently. Cf. *id., at 485*. This is not to deny that a fee may be excessive even if it was negotiated by a board in possession of all relevant information, but such a determination must be based on evidence that the fee "is so disproportionately large that it bears no reasonable relationship to the services rendered and could not have been the product of arm's-length bargaining." *Gartenberg, supra, at 928*.

In contrast, where the board's process was deficient or the adviser withheld important information, the court must take a more rigorous look at the outcome. When an investment adviser fails to disclose material information to the board, greater scrutiny is justified because the withheld information might have hampered the board's ability to function as "an independent check upon the management." *Burks, supra, at 484* (internal quotation marks omitted). "*Section 36(b)* is sharply focused on the question of whether the fees themselves were excessive." *Migdal v. Rowe Price-Fleming Int'l, Inc., 248 F.3d 321, 328 (CA4 2001)*; see also *15 U.S.C. § 80a-35(b)* (imposing a "fiduciary duty with respect to the *receipt of compensation* for services, or of payments of a material natur*e*" (emphasis added)). But an adviser's compliance or noncompliance with its disclosure obligations is a factor that must be considered in calibrating the degree of deference that is due a board's decision to approve an adviser's fees.

It is also important to note that the standard for fiduciary breach under *§ 36(b)* does not call for judicial second-guessing of informed board decisions. See *Daily Income Fund, supra, at 538*; see also *Burks, 441 U.S., at 483* ("Congress consciously chose to address the conflict-of-interest problem through the Act's independent-directors section, rather than through more drastic remedies"). "[P]otential conflicts [of interests] may justify some restraints upon the unfettered discretion of even disinterested mutual fund directors, particularly in their transactions with the investment adviser," but they do not suggest that a court may supplant the judgment of disinterested directors apprised of all relevant information, without additional evidence that the fee exceeds the arm's-length range. *Id., at 481*. In reviewing compensation under *§ 36(b)*, the Act does not require courts to engage in a precise calculation of fees representative of arm's-length bargaining. See *527 F.3d at 633* ("Judicial price-setting does not accompany fiduciary duties"). As recounted above, Congress rejected a "reasonableness" requirement that was criticized as charging the courts with rate-setting responsibilities. See *Daily Income Fund, supra, at 538-540*. Congress' approach recognizes that courts are not well suited to make such precise calculations. Cf.*GMC v. Tracy, 519 U.S. 278, 308 (1997)* ("[T]he Court is institutionally unsuited to gather the facts upon which economic predictions can be made, and professionally untrained to make them"); *Verizon Communs., Inc. v. FCC, 535 U.S. 467, 539 (2002)*; see also *Concord v. Boston Edison Co., 915 F.2d 17, 25 (CA1 1990)* (opinion for the court by Breyer, C. J.) ("[H]ow is a judge or jury to determine a 'fair price'?"). *Gartenberg*'s "so disproportionately large" standard, *694 F.2d at 928*, reflects this congressional choice to "rely largely upon [independent director] 'watchdogs' to protect shareholders interests." *Burks, supra, at 485*.

By focusing almost entirely on the element of disclosure, the Seventh Circuit panel erred. See *527 F.3d at 632* (An investment adviser "must make full disclosure and play no tricks but is not subject to a cap on compensation"). The *Gartenberg* standard, which the panel rejected, may lack sharp analytical clarity, but we believe that it accurately reflects the compromise that is embodied in *§ 36(b)*, and it has provided a workable standard for nearly three decades. The debate between the Seventh Circuit panel and the dissent from the denial of rehearing regarding today's mutual fund market is a matter for Congress, not the courts.

IV

For the foregoing reasons, the judgment of the Court of Appeals is vacated, and the case remanded for further proceedings consistent with this opinion.

It is so ordered.

Securities and Exchange Commission v. Bank of America Corporation

United States District Court, Southern District of New York (2009)

653 F. Supp. 2d 507

■ RAKOFF, DISTRICT JUDGE:

In the Complaint in this case, filed August 3, 2009, the Securities and Exchange Commission ("S.E.C.") alleges, in stark terms, that defendant Bank of America Corporation materially lied to its shareholders in the proxy statement of November 3, 2008 that solicited the shareholders' approval of the $ 50 billion acquisition of Merrill Lynch & Co. ("Merrill"). The essence of the lie, according to the Complaint, was that Bank of America "represented that Merrill had agreed not to pay year-end performance bonuses or other discretionary incentive compensation to its executives prior to the closing of the merger without Bank of America's consent [when] [i]n fact, contrary to the representation ..., Bank of America had agreed that Merrill could pay up to $ 5.8 billion -- nearly 12% of the total consideration to be exchanged in the merger -- in discretionary year-end and other bonuses to Merrill executives for 2008." Compl. P 2. Along with the filing of these very serious allegations, however, the parties, on the very same day, jointly sought this Court's approval of a proposed final Consent Judgment by which Bank of America, without admitting or denying the accusations, would be enjoined from making future false statements in proxy solicitations and would pay to the S.E.C. a fine of $ 33 million.

In other words, the parties were proposing that the management of Bank of America -- having allegedly hidden from the Bank's shareholders that as much as $ 5.8 billion of their money would be given as bonuses to the executives of Merrill who had run that company nearly into bankruptcy -- would now settle the legal consequences of their lying by paying the S.E.C. $ 33 million more of their shareholders' money.

This proposal to have the victims of the violation pay an additional penalty for their own victimization was enough to give the Court pause. The Court therefore heard oral argument on August 10, 2009 and received extensive written submissions on August 24, 2009 and September 9, 2009. Having now carefully reviewed all these materials, the Court concludes that the proposed Consent Judgment must be denied.

In reaching this conclusion, the Court is very mindful of the considerable deference it must accord the parties' proposal, since it would seemingly result in the consensual resolution of the case. Society greatly benefits when lawsuits are amicably resolved, and, for that reason, an ordinary civil settlement that includes dismissal of the underlying action is close to unreviewable. *See Hester Industries, Inc. v. Tyson Foods, Inc., 160 F.3d 911, 916 (2d Cir. 1998)*(citing cases). When, however, as in the case of a typical consent judgment, a federal agency such as the S.E.C. seeks to prospectively invoke the Court's own contempt power by having the Court impose injunctive prohibitions against the defendant, the resolution has aspects of a judicial decree and the Court is therefore obliged to review the proposal a little more closely, to ascertain whether it is within the bounds of fairness, reasonableness, and adequacy --

and, in certain circumstances, whether it serves the public interest. *See S.E.C. v. Randolph, 736 F.2d 525, 529 (9th Cir. 1984); see also S.E.C. v. Wang, 944 F.2d 80, 85 (2d Cir. 1991). See generally, United States v. ITT Continental Baking Co., 420 U.S. 223 (1975); United States v. North Carolina, 180 F.3d 574 (4th Cir. 1999).* But even then, the review is highly deferential. *S.E.C. v. Worldcom, Inc., 273 F. Supp. 2d 431, 436 (S.D.N.Y. 2003).*

Here, however, the Court, even upon applying the most deferential standard of review for which the parties argue, is forced to conclude that the proposed Consent Judgment is neither fair, nor reasonable, nor adequate.

It is not fair, first and foremost, because it does not comport with the most elementary notions of justice and morality, in that it proposes that the shareholders who were the victims of the Bank's alleged misconduct now pay the penalty for that misconduct. The S.E.C. admits that the corporate penalties it here proposes will be "indirectly borne by [the] shareholders." Reply Memorandum of Plaintiff Securities and Exchange Commission in Support of Entry of the Proposed Consent Judgment ("S.E.C. Reply Mem.") at 13. But the S.E.C. argues that this is justified because "[a] corporate penalty ... sends a strong signal to shareholders that unsatisfactory corporate conduct has occurred and allows shareholders to better assess the quality and performance of management." *Id.* This hypothesis, however, makes no sense when applied to the facts here: for the notion that Bank of America shareholders, having been lied to blatantly in connection with the multi-billion-dollar purchase of a huge, nearly-bankrupt company, need to lose another $ 33 million of their money in order to "better assess the quality and performance of management" is absurd.

The S.E.C., while also conceding that its normal policy in such situations is to go after the company executives who were responsible for the lie, rather than innocent shareholders, says it cannot do so here because "[t]he uncontroverted evidence in the investigative record is that lawyers for Bank of America and Merrill drafted the documents at issue and made the relevant decisions concerning disclosure of the bonuses." *Id.* But if that is the case, why are the penalties not then sought from the lawyers? And why, in any event, does that justify imposing penalties on the victims of the lie, the shareholders?

Bank of America, for its part, having originally agreed to remain silent in the face of these charges, now, at the Court's request that it provide the Court with the underlying facts, vigorously asserts that the proxy statement, when read carefully, is neither false nor misleading, *see* Reply Memorandum of Law on Behalf of Bank of America Corporation ("BoA Reply Mem.")at 5, or that, even if it is false or misleading, the misstatements were immaterial because "[it] was widely acknowledged in the period leading up to the shareholder vote that Merrill Lynch intended to pay year-end incentive compensation," *id.* at 19. The S.E.C. responds, however, that these arguments are hollow. The Bank's argument that the proxy statement was not misleading rests in material part on reference to a schedule that was not even attached to the proxy statement, and "[s]hareholders are entitled to rely on the representations in the proxy itself, and are not required to puzzle out material information from a variety of external sources." S.E.C. Reply Mem. at 2. As for the Bank's argument that the investors were not materially misled because the press was already reporting the imminent payment of Merrill bonuses, "investors were not required to ignore Bank of America's express statements in the proxy materials and rely instead on media speculation that may have suggested that these statements were misleading." *Id*. at 9.

Moreover, it is noteworthy that, in all its voluminous papers protesting its innocence, Bank of America never actually provides the Court with the particularized facts that the Court requested, such as precisely how the proxy statement came to be prepared, exactly who made the relevant decisions as to what to include and not include so far as the Merrill bonuses were concerned, etc.

But all of this is beside the point because, if the Bank is innocent of lying to its shareholders, why is it prepared to pay $ 33 million of its shareholders' money as a penalty for lying to them? All the Bank offers in response to this obvious question is the statement in the last footnote of its Reply Memorandum that "Because of the SEC's decision to bring charges, Bank of America would have to spend corporate funds whether or not it settled," BofA Reply Mem. at 28, n. 20 -- the implication being that the payment was simply an exercise of business judgment as to which alternative would cost more: litigating or settling. But, quite aside from the fact that it is difficult to believe that litigating this simple case would cost anything like $ 33 million, it does not appear, so far as one can tell from this single sentence in a footnote, that this decision was made by disinterested parties. It is one thing for management to exercise its business judgment to determine how much of its shareholders money should be used to settle a case brought by former shareholders or third parties. It is quite something else for the very management that is accused of having lied to its shareholders to determine how much of those victims' money should be used to make the case against the management go away.[1] And even if this decision is arguably within their purview, it calls for greater scrutiny by the Court than would otherwise be the case.

Overall, indeed, the parties' submissions, when carefully read, leave the distinct impression that the proposed Consent Judgment was a contrivance designed to provide the S.E.C. with the facade of enforcement and the management of the Bank with a quick resolution of an embarrassing inquiry -- all at the expense of the sole alleged victims, the shareholders. Even under the most deferential review, this proposed Consent Judgment cannot remotely be called fair.

Nor is the proposed Consent Judgment reasonable. Obviously, a proposal that asks the victims to pay a fine for their having been victimized is, for all the reasons already given, as

---

[1] Undoubtedly, the decision to spend this money was made even easier by the fact that the U.S. Government provided the Bank of America with a $ 40 billion or so "bail out," of which $ 20 billion came after the merger. Since $ 3.6 billion of that money had already been spent, indirectly, to compensate the Bank for the Merrill bonuses -- not to mention the $ 20 billion in taxpayer funds that effectively compensated the Bank for the last-minute revelations that Merrill's loss for 2008 was $ 27 billion instead of $ 7 billion -- what impediment could there be to paying a mere $ 33 million (-- or more than most people will see in their lifetimes --) to get rid of a lawsuit saying that the bonuses had been concealed from the shareholders approving the merger? To say, as the Bank now does, that the $ 33 million does not come directly from U.S. funds is simply to ignore the overall economics of the Bank's situation.

unreasonable as it is unfair. But the proposed Consent Judgment is unreasonable in numerous other respects as well.

For example, the Consent Judgment would effectively close the case without the S.E.C. adequately accounting for why, in contravention of its own policy, *see* Order, 8/25/08 (quoting the policy), it did not pursue charges against either Bank management or the lawyers who allegedly were responsible for the false and misleading proxy statements. The S.E.C. says this is because charges against individuals for making false proxy statements require, at a minimum, proof that they participated in the making of the false statements knowing the statements were false or recklessly disregarding the high probability the statements were false. But how can such knowledge be lacking when, as the Complaint in effect alleges, executives at the Bank expressly approved Merrill's making year-end bonuses before they issued the proxy statement denying such approval?[2] The S.E.C. states, as noted, that culpable intent was nonetheless lacking because the lawyers made all the relevant decisions. But, if so, then how can the lawyers be said to lack intent? Under these circumstances, how can a Court find reasonable a proposed Consent Judgment that otherwise violates S.E.C. policy?

To give a different example, the proposed Consent Judgment seeks injunctive relief forbidding the Bank, on pain of contempt of court, from issuing false or misleading statements in the future. On its face, the proposed injunction appears too nebulous to comply with *Rule 65(d) of the Federal Rules of Civil Procedure*, which requires, among other things, that an injunction "describe in reasonable detail ... the act or acts restrained ...." Moreover, since the Bank contends that it never made any false or misleading statements in the past, the Court at this point lacks a factual predicate for imposing such relief.

To be sure, the Bank's initial position was that it neither admitted nor denied the allegations, and such a position, when coupled with proof by the S.E.C. that the alleged violations have occurred, may often be sufficient to support certain forms of injunctive relief. But here the further submissions of the Bank make clear its position that the proxy statement in issue was totally in accordance with the law: meaning that, notwithstanding the injunctive relief here sought by the S.E.C., the Bank would feel free to issue exactly the same kind of proxy statement in the future. Under these circumstances, the broad but vague injunctive relief here sought would be a pointless exercise, since the sanction of contempt may only be imposed for violation of a particularized provision known and reasonably understood by the contemnor, all of which would

---

[2] Lurking in the background is the suggestion, affirmed by the Bank's counsel at the August 10 hearing, that the highest executives of Bank of America, upon learning that Merrill's loss was $ 20 billion more than had been represented at the time the merger was negotiated, were prepared to walk away from the merger until "coerced" by the Government into going through with it, following which the Government provided the Bank with an additional $ 20 billion in bail-out funds. But, quite aside from the fact that none of this appears to have been revealed to the shareholders prior to the merger, neither party suggests that any such coercion played any role in the alleged decision not to reveal the Merrill bonuses. The huge increase in Merrill's losses, however, did arguably render the providing of the bonuses more material, as well as more inexplicable.

be lacking here. *See, e.g., Int'l Longshoreman's Ass'n, Local 1291 v. Philadelphia Marine Trade Ass'n, 389 U.S. 64, 76 (1967)*; *Powell v. Ward, 643 F.2d 924, 931 (2d Cir. 1981)*.

Without multiplying examples further, the point is that the Court finds the proposed Consent Judgment not only unfair but also unreasonable.

Finally, the proposed Consent Judgment is inadequate. The injunctive relief, as noted, is pointless. The fine, if looked at from the standpoint of the violation, is also inadequate, in that $ 33 million is a trivial penalty for a false statement that materially infected a multi-billion-dollar merger. But since the fine is imposed, not on the individuals putatively responsible, but on the shareholders, it is worse than pointless: it further victimizes the victims.

Oscar Wilde once famously said that a cynic is someone "who knows the price of everything and the value of nothing." Oscar Wilde, *Lady Windermere's Fan* (1892). The proposed Consent Judgment in this case suggests a rather cynical relationship between the parties: the S.E.C. gets to claim that it is exposing wrongdoing on the part of the Bank of America in a high-profile merger; the Bank's management gets to claim that they have been coerced into an onerous settlement by overzealous regulators. And all this is done at the expense, not only of the shareholders, but also of the truth.

Yet the truth may still emerge. The Bank of America states unequivocally that if the Court disapproves the Consent Judgment, it is prepared to litigate the charges. BofA Reply Mem. at 5. The S.E.C., having brought the charges, presumably is not about to drop them. Accordingly, the Court, having hereby disapproved the Consent Judgment, directs the parties to file with the Court, no later than one week from today, a jointly proposed Case Management Plan that will have this case ready to be tried on February 1, 2010.

Morrison v. National Australia Bank, Ltd.

Supreme Court of the United States (2010)

130 S. Ct. 2869, 177 L. Ed. 2d 535

- JUSTICE SCALIA delivered the opinion of the Court.

We decide whether *§ 10(b)* of the Securities Exchange Act of 1934 provides a cause of action to foreign plaintiffs suing foreign and American defendants for misconduct in connection with securities traded on foreign exchanges.

I

Respondent National Australia Bank Limited (National) was, during the relevant time, the largest bank in Australia. Its Ordinary Shares -- what in America would be called "common stock" -- are traded on the Australian Stock Exchange Limited and on other foreign securities exchanges, but not on any exchange in the United States. There are listed on the New York Stock Exchange, however, National's American Depositary Receipts (ADRs), which represent the right to receive a specified number of National's Ordinary Shares. 547 F.3d 167, 168, and n. 1 (CA2 2008).

The complaint alleges the following facts, which we accept as true. In February 1998, National bought respondent HomeSide Lending, Inc., a mortgage servicing company headquartered in Florida. HomeSide's business was to receive fees for servicing mortgages (essentially the administrative tasks associated with collecting mortgage payments, see J. Rosenberg, Dictionary of Banking and Financial Services 600 (2d ed. 1985)). The rights to receive those fees, so-called mortgage-servicing rights, can provide a valuable income stream. See 2 The New Palgrave Dictionary of Money and Finance 817 (P. Newman, M. Milgate, & J. Eatwell eds. 1992). How valuable each of the rights is depends, in part, on the likelihood that the mortgage to which it applies will be fully repaid before it is due, terminating the need for servicing. HomeSide calculated the present value of its mortgage-servicing rights by using valuation models designed to take this likelihood into account. It recorded the value of its assets, and the numbers appeared in National's financial statements.

From 1998 until 2001, National's annual reports and other public documents touted the success of HomeSide's business, and respondents Frank Cicutto (National's managing director and chief executive officer), Kevin Race (HomeSide's chief operating officer), and Hugh Harris (HomeSide's chief executive officer) did the same in public statements. But on July 5, 2001, National announced that it was writing down the value of HomeSide's assets by $ 450 million; and then again on September 3, by another $ 1.75 billion. The prices of both Ordinary Shares and ADRs slumped. After downplaying the July write-down, National explained the September write-down as the result of a failure to anticipate the lowering of prevailing interest rates (lower interest rates lead to more refinancings, *i.e.*, more early repayments of mortgages), other mistaken assumptions in the financial models, and the loss of goodwill. According to the complaint, however, HomeSide, Race, Harris, and another HomeSide senior executive who is also a respondent here had manipulated HomeSide's financial models to make the rates of early repayment unrealistically low in order to cause the mortgage-servicing rights to appear more valuable than they really were. The complaint also alleges that National and Cicutto were aware of this deception by July 2000, but did nothing about it.

As relevant here, petitioners Russell Leslie Owen and Brian and Geraldine Silverlock, all Australians, purchased National's Ordinary Shares in 2000 and 2001, before the write-downs.[1] They sued National, HomeSide, Cicutto, and the three HomeSide executives in the United States District Court for the Southern District of New York for alleged violations of §§ *10(b)* and *20(a)* of the Securities and Exchange Act of 1934, 48 Stat. 881, *15 U.S.C. §§ 78j(b)* and *78t(a)*, and SEC *Rule 10b-5, 17 CFR § 240.10b-5 (2009)*, promulgated pursuant to *§ 10(b)*. They sought to represent a class of foreign purchasers of National's Ordinary Shares during a specified period up to the September write-down. 547 F.3d at 169.

Respondents moved to dismiss for lack of subject-matter jurisdiction under *Federal Rule of Civil Procedure 12(b)(1)* and for failure to state a claim under *Rule 12(b)(6)*. The District Court granted the motion on the former ground, finding no jurisdiction because the acts in this country were, "at most, a link in the chain of an alleged overall securities fraud scheme that culminated abroad." *In re National Australia Bank Securities Litigation, No. 03 Civ. 6537 (BSJ), 2006 U.S. Dist. LEXIS 94162, 2006 WL 3844465, *8 (SDNY, Oct. 25, 2006)*. The Court of Appeals for the Second Circuit affirmed on similar grounds. The acts performed in the United States did not "compris[e] the heart of the alleged fraud." *547 F.3d at 175-176*. We granted certiorari, *558 U.S. ___, 130 S. Ct. 783 (2009)*.

II

Before addressing the question presented, we must correct a threshold error in the Second Circuit's analysis. It considered the extraterritorial reach of *§ 10(b)* to raise a question of subject-matter jurisdiction, wherefore it affirmed the District Court's dismissal under *Rule 12(b)(1)*. See *547 F.3d at 177*. In this regard it was following Circuit precedent, see *Schoenbaum v. Firstbrook, 405 F.2d 200, 208*, modified on other grounds en banc, *405 F.2d 215 (1968)*. The Second Circuit is hardly alone in taking this position, see, *e.g., In re CP Ships Ltd. Securities Litigation, 578 F.3d 1306, 1313 (CA11 2009)*; *Continental Grain (Australia) PTY. Ltd. v. Pacific Oilseeds, Inc., 592 F.2d 409, 421 (CA8 1979)*.

But to ask what conduct *§ 10(b)* reaches is to ask what conduct *§ 10(b)* prohibits, which is a merits question. Subject-matter jurisdiction, by contrast, "refers to a tribunal's '"power to hear a case."'" *Union Pacific R. Co. v. Locomotive Engineers and Trainmen Gen. Comm. of Adjustment, Central Region, 558 U.S. ___, ___, (2009)*) (quoting *Arbaugh v. Y & H Corp., 546 U.S. 500, 514 (2006)*, in turn quoting *United States v. Cotton, 535 U.S. 625, 630 (2002)*). It presents an issue quite separate from the question whether the allegations the plaintiff makes

---

[1] Robert Morrison, an American investor in National's ADRs, also brought suit, but his claims were dismissed by the District Court because he failed to allege damages. *In re National Australia Bank Securities Litigation, No. 03 Civ. 6537 (BSJ), 2006 U.S. Dist. LEXIS 94162, 2006 WL 3844465, *9 (SDNY, Oct. 25, 2006)*. Petitioners did not appeal that decision, *547 F.3d 167, 170, n. 3 (CA2 2008)* (case below), and it is not before us. Inexplicably, Morrison continued to be listed as a petitioner in the Court of Appeals and here.

entitle him to relief. See *Bell v. Hood, 327 U.S. 678, 682 (1946)*. The District Court here had jurisdiction under *15 U.S.C. § 78aa* to adjudicate the question whether *§ 10(b)* applies to National's conduct.

In view of this error, which the parties do not dispute, petitioners ask us to remand. We think that unnecessary. Since nothing in the analysis of the courts below turned on the mistake, a remand would only require a new *Rule 12(b)(6)* label for the same *Rule 12(b)(1)* conclusion. As we have done before in situations like this, see, *e.g., Romero v. International Terminal Operating Co., 358 U.S. 354, 359, 381-384 (1959)*, we proceed to address whether petitioners' allegations state a claim.

III

A

It is a "longstanding principle of American law 'that legislation of Congress, unless a contrary intent appears, is meant to apply only within the territorial jurisdiction of the United States.'" *EEOC v. Arabian American Oil Co., 499 U.S. 244, 248 (1991) (Aramco)* (quoting *Foley Bros., Inc. v. Filardo, 336 U.S. 281, 285 (1949)*). This principle represents a canon of construction, or a presumption about a statute's meaning, rather than a limit upon Congress's power to legislate, see *Blackmer v. United States, 284 U.S. 421, 437 (1932)*. It rests on the perception that Congress ordinarily legislates with respect to domestic, not foreign matters. *Smith v. United States, 507 U.S. 197, 204, n. 5 (1993)*. Thus, "unless there is the affirmative intention of the Congress clearly expressed" to give a statute extraterritorial effect, "we must presume it is primarily concerned with domestic conditions." *Aramco, supra, at 248* (internal quotation marks omitted). The canon or presumption applies regardless of whether there is a risk of conflict between the American statute and a foreign law, see *Sale v. Haitian Centers Council, Inc., 509 U.S. 155, 173-174 (1993)*. When a statute gives no clear indication of an extraterritorial application, it has none.

Despite this principle of interpretation, long and often recited in our opinions, the Second Circuit believed that, because the Exchange Act is silent as to the extraterritorial application of *§ 10(b)*, it was left to the court to "discern" whether Congress would have wanted the statute to apply. See *547 F.3d at 170* (internal quotation marks omitted). This disregard of the presumption against extraterritoriality did not originate with the Court of Appeals panel in this case. It has been repeated over many decades by various courts of appeals in determining the application of the Exchange Act, and *§ 10(b)* in particular, to fraudulent schemes that involve conduct and effects abroad. That has produced a collection of tests for divining what Congress would have wanted, complex in formulation and unpredictable in application.

As of 1967, district courts at least in the Southern District of New York had consistently concluded that, by reason of the presumption against extraterritoriality, *§ 10(b)* did not apply when the stock transactions underlying the violation occurred abroad. See *Schoenbaum v. Firstbrook, 268 F. Supp. 385, 392 (1967)* (citing *Ferraoli v. Cantor, CCH Fed. Sec. L. Rep. P91615 (SDNY 1965)* and *Kook v. Crang, 182 F. Supp. 388, 390 (SDNY 1960)*). *Schoenbaum* involved the sale in Canada of the treasury shares of a Canadian corporation whose publicly traded shares (but not, of course, its treasury shares) were listed on both the American Stock Exchange and the Toronto Stock Exchange. Invoking the presumption against extraterritoriality, the court held that *§ 10(b)* was inapplicable (though it incorrectly viewed the defect as jurisdictional). *268 F. Supp. , at 391-392, 393-394.* The decision in *Schoenbaum* was reversed, however, by a Second Circuit opinion which held that "neither the usual presumption against extraterritorial application of legislation nor the specific language of *[§]30(b)* show Congressional intent to preclude application of the Exchange Act to transactions regarding stocks traded in the United States which are effected outside the United States . . . ." *Schoenbaum, 405 F.2d at 206.* It sufficed to apply *§ 10(b)* that, although the transactions in treasury shares took place in Canada, they affected the value of the common shares publicly traded in the United States. See *id., at 208-209.* Application of *§ 10(b)*, the Second Circuit found, was "necessary to protect American investors," *id., at 206.*

The Second Circuit took another step with *Leasco Data Processing Equip. Corp. v. Maxwell, 468 F.2d 1326 (1972)*, which involved an American company that had been fraudulently induced to buy securities in England. There, unlike in *Schoenbaum*, some of the deceptive conduct had occurred in the United States but the corporation whose securities were traded (abroad) was not listed on any domestic exchange. *Leasco* said that the presumption against extraterritoriality applies only to matters over which the United States would not have prescriptive jurisdiction, *468 F.2d at 1334.* Congress had prescriptive jurisdiction to regulate the deceptive conduct in this country, the language of the Act could be read to cover that conduct, and the court concluded that "if Congress had thought about the point," it would have wanted *§ 10(b)* to apply. *Id., at 1334-1337.*

With *Schoenbaum* and *Leasco* on the books, the Second Circuit had excised the presumption against extraterritoriality from the jurisprudence of *§ 10(b)* and replaced it with the inquiry whether it would be reasonable (and hence what Congress would have wanted) to apply the statute to a given situation. As long as there was prescriptive jurisdiction to regulate, the Second Circuit explained, whether to apply *§ 10(b)* even to "predominantly foreign" transactions became a matter of whether a court thought Congress "wished the precious resources of United States courts and law enforcement agencies to be devoted to them rather than leave the problem to foreign countries." *Bersch v. Drexel Firestone, Inc., 519 F.2d 974, 985 (1975)*; see also *IIT v. Vencap, Ltd., 519 F.2d 1001, 1017-1018 (CA2 1975).*

The Second Circuit had thus established that application of *§ 10(b)* could be premised upon either some effect on American securities markets or investors *(Schoenbaum)* or significant conduct in the United States *(Leasco).* It later formalized these two applications into (1) an "effects test," "whether the wrongful conduct had a substantial effect in the United States or upon United States citizens," and (2) a "conduct test," "whether the wrongful conduct occurred in the United States." *SEC v. Berger, 322 F.3d 187, 192-193 (CA2 2003).* These became the north star of the Second Circuit's § 10(b) jurisprudence, pointing the way to what Congress would have wished. Indeed, the Second Circuit declined to keep its two tests distinct on the ground that "an admixture or combination of the two often gives a better picture of whether there is sufficient United States involvement to justify the exercise of jurisdiction by an American court." *Itoba Ltd. v. Lep Group PLC, 54 F.3d 118, 122 (1995).* The Second Circuit never put forward a textual or even extratextual basis for these tests. As early as *Bersch*, it confessed that "if we were asked to point to language in the statutes, or even in the legislative history, that compelled these conclusions, we would be unable to respond," *519 F.2d at 993.*

As they developed, these tests were not easy to administer. The conduct test was held to apply differently depending on whether the harmed investors were Americans or foreigners: When the alleged damages consisted of losses to American investors abroad, it was enough that acts "of material importance" performed in the United States "significantly contributed" to that result; whereas those acts must have "directly caused" the result when losses to foreigners abroad were at issue. See *Bersch, 519 F.2d at 993.* And "merely preparatory activities in the United States" did not suffice "to trigger application of the securities laws for injury to foreigners located abroad." *Id., at 992.* This required the court to distinguish between mere preparation and using the United States as a "base" for fraudulent activities in other countries. *Vencap, supra, at 1017-1018.* But merely satisfying the conduct test was sometimes insufficient without "'some additional factor tipping the scales'" in favor of the application of American law. *Interbrew v. Edperbrascan Corp., 23 F. Supp. 2d 425, 432 (SDNY 1998)* (quoting *Europe & Overseas Commodity Traders, S. A. v. Banque Paribas London, 147 F.3d 118, 129 (CA2 1998)).* District courts have noted the difficulty of applying such vague formulations. See, *e.g., In re Alstom SA, 406 F. Supp. 2d 346, 366-385 (SDNY 2005).* There is no more damning indictment of the "conduct" and "effects" tests than the Second Circuit's own declaration that "the presence or absence of any single factor which was considered significant in other cases . . . is not necessarily dispositive in future cases." *IIT v. Cornfeld, 619 F.2d 909, 918 (1980)* (internal quotation marks omitted).

Other Circuits embraced the Second Circuit's approach, though not its precise application. Like the Second Circuit, they described their decisions regarding the extraterritorial application of *§ 10(b)* as essentially resolving matters of policy. See, *e.g., SEC v. Kasser, 548 F.2d 109, 116 (CA3 1977); Continental Grain, 592 F.2d at 421-422; Grunenthal GmbH v. Hotz, 712 F.2d 421, 424-425 (CA9 1983); Kauthar SDN BHD v. Sternberg, 149 F.3d 659, 667 (CA7 1998).* While applying the same fundamental methodology of balancing interests and arriving at what seemed the best policy, they produced a proliferation of vaguely related variations on the "conduct" and "effects" tests. As described in a leading Seventh Circuit opinion: "Although the circuits . . . seem to agree that there are some transnational situations to which the antifraud provisions of the securities laws are applicable, agreement appears to end at that point." *Id., at 665.* See also *id., at 665-667* (describing the approaches of the various Circuits and adopting yet another variation).

At least one Court of Appeals has criticized this line of cases and the interpretive assumption that underlies it. In *Zoelsch v. Arthur Andersen & Co., 824 F.2d 27, 32 (1987)* (Bork, J.), the District of Columbia Circuit observed that rather than courts' "divining what 'Congress would have wished' if it had addressed the problem[, a] more natural inquiry might be what jurisdiction Congress in fact thought about and conferred." Although tempted to apply the presumption against extraterritoriality and be done with it, see *id., at 31-32,* that court deferred to the Second Circuit because of its "preeminence in the field of securities law," *id., at 32.* See also *Robinson v. TCI/US West Communications Inc., 117 F.3d 900, 906-907 (CA5 1997)* (expressing agreement with *Zoelsch*'s criticism of the emphasis on policy considerations in some of the cases).

Commentators have criticized the unpredictable and inconsistent application of *§ 10(b)* to transnational cases. See, *e.g.,* Choi & Silberman, Transnational Litigation and Global Securities Class-Action Lawsuits, *2009 Wis. L. Rev. 465, 467-468;* Chang, Multinational Enforcement of

U.S. Securities Laws: The Need for the Clear and Restrained Scope of Extraterritorial Subject-Matter Jurisdiction, *9 Fordham J. Corp. & Fin. L. 89, 106-108, 115-116 (2004)*; Langevoort, *Schoenbaum* Revisited: Limiting the Scope of Antifraud Protection in an Internationalized Securities Marketplace, 55 Law & Contemp. Probs. 241, 244-248 (1992). Some have challenged the premise underlying the Courts of Appeals' approach, namely that Congress did not consider the extraterritorial application of *§ 10(b)* (thereby leaving it open to the courts, supposedly, to determine what Congress would have wanted). See, *e.g.,* Sachs, The International Reach of *Rule 10b-5*: The Myth of Congressional Silence, 28 Colum. J. Transnat'l L. 677 (1990) (arguing that Congress considered, but rejected, applying the Exchange Act to transactions abroad). Others, more fundamentally, have noted that using congressional silence as a justification for judge-made rules violates the traditional principle that silence means no extraterritorial application. See, *e.g.,* Note, Let There Be Fraud (Abroad): A Proposal for A New U.S. Jurisprudence with Regard to the Extraterritorial Application of the Anti-Fraud Provisions of the 1933 and 1934 Securities Acts, 28 Law & Pol'y Int'l Bus. 477, 492-493 (1997).

The criticisms seem to us justified. The results of judicial-speculation-made-law -- divining what Congress would have wanted if it had thought of the situation before the court -- demonstrate the wisdom of the presumption against extraterritoriality. Rather than guess anew in each case, we apply the presumption in all cases, preserving a stable background against which Congress can legislate with predictable effects.

B

Rule 10b-5, the regulation under which petitioners have brought suit, was promulgated under *§ 10(b),* and "does not extend beyond conduct encompassed by § 10(b)'s prohibition." *United States v. O'Hagan, 521 U.S. 642, 651 (1997).* Therefore, if *§ 10(b)* is not extraterritorial, neither is *Rule 10b-5.*

On its face, *§ 10(b)* contains nothing to suggest it applies abroad:

> "It shall be unlawful for any person, directly or indirectly, by the use of any means or instrumentality of interstate commerce or of the mails, or of any facility of any national securities exchange . . . [t]o use or employ, in connection with the purchase or sale of any security registered on a national securities exchange or any security not so registered, . . . any manipulative or deceptive device or contrivance in contravention of such rules and regulations as the [Securities and Exchange] Commission may prescribe . . . ." *15 U.S.C. 78j(b).*

Petitioners and the Solicitor General contend, however, that three things indicate that *§ 10(b)* or the Exchange Act in general has at least some extraterritorial application.

First, they point to the definition of "interstate commerce," a term used in *§ 10(b),* which includes "trade, commerce, transportation, or communication . . . between any foreign country and any State." *15 U.S.C. § 78c(a)(17).* But "we have repeatedly held that even statutes that contain broad language in their definitions of 'commerce' that expressly refer to *'foreign* commerce' do not apply abroad." *Aramco, 499 U.S., at 251*; see *id., at 251-252* (discussing cases). The general reference to foreign commerce in the definition of "interstate commerce" does not defeat the presumption against extraterritoriality.

Petitioners and the Solicitor General next point out that Congress, in describing the purposes of the Exchange Act, observed that the "prices established and offered in such transactions are generally disseminated and quoted throughout the United States and foreign countries." *15 U.S.C. § 78b(2)*. The antecedent of "such transactions," however, is found in the first sentence of the section, which declares that "transactions in securities as commonly conducted upon securities exchanges and over-the-counter markets are affected with a national public interest." *§ 78b*. Nothing suggests that this *national* public interest pertains to transactions conducted upon *foreign* exchanges and markets. The fleeting reference to the dissemination and quotation abroad of the prices of securities traded in domestic exchanges and markets cannot overcome the presumption against extraterritoriality.

Finally, there is *§ 30(b)* of the Exchange Act, *15 U.S.C. § 78dd(b)*, which *does* mention the Act's extraterritorial application: "The provisions of [the Exchange Act] or of any rule or regulation thereunder shall not apply to any person insofar as he transacts a business in securities without the jurisdiction of the United States," unless he does so in violation of regulations promulgated by the Securities and Exchange Commission "to prevent . . . evasion of [the Act]." (The parties have pointed us to no regulation promulgated pursuant to *§ 30(b)*.) The Solicitor General argues that "[this] exemption would have no function if the Act did not apply in the first instance to securities transactions that occur abroad." Brief for United States as *Amicus Curiae* 14.

We are not convinced. In the first place, it would be odd for Congress to indicate the extraterritorial application of the whole Exchange Act by means of a provision imposing a condition precedent to its application abroad. And if the whole Act applied abroad, why would the Commission's enabling regulations be limited to those preventing "evasion" of the Act, rather than all those preventing "violation"? The provision seems to us directed at actions abroad that might conceal a domestic violation, or might cause what would otherwise be a domestic violation to escape on a technicality. At most, the Solicitor General's proposed inference is possible; but possible interpretations of statutory language do not override the presumption against extraterritoriality. See *Aramco, supra, at 253*.

The Solicitor General also fails to account for *§ 30(a)*, which reads in relevant part as follows:

> "It shall be unlawful for any broker or dealer . . . to make use of the mails or of any means or instrumentality of interstate commerce for the purpose of effecting on an exchange not within or subject to the jurisdiction of the United States, any transaction in any security the issuer of which is a resident of, or is organized under the laws of, or has its principal place of business in, a place within or subject to the jurisdiction of the United States, in contravention of such rules and regulations as the Commission may prescribe . . . ." *15 U.S.C. § 78dd(a)*.

Subsection 30(a) contains what *§ 10(b)* lacks: a clear statement of extraterritorial effect. Its explicit provision for a specific extraterritorial application would be quite superfluous if the rest of the Exchange Act already applied to transactions on foreign exchanges -- and its limitation of that application to securities of domestic issuers would be inoperative. Even if that were not true, when a statute provides for some extraterritorial application, the presumption against extraterritoriality operates to limit that provision to its terms. See *Microsoft Corp. v. AT&T Corp., 550 U.S. 437, 455-456 (2007)*. No one claims that *§ 30(a)* applies here.

The concurrence claims we have impermissibly narrowed the inquiry in evaluating whether a statute applies abroad, citing for that point the dissent in *Aramco*, see *post*, at 6. But we do not say, as the concurrence seems to think, that the presumption against extraterritoriality is a "clear statement rule," *ibid.*, if by that is meant a requirement that a statute say "this law applies abroad." Assuredly context can be consulted as well. But whatever sources of statutory meaning one consults to give "the most faithful reading" of the text, *post*, at 7, there is no clear indication of extraterritoriality here. The concurrence does not even try to refute that conclusion, but merely puts forward the same (at best) uncertain indications relied upon by petitioners and the Solicitor General. As the opinion *for the Court* in *Aramco* (which we prefer to the dissent) shows, those uncertain indications do not suffice.

In short, there is no affirmative indication in the Exchange Act that *§ 10(b)* applies extraterritorially, and we therefore conclude that it does not.

IV

A

Petitioners argue that the conclusion that *§ 10(b)* does not apply extraterritorially does not resolve this case. They contend that they seek no more than domestic application anyway, since Florida is where HomeSide and its senior executives engaged in the deceptive conduct of manipulating HomeSide's financial models; their complaint also alleged that Race and Hughes made misleading public statements there. This is less an answer to the presumption against extraterritorial application than it is an assertion -- a quite valid assertion -- that that presumption here (as often) is not self-evidently dispositive, but its application requires further analysis. For it is a rare case of prohibited extraterritorial application that lacks *all* contact with the territory of the United States. But the presumption against extraterritorial application would be a craven watchdog indeed if it retreated to its kennel whenever *some* domestic activity is involved in the case. The concurrence seems to imagine just such a timid sentinel, see *post*, at 7-8, but our cases are to the contrary. In *Aramco*, for example, the Title VII plaintiff had been hired in Houston, and was an American citizen. See *499 U.S., at 247*. The Court concluded, however, that neither that territorial event nor that relationship was the "focus" of congressional concern, *id., at 255*, but rather domestic employment. See also *Foley Bros., 336 U.S., at 283, 285-286*.

Applying the same mode of analysis here, we think that the focus of the Exchange Act is not upon the place where the deception originated, but upon purchases and sales of securities in the United States. *Section 10(b)* does not punish deceptive conduct, but only deceptive conduct "in connection with the purchase or sale of any security registered on a national securities exchange or any security not so registered." *15 U.S.C. § 78j(b)*. See *SEC v. Zandford, 535 U.S. 813, 820 (2002)*. Those purchase-and-sale transactions are the objects of the statute's solicitude. It is those transactions that the statute seeks to "regulate," see *Superintendent of Ins. of N. Y. v. Bankers Life & Casualty Co., 404 U.S. 6, 12 (1971)*; it is parties or prospective parties to those transactions that the statute seeks to "protec[t]," *id., at 10*. See also *Ernst & Ernst v. Hochfelder, 425 U.S. 185, 195 (1976)*. And it is in our view only transactions in securities listed on domestic exchanges, and domestic transactions in other securities, to which *§ 10(b)* applies.

The primacy of the domestic exchange is suggested by the very prologue of the Exchange Act, which sets forth as its object "[t]o provide for the regulation of securities exchanges . . . operating in interstate and foreign commerce and through the mails, to prevent inequitable and unfair practices on such exchanges . . . ." 48 Stat. 881. We know of no one who thought that the Act was intended to "regulat[e]" *foreign* securities exchanges -- or indeed who even believed that under established principles of international law Congress had the power to do so. The Act's registration requirements apply only to securities listed on national securities exchanges. *15 U.S.C. § 78l(a)*.

With regard to securities *not* registered on domestic exchanges, the exclusive focus on *domestic* purchases and sales[10] is strongly confirmed by *§ 30(a)* and *(b)*, discussed earlier. The former extends the normal scope of the Exchange Act's prohibitions to acts effecting, in violation of rules prescribed by the Commission, a "transaction" in a United States security "on an exchange not within or subject to the jurisdiction of the United States." *§ 78dd(a)*. And the latter specifies that the Act does not apply to "any person insofar as he transacts a business in securities without the jurisdiction of the United States," unless he does so in violation of regulations promulgated by the Commission "to prevent evasion [of the Act]." *§ 78dd(b)*. Under both provisions it is the foreign location of the *transaction* that establishes (or reflects the presumption of) the Act's inapplicability, absent regulations by the Commission.

The same focus on domestic transactions is evident in the Securities Act of 1933, 48 Stat. 74, enacted by the same Congress as the Exchange Act, and forming part of the same comprehensive regulation of securities trading. See *Central Bank of Denver, N. A. v. First Interstate Bank of Denver, N. A., 511 U.S. 164, 170-171 (1994)*. That legislation makes it unlawful to sell a security, through a prospectus or otherwise, making use of "any means or instruments of transportation or communication in interstate commerce or of the mails," unless a registration statement is in effect. *15 U.S.C. § 77e(a)(1)*. The Commission has interpreted that requirement "not to include . . . sales that occur outside the United States." *17 CFR § 230.901 (2009)*.

Finally, we reject the notion that the Exchange Act reaches conduct in this country affecting exchanges or transactions abroad for the same reason that *Aramco* rejected overseas application

---

[10] That is in our view the meaning which the presumption against extraterritorial application requires for the words "purchase or sale, of . . . any security not so registered" in § 10(b)'s phrase "in connection with the purchase or sale of any security registered on a national securities exchange *or any security not so registered*" (emphasis added). Even without the presumption against extraterritorial application, the only alternative to that reading makes nonsense of the phrase, causing it to cover all purchases and sales of registered securities, and all purchases and sales of nonregistered securities -- a thought which, if intended, would surely have been expressed by the simpler phrase "all purchases and sales of securities."

of Title VII to all domestically concluded employment contracts or all employment contracts with American employers: The probability of incompatibility with the applicable laws of other countries is so obvious that if Congress intended such foreign application "it would have addressed the subject of conflicts with foreign laws and procedures." *499 U.S., at 256.* Like the United States, foreign countries regulate their domestic securities exchanges and securities transactions occurring within their territorial jurisdiction. And the regulation of other countries often differs from ours as to what constitutes fraud, what disclosures must be made, what damages are recoverable, what discovery is available in litigation, what individual actions may be joined in a single suit, what attorney's fees are recoverable, and many other matters. See, *e.g.,* Brief for United Kingdom of Great Britain and Northern Ireland as *Amicus Curiae* 16-21. The Commonwealth of Australia, the United Kingdom of Great Britain and Northern Ireland, and the Republic of France have filed *amicus* briefs in this case. So have (separately or jointly) such international and foreign organizations as the International Chamber of Commerce, the Swiss Bankers Association, the Federation of German Industries, the French Business Confederation, the Institute of International Bankers, the European Banking Federation, the Australian Bankers' Association, and the Association Francaise des Entreprises Privees. They all complain of the interference with foreign securities regulation that application of § 10(b) abroad would produce, and urge the adoption of a clear test that will avoid that consequence. The transactional test we have adopted -- whether the purchase or sale is made in the United States, or involves a security listed on a domestic exchange -- meets that requirement.

B

The Solicitor General suggests a different test, which petitioners also endorse: "[A] transnational securities fraud violates *[§]10(b)* when the fraud involves significant conduct in the United States that is material to the fraud's success." Brief for United States as *Amicus Curiae* 16; see Brief for Petitioners 26. Neither the Solicitor General nor petitioners provide any textual support for this test. The Solicitor General sets forth a number of purposes such a test would serve: achieving a high standard of business ethics in the securities industry, ensuring honest securities markets and thereby promoting investor confidence, and preventing the United States from becoming a "Barbary Coast" for malefactors perpetrating frauds in foreign markets. Brief for United States as *Amicus Curiae* 16-17. But it provides no textual support for the last of these purposes, or for the first two as applied to the foreign securities industry and securities markets abroad. It is our function to give the statute the effect its language suggests, however modest that may be; not to extend it to admirable purposes it might be used to achieve.

If, moreover, one is to be attracted by the desirable consequences of the "significant and material conduct" test, one should also be repulsed by its adverse consequences. While there is no reason to believe that the United States has become the Barbary Coast for those perpetrating frauds on foreign securities markets, some fear that it has become the Shangri-La of class-action litigation for lawyers representing those allegedly cheated in foreign securities markets. See Brief for Infineon Technologies AG as *Amicus Curiae* 1-2, 22-25; Brief for European Aeronautic Defence & Space Co. N. V. et al. as *Amici Curiae* 2-4; Brief for Securities Industry and Financial Markets Association et al. as *Amici Curiae* 10-16; Coffee, Securities Policeman to the World? The Cost of Global Class Actions, N. Y. L. J. 5 (2008); S. Grant & D. Zilka, The Current Role of Foreign Investors in Federal Securities Class Actions, PLI Corporate Law and Practice

Handbook Series, PLI Order No. 11072, pp. 15-16 (Sept.-Oct. 2007); Buxbaum, Multinational Class Actions Under Federal Securities Law: Managing Jurisdictional Conflict, *46 Colum. J. Transnat'l L. 14, 38-41 (2007)*.

As case support for the "significant and material conduct" test, the Solicitor General relies primarily on *Pasquantino v. United States, 544 U.S. 349 (2005)*. In that case we concluded that the wire-fraud statute, *18 U.S.C. § 1343 (2009 ed., Supp. II)*, was violated by defendants who ordered liquor over the phone from a store in Maryland with the intent to smuggle it into Canada and deprive the Canadian Government of revenue. *544 U.S., at 353, 371. Section 1343* prohibits "any scheme or artifice to defraud," -- fraud *simpliciter*, without any requirement that it be "in connection with" any particular transaction or event. The *Pasquantino* Court said that the petitioners'"offense was complete the moment they executed the scheme inside the United States," and that it was "[t]his domestic element of petitioners' conduct [that] the Government is punishing." *544 U.S., at 371. Section 10(b)*, by contrast, punishes not all acts of deception, but only such acts "in connection with the purchase or sale of any security registered on a national securities exchange or any security not so registered." Not deception alone, but deception with respect to certain purchases or sales is necessary for a violation of the statute.

The Solicitor General points out that the "significant and material conduct" test is in accord with prevailing notions of international comity. If so, that proves that *if* the United States asserted prescriptive jurisdiction pursuant to the "significant and material conduct" test it would not violate customary international law; but it in no way tends to prove that that is what Congress has done.

Finally, the Solicitor General argues that the Commission has adopted an interpretation similar to the "significant and material conduct" test, and that we should defer to that. In the two adjudications the Solicitor General cites, however, the Commission did not purport to be providing its own interpretation of the statute, but relied on decisions of federal courts -- mainly Court of Appeals decisions that in turn relied on the *Schoenbaum* and *Leasco* decisions of the Second Circuit that we discussed earlier. See *In re United Securities Clearing Corp., 52 S. E. C. 92, 95, n. 14, 96, n. 16 (1994)*; *In re Robert F. Lynch, 46 S.E.C. 5, 10 n. 15 (1975)*. We need "accept only those agency interpretations that are reasonable in light of the principles of construction courts normally employ." *Aramco, 499 U.S., at 260* (SCALIA, J., concurring in part and concurring in judgment). Since the Commission's interpretations relied on cases we disapprove, which ignored or discarded the presumption against extraterritoriality, we owe them no deference.

* * *

Section 10(b) reaches the use of a manipulative or deceptive device or contrivance only in connection with the purchase or sale of a security listed on an American stock exchange, and the purchase or sale of any other security in the United States. This case involves no securities listed on a domestic exchange, and all aspects of the purchases complained of by those petitioners who still have live claims occurred outside the United States. Petitioners have therefore failed to state a claim on which relief can be granted. We affirm the dismissal of petitioners' complaint on this ground.

It is so ordered.

JUSTICE SOTOMAYOR took no part in the consideration or decision of this case.

JUSTICE BREYER, concurring in part and concurring in the judgment.

Section 10(b) of the Securities Exchange Act of 1934 applies to fraud "in connection with" two categories of transactions: (1) "the purchase or sale of any security registered on a national securities exchange" or (2) "the purchase or sale of . . . any security not so registered." *15 U.S.C. § 78j(b)*. In this case, the purchased securities are listed only on a few foreign exchanges, none of which has registered with the Securities and Exchange Commission as a "national securities exchange." See *§ 78f*. The first category therefore does not apply. Further, the relevant purchases of these unregistered securities took place entirely in Australia and involved only Australian investors. And in accordance with the presumption against extraterritoriality, I do not read the second category to include such transactions. Thus, while state law or other federal fraud statutes, see, *e.g., 18 U.S.C. § 1341* (mail fraud), *§ 1343* (wire fraud), may apply to the fraudulent activity alleged here to have occurred in the United States, I believe that *§ 10(b)* does not. This case does not require us to consider other circumstances.

To the extent the Court's opinion is consistent with these views, I join it.

JUSTICE STEVENS, with whom JUSTICE GINSBURG joins, concurring in the judgment.

While I agree that petitioners have failed to state a claim on which relief can be granted, my reasoning differs from the Court's. I would adhere to the general approach that has been the law in the Second Circuit, and most of the rest of the country, for nearly four decades.

I

Today the Court announces a new "transactional test," *ante*, at 21, for defining the reach of *§ 10(b)* of the Securities Exchange Act of 1934 (Exchange Act), *15 U.S.C. § 78j(b)*, and SEC *Rule 10b-5, 17 CFR § 240.10b-5(b) (2009)*: Henceforth, those provisions will extend only to "transactions in securities listed on domestic exchanges . . . and domestic transactions in other securities," *ante*, at 18. If one confines one's gaze to the statutory text, the Court's conclusion is a plausible one. But the federal courts have been construing *§ 10(b)* in a different manner for a long time, and the Court's textual analysis is not nearly so compelling, in my view, as to warrant the abandonment of their doctrine.

The text and history of *§ 10(b)* are famously opaque on the question of when, exactly, transnational securities frauds fall within the statute's compass. As those types of frauds became more common in the latter half of the 20th century, the federal courts were increasingly called upon to wrestle with that question. The Court of Appeals for the Second Circuit, located in the Nation's financial center, led the effort. Beginning in earnest with *Schoenbaum v. Firstbrook, 405 F.2d 200*, rev'd on rehearing on other grounds, *405 F.2d 215 (1968)* (en banc), that court strove, over an extended series of cases, to "discern" under what circumstances "Congress would have wished the precious resources of the United States courts and law enforcement agencies to be devoted to [transnational] transactions," *547 F.3d 167, 170 (2008)* (internal quotation marks omitted). Relying on opinions by Judge Henry Friendly,[1] the Second Circuit eventually settled on a conduct-and-effects test. This test asks "(1) whether the wrongful conduct occurred in the Unites States, and (2) whether the wrongful conduct had a substantial effect in the United States or upon United States citizens." *Id., at 171.* Numerous cases flesh out the proper application of each prong.

The Second Circuit's test became the "north star" of § 10(b) jurisprudence, *ante*, at 8, not just regionally but nationally as well. With minor variations, other courts converged on the same basic approach. See Brief for United States as *Amicus Curiae* 15 ("The courts have uniformly agreed that *Section 10(b)* can apply to a transnational securities fraud either when fraudulent conduct has effects in the United States or when sufficient conduct relevant to the fraud occurs in the United States"); see also 1 *Restatement (Third) of Foreign Relations Law of the United States § 416* (1986) (setting forth conduct-and-effects test). Neither Congress nor the Securities Exchange Commission (Commission) acted to change the law. To the contrary, the Commission largely adopted the Second Circuit's position in its own adjudications. See *ante*, at 23-24.

In light of this history, the Court's critique of the decision below for applying "judge-made rules" is quite misplaced. *Ante*, at 11. This entire area of law is replete with judge-made rules, which give concrete meaning to Congress' general commands. "When we deal with private actions under *Rule 10b-5*," then-Justice Rehnquist wrote many years ago, "we deal with a judicial oak which has grown from little more than a legislative acorn." *Blue Chip Stamps v. Manor Drug Stores, 421 U.S. 723, 737 (1975).* The "'Mother Court'" of securities law tended to that oak. *Id., at 762* (Blackmun, J., dissenting) (describing the Second Circuit). One of our greatest jurists -- the judge who, "without a doubt, did more to shape the law of securities regulation than any [other] in the country" -- was its master arborist.

The development of § 10(b) law was hardly an instance of judicial usurpation. Congress invited an expansive role for judicial elaboration when it crafted such an open-ended statute in 1934. And both Congress and the Commission subsequently affirmed that role when they left intact the relevant statutory and regulatory language, respectively, throughout all the years that followed. See Brief for Alecta pensionsforsakring, omsesidigt et al. as *Amici Curiae* 31-33; cf. *Musick, Peeler & Garrett v. Employers Ins. of Wausau, 508 U.S. 286, 294 (1993)* (inferring from recent legislation Congress' desire to "acknowledg[e]" the 10b-5 action without "entangling" itself in the precise formulation thereof). Unlike certain other domains of securities law, this is "a case in which Congress has enacted a regulatory statute and then has accepted, over a long period of time, broad judicial authority to define substantive standards of conduct and liability," and much else besides. *Stoneridge Investment Partners, LLC v. Scientific-Atlanta, Inc., 552 U.S. 148, 163 (2008).*

    . . . .

---

[1] See, *e.g., IIT, Int'l Inv. Trust v. Cornfeld, 619 F.2d 909 (CA2 1980); IIT v. Vencap, Ltd., 519 F.2d 1001 (CA2 1975); Bersch v. Drexel Firestone, Inc., 519 F.2d 974 (CA2 1975); Leasco Data Processing Equip. Corp. v. Maxwell, 468 F.2d 1326 (CA2 1972).*

Thus, while the Court devotes a considerable amount of attention to the development of the case law, *ante*, at 6-10, it draws the wrong conclusions. The Second Circuit refined its test over several decades and dozens of cases, with the tacit approval of Congress and the Commission and with the general assent of its sister Circuits. That history is a reason we should give additional weight to the Second Circuit's "judge-made" doctrine, not a reason to denigrate it. "The longstanding acceptance by the courts, coupled with Congress' failure to reject [its] reasonable interpretation of the wording of § 10(b), . . . argues significantly in favor of acceptance of the [Second Circuit] rule by this Court." *Blue Chip, 421 U.S., at 733.*

II

The Court's other main critique of the Second Circuit's approach -- apart from what the Court views as its excessive reliance on functional considerations and reconstructed congressional intent -- is that the Second Circuit has "disregard[ed]" the presumption against extraterritoriality. *Ante*, at 6. It is the Court, however, that misapplies the presumption, in two main respects.

First, the Court seeks to transform the presumption from a flexible rule of thumb into something more like a clear statement rule. We have been here before. In the case on which the Court primarily relies, *EEOC v. Arabian American Oil Co., 499 U.S. 244 (1991) (Aramco)*, Chief Justice Rehnquist's majority opinion included a sentence that appeared to make the same move. See *id., at 258* ("Congress' awareness of the need to make a clear statement that a statute applies overseas is amply demonstrated by the numerous occasions on which it has expressly legislated the extraterritorial application of a statute"). Justice Marshall, in dissent, vigorously objected. See *id., at 261* ("[C]ontrary to what one would conclude from the majority's analysis, this canon is *not* a 'clear statement' rule, the application of which relieves a court of the duty to give effect to all available indicia of the legislative will").

Yet even *Aramco* -- surely the most extreme application of the presumption against extraterritoriality in my time on the Court -- contained numerous passages suggesting that the presumption may be overcome without a clear directive. See *id., at 248-255* (majority opinion) (repeatedly identifying congressional "intent" as the touchstone of the presumption). And our cases both before and after *Aramco* make perfectly clear that the Court continues to give effect to "*all available evidence* about the meaning" of a provision when considering its extraterritorial application, lest we defy Congress' will. *Sale v. Haitian Centers Council, Inc., 509 U.S. 155, 177 (1993)* (emphasis added). Contrary to JUSTICE SCALIA's personal view of statutory interpretation, that evidence legitimately encompasses more than the enacted text. Hence, while the Court's dictum that "[w]hen a statute gives no clear indication of an extraterritorial application, it has none," *ante*, at 6, makes for a nice catchphrase, the point is overstated. The presumption against extraterritoriality can be useful as a theory of congressional purpose, a tool for managing international conflict, a background norm, a tiebreaker. It does not relieve courts of their duty to give statutes the most faithful reading possible.

Second, and more fundamentally, the Court errs in suggesting that the presumption against extraterritoriality is fatal to the Second Circuit's test. For even if the presumption really were a clear statement (or "clear indication," *ante*, at 6, 16) rule, it would have only marginal relevance to this case.

It is true, of course, that "this Court ordinarily construes ambiguous statutes to avoid unreasonable interference with the sovereign authority of other nations," *F. Hoffmann-La Roche Ltd v. Empagran S. A., 542 U.S. 155, 164 (2004)*, and that, absent contrary evidence, we presume "Congress is primarily concerned with domestic conditions," *Foley Bros., Inc. v. Filardo, 336 U.S. 281, 285 (1949)*. Accordingly, the presumption against extraterritoriality "provides a sound basis for concluding that *Section 10(b)* does not apply when a securities fraud with no effects in the United States is hatched and executed entirely outside this country." Brief for United States as *Amicus Curiae* 22. But that is just about all it provides a sound basis for concluding. And the conclusion is not very illuminating, because no party to the litigation disputes it. No one contends that § *10(b)* applies to wholly foreign frauds.

Rather, the real question in this case is how much, and what kinds of, *domestic* contacts are sufficient to trigger application of § *10(b)*. In developing its conduct-and-effects test, the Second Circuit endeavored to derive a solution from the Exchange Act's text, structure, history, and purpose. Judge Friendly and his colleagues were well aware that United States courts "cannot and should not expend [their] resources resolving cases that do not affect Americans or involve fraud emanating from America." *547 F.3d at 175*; see also *id., at 171* (overriding concern is "'whether there is sufficient United States involvement'" (quoting *Itoba Ltd. v. Lep Group PLC, 54 F.3d 118, 122 (CA2 1995))).

. . . .

This approach is consistent with the understanding shared by most scholars that Congress, in passing the Exchange Act, "expected U.S. securities laws to apply to certain international transactions or conduct." Buxbaum, Multinational Class Actions Under Federal Securities Law: Managing Jurisdictional Conflict, *46 Colum. J. Transnat'l L. 14, 19 (2007)*; see also *Leasco Data Processing Equip. Corp. v. Maxwell, 468 F.2d 1326, 1336 (CA2 1972)* (Friendly, J.) (detailing evidence that Congress "meant § *10(b)* to protect against fraud in the sale or purchase of securities whether or not these were traded on organized United States markets"). It is also consistent with the traditional understanding, regnant in the 1930's as it is now, that the presumption against extraterritoriality does not apply "when the conduct [at issue] occurs within the United States," and has lesser force when "the failure to extend the scope of the statute to a foreign setting will result in adverse effects within the United States." *Environmental Defense Fund, Inc. v. Massey, 986 F.2d 528, 531 (CADC 1993)*; accord, Restatement (Second) of Foreign Relations Law of the United States § 38 (1964-1965); cf. *Small v. United States, 544 U.S. 385, 400 (2005)* (THOMAS, J., joined by SCALIA and KENNEDY, JJ., dissenting) (presumption against extraterritoriality "lend[s] no support" to a "rule restricting a federal statute from reaching conduct *within U.S. borders*"); *Continental Ore Co. v. Union Carbide & Carbon Corp., 370 U.S. 690, 705 (1962)* (presumption against extraterritoriality not controlling "[s]ince the activities of the defendants had an impact within the United States and upon its foreign trade"). And it strikes a reasonable balance between the goals of "preventing the export of fraud from America," protecting shareholders, enhancing investor confidence, and deterring corporate misconduct, on the one hand, and conserving United States resources and limiting conflict with foreign law, on the other. *547 F.3d at 175*.

Thus, while *§ 10(b)* may not give any "clear indication" on its face as to how it should apply to transnational securities frauds, *ante*, at 6, 16, it does give strong clues that it should cover at least some of them, see n. 9, *supra*. And in my view, the Second Circuit has done the best job of discerning what sorts of transnational frauds Congress meant in 1934 -- and still means today -- to regulate. I do not take issue with the Court for beginning its inquiry with the statutory text, rather than the doctrine in the Courts of Appeals. Cf. *ante*, at 18, n. 9. I take issue with the Court for beginning *and ending* its inquiry with the statutory text, when the text does not speak with geographic precision, and for dismissing the long pedigree of, and the persuasive account of congressional intent embodied in, the Second Circuit's rule.

Repudiating the Second Circuit's approach in its entirety, the Court establishes a novel rule that will foreclose private parties from bringing § 10(b) actions whenever the relevant securities were purchased or sold abroad and are not listed on a domestic exchange.[12] The real motor of the Court's opinion, it seems, is not the presumption against extraterritoriality but rather the Court's belief that transactions on domestic exchanges are "the focus of the Exchange Act" and "the objects of [its] solicitude." *Ante*, at 17, 18. In reality, however, it is the "public interest" and "the interests of investors" that are the objects of the statute's solicitude. *Europe & Overseas Commodity Traders, S. A. v. Banque Paribas London, 147 F.3d 118, 125 (CA2 1998)* (citing H. R. Rep. No. 1838, 73d Cong., 2d Sess., 32-33 (1934)); see also *Basic Inc. v. Levinson, 485 U.S. 224, 230 (1988)* ("The 1934 Act was designed to protect investors against manipulation of stock prices" (citing S. Rep. No. 792, 73d Cong., 2d Sess., 1-5 (1934)); *Ernst & Ernst v. Hochfelder, 425 U.S. 185, 195 (1976)* ("The 1934 Act was intended principally to protect investors . . . "); S. Rep. No. 1455, 73d Cong., 2d Sess., 68 (1934) ("The Securities Exchange Act of 1934 aims to protect the interests of the public against the predatory operations of directors, officers, and principal stockholders of corporations . . . "). And while the clarity and simplicity of the Court's test may have some salutary consequences, like all bright-line rules it also has drawbacks.

Imagine, for example, an American investor who buys shares in a company listed only on an overseas exchange. That company has a major American subsidiary with executives based in New York City; and it was in New York City that the executives masterminded and implemented a massive deception which artificially inflated the stock price -- and which will, upon its disclosure, cause the price to plummet. Or, imagine that those same executives go knocking on doors in Manhattan and convince an unsophisticated retiree, on the basis of material

---

[12] The Court's opinion does not, however, foreclose the Commission from bringing enforcement actions in additional circumstances, as no issue concerning the Commission's authority is presented by this case. The Commission's enforcement proceedings not only differ from private § 10(b) actions in numerous potentially relevant respects, see Brief for United States as *Amicus Curiae* 12-13, but they also pose a lesser threat to international comity, *id.*, at 26-27; cf. *Empagran, 542 U.S., at 171* ("'[P]rivate plaintiffs often are unwilling to exercise the degree of self-restraint and consideration of foreign governmental sensibilities generally exercised by the U.S. Government'" (quoting Griffin, Extraterritoriality in U.S. and EU Antitrust Enforcement, *67 Antitrust L. J. 159, 194 (1999)*; alteration in original)).

misrepresentations, to invest her life savings in the company's doomed securities. Both of these investors would, under the Court's new test, be barred from seeking relief under *§ 10(b)*.

The oddity of that result should give pause. For in walling off such individuals from *§ 10(b)*, the Court narrows the provision's reach to a degree that would surprise and alarm generations of American investors -- and, I am convinced, the Congress that passed the Exchange Act. Indeed, the Court's rule turns § 10(b) jurisprudence (and the presumption against extraterritoriality) on its head, by withdrawing the statute's application from cases in which there is *both* substantial wrongful conduct that occurred in the United States *and* a substantial injurious effect on United States markets and citizens.

III

In my judgment, if petitioners' allegations of fraudulent misconduct that took place in Florida are true, then respondents may have violated *§ 10(b)*, and could potentially be held accountable in an enforcement proceeding brought by the Commission. But it does not follow that shareholders who have failed to allege that the bulk or the heart of the fraud occurred in the United States, or that the fraud had an adverse impact on American investors or markets, may maintain a private action to recover damages they suffered abroad. Some cases involving foreign securities transactions have extensive links to, and ramifications for, this country; this case has Australia written all over it. Accordingly, for essentially the reasons stated in the Court of Appeals' opinion, I would affirm its judgment.

The Court instead elects to upend a significant area of securities law based on a plausible, but hardly decisive, construction of the statutory text. In so doing, it pays short shrift to the United States' interest in remedying frauds that transpire on American soil or harm American citizens, as well as to the accumulated wisdom and experience of the lower courts. I happen to agree with the result the Court reaches in this case. But "I respectfully dissent," once again, "from the Court's continuing campaign to render the private cause of action under *§ 10(b)* toothless." *Stoneridge, 552 U.S., at 175* (STEVENS, J., dissenting).

Justice Stevens' concern that the majority's test in <u>Morrison</u> for the extraterritorial reach of Rule 10b-5 could also divest the SEC of jurisdiction to challenge fraudulent conduct occurring in the United States (where the securities were traded only abroad) has seemingly been rendered moot by the Dodd-Frank Act, which amends Section 22 of the Securities Act of 1933 and Section 27 of the Securities Exchange Act to authorize the SEC to sue when "conduct within the United States . . . constitutes significant steps in furtherance of the violation" (even though the securities trade only abroad).

OPENTABLE, INC.
REGISTRATION STATEMENT,
MAY 21, 2009

POS AM 1 a2193227zposam.htm POS AM

Use these links to rapidly review the document

Table of Contents

As filed with the Securities and Exchange Commission on May 21, 2009

Registration No. 333-157034

UNITED STATES
SECURITIES AND EXCHANGE COMMISSION
WASHINGTON, D.C. 20549

POST-EFFECTIVE
AMENDMENT NO. 2
TO
FORM S-1
REGISTRATION STATEMENT
UNDER
THE SECURITIES ACT OF 1933

OPENTABLE, INC.
(Exact name of registrant as specified in its charter)

Delaware	7389	94-3374049
(State or other jurisdiction of incorporation or organization)	(Primary Standard Industrial Classification Code Number)	(I.R.S. Employer Identification Number)

799 Market Street, 4th Floor
San Francisco, CA 94103
(415) 344-4200
(Address, including zip code, and telephone number, including
area code, of registrant's principal executive offices)

Jeffrey D. Jordan
Chief Executive Officer
OpenTable, Inc.
799 Market Street, 4th Floor
San Francisco, CA 94103
(415) 344-4200
(Name, address, including zip code, and telephone number, including area code, of agent for service)

Copies To:

Patrick A. Pohlen, Esq.	Alan F. Denenberg, Esq.
Latham & Watkins LLP	Davis Polk & Wardwell
140 Scott Drive	1600 El Camino Real
Menlo Park, California 94025	Menlo Park, California 94025
(650) 328-4600	(650) 752-2000

Approximate date of commencement of the proposed sale to the public:
As soon as practicable after this Registration Statement becomes effective.

If any of the securities being registered on this form are to be offered on a delayed or continuous basis pursuant to Rule 415 under the Securities Act of 1933, check the following box. ☐

If this Form is filed to register additional securities for an offering pursuant to Rule 462(b) under the Securities Act, check the following box and list the Securities Act registration statement number of the earlier effective registration statement for the same offering. ☐

If this Form is a post-effective amendment filed pursuant to Rule 462(c) under the Securities Act, check the following box and list the Securities Act registration statement number of the earlier effective registration statement for the same offering. ☐

If this Form is a post-effective amendment filed pursuant to Rule 462(d) under the Securities Act, check the following box and list the Securities Act registration statement number of the earlier effective registration statement for the same offering. ☐

Indicate by check mark whether the registrant is a large accelerated filer, an accelerated filer, a non-accelerated filer, or a smaller reporting company. See definitions of "large accelerated filer," "accelerated filer," and "smaller reporting company" in Rule 12b-2 of the Exchange Act. (Check one):

Large accelerated filer ☐   Accelerated filer ☐   Non-accelerated filer ☒   Smaller reporting company ☐
                                                                 (Do not check if a smaller
                                                                 reporting company)

The Registrant hereby amends this Registration Statement on such date or dates as may be necessary to delay its effective date until the Registrant shall file a further amendment which specifically states that this Registration Statement shall thereafter become effective in accordance with Section 8(a) of the Securities Act of 1933 or until the Registration Statement shall become effective on such date as the Commission, acting pursuant to said Section 8(a), may determine.

The information in this prospectus is not complete and may be changed. We and the selling stockholders may not sell these securities until the registration statement filed with the Securities and Exchange Commission is effective. This prospectus is not an offer to sell these securities and we are not soliciting an offer to buy these securities in any jurisdiction where the offer or sale is not permitted.

Subject to Completion
Preliminary Prospectus dated May 21, 2009

PROSPECTUS

3,000,000 Shares

Common Stock

This is the initial public offering of our common stock. Prior to this offering, there has been no public market for our common stock. We are offering 1,572,684 shares of the common stock offered by this prospectus, and the selling stockholders are offering 1,427,316 shares. We will not receive any proceeds from the sale of shares to be offered by the selling stockholders. The initial public offering price of our common stock is expected to be between $16.00 and $18.00 per share. Our common stock has been approved for listing on The Nasdaq Global Market under the symbol "OPEN," subject to official notice of issuance.

Investing in our common stock involves a high degree of risk. See "Risk Factors" on page 10 of this prospectus.

	Per Share	Total
Public offering price	$	$
Underwriting discount	$	$
Proceeds, before expenses, to OpenTable, Inc.	$	$
Proceeds, before expenses, to the selling stockholders	$	$

The underwriters have a 30-day option to purchase up to an additional 450,000 shares of common stock from us to cover overallotments, if any.

Neither the Securities and Exchange Commission nor any state securities commission nor any other regulatory body has approved or disapproved of these securities or determined if this prospectus is truthful or complete. Any representation to the contrary is a criminal offense.

The shares will be ready for delivery on or about   , 2009.

Merrill Lynch & Co.

Allen & Company LLC

Stifel Nicolaus   **ThinkEquity LLC**

The date of this prospectus is _____ , 2009.

 OpenTable®

We provide solutions that form an online network connecting reservation-taking restaurants and people who dine at those restaurants.

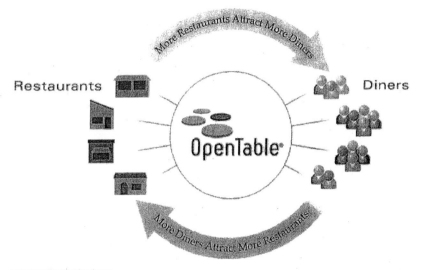

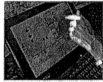

For restaurants, we provide the OpenTable Electronic Reservation Book, an integrated software and hardware solution that replaces traditional pen-and-paper reservation books at the restaurant host stand. Our solution enables restaurants to manage their phone reservations as well as accept online reservations through OpenTable.com.

For diners, we operate OpenTable.com, a popular restaurant reservation website that enables diners to find, choose and book tables at restaurants on the OpenTable network in real time. OpenTable.com helps diners overcome the inefficiencies of reserving by phone and helps restaurants fill their seats.

TABLE OF CONTENTS

You should rely only on the information contained in this prospectus or contained in any free writing prospectus filed with the Securities and Exchange Commission. Neither we, the selling stockholders nor the underwriters have authorized anyone to provide you with additional information or information different from that contained in this prospectus or in any free writing prospectus filed with the Securities and Exchange Commission. We and the selling stockholders are offering to sell, and seeking offers to buy, our common stock only in jurisdictions where offers and sales are permitted. The information contained in this prospectus is accurate only as of the date of this prospectus, regardless of the time of delivery of this prospectus or of any sale of our common stock.

PROSPECTUS SUMMARY

This summary highlights information contained elsewhere in this prospectus and does not contain all of the information that you should consider in making your investment decision. Before investing in our common stock, you should carefully read this entire prospectus, including our consolidated financial statements and the related notes included in this prospectus and the information set forth under the headings "Risk Factors" and "Management's Discussion and Analysis of Financial Condition and Results of Operations."

Our Company

We provide solutions that form an online network connecting reservation-taking restaurants and people who dine at those restaurants. Our solutions for restaurants include our Electronic Reservation Book, or ERB, which combines proprietary software and computer hardware that computerizes restaurant host-stand operations and replaces traditional pen-and-paper reservation books. Our ERB streamlines and enhances a number of business-critical functions and processes for restaurants, including reservation management, table management, guest recognition and email marketing. The ERBs at our restaurant customers connect via the Internet to form an online network of restaurant reservation books. Our solutions for diners include our popular restaurant reservation website, www.opentable.com, which enables diners to find, choose and book tables at restaurants on the OpenTable network in real time, overcoming the inefficiencies associated with the traditional process of reserving by phone. Restaurants pay us a one-time installation fee for onsite installation and training, a monthly subscription fee for the use of our software and hardware and a fee for each restaurant guest seated through online reservations. Our online reservation service is free to diners.

We initially focused on acquiring a critical mass of local restaurant customers in four metropolitan areas: Chicago, New York, San Francisco and Washington, D.C. These markets have since developed into active, local networks of restaurants and diners that continue to grow. We have applied and continue to apply the same fundamental strategy in developing and penetrating our other markets. As of March 31, 2009, the OpenTable network included approximately 10,000 OpenTable restaurant customers spanning all 50 states as well as select markets outside of the United States. Since our inception in 1998, we have seated approximately 100 million diners through OpenTable reservations, and during the three months ended March 31, 2009, we seated an average of approximately three million diners per month. For the twelve months ended December 31, 2007 and 2008, our revenues were $41.1 million and $55.8 million, respectively. For the twelve months ended December 31, 2007 and 2008, our subscription revenues accounted for 55% and 54% of our total revenues, respectively, and our reservation revenues accounted for 41% and 41% of our total revenues, respectively. For the three months ended March 31, 2008 and 2009, our subscription revenues accounted for 52% and 52% of our total revenues, respectively, and our reservation revenues accounted for 44% and 43% of our total revenues, respectively.

Market Opportunity

We target our solutions, by which we mean our ERB and the OpenTable website, to reservation-taking restaurants and diners, respectively. We believe based on our internal estimates that there are approximately 30,000 reservation-taking restaurants in North America that seat approximately 600 million diners through reservations annually, though this number fluctuates with economic and other conditions.

The ability of the restaurant industry to leverage the power of the Internet for reservation transactions has been inhibited by two key characteristics. First, the reservation-taking restaurant industry has been slow to computerize host-stand operations. Restaurant reservations historically have been largely handled by the traditional pen-and-paper reservation book, despite the inherent operational inefficiencies and potential for error. Second, the reservation-taking restaurant industry is

1

highly fragmented, with independent restaurants and small, local restaurant groups comprising a significant majority of restaurant locations. The restaurant industry is also inherently local, making it time-consuming and costly to aggregate the breadth of local restaurant table inventory required to attract a critical mass of diners to make reservations online and create an online restaurant reservation network.

Historically, diners learned about restaurants through word of mouth and local print media, such as dining guides, newspapers and magazines. While diners continue to value personal recommendations, the Internet now puts a wealth of restaurant information at their fingertips. However, the ability to book restaurant reservations has largely been missing from online dining sources. Moreover, reserving by phone remains a highly inefficient and inconvenient process. In order for diners to fully embrace online restaurant reservations, they need real-time access to table inventory across a broad selection of local restaurants and the ability to instantly book confirmed reservations around-the-clock.

We believe the Internet can streamline operations and fill additional seats for reservation-taking restaurants and redefine the reservation experience for diners. In addition, we believe that there is a significant opportunity to provide solutions to reservation-taking restaurants and diners, as the network connecting the two groups is created and expanded.

Our Solution

Reservation-taking restaurants and diners have interconnected needs. Restaurants require cost-effective ways to attract guests and manage their reservations, while diners seek convenient ways to find available restaurants, choose among them and secure reservations. By creating an online network of restaurants and diners that transact with each other through real-time reservations, we have developed a specialized platform for addressing the needs of both.

Essential to this network is building a critical mass of local, computerized restaurant reservation books. We achieve this by offering software that provides important operational benefits for the restaurant, bundling it with computer hardware and installing this solution at the restaurant host stand, thereby creating a compelling solution for restaurants. We provide our solutions to individual restaurants within a market, one by one, via a direct sales force. We believe that we deliver a strong return on investment for our restaurant customers by streamlining their operations, filling additional seats and improving their quality of service. As a result, we have historically enjoyed high customer satisfaction and retention rates.

The OpenTable website gives diners real-time access to tables at restaurants on the OpenTable network. As more local restaurants are added to the network, the utility provided to diners increases and more diners discover the benefits of researching restaurants and making reservations on our website. The more diners who use our website to make their dining decisions, the more value we deliver to our restaurant customers and the more restaurants are attracted to our network.

Benefits of OpenTable to Reservation-Taking Restaurants

In response to the needs of reservation-taking restaurants, we offer the OpenTable ERB, a bundled solution consisting of proprietary OpenTable software, which is installed on a touch-screen computer system and supported by various asset-protection and security tools. Additionally, we provide restaurants with access to diners via our website as well as through reservation links on our partners' websites and on restaurants' own websites. Our solutions help restaurants participating in the OpenTable network to:

- fill seats that might otherwise remain empty and minimize "no-shows" by offering the convenience of online reservations directly through the OpenTable website as well as indirectly through the websites of our partners and restaurant customers;

2

- create operational efficiencies by replacing the restaurant's pen-and-paper system with a computerized reservation book and helping restaurants maximize seat utilization, facilitate server rotations and improve table turns;

- boost guest recognition and overall guest service by recording diner preferences and histories and by collecting and delivering feedback from OpenTable diners;

- computerize their host-stand operations by providing a solution that combines proprietary software and computer hardware and customized, on-site installation, training and technical support; and

- market to a targeted audience with measurable results by giving restaurants valuable marketing exposure during the diners' decision-making process and requiring payment by restaurants only for those diners whom they ultimately serve.

Benefits of OpenTable to Diners

In response to the needs of diners, we offer the OpenTable website, a destination website for those seeking a convenient way to research restaurants and make reservations. Our website enables diners to:

- find available tables by allowing diners to search for reservations by location, date, time and party size and view real-time table availability across a variety of restaurants;

- choose a restaurant by providing diners with restaurant information such as restaurant descriptions, photos and menus as well as lists of restaurants that are most highly rated by OpenTable diners in different categories; and

- book instantly-confirmed reservations for free by allowing diners to make reservations through the OpenTable website, which are instantly recorded in the ERB located at the restaurant.

Our Strategy

As our network of reservation-taking restaurants and diners grows, the value we deliver grows as well. Because the foundation of our network is building a critical mass of computerized reservation books, we enhance our offering to diners by adding new restaurant customers. In turn, as more diners use the OpenTable website to make their dining decisions and book their reservations, we deliver more value to our restaurant customers by helping them fill more of their seats. In this process, we grow the value of our business. The key elements of this strategy include:

Continue to Build the OpenTable Network in North America

The value of the OpenTable network grows as participation among restaurants and diners grows. Experience in our earliest markets provided a successful model that we have implemented while entering new markets, and, as a result, our newer North American markets have grown relatively predictably over time. We intend to continue to build our North American network in the United States, Canada and Mexico by employing this proven model, which includes the following elements:

- producing and maintaining superior solutions by continuing to evolve our ERB based on nearly a decade of in-field experience as well as feedback from our installed base of approximately 10,000 restaurant customers, and optimizing our website through insights gained from the experience of seating approximately 100 million diners through online reservations;

- providing excellent customer service and support by continuing to employ highly trained operational teams to provide installation and training services for our restaurant customers

3

and continuing to augment our in-house support staff with contract support services to deliver superior customer assistance;

- leveraging our direct sales force, which is experienced in selling the benefits of OpenTable to reservation-taking restaurants, which operate in a highly fragmented industry; and

- continuing to attract diners to our website by offering the best reservation experience through enhanced ease of use and restaurant content, thereby increasing market adoption of our solutions, building our brand awareness and driving word-of-mouth referrals to our website.

Expand Internationally

We intend to augment our growing North American business by selectively expanding into countries outside of North America that are characterized by large numbers of online consumer transactions and reservation-taking restaurants. We currently have operations in Germany, Japan and the United Kingdom, each supported with a direct sales force and operational staff. We have approximately 1,000 restaurant customers in these markets. In general, our strategy internationally is to replicate the model we have successfully employed in North America. In particular, our initial focus in new international markets is to increase our restaurant customer base, and we believe the localized versions of our software solution will compete favorably against competitive software offerings, enabling us to expand our network of computerized reservation books across a broad selection of local restaurants.

Risk Factors

Our business is subject to numerous risks and uncertainties, including those highlighted in the section entitled "Risk Factors" immediately following this prospectus summary, that primarily represent challenges we face in connection with the successful implementation of our strategy and the growth of our business. Our limited operating history makes it difficult for us to accurately forecast revenues and appropriately plan our expenses. We expect a number of factors to cause our operating results to fluctuate on a quarterly and annual basis, which may make it difficult to predict our future performance. Such factors include deteriorating global economic conditions and our ability to maintain an adequate rate of growth, effectively manage our growth, retain and attract restaurant customers and visitors to our website, provide a high-quality customer experience through our website and ERB and successfully enter new markets and manage our international expansion.

Corporate Information

We were originally incorporated as easyeats.com, Inc., a California corporation, on October 13, 1998. On June 2, 1999, we changed our name to OpenTable.com, Inc. We subsequently reincorporated in Delaware on September 20, 2000 under our current name, OpenTable, Inc. Our principal executive offices are located at 799 Market Street, 4th Floor, San Francisco, California 94103, and our telephone number is (415) 344-4200. Our website address is www.opentable.com. Information contained on our website is not a part of this prospectus and the inclusion of our website address in this prospectus is an inactive textual reference only. Unless the context requires otherwise, the words "OpenTable," "we," "company," "us" and "our" refer to OpenTable, Inc. and our wholly owned subsidiaries.

OpenTable®, the OpenTable logo and other trademarks or service marks of OpenTable appearing in this prospectus are the property of OpenTable. Trade names, trademarks and service marks of other companies appearing in this prospectus are the property of the respective holders.

4

THE OFFERING

Common stock offered:

By OpenTable, Inc.	1,572,684 shares (or 2,022,684 shares if the underwriters exercise their overallotment option in full)
By the selling stockholders	1,427,316 shares

Shares outstanding after the offering

21,604,587 shares (or 22,054,587 shares if the underwriters exercise their overallotment option in full)

Use of proceeds

We expect the net proceeds to us from this offering, after expenses, to be approximately $21.9 million based on an assumed initial public offering price of $17.00 per share and after deducting underwriting discounts and commissions and estimated offering expenses payable by us. We intend to use the net proceeds from this offering for general corporate purposes, including working capital, sales and marketing activities, general and administrative matters and capital expenditures. We may also use a portion of the net proceeds to acquire or invest in complementary technologies, solutions or businesses or to obtain rights to such complementary technologies, solutions or businesses. There are no agreements or understandings with respect to such a transaction at this time.

Risk factors

See "Risk Factors" beginning on page 10 and the other information included in this prospectus for a discussion of factors you should carefully consider before deciding to invest in our common stock.

Proposed Nasdaq Global Market symbol

"OPEN"

The number of shares of our common stock outstanding after this offering is based on 20,031,903 shares outstanding as of March 31, 2009, and excludes:

- an aggregate of 162,836 shares of common stock reserved for issuance under our 1999 Stock Plan;

- 1,240,104 additional shares of common stock, subject to increase on an annual basis, reserved for issuance under our 2009 Equity Incentive Award Plan, which we plan to adopt in connection with this offering;

- 2,402,605 shares of common stock issuable upon the exercise of outstanding options to purchase our common stock granted pursuant to our 1999 Stock Plan at a weighted average exercise price of $7.33 per share; and

- 182,059 shares of common stock issuable upon the exercise of outstanding warrants at a weighted average exercise price of $3.85 per share.

5

Except as otherwise indicated, information in this prospectus reflects or assumes the following:

- a 1-for-12.5 reverse stock split of our common stock and preferred stock to be effected immediately prior to the effectiveness of our initial public offering registration statement;

- that our amended and restated certificate of incorporation, which we will file in connection with the completion of this offering, is in effect;

- the automatic conversion of all of our outstanding preferred stock into an aggregate of 9,075,737 shares of common stock upon completion of this offering; and

- no exercise of the underwriters' overallotment option to purchase up to 450,000 additional shares of our common stock.

Directors A. George "Skip" Battle, Michelle Peluso and Paul Pressler have indicated an interest in purchasing up to an aggregate of 58,822 shares of common stock in this offering, based on an assumed initial public offering price of $17.00 per share. However, because indications of interest are not binding agreements or commitments to purchase, these directors may elect not to purchase any shares in this offering. The shares would be sold to these investors at the same price and on the same terms as the other investors in this offering.

6

SUMMARY CONSOLIDATED FINANCIAL DATA

The following tables summarize the consolidated financial data for our business. You should read this summary financial data in conjunction with "Management's Discussion and Analysis of Financial Condition and Results of Operations" and our consolidated financial statements and related notes, all included elsewhere in this prospectus.

We derived the consolidated statements of operations data for the years ended December 31, 2006, 2007 and 2008 from our audited consolidated financial statements included elsewhere in this prospectus. The unaudited consolidated statements of operations data for the three months ended March 31, 2008 and 2009, and the unaudited consolidated balance sheet data as of March 31, 2009, are derived from our unaudited consolidated financial statements included elsewhere in this prospectus. We have prepared the unaudited information on the same basis as the audited consolidated financial statements and have included, in our opinion, all adjustments, consisting only of normal recurring adjustments, that we consider necessary for a fair presentation of the financial information set forth in those statements and assumes a 1-for-12.5 reverse stock split of our common stock and preferred stock to be effected immediately prior to the effectiveness of our initial public offering registration statement. Results for the three months ended March 31, 2009 are not necessarily indicative of the results to be expected for the fiscal year ending December 31, 2009. Our historical results are not necessarily indicative of the results to be expected in the future.

Pro forma basic net income (loss) per share has been calculated assuming the conversion of all outstanding shares of our preferred stock into 9,075,737 shares of common stock upon the completion of this offering. The balance sheet data as of March 31, 2009 is presented:

- on an actual basis;

- on a pro forma basis to reflect a 1-for-12.5 reverse stock split of our common stock and preferred stock to be effected immediately prior to the effectiveness of our initial public offering registration statement and the automatic conversion of all outstanding shares of our preferred stock into 9,075,737 shares of common stock in connection with the completion of this offering; and

- on a pro forma as adjusted basis to reflect the pro forma adjustments and the sale by us of 1,572,684 shares of common stock offered by this prospectus at an assumed initial public offering price of $17.00 per share after deducting underwriting discounts and commissions and estimated offering expenses payable by us.

7

	Years Ended December 31,			Three Months Ended March 31,	
	2006	2007	2008	2008	2009
	(In thousands, except per share amounts)				
Consolidated Statements of Operations Data:					
REVENUES	$27,168	$41,148	$55,844	$13,263	$15,995
COSTS AND EXPENSES:					
Operations and support(1)	9,548	12,603	17,760	4,012	5,106
Sales and marketing(1)	7,675	11,326	14,830	3,591	3,798
Technology(1)	4,024	5,863	9,511	2,175	2,712
General and administrative(1)	5,972	12,212	13,117	3,144	3,547
Total costs and expenses	27,219	42,004	55,218	12,922	15,163
Income (loss) from operations	(51)	(856)	626	341	832
Other income, net	421	951	468	180	55
Income before taxes	370	95	1,094	521	887
Income tax expense (benefit)	176	(9,121)	2,118	608	521
NET INCOME (LOSS)	$ 194	$ 9,216	$(1,024)	$ (87)	$ 366
Net income (loss) per share:					
Basic	$ 0.02	$ 0.97	$ (0.10)	$ (0.01)	$ 0.04
Diluted	$ 0.01	$ 0.46	$ (0.10)	$ (0.01)	$ 0.02
Weighted average shares outstanding:					
Basic	9,132	9,522	10,016	9,850	10,276
Diluted	19,523	20,019	10,016	9,850	21,017
Pro forma net income (loss) per share—basic and diluted (unaudited)			$ (0.05)		$ 0.02
Pro forma weighted average shares outstanding used in calculating net income (loss) per share (unaudited):					
Basic			19,092		19,352
Diluted			19,092		21,017

(1) Stock-based compensation included in above line items:

Operations and support	$ 58	$ 290	$ 339	$ 77	$ 86
Sales and marketing	67	709	878	228	223
Technology	64	288	694	132	174
General and administrative	520	1,816	2,059	547	476
Total	$ 709	$3,103	$3,970	$ 984	$ 959
Other Operational Data:					
Installed restaurants (at period end):					
North America	5,583	7,391	9,295	7,823	9,548
International	204	470	1,040	581	1,097
Total	5,787	7,861	10,335	8,404	10,645
Seated diners (in thousands):					
North America	15,171	24,614	33,636	8,395	9,922
International	84	244	542	123	186
Total	15,255	24,858	34,178	8,518	10,108
Headcount (at period end):					
North America	152	192	238	206	245
International	16	34	59	42	55
Total	168	226	297	248	300

8

	Years Ended December 31,			Three Months Ended March 31,	
	2006	2007	2008	2008	2009
			(In thousands)		
Additional Financial Data:					
Revenues:					
North America	$26,654	$39,601	$53,065	$12,667	$15,189
International	514	1,547	2,779	596	806
Total	$27,168	$41,148	$55,844	$13,263	$15,995
Income (loss) from operations:					
North America	$ 3,106	$ 4,974	$ 9,088	$ 2,409	$ 2,326
International	(3,157)	(5,830)	(8,462)	(2,068)	(1,494)
Total	$ (51)	$ (856)	$ 626	$ 341	$ 832
Depreciation and amortization:					
North America	$ 2,029	$ 2,817	$ 4,026	$ 877	$ 1,159
International	89	184	350	74	104
Total	$ 2,118	$ 3,001	$ 4,376	$ 951	$ 1,263

	As of March 31, 2009		
	Actual	Pro Forma	Pro Forma as Adjusted(1)
		(In thousands)	
Consolidated Balance Sheet Data:			
Cash and cash equivalents	$12,010	$ 12,010	$ 33,918
Short-term investments	13,194	13,194	13,194
Property and equipment, net	11,069	11,069	11,069
Working capital	15,835	15,835	37,743
Total assets	54,587	54,587	76,495
Dining rewards payable	9,221	9,221	9,221
Convertible preferred stock	21,909	—	—
Total stockholders' equity	28,405	28,405	50,313

(1) A $1.00 increase or decrease in the assumed initial public offering price of $17.00 per share would increase or decrease pro forma as adjusted cash and cash equivalents, working capital, total assets and total stockholders' equity by $1.5 million, assuming the number of shares offered by us, as shown on the cover of this prospectus, remains the same and after deducting the underwriting discounts and commissions and estimated offering expenses payable by us.

9

RISK FACTORS

Investing in our common stock involves a high degree of risk. You should carefully consider the risks described below and the other information in this prospectus before making a decision to invest in our common stock. If any of such risks actually occur, our business, operating results or financial condition could be adversely affected. In those cases, the trading price of our common stock could decline and you may lose all or part of your investment.

Risks Related to Our Business

Our limited operating history makes it difficult for us to accurately forecast revenues and appropriately plan our expenses.

We were formed in October 1998 and have a limited operating history. As a result, it is difficult to accurately forecast our revenues and plan our operating expenses. We base our current and future expense levels on our operating forecasts and estimates of future revenues from restaurants, which pay us an installation fee for our Electronic Reservation Book, or ERB, a monthly subscription fee and a fee for each restaurant guest seated through online reservations. Revenues and operating results are difficult to forecast due to the uncertainty of the volume and timing of obtaining new restaurant customers and of diners seated through OpenTable reservations. Some of our expenses are fixed, and, as a result, we may be unable to adjust our spending in a timely manner to compensate for any unexpected shortfall in revenues. This inability could cause our net income in a given quarter to be lower than expected.

The impact of worldwide economic conditions, including the resulting effect on consumer spending, may adversely affect our business, operating results and financial condition.

Our performance is subject to worldwide economic conditions and their impact on levels of consumer spending, which have recently deteriorated significantly and may remain depressed, or be subject to further deterioration, for the foreseeable future. Some of the factors having an impact on discretionary consumer spending include general economic conditions, unemployment, consumer debt, reductions in net worth based on recent severe market declines, residential real estate and mortgage markets, taxation, energy prices, interest rates, consumer confidence and other macroeconomic factors. There can be no assurances that government responses to the disruptions in the financial markets and other factors contributing to the recession we are currently experiencing will restore consumer confidence and positively impact consumer spending.

Consumer purchases of discretionary items generally decline during recessionary periods and other periods in which disposable income is adversely affected. Because spending for restaurant dining is generally considered to be discretionary, declines in consumer spending may have a more negative effect on our business than on those businesses that sell products or services considered to be necessities. In particular, a significant majority of our restaurant customers are fine-dining restaurants which have been particularly affected by economic downturns such as the one we are currently experiencing. We believe that the total number of reservations, including reservations by phone, seated by our restaurant customers has decreased approximately 10% to 15% for the fourth quarter of 2008 from the same period in 2007.

Unfavorable changes in the above factors or in other business and economic conditions affecting our restaurant customers and diners could result in continued reduced traffic in some or all of the restaurants that use our solutions, result in fewer reservations made through our website or the websites of our partners or restaurant customers and lower our profit margins, cause our restaurant customers to go out of business, cause our restaurant customers to terminate their subscriptions to our solutions or default on their payment obligations to us and have a material adverse effect on our financial condition and operating results.

10

Moreover, the majority of our restaurant customers are located in major metropolitan areas like New York City and the San Francisco Bay Area, and to the extent any one of these geographic areas experiences any of the above described conditions to a greater extent than other geographic areas, the material adverse effect on our financial condition and operating results could be exacerbated.

We expect a number of factors to cause our operating results to fluctuate on a quarterly and annual basis, which may make it difficult to predict our future performance.

Our revenues and operating results could vary significantly from quarter to quarter and year to year because of a variety of factors, many of which are outside of our control. As a result, comparing our operating results on a period-to-period basis may not be meaningful. In addition to other risk factors discussed in this section, factors that may contribute to the variability of our quarterly and annual results include:

- our ability to accurately forecast revenues and appropriately plan our expenses;

- the impact of worldwide economic conditions, including the resulting effect on consumer spending;

- our ability to maintain an adequate rate of growth;

- our ability to effectively manage our growth;

- our ability to attract new restaurant customers;

- our ability to increase the number of visitors to our website and convert those visitors into diners who reserve a table using our website and then dine with our restaurant customers;

- our ability to retain existing restaurant customers and diners or encourage repeat reservations;

- our ability to provide a high-quality customer experience through our website and ERB;

- our ability to successfully enter new markets and manage our international expansion;

- the impact of fluctuations in currency exchange rates;

- the effects of increased competition in our business;

- our ability to keep pace with changes in technology and our competitors;

- our ability to successfully manage any future acquisitions of businesses, solutions or technologies;

- the success of our marketing efforts;

- changes in consumer behavior and any related impact on the restaurant industry, especially in the geographic markets where we operate;

- seasonal patterns in restaurant dining;

- interruptions in service and any related impact on our reputation;

- the attraction and retention of qualified employees and key personnel;

- our ability to protect our intellectual property, including our proprietary ERB;

- costs associated with defending intellectual property infringement and other claims;

- the effects of natural or man-made catastrophic events;

11

- the effectiveness of our internal controls; and

- changes in government regulation affecting our business.

As a result of these and other factors, the results of any prior quarterly or annual periods should not be relied upon as indications of our future operating performance. In addition, our operating results may not meet the expectations of investors or public market analysts who follow our company.

Our recent growth rate will likely not be sustainable and a failure to maintain an adequate growth rate will adversely affect our net income and our business.

Our revenues have grown rapidly, increasing from $27.2 million in 2006 to $41.1 million in 2007 to $55.8 million in 2008, representing a compound annual growth rate of 43%. We do not expect to sustain our recent growth rate in future periods, and you should not rely on the revenue growth of any prior quarterly or annual periods as an indication of our future performance. If we are unable to maintain adequate revenue growth, our net income will be adversely affected, and we may not have adequate resources to execute our business strategy.

Growth may place significant demands on our management and our infrastructure.

We have experienced substantial growth in our business. This growth has placed and may continue to place significant demands on our management and our operational and financial infrastructure. As our operations grow in size, scope and complexity, we will need to improve and upgrade our systems and infrastructure to offer an increasing number of customers enhanced solutions, features and functionality. The expansion of our systems and infrastructure will require us to commit substantial financial, operational and technical resources in advance of an increase in the volume of business, with no assurance that the volume of business will increase. Continued growth could also strain our ability to maintain reliable service levels for our customers, develop and improve our operational, financial and management controls, enhance our reporting systems and procedures and recruit, train and retain highly skilled personnel.

Managing our growth will require significant expenditures and allocation of valuable management resources. If we fail to achieve the necessary level of efficiency in our organization as it grows, our business, operating results and financial condition would be harmed.

If we fail to increase the number of our customers or retain existing customers, our revenues and our business will be harmed.

In 2008, almost all of our revenues were generated by our restaurant customers, which pay us a one-time installation fee, a monthly subscription fee for our ERB and a fee for each restaurant guest seated through online reservations. Our growth depends in large part on increasing the number of our restaurant customers, increasing the number of visitors to our website and then converting those visitors into diners who use our website to make restaurant reservations. Either category of customers may decide not to continue to use our solutions in favor of other means of reserving tables or because of budgetary constraints or other reasons.

To grow our base of restaurant customers, we must convince prospective restaurant customers of the benefits of our ERB and related solutions and encourage them to forego the traditional pen-and-paper reservation book to which they are likely accustomed. Due to the fragmented nature of the restaurant industry, many prospective restaurant customers may not be familiar with our solutions and will generally favor using more traditional methods of taking reservations.

To increase the number of diners who use our website, we must convince them of the value of our solutions. Our ability to do so is driven in large part by increasing the number of restaurant listings

12

available on our website and also by making the diner's visit to our website a convenient and user-friendly experience.

We cannot assure you that we will be successful in continuing to expand our restaurant customer base or in continuing to attract diners to make reservations on our website. Our future sales and marketing efforts may be ineffective. If diners choose not to use our solutions or decrease their use of our solutions or we are unable to attract new diners, listings on our website could be reduced, search activity on our website could decline, the usefulness of our solutions could be diminished and we could experience declining revenues.

We may be unable to successfully execute our business strategy if we fail to continue to provide our customers with a high-quality customer experience.

A critical component of our strategy is providing a high-quality customer experience for both restaurants and diners. Accordingly, the effective performance, reliability and availability of our ERB, website and network infrastructure are critical to our reputation and our ability to attract and retain customers. In order to provide a high-quality customer experience, we have invested and will continue to invest substantial resources in our ERB, website development and functionality and customer service operations. If we do not continue to make such investments and as a result, or due to other reasons, fail to provide a high-quality customer experience, we may lose restaurants and diners from our network, which could significantly decrease the value of our solutions to both groups. Moreover, failure to provide our customers with high-quality customer experiences for any reason could substantially harm our reputation and adversely affect our efforts to develop as a trusted website.

We may be unsuccessful in expanding our operations internationally, which could harm our business, operating results and financial condition.

In 2004, we established our European headquarters in London and expanded our North American presence in Canada. In 2006, we opened an office in Tokyo and further expanded our North American presence in Mexico. In 2007, we expanded our European presence with offices in France, Germany and Spain. Our ability to expand internationally involves various risks, including the need to invest significant resources in such expansion, the possibility that returns on such investments will not be achieved in the near future and competitive environments with which we are unfamiliar. Our international operations may not prove to be successful in certain markets. For example, in 2008, we decided to close our offices in France and Spain. In addition, we have incurred and expect to continue to incur significant expenses in advance of generating material revenues as we attempt to establish our presence in particular international markets. Our current and any future international expansion plans we choose to undertake will require management attention and resources and may be unsuccessful. We do not have substantial experience in selling our solutions in international markets or in conforming to the local cultures, standards or policies necessary to successfully compete in those markets, and we must invest significant resources in order to build a direct sales force and operational infrastructure in such markets. Furthermore, in many international markets we are not the first entrant and there exists greater competition with stronger brand names than we have faced in North American markets. Our ability to expand internationally will also be limited by the demand for our solutions and the adoption of the Internet in these markets. Different privacy, censorship and liability standards and regulations and different intellectual property laws in foreign countries may cause our business and operating results to suffer.

Any future international operations may also fail to succeed due to other risks inherent in foreign operations, including:

- difficulties or delays in acquiring a network of restaurant customers in one or more international markets;

13

- different restaurant preferences and dining patterns than those in North America;

- varied, unfamiliar and unclear legal and regulatory restrictions;

- unexpected changes in international regulatory requirements and tariffs;

- legal, political or systemic restrictions on the ability of U.S. companies to market services or otherwise do business in foreign countries;

- less extensive adoption of the Internet as a commerce medium or information source and increased restriction on the content of websites;

- difficulties in staffing and managing foreign operations;

- greater difficulty in accounts receivable collection;

- currency fluctuations;

- potential adverse tax consequences;

- lack of infrastructure to adequately conduct electronic commerce transactions; and

- price controls or other restrictions on foreign currency.

As a result of these obstacles, we may find it impossible or prohibitively expensive to expand internationally or we may be unsuccessful in our attempt to do so, which could harm our business, operating results and financial condition.

We face risks associated with currency exchange rate fluctuations.

For the three months ended March 31, 2009, we incurred approximately 18% of our operating expenses in pounds sterling, euros, yen and other foreign currencies, while most of our revenues were denominated in U.S. dollars. Conducting business in currencies other than U.S. dollars subjects us to fluctuations in currency exchange rates that could have a negative impact on our reported operating results. Fluctuations in the value of the U.S. dollar relative to other currencies affect our revenues, costs and expenses, and operating margins, and result in foreign currency transaction gains and losses. To date, we have not engaged in exchange rate hedging activities. Even if we were to implement hedging strategies to mitigate this risk, these strategies might not eliminate our exposure to foreign exchange rate fluctuations and would involve costs and risks of their own, such as ongoing management time and expertise, external costs to implement the hedging activities and potential accounting implications.

The markets for our solutions in North America may become more competitive, and there can be no certainty that we will maintain our current restaurant customers and diners or attract new restaurants and diners or that our operating margins will not be affected by competition.

We expect that the competitive environment for our solutions may become more intense as additional companies enter our North American markets. Currently, our primary competitors in North America are the pen-and-paper reservation book used by most restaurants and the phone used by diners. Secondary competitors include companies who provide computerized reservation management systems with a variety of technologies, as well as allocation-based reservation-taking websites that offer diners the ability to book reservations for a limited selection of restaurant table inventory. These secondary competitors may enhance their technologies to be more competitive, and additional competitors may enter our markets in North America. Any new competitors could have greater name recognition among restaurants and diners and greater financial, technical and marketing resources. Greater financial resources and product development capabilities may allow these competitors to respond more quickly to new or emerging technologies and changes in restaurant and diner requirements that may render our solutions obsolete. These competitors could introduce new solutions with competitive price and performance characteristics or undertake more aggressive marketing campaigns than ours. If we lose existing restaurant customers and diners or fail to attract new

14

restaurants and diners as a result of increased competition, our business, operating results and financial condition could be adversely affected.

Rapid technological changes may render our technology obsolete or decrease the attractiveness of our solutions to our customers.

To remain competitive, we must continue to enhance and improve the functionality and features of our website and ERB. The Internet and the online commerce industry are rapidly changing. If competitors introduce new solutions embodying new technologies, or if new industry standards and practices emerge, our existing website, technology and ERB may become obsolete. Our future success will depend on our ability to:

- enhance our existing solutions;

- develop and potentially license new solutions and technologies that address the increasingly sophisticated and varied needs of our prospective customers; and

- respond to technological advances and emerging industry standards and practices on a cost-effective and timely basis.

Developing our ERB, website and other technology entails significant technical and business risks. We may use new technologies ineffectively, or we may fail to adapt our website, transaction processing systems and network infrastructure to consumer requirements or emerging industry standards. For example, our website functionality that allows searches and displays of reservation availability is a critical part of our service, and it may become out-of-date or insufficient from our customers' perspective or in relation to the search and display functionality of our competitors' websites. If we face material delays in introducing new or enhanced solutions, our customers may forego the use of our solutions in favor of those of our competitors.

Future acquisitions could disrupt our business and harm our financial condition and operating results.

Our success will depend, in part, on our ability to expand our offerings and markets and grow our business in response to changing technologies, customer demands and competitive pressures. In some circumstances, we may determine to do so through the acquisition of complementary businesses, solutions or technologies rather than through internal development. The identification of suitable acquisition candidates can be difficult, time-consuming and costly, and we may not be able to successfully complete identified acquisitions. Furthermore, even if we successfully complete an acquisition, we may not be able to successfully assimilate and integrate the business, technologies, solutions, personnel or operations of the company that we acquired, particularly if key personnel of an acquired company decide not to work for us. In addition, we may issue equity securities to complete an acquisition, which would dilute our stockholders' ownership and could adversely affect the price of our common stock. Acquisitions may also involve the entry into geographic or business markets in which we have little or no prior experience. Consequently, we may not achieve anticipated benefits of the acquisitions which could harm our operating results.

We rely on our marketing efforts to attract new customers and must do so in a cost-effective manner; otherwise our operations will be harmed.

A significant component of our business strategy is the promotion of the OpenTable website and ERB. We believe that the attractiveness of our solutions to our current and potential customers, both restaurants and diners, will increase as new restaurants provide additional restaurant listings and diners increasingly use our website to conduct searches and make restaurant reservations. This is because an increase in the number of restaurant listings and the number of diners searching those listings increases the utility of our website and its associated search, listing and reservation services. If

15

we do not continue to grow the use of our website and ERB, we may fail to build the critical mass of both restaurant customers and diners required to substantially increase our revenues.

While our marketing efforts do not currently involve significant expenditures, in the future we may find it necessary to invest more heavily in direct marketing or online or traditional advertising. If we are unable to effectively market our solutions to new customers or are unable to do so in a cost-effective manner, our operating results could be adversely affected.

System interruptions that impair access to our website would damage our reputation and brand and substantially harm our business and operating results.

The satisfactory performance, reliability and availability of our ERB, website and network infrastructure are critical to our reputation, our ability to attract and retain both restaurant customers and diners and our ability to maintain adequate customer service levels. Any systems interruption that results in the unavailability of our website or any restaurant connected to our website could result in negative publicity, damage our reputation and brand and cause our business and operating results to suffer. We may experience temporary system interruptions (either to our website or at our restaurant customer locations) for a variety of reasons, including network failures, power failures, software errors or an overwhelming number of visitors trying to reach our website during periods of strong demand. In addition, our primary data center is hosted by a third party. Because we are dependent in part on third parties for the implementation and maintenance of certain aspects of our systems and because some of the causes of system interruptions may be outside of our control, we may not be able to remedy such interruptions in a timely manner, or at all.

We depend on key and highly skilled personnel to operate our business, and if we are unable to retain our current personnel or hire additional personnel our ability to develop and successfully market our business could be harmed.

We believe our future success will depend in large part upon our ability to attract and retain highly skilled managerial, technical, finance, creative and sales and marketing personnel. Moreover, we believe that our future success is highly dependent on the contributions of our named executive officers, as defined in "Management-Executive Compensation." All of our U.S. officers and other employees are at-will employees, which means they may terminate their employment relationship with us at any time, and their knowledge of our business and industry would be extremely difficult to replace. In addition, the loss of any key employees or the inability to attract or retain qualified personnel could delay the development and introduction of, and harm our ability to sell, our solutions and harm the market's perception of us. Competition for qualified personnel is particularly intense in the San Francisco Bay Area, where our headquarters are located. Further, our principal overseas operations are based in London and Tokyo, which are cities that, similar to our headquarters region, have high costs of living and consequently high compensation standards. Qualified individuals are in high demand, and we may incur significant costs to attract them. We may be unable to attract and retain suitably qualified individuals who are capable of meeting our growing sales, operational and managerial requirements, or may be required to pay increased compensation in order to do so. If we are unable to attract and retain the qualified personnel we need to succeed, our business will suffer.

Volatility or lack of performance in our stock price may also affect our ability to attract and retain our key employees. Our named executive officers have become, or will soon become, vested in a substantial amount of stock or stock options. Employees may be more likely to leave us if the shares they own or the shares underlying their options have significantly appreciated in value relative to the original purchase prices of the shares or the exercise prices of the options, or if the exercise prices of the options that they hold are significantly above the market price of our common stock. If we are unable to retain our employees, our business, operating results and financial condition will be harmed.

16

Failure to adequately protect our intellectual property could substantially harm our business and operating results.

Because our business is heavily dependent on our intellectual property, including our proprietary software, the protection of our intellectual property rights is crucial to the success of our business. We rely on a combination of patent, trademark, trade secret and copyright law and contractual restrictions to protect our intellectual property. These afford only limited protection. Despite our efforts to protect our proprietary rights, unauthorized parties may attempt to copy aspects of our website features, software and functionality or obtain and use information that we consider proprietary, such as the technology used to operate our website, our content and our trademarks. Moreover, policing our proprietary rights is difficult and may not always be effective. In particular, because we sell our solutions internationally, we may need to enforce our rights under the laws of countries that do not protect proprietary rights to as great an extent as do the laws of the United States.

We have registered "OpenTable" and our other trademarks as trademarks in the United States and in certain other countries. Competitors may adopt service names similar to ours, thereby impeding our ability to build brand identity and possibly leading to customer confusion. In addition, there could be potential trade name or trademark infringement claims brought by owners of other registered trademarks or trademarks that incorporate variations of the term OpenTable or our other trademarks. From time to time, we have acquired Internet domain names held by others when such names were causing consumer confusion or had the potential to cause consumer confusion.

We currently hold the "OpenTable.com" Internet domain name and various other related domain names. Domain names generally are regulated by Internet regulatory bodies. If we lose the ability to use a domain name in a particular country, we would be forced to either incur significant additional expenses to market our solutions within that country, including the development of a new brand and the creation of new promotional materials, or elect not to sell solutions in that country. Either result could substantially harm our business and operating results. The regulation of domain names in the United States and in foreign countries is subject to change. Regulatory bodies could establish additional top-level domains, appoint additional domain name registrars or modify the requirements for holding domain names. As a result, we may not be able to acquire or maintain the domain names that utilize the name OpenTable in all of the countries in which we currently conduct or intend to conduct business.

Litigation or proceedings before the U.S. Patent and Trademark Office or other governmental authorities and administrative bodies in the United States and abroad may be necessary in the future to enforce our intellectual property rights, to protect our patent rights, trade secrets and domain names and to determine the validity and scope of the proprietary rights of others. Our efforts to enforce or protect our proprietary rights may be ineffective and could result in substantial costs and diversion of resources and could substantially harm our operating results.

Assertions by third parties of infringement by us of their intellectual property rights could result in significant costs and substantially harm our business and operating results.

Other parties have asserted, and may in the future assert, that we have infringed their intellectual property rights. Such litigation may involve patent holding companies or other adverse patent owners who have no relevant product revenue, and therefore our own issued and pending patents may provide little or no deterrence. For example, on May 12, 2009, Mount Hamilton Partners, LLC, or Mount Hamilton, filed a patent infringement lawsuit against us in the United States District Court for the Northern District of California, seeking, among other things, a judgment that we have infringed a certain patent held by Mount Hamilton, an injunctive order against the alleged infringing activities and an award for damages. If an injunction is granted, it could force us to stop or alter certain of our business activities, such as certain aspects of our points-based loyalty program,

17

OpenTable Dining Rewards. We could also be required to pay damages in an unspecified amount. Neither the outcome of the litigation nor the amount and range of potential damages or exposure associated with the litigation can be assessed with certainty.

Furthermore, we cannot predict whether assertions of third party intellectual property rights or claims arising from such assertions will substantially harm our business and operating results. If we are forced to defend against any infringement claims, including the alleged infringement claims of Mount Hamilton, whether they are with or without merit or are determined in our favor, we may face costly litigation and diversion of technical and management personnel. Furthermore, an adverse outcome of a dispute may require us to pay damages, potentially including treble damages and attorneys' fees, if we are found to have willfully infringed a party's patent or copyright rights; cease making, licensing or using solutions that are alleged to incorporate the intellectual property of others; expend additional development resources to redesign our solutions; and enter into potentially unfavorable royalty or license agreements in order to obtain the right to use necessary technologies. Royalty or licensing agreements, if required, may be unavailable on terms acceptable to us, or at all. In any event, we may need to license intellectual property which would require us to pay royalties or make one-time payments.

We depend in part on licenses of technologies from third parties in order to deliver our solutions, and, as a result, our business is dependent in part on the availability of such licenses on commercially reasonable terms.

We currently, and will continue to, license certain technologies from third parties. We cannot be certain that these third-party content licenses will be available to us on commercially reasonable terms or that we will be able to successfully integrate the technology into our solutions. These third-party in-licenses may expose us to increased risk, including risks associated with the assimilation of new technology sufficient to offset associated acquisition and maintenance costs. The inability to obtain any of these licenses could result in delays in solution development until equivalent technology can be identified and integrated. Any such delays in services could cause our business, operating results and financial condition to suffer.

Confidentiality agreements with employees and others may not adequately prevent disclosure of trade secrets and other proprietary information.

We have devoted substantial resources to the development of our proprietary technology, including the proprietary software component of our ERB, and related processes. In order to protect our proprietary technology and processes, we rely in part on confidentiality agreements with our employees, licensees, independent contractors and other advisors. These agreements may not effectively prevent disclosure of confidential information and may not provide an adequate remedy in the event of unauthorized disclosure of confidential information. In addition, others may independently discover trade secrets and proprietary information, and in such cases we could not assert any trade secret rights against such parties. Costly and time-consuming litigation could be necessary to enforce and determine the scope of our proprietary rights, and failure to obtain or maintain trade secret protection could adversely affect our competitive business position.

Our failure to protect confidential information of our customers and our network against security breaches could damage our reputation and brand and substantially harm our business and operating results.

Currently, some of our restaurant customers require that diners enter their credit card information to hold a reservation. We rely on encryption and authentication technology licensed from third parties to effect secure transmission of confidential information, including credit card numbers. Advances in computer capabilities, new discoveries in the field of cryptography or other developments may result in a compromise or breach of the technology used by us to protect customer transaction

18

data. Any such compromise of our security could damage our reputation and brand and expose us to a risk of loss or litigation and possible liability which would substantially harm our business and operating results. We may need to expend significant resources to protect against security breaches or to address problems caused by breaches.

We rely on a third-party customer support service provider for the majority of our customer service calls. If this service provider experiences operational difficulties or disruptions, our business could be adversely affected.

We depend on a U.S.-based third-party customer support service provider to handle most of our routine support cases. While we have a small customer service center in our San Francisco headquarters, if our customer support service provider experienced operational difficulties, our ability to respond to customer service calls in a timely manner and the quality of our customer service would be adversely affected, which in turn could affect our reputation and results of operations. While we have a contract with our customer support service provider, either party may terminate the contract for convenience by providing the other party at least 90 days prior notice of its intent to terminate. If for any reason our relationship with our customer support service provider were to end, it would require a significant amount of time to either scale up our San Francisco call center or to hire and train a new customer support service provider.

We outsource a portion of our software development to a third-party service provider located in India. Any interruption in our relationship with this service provider could adversely affect our business.

If for any reason our relationship with our third-party software development service provider were to end, it would require a significant amount of time to transition the software development work either in-house or to a new third-party service provider. Our contract with this software development service provider has a term ending on January 31, 2010. Either party may terminate the contract at any time by providing the other party at least 30 days prior notice of its intent to terminate. If our third-party software development service provider fails to perform its obligations in a timely manner or at satisfactory quality levels, our ability to bring solutions to market and our reputation could suffer. In addition, our third-party software development service provider is located in India and, as a result, may be subject to geopolitical uncertainty.

We may require additional capital to respond to business opportunities, challenges, acquisitions or unforeseen circumstances. If such capital is not available to us, our business, operating results and financial condition may be harmed.

We may require additional capital to expand our business. However, additional funds may not be available when we need them, on terms that are acceptable to us, or at all. For example, any debt financing secured by us in the future could involve restrictive covenants relating to our capital raising activities and other financial and operational matters, which may make it more difficult for us to obtain additional capital and to pursue business opportunities, including potential acquisitions. If we do not have funds available to enhance our solutions, maintain the competitiveness of our technology or pursue business opportunities, we may not be able to service our existing customers or acquire new customers. In addition, if we do not have funds available to make strategic acquisitions, we may not be able to expand our business. The inability to raise additional capital could have an adverse effect on our business, operating results and financial condition.

If we issue additional shares of common stock to raise capital, it may have a dilutive effect on your investment.

If we raise additional capital through further issuances of equity or convertible debt securities, our existing stockholders could suffer significant dilution in their percentage ownership of us.

19

Moreover, any new equity securities we issue could have rights, preferences and privileges senior to those of holders of our common stock, including shares of common stock sold in this offering.

A further tightening of the credit markets may have an adverse effect on our ability to obtain short-term debt financing.

The recent deterioration of the global economy threatens to cause further tightening of the credit markets, more stringent lending standards and terms and higher volatility in interest rates. Persistence of these conditions could have a material adverse effect on our access to short-term debt and the terms and cost of that debt. As a result, we may not be able to secure additional financing in a timely manner, or at all, to meet our future capital needs which may have an adverse effect on our business, operating results and financial condition.

Our business is subject to the risks of earthquakes, fires, floods and other natural catastrophic events and to interruption by man-made problems such as computer viruses or terrorism.

Our systems and operations are vulnerable to damage or interruption from earthquakes, fires, floods, power losses, telecommunications failures, terrorist attacks, acts of war, human errors, break-ins and similar events. For example, a significant natural disaster, such as an earthquake, fire or flood, could have a material adverse impact on our business, operating results and financial condition, and our insurance coverage may be insufficient to compensate us for losses that may occur. Our U.S. corporate offices and the facility we lease to house our computer and telecommunications equipment are located in the San Francisco Bay Area, a region known for seismic activity. In addition, acts of terrorism, which may be targeted at metropolitan areas which have higher population density than rural areas, could cause disruptions in our or our restaurant customers' businesses or the economy as a whole. Our servers may also be vulnerable to computer viruses, break-ins and similar disruptions from unauthorized tampering with our computer systems, which could lead to interruptions, delays, loss of critical data or the unauthorized disclosure of confidential customer data. We may not have sufficient protection or recovery plans in certain circumstances, such as natural disasters affecting the San Francisco Bay Area, and our business interruption insurance may be insufficient to compensate us for losses that may occur. As we rely heavily on our servers, computer and communications systems and the Internet to conduct our business and provide high quality customer service, such disruptions could negatively impact our ability to run our business and either directly or indirectly disrupt our restaurant customers' businesses, which could have an adverse affect on our business, operating results and financial condition.

We will incur increased costs as a result of being a public company, which may adversely affect our operating results and financial condition.

As a public company, we will incur significant accounting, legal and other expenses that we did not incur as a private company. We will incur costs associated with our public company reporting requirements. We also anticipate that we will incur costs associated with corporate governance requirements, including requirements under the Sarbanes-Oxley Act of 2002, as well as rules implemented by the SEC and The Nasdaq Stock Market. We expect these rules and regulations to increase our legal and financial compliance costs and to make some activities more time-consuming and costly. Furthermore, these laws and regulations could make it more difficult or more costly for us to obtain certain types of insurance, including director and officer liability insurance, and we may be forced to accept reduced policy limits and coverage or incur substantially higher costs to obtain the same or similar coverage. The impact of these requirements could also make it more difficult for us to attract and retain qualified persons to serve on our board of directors, our board committees or as executive officers. We cannot predict or estimate the amount or timing of additional costs we may incur to respond to these requirements. We are currently evaluating and monitoring developments with

20

respect to these rules, and we cannot predict or estimate the amount of additional costs we may incur or the timing of such costs.

New laws and regulations as well as changes to existing laws and regulations affecting public companies, including the provisions of the Sarbanes-Oxley Act of 2002 and rules adopted by the SEC and by The Nasdaq Stock Market, would likely result in increased costs to us as we respond to their requirements.

Risks Related to Our Industry

Seasonality may cause fluctuations in our financial results.

We generally experience some effects of seasonality due to increases in restaurant dining tied to certain holidays and restaurant industry promotions. Accordingly, the number of reservations made through our system has generally increased at a higher rate in the first and fourth quarters compared to the second and third quarters. Although historically our revenue has increased in each quarter as we have added restaurant customers and diners, in the future this seasonality may cause fluctuations in our financial results. In addition, other seasonality trends may develop and the existing seasonality and consumer behavior that we experience may change.

If use of the Internet, particularly with respect to online restaurant reservations, does not continue to increase as rapidly as we anticipate, our business will be harmed.

Our future net profits are substantially dependent upon the continued use of the Internet as an effective medium of business and communication by our target customers. Internet use may not continue to develop at historical rates, and consumers may not continue to use the Internet and other online services as a medium for commerce. In addition, the Internet may not be accepted as a viable long-term marketplace or resource for a number of reasons, including:

- actual or perceived lack of security of information or privacy protection;

- possible disruptions, computer viruses or other damage to Internet servers or to users' computers; and

- excessive governmental regulation.

Our success will depend, in large part, upon third parties maintaining the Internet infrastructure to provide a reliable network backbone with the speed, data capacity, security and hardware necessary for reliable Internet access and services. Our business, which relies on a contextually rich website that requires the transmission of substantial data, is also significantly dependent upon the availability and adoption of broadband Internet access and other high-speed Internet connectivity technologies.

Government regulation of the Internet is evolving, and unfavorable changes could substantially harm our business and operating results.

We are subject to general business regulations and laws as well as regulations and laws specifically governing the Internet. Existing and future laws and regulations may impede the growth of the Internet or other online services. These regulations and laws may cover taxation, tariffs, user privacy, data protection, pricing, content, copyrights, distribution, electronic contracts and other communications, consumer protection, broadband residential Internet access and the characteristics and quality of services. It is not clear how existing laws governing issues such as property ownership, sales and other taxes, libel and personal privacy apply to the Internet. Unfavorable resolution of these issues may substantially harm our business and operating results.

21

Risks Related to Owning Our Common Stock

An active, liquid and orderly market for our common stock may never develop or be sustained.

Prior to this offering there has been no market for shares of our common stock. An active trading market for our common stock may never develop or be sustained, which could depress the market price of our common stock and could affect your ability to sell your shares. The initial public offering price will be determined through negotiations between us and the representative of the underwriters and may bear no relationship to the price at which our common stock will trade following the completion of this offering. The trading price of our common stock following this offering is likely to be highly volatile and could be subject to wide fluctuations in response to various factors, some of which are beyond our control. In addition to the factors discussed in this "Risk Factors" section and elsewhere in this prospectus, these factors include:

- our operating performance and the operating performance of similar companies;

- the overall performance of the equity markets;

- the number of shares of our common stock publicly owned and available for trading;

- threatened or actual litigation;

- changes in laws or regulations relating to our solutions;

- any major change in our board of directors or management;

- publication of research reports about us or our industry or positive or negative recommendations or withdrawal of research coverage by securities analysts;

- large volumes of sales of our shares of common stock by existing stockholders; and

- general political and economic conditions.

In addition, the stock market in general, and the market for Internet-related companies in particular, has experienced extreme price and volume fluctuations that have often been unrelated or disproportionate to the operating performance of those companies. These fluctuations may be even more pronounced in the trading market for our stock shortly following this offering. Securities class action litigation has often been instituted against companies following periods of volatility in the overall market and in the market price of a company's securities. This litigation, if instituted against us, could result in very substantial costs, divert our management's attention and resources and harm our business, operating results and financial condition. In addition, the recent distress in the financial markets has also resulted in extreme volatility in security prices.

Our directors, executive officers and principal stockholders will continue to have substantial control over us after this offering and could delay or prevent a change in corporate control.

After this offering, our directors, executive officers and holders of more than 5% of our common stock, together with their affiliates, will beneficially own, in the aggregate, approximately 78.28% of our outstanding common stock, assuming no exercise of the underwriters' option to purchase additional shares of our common stock in this offering and assuming the purchase of an aggregate of 58,822 shares of common stock in this offering by members of our board of directors. As a result, these stockholders, acting together, would have the ability to control the outcome of matters submitted to our stockholders for approval, including the election of directors and any merger, consolidation or sale of all or substantially all of our assets. In addition, these stockholders, acting together, would have the ability to control the management and affairs of our company. Accordingly, this concentration of ownership might harm the market price of our common stock by:

- delaying, deferring or preventing a change in corporate control;

- impeding a merger, consolidation, takeover or other business combination involving us; or

22

- discouraging a potential acquirer from making a tender offer or otherwise attempting to obtain control of us.

Future sales of shares of our common stock by existing stockholders could depress the price of our common stock.

If our existing stockholders sell, or indicate an intent to sell, substantial amounts of our common stock in the public market after the 180-day contractual lock-up and other legal restrictions on resale discussed in this prospectus lapse, the trading price of our common stock could decline significantly and could decline below the initial public offering price. Based on shares outstanding as of March 31, 2009, upon completion of this offering, we will have outstanding approximately 21,604,587 shares of common stock, assuming no exercise of the underwriters' overallotment option and no exercise of outstanding options and warrants. Assuming the purchase of an aggregate of 58,822 shares of common stock in this offering by members of our board of directors, 2,941,178 shares of common stock, plus any shares sold upon exercise of the underwriters' overallotment option, will be immediately freely tradable, without restriction, in the public market. Merrill Lynch may, in its sole discretion, permit our officers, directors, employees and current stockholders to sell shares prior to the expiration of the lock-up agreements.

After the lock-up agreements pertaining to this offering expire and based on shares outstanding as of March 31, 2009, an additional 18,604,587 shares will be eligible for sale in the public market. In addition, (i) the 2,402,605 shares subject to outstanding options under our 1999 Stock Plan, as amended, as of March 31, 2009, (ii) the 1,240,104 shares reserved for future issuance under our 2009 Equity Incentive Award Plan and (iii) the 162,836 shares remaining available for issuance under our 1999 Stock Plan, as amended, as of March 31, 2009, that will become available for issuance under our 2009 Equity Incentive Award Plan, will become eligible for sale in the public market in the future, subject to certain legal and contractual limitations. If these additional shares are sold, or if it is perceived that they will be sold, in the public market, the price of our common stock could decline substantially.

If securities or industry analysts do not publish research or publish inaccurate or unfavorable research about our business, our stock price and trading volume could decline.

The trading market for our common stock will depend in part on the research and reports that securities or industry analysts publish about us or our business. Securities and industry analysts do not currently, and may never, publish research on our company. If no securities or industry analysts commence coverage of our company, the trading price for our stock would likely be negatively impacted. In the event securities or industry analysts initiate coverage, if one or more of the analysts who cover us downgrade our stock or publish inaccurate or unfavorable research about our business, our stock price would likely decline. If one or more of these analysts cease coverage of our company or fail to publish reports on us regularly, demand for our stock could decrease, which might cause our stock price and trading volume to decline.

Our management will have broad discretion over the use of the proceeds we receive in this offering and might not apply the proceeds in ways that increase the value of your investment.

Our management will have broad discretion to use the net proceeds to us from this offering, and you will be relying on the judgment of our management regarding the application of these proceeds. Our management might not apply the net proceeds from this offering in ways that increase the value of your investment. We expect to use the net proceeds to us from this offering for working capital and other general corporate purposes, including the funding of our marketing activities and the costs of operating as a public company, as well as further investment in the development of our proprietary technologies. We may also use a portion of the net proceeds for the acquisition of businesses, solutions and technologies that we believe are complementary to our own, although we have

23

no agreements or understandings with respect to any acquisition at this time. We have not allocated the net proceeds from this offering for any specific purposes. Until we use the net proceeds to us from this offering, we plan to invest them, and these investments may not yield a favorable rate of return. If we do not invest or apply the net proceeds from this offering in ways that enhance stockholder value, we may fail to achieve expected financial results, which could cause our stock price to decline.

Certain provisions in our charter documents and Delaware law could discourage takeover attempts and lead to management entrenchment.

Our certificate of incorporation and bylaws that will be in effect prior to the closing of this offering will contain provisions that could have the effect of delaying or preventing changes in control or changes in our management without the consent of our board of directors. These provisions will include:

- a classified board of directors with three-year staggered terms, which may delay the ability of stockholders to change the membership of a majority of our board of directors;

- no cumulative voting in the election of directors, which limits the ability of minority stockholders to elect director candidates;

- the exclusive right of our board of directors to elect a director to fill a vacancy created by the expansion of the board of directors or the resignation, death or removal of a director, which prevents stockholders from being able to fill vacancies on our board of directors;

- the ability of our board of directors to determine to issue shares of preferred stock and to determine the price and other terms of those shares, including preferences and voting rights, without stockholder approval, which could be used to significantly dilute the ownership of a hostile acquirer;

- a prohibition on stockholder action by written consent, which forces stockholder action to be taken at an annual or special meeting of our stockholders;

- the requirement that a special meeting of stockholders may be called only by the chairman of the board of directors, the chief executive officer or the board of directors, which may delay the ability of our stockholders to force consideration of a proposal or to take action, including the removal of directors; and

- advance notice procedures that stockholders must comply with in order to nominate candidates to our board of directors or to propose matters to be acted upon at a stockholders' meeting, which may discourage or deter a potential acquiror from conducting a solicitation of proxies to elect the acquiror's own slate of directors or otherwise attempting to obtain control of us.

We are also subject to certain anti-takeover provisions under Delaware law. Under Delaware law, a corporation may not, in general, engage in a business combination with any holder of 15% or more of its capital stock unless the holder has held the stock for three years or, among other things, the board of directors has approved the transaction.

24

SPECIAL NOTE REGARDING FORWARD-LOOKING STATEMENTS

This prospectus includes forward-looking statements. We have based these forward-looking statements largely on our current expectations and projections about future events and financial trends affecting the financial condition of our business. Forward-looking statements should not be read as a guarantee of future performance or results, and will not necessarily be accurate indications of the times at, or by, which such performance or results will be achieved. Forward-looking statements are based on information available at the time those statements are made and/or management's good faith belief as of that time with respect to future events, and are subject to risks and uncertainties that could cause actual performance or results to differ materially from those expressed in or suggested by the forward-looking statements. Important factors that could cause such differences include, but are not limited to:

- our ability to accurately forecast revenues and appropriately plan our expenses;

- the impact of worldwide economic conditions, including the resulting effect on consumer spending;

- our ability to maintain an adequate rate of growth;

- our ability to effectively manage our growth;

- our ability to attract new restaurant customers;

- our ability to increase the number of visitors to our website and convert those visitors into diners who reserve a table using our website and then dine with our restaurant customers;

- our ability to retain existing restaurant customers and diners or encourage repeat reservations;

- our ability to provide a high-quality customer experience through our website and ERB;

- our ability to successfully enter new markets and manage our international expansion;

- the impact of fluctuations in currency exchange rates;

- the effects of increased competition in our business;

- our ability to keep pace with changes in technology and our competitors;

- our ability to successfully manage any future acquisitions of businesses, solutions or technologies;

- the success of our marketing efforts;

- interruptions in service and any related impact on our reputation;

- the attraction and retention of qualified employees and key personnel;

- our ability to protect our intellectual property, including our proprietary ERB;

- costs associated with defending intellectual property infringement and other claims;

- the effects of natural or man-made catastrophic events;

- the effectiveness of our internal controls;

- changes in government regulation affecting our business; and

- other risk factors included under "Risk Factors" in this prospectus.

25

In addition, in this prospectus, the words "believe," "may," "will," "estimate," "continue," "anticipate," "intend," "expect," "predict," "potential" and similar expressions, as they relate to our company, our business and our management, are intended to identify forward-looking statements. In light of these risks and uncertainties, the forward-looking events and circumstances discussed in this prospectus may not occur and actual results could differ materially from those anticipated or implied in the forward-looking statements.

Forward-looking statements speak only as of the date of this prospectus. You should not put undue reliance on any forward-looking statements. We assume no obligation to update forward-looking statements to reflect actual results, changes in assumptions or changes in other factors affecting forward-looking information, except to the extent required by applicable laws. If we update one or more forward-looking statements, no inference should be drawn that we will make additional updates with respect to those or other forward-looking statements.

26

USE OF PROCEEDS

We estimate that the net proceeds to us from the sale of the shares of common stock offered by us will be approximately $21.9 million, or approximately $29.0 million if the underwriters' overallotment option is exercised in full, based on an assumed initial public offering price of $17.00 per share and after deducting underwriting discounts and commissions and estimated offering expenses payable by us. We will not receive any proceeds from the sale of common stock by the selling stockholders.

A $1.00 increase (decrease) in the assumed initial public offering price of $17.00 per share would increase (decrease) the net proceeds to us from this offering by approximately $1.5 million, assuming the number of shares offered by us, as set forth on the cover page of this prospectus, remains the same, or approximately $1.9 million if the underwriters' overallotment option is exercised in full, and after deducting underwriting discounts and commissions and estimated offering expenses payable by us.

We currently intend to use the net proceeds to us from this offering primarily for general corporate purposes, including working capital, sales and marketing activities, general and administrative matters and capital expenditures. We may also use a portion of the net proceeds for the acquisition of, or investment in, technologies, solutions or businesses that complement our business. We have no present understandings, commitments or agreements to enter into any acquisitions or investments. Our management will have broad discretion over the uses of the net proceeds in this offering. Pending these uses, we intend to invest the net proceeds from this offering in short-term, investment-grade interest-bearing securities such as money market accounts, certificates of deposit, commercial paper and guaranteed obligations of the U.S. government.

By establishing a public market for our common stock, this offering is also intended to facilitate our future access to public markets.

DIVIDEND POLICY

We have never declared or paid, and do not anticipate declaring or paying, any cash dividends on our common stock. Any future determination as to the declaration and payment of dividends, if any, will be at the discretion of our board of directors and will depend on then existing conditions, including our financial condition, operating results, contractual restrictions, capital requirements, business prospects and other factors our board of directors may deem relevant.

27

CAPITALIZATION

The following table shows:

- our capitalization as of March 31, 2009;

- our capitalization as of March 31, 2009, on a pro forma basis, giving effect to the automatic conversion of all outstanding preferred stock into an aggregate of 9,075,737 shares of common stock as if such conversions had occurred on March 31, 2009; and

- our capitalization as of March 31, 2009, on a pro forma as adjusted basis, giving effect to the sale by us of 1,572,684 shares of common stock in this offering, at an assumed initial public offering price of $17.00 per share, after deducting underwriting discounts and commissions and estimated offering expenses payable by us.

	As of March 31, 2009		
	Actual	Pro Forma	Pro Forma, as Adjusted(1)
		(In thousands)	
Cash, cash equivalents and short-term investments	$ 25,204	$ 25,204	$ 47,112
Stockholders' equity:			
Convertible preferred stock	$ 21,909	$ —	$ —
Common stock	1	2	2
Additional paid-in capital	65,361	87,269	109,177
Treasury stock	(647)	(647)	(647)
Accumulated other comprehensive loss	(242)	(242)	(242)
Accumulated deficit	(57,977)	(57,977)	(57,977)
Total stockholders' equity	28,405	28,405	50,313
Total capitalization	$ 28,405	$ 28,405	$ 50,313

(1) A $1.00 increase (decrease) in the assumed initial public offering price of $17.00 per share would increase (decrease) the amount of additional paid-in capital, total stockholders' equity and total capitalization by approximately $1.5 million, assuming the number of shares offered by us, as set forth on the cover page of this prospectus, remains the same and after deducting underwriting discounts and commissions and estimated offering expenses payable by us.

The outstanding share information set forth above is as of March 31, 2009 and excludes:

- an aggregate of 162,836 shares of common stock reserved for issuance under our 1999 Stock Plan;

- 1,240,104 additional shares of common stock, subject to increase on an annual basis, reserved for issuance under our 2009 Equity Incentive Award Plan, which we plan to adopt in connection with this offering;

- 2,402,605 shares of common stock issuable upon the exercise of outstanding options to purchase our common stock granted pursuant to our 1999 Stock Plan at a weighted average exercise price of $7.33 per share; and

- 182,059 shares of common stock issuable upon the exercise of outstanding warrants at a weighted average exercise price of $3.85 per share.

28

DILUTION

If you invest in our common stock, your interest will be diluted to the extent of the difference between the public offering price per share of our common stock and the pro forma net tangible book value per share of our common stock immediately after the offering.

The historical net tangible book value of our common stock as of March 31, 2009 was $28.4 million, or $2.59 per share. Historical net tangible book value per share is determined by dividing the net tangible book value by the number of shares of outstanding common stock. If you invest in our common stock in this offering, your ownership interest will be immediately diluted to the extent of the difference between the initial public offering price per share and the pro forma as adjusted net tangible book value per share of our common stock.

After giving effect to the (i) a 1-for-12.5 reverse stock split of our common stock and preferred stock to be effected immediately prior to the effectiveness of our initial public offering registration statement, (ii) automatic conversion of our outstanding preferred stock into common stock in connection with this offering and (iii) receipt of the net proceeds from our sale of 1,572,684 shares of common stock in this offering at an assumed initial public offering price of $17.00 per share, after deducting underwriting discounts and commissions and estimated offering expenses payable by us, our pro forma as adjusted net tangible book value as of March 31, 2009 would have been approximately $50.3 million, or $2.33 per share. This represents an immediate increase in pro forma as adjusted net tangible book value of $0.64 per share to existing stockholders and an immediate dilution of $10.94 per share to new investors purchasing common stock in this offering.

The following table illustrates this dilution on a per share basis to new investors:

Assumed initial public offering price		$17.00
Net tangible book value per share as of March 31, 2009	$ 2.59	
Decrease per share attributable to conversion of preferred stock	(1.17)	
Pro forma net tangible book value before this offering	1.42	
Increase per share attributable to this offering	0.91	
Pro forma net tangible book value, as adjusted to give effect to this offering		2.33
Dilution in pro forma net tangible book value per share to new investors in this offering		$14.67

A $1.00 increase (decrease) in the assumed initial public offering price of $17.00 per share would increase (decrease) the pro forma net tangible book value, as adjusted to give effect to this offering, by $0.07 per share and the dilution to new investors by $0.93 per share, assuming the number of shares offered by us, as set forth on the cover page of this prospectus, remains the same and after deducting underwriting discounts and commissions and estimated expenses payable by us.

The table below summarizes as of March 31, 2009, on a pro forma as adjusted basis described above, the number of shares of our common stock, the total consideration and the average price per share (i) paid to us by existing stockholders and (ii) to be paid by new investors purchasing our common stock in this offering at an assumed initial public offering price of $17.00 per share.

	Shares Purchased		Total Consideration		Average Price
	Number	Percent	Amount	Percent	Per Share
	(In thousands, other than percentages)				
Existing stockholders	20,032	92.7%	$ 78,632	74.6%	$ 3.93
New investors	1,573	7.3	26,736	25.4	17.00
Total	21,605	100.0%	$105,368	100.0%	

29

The above discussion and tables are based on 20,031,903 shares of common stock issued and outstanding as of March 31, 2009 and excludes:

- an aggregate of 162,836 additional shares of common stock reserved for issuance under our 1999 Stock Plan;

- 1,240,104 additional shares of common stock, subject to increase on an annual basis, reserved for issuance under our 2009 Equity Incentive Award Plan, which we plan to adopt in connection with this offering;

- 2,402,605 shares of common stock issuable upon the exercise of outstanding options to purchase our common stock granted pursuant to our 1999 Stock Plan at a weighted average exercise price of $7.33 per share; and

- 182,059 shares of common stock issuable upon the exercise of outstanding warrants at a weighted average exercise price of $3.85 per share.

Sales by the selling stockholders in this offering will cause the number of shares held by existing stockholders to be reduced to 18,604,587 shares or 86.1% of the total number of shares of our common stock outstanding after this offering. If the underwriters' overallotment option is exercised in full, the number of shares held by the existing stockholders after this offering would be reduced to 84.4% of the total number of shares of our common stock outstanding after this offering, and the number of shares held by new investors would increase to 3,450,000 or 15.6% of the total number of shares of our common stock outstanding after this offering.

To the extent that any outstanding options or warrants are exercised, new investors will experience further dilution.

30

SELECTED CONSOLIDATED FINANCIAL DATA

You should read the following selected historical consolidated financial data below in conjunction with "Management's Discussion and Analysis of Financial Condition and Results of Operations" and the consolidated financial statements, related notes and other financial information included in this prospectus. The selected consolidated financial data in this section are not intended to replace the consolidated financial statements and are qualified in their entirety by the consolidated financial statements and related notes included in this prospectus.

The consolidated statements of operations data for the years ended December 31, 2006, 2007 and 2008 and the consolidated balance sheets data as of December 31, 2007 and 2008 are derived from our audited consolidated financial statements included in this prospectus. The consolidated statements of operations data for the years ended December 31, 2004 and 2005 and the consolidated balance sheets data as of December 31, 2004, 2005 and 2006 are derived from our audited consolidated financial statements not included in this prospectus. The unaudited consolidated statements of operations data for the three months ended March 31, 2008 and 2009, and the unaudited consolidated balance sheet data as of March 31, 2009, are derived from our unaudited consolidated financial statements that are included elsewhere in the prospectus. We have prepared the unaudited information on the same basis as the audited consolidated financial statements and have included, in our opinion, all adjustments, consisting only of normal recurring adjustments, that we consider necessary for a fair presentation of the financial information set forth in those statements and assumes a 1-for-12.5 reverse stock split of our common stock and preferred stock to be effected immediately prior to the effectiveness of our initial public offering registration statement. Results for the three months ended March 31, 2009 are not necessarily indicative of the results to be expected for the fiscal year ending December 31, 2009. Historical results are not necessarily indicative of the results to be expected in the future.

Pro forma basic net income (loss) per share has been calculated assuming the conversion of all outstanding shares of our preferred stock into 9,075,737 shares of common stock upon the completion of this offering.

31

	Years Ended December 31,					Three Months Ended March 31,	
	2004	2005	2006	2007	2008	2008	2009
			(In thousands, except per share amounts)				
Consolidated Statements of Operations Data:							
REVENUES	$10,142	$16,715	$27,168	$41,148	$55,844	$13,263	$15,995
COSTS AND EXPENSES:							
Operations and support(1)	5,588	8,016	9,548	12,603	17,760	4,012	5,106
Sales and marketing(1)	4,944	6,529	7,675	11,326	14,830	3,591	3,798
Technology(1)	2,165	2,969	4,024	5,863	9,511	2,175	2,712
General and administrative(1)	2,898	4,191	5,972	12,212	13,117	3,144	3,547
Total costs and expenses	15,595	21,705	27,219	42,004	55,218	12,922	15,163
Income (loss) from operations	(5,453)	(4,990)	(51)	(856)	626	341	832
Other income, net	(3)	323	421	951	468	180	55
Income (loss) before taxes	(5,456)	(4,667)	370	95	1,094	521	887
Income tax expense (benefit)	—	—	176	(9,121)	2,118	608	521
NET INCOME (LOSS)	$(5,456)	$(4,667)	$ 194	$ 9,216	$(1,024)	$ (87)	$ 366
Net income (loss) per share:							
Basic	$ (0.73)	$ (0.55)	$ 0.02	$ 0.97	$ (0.10)	$ (0.01)	$ 0.04
Diluted	$ (0.73)	$ (0.55)	$ 0.01	$ 0.46	$ (0.10)	$ (0.01)	$ 0.02
Weighted average shares outstanding:							
Basic	7,496	8,487	9,132	9,522	10,016	9,850	10,276
Diluted	7,496	8,487	19,523	20,019	10,016	9,850	21,017
Pro forma net income (loss) per share—basic and diluted (unaudited)					$ (0.05)		$ 0.02
Pro forma weighted average shares outstanding used in calculating net income (loss) per share (unaudited)							
Basic					19,092		19,352
Diluted					19,092		21,017

(1)   Stock-based compensation included in above line items:

	2004	2005	2006	2007	2008	2008	2009
Operations and support	$ 31	$ 23	$ 58	$ 290	$ 339	$ 77	$ 86
Sales and marketing	50	36	67	709	878	228	223
Technology	30	50	64	288	694	132	174
General and administrative	76	187	520	1,816	2,059	547	476
Total	$ 187	$ 296	$ 709	$3,103	$3,970	$ 984	$ 959

32

	Years Ended December 31,					Three Months Ended March 31,	
	2004	2005	2006	2007	2008	2008	2009
Other Operational Data:							
Installed restaurants (at period end):							
North America	2,423	3,873	5,583	7,391	9,295	7,823	9,548
International	—	71	204	470	1,040	581	1,097
Total	2,423	3,944	5,787	7,861	10,335	8,404	10,645
Seated diners (in thousands):							
North America	4,574	8,322	15,171	24,614	33,636	8,395	9,922
International	—	10	84	244	542	123	186
Total	4,574	8,332	15,255	24,858	34,178	8,518	10,108
Headcount (at period end):							
North America	128	143	152	192	238	206	245
International	3	9	16	34	59	42	55
Total	131	152	168	226	297	248	300

(In thousands)

	2004	2005	2006	2007	2008	2008	2009
Additional Financial Data:							
Revenues:							
North America	$10,142	$16,618	$26,654	$39,601	$53,065	$12,667	$15,189
International	—	97	514	1,547	2,779	596	806
Total	$10,142	$16,715	$27,168	$41,148	$55,844	$13,263	$15,995
Income (loss) from operations:							
North America	$(5,326)	$(3,373)	$ 3,106	$ 4,974	$ 9,088	$ 2,409	$ 2,326
International	(127)	(1,617)	(3,157)	(5,830)	(8,462)	(2,068)	(1,494)
Total	$(5,453)	$(4,990)	$ (51)	$ (856)	$ 626	$ 341	$ 832
Depreciation and amortization:							
North America	$ 645	$ 1,260	$ 2,029	$ 2,817	$ 4,026	$ 877	$ 1,159
International	—	21	89	184	350	74	104
Total	$ 645	$ 1,281	$ 2,118	$ 3,001	$ 4,376	$ 951	$ 1,263

	As of December 31,					March 31,
	2004	2005	2006	2007	2008	2009
			(In thousands)			
Consolidated Balance Sheets Data:						
Cash and cash equivalents	$ 2,475	$ 8,076	$10,264	$21,661	$ 5,528	$ 12,010
Short-term investments	12,000	504	—	—	17,259	13,194
Property and equipment, net	2,316	4,619	6,019	8,378	11,125	11,069
Working capital	12,456	5,389	5,655	9,759	14,745	15,835
Total assets	19,816	17,248	21,124	45,814	50,883	54,587
Dining rewards payable	1,224	2,021	3,499	5,836	8,462	9,221
Convertible preferred stock	21,909	21,909	21,909	21,909	21,909	21,909
Total stockholders' equity	12,552	8,324	8,907	22,485	26,684	28,405

33

MANAGEMENT'S DISCUSSION AND ANALYSIS OF
FINANCIAL CONDITION AND RESULTS OF OPERATIONS

You should read the following discussion of our financial condition and results of operations in conjunction with the financial statements and the notes thereto included elsewhere in this prospectus. The following discussion contains forward-looking statements that reflect our plans, estimates and beliefs. Our actual results could differ materially from those discussed in the forward-looking statements. Factors that could cause or contribute to these differences include those discussed below and elsewhere in this prospectus, particularly in "Risk Factors."

Overview

We provide solutions that form an online network connecting reservation-taking restaurants and people who dine at those restaurants. Our solutions include our proprietary Electronic Reservation Book, or ERB, for restaurant customers and www.opentable.com, a popular restaurant reservation website for diners. The OpenTable network includes approximately 10,000 OpenTable restaurant customers spanning all 50 states as well as select markets outside of the United States. Since our inception in 1998, we have seated approximately 100 million diners through OpenTable reservations; during the three months ended March 31, 2009, we seated an average of approximately three million diners per month. Restaurants pay us a one-time installation fee for onsite installation and training, a monthly subscription fee for the use of our software and hardware and a fee for each restaurant guest seated through online reservations. Our online restaurant reservation service is free to diners. For the twelve months ended December 31, 2008 and the three months ended March 31, 2009, our net revenues were $55.8 million and $16.0 million, respectively. For the twelve months ended December 31, 2008 and the three months ended March 31, 2009, our subscription revenues accounted for 54% and 52% of our total revenues, respectively, and our reservation revenues accounted for 41% and 43% of our total revenues, respectively.

In 2004, we began to selectively expand outside of North America into countries that are characterized by large numbers of online consumer transactions and reservation-taking restaurants. To date, we have concentrated our international efforts in Germany, Japan and the United Kingdom. Our revenues outside of North America for the twelve months ended December 31, 2008 and the three months ended March 31, 2009, were $2.8 million and $0.8 million, respectively, or 5% and 5% of our total revenues, respectively. We intend to continue to incur substantial expenses in advance of recognizing material related revenues as we attempt to further penetrate our existing international markets and selectively enter new markets. Some international markets may fail to meet our expectations, and we may decide to realign our focus, as we did when we closed our offices in Spain and France in the fourth quarter of 2008.

Basis of Presentation

General

We report consolidated operations in U.S. dollars and operate in two geographic segments: North America and International. The North America segment is comprised of all of our operations in the United States, Canada and Mexico, and the International segment is comprised of all non-North America operations, which includes operations in Europe and Asia.

Revenues

We generate substantially all of our revenues from our restaurant customers; we do not charge any fees to diners. Our revenues include installation fees for our ERB (including training), monthly subscription fees and a fee for each restaurant guest seated through online reservations. Installation fees are recognized on a straight-line basis over an estimated customer life of approximately seven

34

years. Subscription revenues are recognized on a straight-line basis during the contractual period over which the service is delivered to our restaurant customers. Revenues from online reservations are recognized on a transaction basis as the diners are seated by the restaurant. Revenues are shown net of redeemable Dining Points issued to diners as described below in "Dining Rewards Loyalty Program." See "Critical Accounting Policies and Estimates—Dining Rewards Loyalty Program" below.

Costs and Expenses

Operations and support. Our operations and support expenses consist primarily of payroll and related costs, including bonuses and stock-based compensation, for those employees associated with installation, support and maintenance for our restaurant customers, as well as costs related to our outsourced call center. Operations and support expenses also include restaurant equipment costs, such as depreciation on restaurant-related hardware, shipping costs related to restaurant equipment, restaurant equipment costs that do not meet the capitalization threshold, referral payments and website connectivity costs. Operations and support expenses also include amortization of capitalized website and development costs (see "Critical Accounting Policies and Estimates—Website and Software Development Costs" below). Also included in operations and support expenses are travel and related expenses incurred by the employees providing installation and support services for our restaurant customers, plus allocated facilities costs.

Sales and marketing. Our sales and marketing expenses consist primarily of salaries, benefits and incentive compensation for sales and marketing employees, including stock-based compensation. Also included are expenses for trade shows, public relations and other promotional and marketing activities, travel and entertainment expenses and allocated facilities costs.

Technology. Our technology expenses consist primarily of salaries and benefits, including bonuses and stock-based compensation, for employees and contractors engaged in the development and ongoing maintenance of our website, infrastructure and software, as well as allocated facilities costs.

General and administrative. Our general and administrative costs consist primarily of salaries and benefits, including stock-based compensation, for general and administrative employees and contractors involved in executive, finance, accounting, risk management, human resources and legal roles. In addition, general and administrative costs include consulting, legal, accounting and other professional fees. Bad debt, third party payment processor, credit card, bank processing fees and allocated facilities costs are also included in general and administrative expenses.

Headcount consists of full-time equivalent employees, as well as full-time equivalent contractors, in all of the sections noted below.

Other Income, Net

Other income, net consists primarily of the interest income earned on our cash accounts. Foreign exchange gains and losses are also included in other income, net.

Income Taxes

We are subject to tax in the United States as well as other tax jurisdictions or countries in which we conduct business. Earnings from our non-U.S. activities are subject to local country income tax and may be subject to current U.S. income tax.

As of December 31, 2008, for federal and state tax purposes, we had $10.4 million of federal and $9.8 million of state net operating loss carryforwards available to reduce future taxable income. These net operating loss carryforwards begin to expire in 2023 and 2009 for federal and state tax purposes, respectively. Our ability to use our net operating loss carryforwards to offset any future taxable income will be subject to limitations attributable to equity transactions that resulted in a change of ownership as defined by Section 382 of the Internal Revenue Code of 1986, as amended, or the Internal Revenue Code. We have $15.0 million in unrecognized tax benefits primarily as a result of the limitations on our net operating loss carryforwards. In the event that any unrecognized tax benefits are recognized, the effective tax rate will be affected. Approximately $14.3 million of the unrecognized tax benefit would impact the effective tax rate if recognized. Our policy is to classify interest accrued or penalties related to unrecognized tax benefits as a component of income tax expense. No such interest or penalties have been recorded to date.

Our net deferred tax assets consist primarily of net operating loss carryforwards generated before we achieved profitability. During the fourth quarter of 2007, we concluded that it was more likely than not that we would be able to realize the benefit of these deferred tax assets in the future. Consequently, we recognized a net tax benefit of $9.4 million in the fourth quarter of 2007 resulting primarily from the release of substantially all of the net deferred tax valuation allowance. We based this conclusion on historical and projected operating performance, as well as our expectation that our operations will generate sufficient taxable income in future periods to be able to realize a portion of the tax benefits associated with the deferred tax assets. We will continue to assess the need for a valuation allowance on the deferred tax asset by evaluating both positive and negative evidence that may exist. Any adjustment to the deferred tax asset valuation allowance would be recorded in the income statement of the periods that the adjustment is determined to be required.

Critical Accounting Policies and Estimates

Our consolidated financial statements are prepared in accordance with U.S. Generally Accepted Accounting Principles (GAAP). The preparation of these consolidated financial statements requires us to make estimates and assumptions that affect the reported amounts of assets, liabilities, revenues, expenses and related disclosures. We evaluate our estimates and assumptions on an ongoing basis. Our estimates are based on historical experience and various other assumptions that we believe to be reasonable under the circumstances. Our actual results could differ from these estimates.

We believe that the assumptions and estimates associated with revenue recognition, the points-based loyalty program, website and software development costs, income taxes and stock-based compensation have the greatest potential impact on our consolidated financial statements. Therefore, we consider these to be our critical accounting policies and estimates. For further information on all of our significant accounting policies, please see Note 2 of the accompanying notes to our consolidated financial statements.

Revenue Recognition

Our revenues include installation fees for our ERB (including training), monthly subscription fees and a fee for each restaurant guest seated through online reservations. We provide our application as a service, and follow the provisions of SEC Staff Accounting Bulletin No. 104, *Revenue Recognition* (SAB No. 104) and FASB Emerging Issues Task Force Issue No. 00-21, *Revenue Arrangements with Multiple Deliverables* (EITF No. 00-21). We recognize revenue when all of the following conditions are met: there is persuasive evidence of an arrangement; the service has been provided to the customer; the collection of the fees is reasonably assured; and the amount of fees to be paid by the customer is fixed or determinable. Amounts paid by the customer include the right to use our hardware during the service period. Proportionate revenue related to the right to use our hardware accounts for less than 10% of revenues for the periods presented.

Revenues from the installation of our ERB are recognized on a straight-line basis over the estimated customer life, commencing with customer acceptance. The estimated customer life is approximately six years, based on historical restaurant customer termination activity. Estimates made by

36

us may differ from actual customer lives. These differences may materially impact installation and other revenue by increasing or decreasing revenue, depending on whether the estimated customer life decreases or increases. A change in the estimated customer life by one year in either direction would have a minimal impact to total revenue of less than 1%. Subscription revenues are recognized on a straight-line basis during the contractual period over which the service is delivered. Reservation revenues (or per seated diner fees) are recognized on a transaction-by-transaction basis as diners are seated by our restaurant customers. Amounts that have been invoiced are recorded in accounts receivable and in deferred revenues or revenues, depending on whether the revenue recognition criteria have been met. Revenues are shown net of redeemable Dining Points issued to diners (as described below).

Dining Rewards Loyalty Program

We provide a points-based loyalty program, OpenTable Dining Rewards, to registered diners who book and honor reservations through the OpenTable website. OpenTable Dining Rewards involves the issuance of "Dining Points," which can be accumulated and redeemed for "Dining Cheques." The standard award is 100 points per reservation, but diners can earn 1,000 points for reservations during featured times under the OpenTable Dining Rewards program. When a diner accumulates a minimum of 2,000 points, he or she may redeem them for a $20 Dining Cheque. Every 100 Dining Points is equal to one dollar. Diners may present Dining Cheques at any OpenTable restaurant and their bill is reduced by the cheque amount. The restaurant then deposits the Dining Cheque to its bank.

If a diner does not make a seated reservation within any 12-month period, then his or her account is considered inactive and the Dining Points balance is reset to zero. As is typical with points-based incentive programs, many Dining Points expire unused. In addition, some Dining Cheques are never used. The recorded expense is an estimate of the eventual cash outlay related to the issued Dining Points and is booked at the time the points are earned by the diner (i.e., when the diner is "seated" by the restaurant). We estimate the cost of the issued Dining Points by analyzing historical patterns of redemption and cheque cashing activity. These historical patterns are evaluated in light of any current or proposed program changes that may impact future point redemption. Actual redemption rates could differ from our estimates used in assessing the contra-revenue amounts and corresponding liability. These differences could materially impact reservation revenues. For example, an increase of 10% in the redemption rate as of March 31, 2009 would result in a reduction in revenues of $1.7 million and an increase in the dining rewards payable liability of 18%.

We recognize the cost and a corresponding liability associated with Dining Points as contra-revenue in accordance with EITF Issue No. 01-09, *Accounting for Consideration Given by a Vendor to a Customer (Including a Reseller of the Vendor's Products)* (EITF 01-09) and EITF Issue No. 00-22, *Accounting for "Points" and Certain Other Time- or Volume-Based Sales Incentive Offers, and Offers for Free Products or Services to be Delivered in the Future* (EITF 00-22).

Website and Software Development Costs

Costs related to website and internal-use software are accounted for in accordance with American Institute of Certified Public Accountants Statement of Position 98-1, *Accounting for the Costs of Computer Software Developed or Obtained for Internal Use* (SOP 98-1) and EITF Issue No. 00-2, *Accounting for Website Development Costs* (EITF 00-2). Such software is primarily related to our website, including support systems. In accordance with SOP 98-1 and EITF 00-2, we capitalize our costs to develop software when preliminary development efforts are successfully completed, management has authorized and committed project funding and it is probable that the project will be completed and the software will be used as intended. Such costs are amortized on a straight-line basis over the estimated useful life of the related asset, generally estimated between two to four years. Costs incurred prior to meeting these criteria are expensed as incurred. Costs incurred for enhancements that are expected to

37

result in additional features or functionality are capitalized and expensed over the estimated useful life of the enhancements.

We follow the guidance in Statement of Financial Accounting Standard No. 86, *Accounting for the Costs of Computer Software to Be Sold, Leased, or Otherwise Marketed* (SFAS 86) in accounting for costs incurred in connection with development of the software contained in the ERB used by all restaurant customers, and in a limited number of certain transactions we sell reservation systems that do not include our ongoing service. All costs incurred to establish the technological feasibility of a computer product to be sold, leased or otherwise marketed are expensed as incurred. Costs incurred subsequent to establishing technological feasibility and through general product release are capitalized and amortized over the estimated product life. The period between technological feasibility and general product release is extremely short for us, and the costs incurred during this stage are not considered to be material and are expensed as incurred.

Income Taxes

We record income taxes using the asset and liability method, which requires the recognition of deferred tax assets and liabilities for the expected future tax consequences of events that have been recognized in our financial statements or tax returns. In estimating future tax consequences, generally all expected future events other than enactments or changes in the tax law or rates are considered. Valuation allowances are provided when necessary to reduce deferred tax assets to the amount expected to be realized.

We operate in various tax jurisdictions and are subject to audit by various tax authorities. We provide for tax contingencies whenever it is deemed probable that a tax asset has been impaired or a tax liability has been incurred for events such as tax claims or changes in tax laws. Tax contingencies are based upon their technical merits, relevant tax law and the specific facts and circumstances as of each reporting period. Changes in facts and circumstances could result in material changes to the amounts recorded for such tax contingencies.

On January 1, 2007, we adopted Financial Accounting Standards Board (FASB) Interpretation No. 48, *Accounting for Uncertainty in Income Taxes—an interpretation of FASB Statement No. 109* (FIN 48), which supplements FASB Statement No. 109 by defining the confidence level that a tax position must meet in order to be recognized in the financial statements. FIN 48 requires that the tax effects of a position be recognized only if it is "more likely than not" to be sustained based solely on its technical merits as of the reporting date. We consider many factors when evaluating and estimating our tax positions and tax benefits, which may require periodic adjustments and which may not accurately anticipate actual outcomes.

With the adoption of FIN 48, companies are required to adjust their financial statements to reflect only those tax positions that are more likely than not to be sustained. Any necessary adjustment would be recorded directly to retained earnings and reported as a change in accounting principle as of the date of adoption. FIN 48 prescribes a comprehensive model for the financial statement recognition, measurement, presentation and disclosure of uncertain tax positions taken or expected to be taken in income tax returns.

Stock-based Compensation

Prior to January 1, 2006, we accounted for stock-based employee compensation arrangements using the intrinsic value method of Accounting Principles Board Opinion No. 25, *Accounting for Stock Issued to Employees* (APB 25) and related interpretations, and complied with the disclosure-only provisions of SFAS No. 123, *Accounting for Stock-Based Compensation* (SFAS 123) as amended by SFAS No. 148, *Accounting for Stock-Based Compensation, Transition and Disclosure, an amendment to SFAS Statement No. 123* (SFAS 148). Under APB 25 compensation expense for employees is based on

38

the excess, if any, of the fair value of our common stock over the exercise price of the option on the date of grant.

Effective January 1, 2006, we adopted SFAS No. 123R, *Share-Based Payment* (SFAS No. 123R), which requires compensation expense related to share-based transactions, including employee stock options, to be measured and recognized in the financial statements based on fair value. SFAS No. 123R revises SFAS No. 123, as amended, and supersedes APB 25. We adopted SFAS No. 123R using the modified prospective method. Under modified prospective application, SFAS No. 123R applies to new awards and to awards modified, repurchased or cancelled after the required effective date. Additionally, compensation cost for the portion of awards for which the requisite service has not been rendered that are outstanding as of the required effective date are recognized as the requisite service is rendered on or after the required effective date. The compensation expense for that portion of awards is based on the grant-date fair value of those awards. The compensation expense for awards with grant dates prior to January 1, 2006, are attributed to periods beginning on or after the effective date using the attribution method that was used under SFAS No. 123, except that the method of recognizing forfeitures only as they occur is not continued.

We are using the graded vesting attribution method prescribed by SFAS No. 123R, over the option vesting period, for all options granted on or after January 1, 2006. All options granted prior to 2006 are being amortized using a straight-line method.

The fair values of the common stock underlying stock options granted during the fourth quarter of 2007 and 2008 were estimated by our board of directors, which intended all options granted to be exercisable at a price per share not less than the per share fair value of our common stock underlying those options on the date of grant. In the absence of a public trading market, our board of directors considered numerous objective and subjective factors to determine its best estimate of the fair market value of our common stock as of the date of each option grant, including but not limited to, the following factors: (i) the rights, preferences and privileges of our preferred stock relative to the common stock; (ii) our performance and stage of development; (iii) valuations of our common stock; and (iv) the likelihood of achieving a liquidity event for the shares of common stock underlying these stock options, such as an initial public offering or sale of our company, given prevailing market conditions. The assumptions we use in the valuation model are based on subjective future expectations combined with management judgment. If any of the assumptions used in the Black-Scholes model changes significantly, stock-based compensation for future awards may differ materially compared with the awards granted previously.

In April 2008, in connection with the preparation of our consolidated financial statements, we performed a retrospective analysis to reassess the fair value of our common stock at certain option grant dates for financial reporting purposes. We performed a retrospective valuation analysis as of December 2007 and March 2008. The valuation analysis consisted of two major steps: the estimation of the aggregate value of the entire company (referred to as Business Enterprise Value, or BEV) and the allocation of this aggregate value to each element of the contemporary capital structure (preferred stock, common stock, options and warrants). As described below, the BEV was estimated using a combination of income and market-based methods. The allocation of the BEV to equity classes was performed using an option-based method as of each valuation date.

Significant Factors, Assumptions and Methodologies Used in Determining Fair Value

In determining the fair value of our BEV and common stock, we used a combination of the income approach and the market approach to estimate our aggregate BEV at each valuation date: December 2007 and March 2008.

The income approach is an estimate of the present value of the future monetary benefits expected to flow to the owners of a business. It requires a projection of the cash flows that the business

39

is expected to generate over a forecast period and an estimate of the present value of cash flows beyond that period, which is referred to as residual value. These cash flows are converted to present value by means of discounting, using a rate of return that accounts for the time value of money and the appropriate degree of risks inherent in the business. The market approach considers multiples of financial metrics based on both acquisitions and trading multiples of a peer group of companies. These multiples are then applied to our financial metrics to derive an indication of value.

Our indicated BEV at each valuation date was then allocated to the shares of redeemable convertible preferred stock, warrants to purchase shares of redeemable convertible preferred stock, and common stock, using a contingent claim methodology. This methodology treats the various components of our capital structure as a series of call options on the proceeds expected from the sale of the company or the liquidation of our assets at some future date. These call options are then valued using the Black-Scholes option pricing model. This model defines the securities' fair values as functions of the current fair value of the company and assumptions based on the securities' rights and preferences. As a result, the option-pricing method requires assumptions regarding the anticipated timing of a potential liquidity event, such as an initial public offering, and the estimated volatility of our equity securities. The anticipated timing of a liquidity event utilized in these valuations was based on then current plans and estimates of our board of directors and management regarding an initial public offering. Estimates of the volatility of our stock were based on available information on the volatility of capital stock of comparable publicly traded companies.

Common Stock Valuations

We granted stock options with the following exercise prices during the twelve months ended December 31, 2008:

Option Grant Dates	Number of Shares Underlying Options	Exercise Price Per Share	Fair Market Value Per Underlying Share as of Grant Date	Intrinsic Value
March 2008	398,446	$ 7.75	$ 10.63	$ 2.88
May 2008	48,000	10.63	10.63	—
December 2008	115,400	10.63	10.63	—

No stock options were granted in the three months ended March 31, 2009.

In determining the fair value of our BEV and common stock, we conducted retrospective valuations using the approaches mentioned above. These valuations resulted in estimated fair value of our common stock for accounting purposes of $10.63 per share at March 2008.

Under SFAS No. 123R, the fair value of each option award is estimated on the date of grant using the Black-Scholes option pricing model. We determined weighted average valuation assumptions as follows:

- *Volatility.* As we do not have a trading history for our common stock, the expected stock price volatility for our common stock was estimated by taking the median historic price volatility for industry peers based on daily price observations over a period equivalent to the expected term of the stock option grants. Industry peers consist of several public companies in the technology industry similar in size, stage of life cycle and financial leverage. We did not rely on implied volatilities of traded options in our industry peers' common stock because the volume of activity was relatively low.

- *Expected term.* The expected term was estimated using the simplified method allowed under SEC Staff Accounting Bulletin No. 107, *Share-Based Payment.*

40

- *Risk free rate.* The risk free interest rate is based on the yields of U.S. Treasury securities with maturities similar to the expected term of the options for each option group.

- *Forfeiture rate.* We estimated the forfeiture rate using our historical experience with forfeitures. We review the estimated forfeiture rates each period end and make changes as factors affecting the forfeiture rate calculations and assumptions change.

- *Dividend yield.* We have never declared or paid any cash dividends and do not presently plan to pay cash dividends in the foreseeable future. Consequently, we used an expected dividend yield of zero.

The following table summarizes the assumptions relating to our stock options for the year ended December 31, 2008:

	Year Ended December 31, 2008
Dividend yield	0%
Volatility	55%
Risk free interest rate	1.54%-3.34%
Expected term, in years	5.92-6.53

No stock options were granted in the three months ended March 31, 2009.

Using the Black-Scholes option pricing model, we recorded non-cash stock-based compensation expenses related to employee stock options granted of approximately $4.0 million in 2008 and approximately $1.0 million for the three months ended March 31, 2009, in accordance with the requirements of SFAS No. 123R.

41

Results of Operations

The following tables set forth our results of operations for the periods presented and as a percentage of our revenues for those periods. The period-to-period comparison of financial results is not necessarily indicative of future results.

	Years Ended December 31,			Three Months Ended March 31,	
	2006	2007	2008	2008	2009
	(In thousands, except per share amounts)				
REVENUES	$27,168	$41,148	$55,844	$13,263	$15,995
COSTS AND EXPENSES:					
Operations and support(1)	9,548	12,603	17,760	4,012	5,106
Sales and marketing(1)	7,675	11,326	14,830	3,591	3,798
Technology(1)	4,024	5,863	9,511	2,175	2,712
General and administrative(1)	5,972	12,212	13,117	3,144	3,547
Total costs and expenses	27,219	42,004	55,218	12,922	15,163
Income (loss) from operations	(51)	(856)	626	341	832
Other income, net	421	951	468	180	55
Income before taxes	370	95	1,094	521	887
Income tax expense (benefit)	176	(9,121)	2,118	608	521
NET INCOME (LOSS)	$ 194	$ 9,216	$(1,024)	$ (87)	$ 366
Net income (loss) per share:					
Basic	$ 0.02	$ 0.97	$ (0.10)	$ (0.01)	$ 0.04
Diluted	$ 0.01	$ 0.46	$ (0.10)	$ (0.01)	$ 0.02
Weighted average shares outstanding:					
Basic	9,132	9,522	10,016	9,850	10,276
Diluted	19,523	20,019	10,016	9,850	21,017

(1) Stock-based compensation included in above line items:

Operations and support	$ 58	$ 290	$ 339	$ 77	$ 86
Sales and marketing	67	709	878	228	223
Technology	64	288	694	132	174
General and administrative	520	1,816	2,059	547	476
Total	$ 709	$ 3,103	$ 3,970	$ 984	$ 959

42

	Years Ended December 31,			Three Months Ended March 31,	
	2006	2007	2008	2008	2009
Other Operational Data:					
Installed restaurants (at period end):					
North America	5,583	7,391	9,295	7,823	9,548
International	204	470	1,040	581	1,097
Total	5,787	7,861	10,335	8,404	10,645
Seated diners (in thousands):					
North America	15,171	24,614	33,636	8,395	9,922
International	84	244	542	123	186
Total	15,255	24,858	34,178	8,518	10,108
Headcount (at period end):					
North America	152	192	238	206	245
International	16	34	59	42	55
Total	168	226	297	248	300

	(In thousands)				
Additional Financial Data:					
Revenues:					
North America	$26,654	$39,601	$53,065	$12,667	$15,189
International	514	1,547	2,779	596	806
Total	$27,168	$41,148	$55,844	$13,263	$15,995
Income (loss) from operations:					
North America	$ 3,106	$ 4,974	$ 9,088	$ 2,409	$ 2,326
International	(3,157)	(5,830)	(8,462)	(2,068)	(1,494)
Total	$ (51)	$ (856)	$ 626	$ 341	$ 832
Depreciation and amortization:					
North America	$ 2,029	$ 2,817	$ 4,026	$ 877	$ 1,159
International	89	184	350	74	104
Total	$ 2,118	$ 3,001	$ 4,376	$ 951	$ 1,263

	Years Ended December 31,			Three Months Ended March 31,	
	2006	2007	2008	2008	2009
	(As a percentage of revenues)				
REVENUES	100%	100%	100%	100%	100%
COSTS AND EXPENSES:					
Operations and support	35	31	32	30	32
Sales and marketing	28	27	27	28	24
Technology	15	14	17	16	17
General and administrative	22	30	23	24	22
Total costs and expenses	100	102	99	98	95
Income (loss) from operations	(0)	(2)	1	2	5
Other income, net	2	2	1	2	0
Income before taxes	2	0	2	4	5

Income tax expense (benefit)	1	(22)	4	5	3
NET INCOME (LOSS)	1%	22%	(2)%	(1)%	2%

43

Three Months Ended March 31, 2008 and 2009

Revenues

	Three Months Ended March 31,		% Change
	2008	2009	
	(Dollars in thousands)		
Installed restaurants (at period end):			
North America	7,823	9,548	22%
International	581	1,097	89
Total	8,404	10,645	27%
Seated diners (in thousands):			
North America	8,395	9,922	18%
International	123	186	51
Total	8,518	10,108	19%
Revenues by type:			
Subscription	$ 6,887	$ 8,389	22%
Reservation	5,830	6,904	18
Installation and other	546	702	29
Total	$13,263	$15,995	21%
Percentage of revenues by type:			
Subscription	52%	52%	
Reservation	44	43	
Installation and other	4	5	
Total	100%	100%	
Revenues by location:			
North America	$12,667	$15,189	20%
International	596	806	35
Total	$13,263	$15,995	21%
Percentage of revenues by location:			
North America	96%	95%	
International	4	5	
Total	100%	100%	

Total revenues increased $2.7 million, or 21%, from the three months ended March 31, 2008, to the three months ended March 31, 2009. Subscription revenues increased to $8.4 million in 2009, from $6.9 million in 2008, an increase of $1.5 million or 22%. Subscription revenues increased as a result of the increase in the installed base of restaurants. Reservation revenues increased to $6.9 million in 2009, from $5.8 million in 2008, an increase of $1.1 million or 18%. Reservation revenues increased as a result of the increase in seated diners.

44

Costs and Expenses

Operations and Support

| | Three Months Ended March 31, | | |
	2008	2009	% Change
	(Dollars in thousands)		
Operations and support	$4,012	$5,106	27%
Headcount (at period end):			
North America	69	75	9
International	20	25	25
Total	89	100	12%

Our operations and support expenses increased $1.1 million, or 27%, from the three months ended March 31, 2008, to the three months ended March 31, 2009. The increase in operations and support expenses was primarily attributable to an increase of $0.5 million in headcount related costs due to an increase in operations and support headcount and a $0.4 million increase in restaurant equipment costs including depreciation on restaurant hardware, equipment and shipping costs in connection with the increase in the installed base of restaurants.

Sales and Marketing

| | Three Months Ended March 31, | | |
	2008	2009	% Change
	(Dollars in thousands)		
Sales and marketing	$3,591	$3,798	6%
Headcount (at period end):			
North America	45	57	27
International	19	24	26
Total	64	81	27%

Our sales and marketing expenses increased $0.2 million, or 6%, from the three months ended March 31, 2008, to the three months ended March 31, 2009. The increase in sales and marketing expenses was primarily attributable to a $0.2 million increase in headcount related costs as a result of increases in headcount.

Technology

| | Three Months Ended March 31, | | |
	2008	2009	% Change
	(Dollars in thousands)		
Technology	$2,175	$2,712	25%
Headcount (at period end):			
North America	61	69	13
International	—	—	
Total	61	69	13%

45

Our technology expenses increased $0.5 million, or 25%, from the three months ended March 31, 2008, to the three months ended March 31, 2009. The increase in technology expenses was primarily attributable to a $0.4 million increase in headcount related costs, resulting from an increase in technology headcount. We increased our technology headcount to address website and ERB enhancements, internationalization of our solutions and website, and system control enhancements.

General and Administrative

	Three Months Ended March 31,		% Change
	2008	2009	
	(Dollars in thousands)		
General and administrative	$3,144	$3,547	13%
Headcount (at period end):			
North America	31	44	42
International	3	6	100
Total	34	50	47%

Our general and administrative expenses increased $0.4 million, or 13%, from the three months ended March 31, 2008, to the three months ended March 31, 2009. The increase was primarily attributable to a $0.2 million increase in headcount related costs as a result of increases in headcount, and a $0.2 million increase in bad debt expense.

Other Income, Net

	Three Months Ended March 31,		% Change
	2008	2009	
	(Dollars in thousands)		
Other income, net	$180	$55	(69)%

Other income, net decreased $0.1 million, or 69%, from the three months ended March 31, 2008, to the three months ended March 31, 2009. The decrease was the result of less interest income being earned on cash, cash equivalents and short-term investments in 2009, as a result of lower short-term interest rates in 2009 compared to 2008.

Income Taxes

	Three Months Ended March 31,		% Change
	2008	2009	
	(Dollars in thousands)		
Income tax expense	$608	$521	(14)%

Income tax expense decreased $0.1 million, or 14%, from the three months ended March 31, 2008, to the three months ended March 31, 2009. Our effective tax rate is expected to be lower in 2009 than 2008 due to our largest permanent difference, non-deductible stock-based compensation, being a smaller percentage of taxable income, than experienced in 2008.

46

Years ended December 31, 2006, 2007 and 2008

Revenues

	Years Ended December 31,			2006 to 2007% Change	2007 to 2008% Change
	2006	2007	2008		
	(Dollars in thousands)				
Installed restaurants (at period end):					
North America	5,583	7,391	9,295	32%	26%
International	204	470	1,040	130	121
Total	5,787	7,861	10,335	36%	31%
Seated diners (in thousands):					
North America	15,171	24,614	33,636	62%	37%
International	84	244	542	190	122
Total	15,255	24,858	34,178	63%	37%
Revenues by type:					
Subscription	$15,454	$22,434	$30,293	45%	35%
Reservation	10,664	17,010	23,135	60	36
Installation and other	1,050	1,704	2,416	62	42
Total	$27,168	$41,148	$55,844	51%	36%
Percentage of revenues by type:					
Subscription	57%	55%	54%		
Reservation	39	41	41		
Installation and other	4	4	5		
Total	100%	100%	100%		
Revenues by location:					
North America	$26,654	$39,601	$53,065	49%	34%
International	514	1,547	2,779	201	80
Total	$27,168	$41,148	$55,844	51%	36%
Percentage of revenues by location:					
North America	98%	96%	95%		
International	2	4	5		
Total	100%	100%	100%		

2007 compared to 2008. Total revenues increased $14.7 million, or 36%, from 2007 to 2008. Subscription revenues increased to $30.3 million in 2008 from $22.4 million in 2007, an increase of $7.9 million, or 35%. Subscription revenues increased due to the increase in installed restaurants. Reservation revenues increased to $23.1 million in 2008 from $17.0 million in 2007, an increase of $6.1 million, or 36%. Reservation revenues increased as a result of an increase in seated diners.

2006 compared to 2007. Total revenues increased $14.0 million, or 51%, from 2006 to 2007. Subscription revenues increased to $22.4 million in 2007 from $15.5 million in 2006, an increase of $7.0 million, or 45%. Subscription revenues increased due to the increase in installed restaurants. Reservation revenues increased to $17.0 million in 2007 from $10.7 million in 2006, an increase of $6.3 million, or 60%. Reservation revenues increased as a result of an increase in seated diners.

47

Costs and Expenses

Operations and Support

| | Years Ended December 31, | | | 2006 to 2007 | 2007 to 2008 |
	2006	2007	2008	% Change	% Change
	(Dollars in thousands)				
Operations and support	$9,548	$12,603	$17,760	32%	41%
Headcount (at period end):					
North America	58	63	78	9	24
International	5	16	28	220	75
Total	63	79	106	25%	34%

2007 compared to 2008. Operations and support expenses for the year ended December 31, 2008 were $17.8 million compared to $12.6 million for the year ended December 31, 2007, an increase of $5.2 million, or 41%. The increase in operations and support expenses was primarily attributable to a $1.9 million increase in headcount related expenses, including a $0.4 million increase in cost at our outsourced customer support center, plus a $1.6 million increase in restaurant equipment costs, including depreciation on restaurant hardware, equipment and shipping costs in connection with the increase in the installed base of restaurants.

2006 compared to 2007. Operations and support expenses for the year ended December 31, 2007 were $12.6 million compared to $9.5 million for the year ended December 31, 2006, an increase of $3.1 million, or 32%. The increase in operations and support expenses was primarily attributable to a $1.6 million increase in headcount related expenses related to our expansion into international markets, including a $0.5 million increase in capacity at our outsourced customer support center, plus a $0.7 million increase in depreciation on restaurant hardware in connection with the increase in the installed customer base. The increase in both internal and external resources was a result of increasing capacity to meet the growth of new restaurant customers and an increase in the number of customers with more complex implementation requirements.

Sales and Marketing

| | Years Ended December 31, | | | 2006 to 2007 | 2007 to 2008 |
	2006	2007	2008	% Change	% Change
	(Dollars in thousands)				
Sales and marketing	$7,675	$11,326	$14,830	48%	31%
Headcount (at period end):					
North America	35	40	50	14	25
International	7	15	24	114	60
Total	42	55	74	31%	35%

2007 compared to 2008. Sales and marketing expenses for the year ended December 31, 2007 were $14.8 million compared to $11.3 million for the year ended December 31, 2007, an increase of $3.5 million, or 31%. The increase in sales and marketing expenses was primarily attributable to a $2.5 million increase in headcount related costs, consistent with the increase in headcount. Also included in headcount and related costs was an increase in commissions of $0.3 million consistent with the increase in newly contracted restaurant customers compared to the prior year.

2006 compared to 2007. Sales and marketing expenses for the year ended December 31, 2007 were $11.3 million compared to $7.7 million for the year ended December 31, 2006, an increase of $3.7 million, or 48%. The increase in sales and marketing expenses was primarily attributable to a

48

$3.1 million increase in headcount related costs, consistent with the increase in headcount. Also included in headcount and related costs was an increase in commissions of $1.0 million consistent with the increase in newly contracted restaurant customers compared to the prior year.

Technology

	Years Ended December 31,			2006 to 2007 % Change	2007 to 2008 % Change
	2006	2007	2008		
	(Dollars in thousands)				
Technology	$4,024	$5,863	$9,511	46%	62%
Headcount (at period end):					
North America	35	59	67	69	14
International	—	—	—		
Total	35	59	67	69%	14%

2007 compared to 2008. Technology expenses for the year ended December 31, 2008 were $9.5 million compared to $5.9 million for the year ended December 31, 2007, an increase of $3.6 million, or 62%. The increase in technology expenses was primarily attributable to a $3.2 million increase in headcount related costs, consistent with the increase in headcount that began in the second half of 2007.

2006 compared to 2007. Technology expenses for the year ended December 31, 2007 were $5.9 million compared to $4.0 million for the year ended December 31, 2006, an increase of $1.8 million, or 46%. The increase in technology expenses was primarily attributable to a $1.6 million increase in headcount related costs, consistent with the increase in headcount. We significantly increased the size of our technology team during 2007 to support website and ERB enhancements, the international expansion of our solutions and website, and system control enhancements.

General and Administrative

	Years Ended December 31,			2006 to 2007 % Change	2007 to 2008 % Change
	2006	2007	2008		
	(Dollars in thousands)				
General and administrative	$5,972	$12,212	$13,117	104%	7%
Headcount (at period end):					
North America	24	30	43	25	43
International	4	3	7	(25)	133
Total	28	33	50	18%	52%

2007 compared to 2008. General and administrative expenses for the year ended December 31, 2008 were $13.1 million compared to $12.2 million for the year ended December 31, 2007, an increase of $0.9 million, or 7%. The increase in general and administrative expenses was primarily the result of an increase of $1.6 million in headcount related costs and a $0.6 million increase in bad debt expense. These amounts were offset by a one-time legal settlement in the amount of $1.6 million included in the 2007 period.

2006 compared to 2007. General and administrative expenses for the year ended December 31, 2007 were $12.2 million compared to $6.0 million for the year ended December 31, 2006, an increase of $6.2 million, or 104%. The increase in general and administrative expenses was primarily the result of an increase of $2.3 million in headcount related costs, as a result of increased headcount, and an increase in professional services of $1.7 million to support international accounting efforts. A one-time $1.6 million legal settlement was also included in the 2007 period. Excluding the one-time

49

legal settlement costs, general and administrative costs increased as a result of the growth of our financial and accounting resources.

Other Income, Net

	Years Ended December 31,			2006 to 2007	2007 to 2008
	2006	2007	2008	% Change	% Change
	(Dollars in thousands)				
Other income, net	$421	$951	$468	126%	(51)%

2007 compared to 2008.   Other income, net for the year ended December 31, 2008 was $0.5 million compared to $1.0 million for the year ended December 31, 2007, a decrease of $0.5 million, or 51%. The decrease in other income, net was primarily the result of a $0.2 million decrease in interest income earned on cash, cash equivalents and short-term investments as a result of experiencing lower short-term borrowing interest rates, and a $0.3 million increase in foreign exchange transaction loss.

2006 compared to 2007.   Other income, net for the year ended December 31, 2007 was $1.0 million compared to $0.4 million for the year ended December 31, 2006, an increase of $0.5 million, or 126%. The increase in other income, net was primarily the result of a $0.4 million increase in interest income earned on cash, cash equivalents and short-term investments. Cash increased $11.4 million from 2006 to 2007, which together with higher short-term interest rates during the first half of 2007 resulted in significantly higher interest income.

Income Taxes

	Years Ended December 31,		
	2006	2007	2008
	(Dollars in thousands)		
Income tax expense (benefit)	$176	$(9,121)	$2,118

2007 compared to 2008.   Income tax expense for the year ended December 31, 2008 was $2.1 million compared to an income tax benefit of $9.1 million for the year ended December 31, 2007. Our income tax expense in 2008 was higher than the amount using the expected statutory rate by $1.6 million due to permanent differences, the largest of which was non-deductible stock-based compensation. The income tax benefit in 2007 was primarily the result of releasing substantially all of the valuation allowance against our deferred tax asset.

2006 compared to 2007.   In 2006, we recorded income taxes that were principally attributable to foreign taxes and other minimum corporate taxes. In those periods, we offset our taxable income through the utilization of net operating loss carryforwards. In the fourth quarter of 2007, we determined that it would be more likely than not that the cumulative net operating losses and other deferred tax benefits would be realizable by us, creating a $9.1 million income tax benefit due to the deferred tax asset recorded on our balance sheet at the end of 2007.

50

Quarterly Results of Operations Data

The following tables set forth our unaudited quarterly consolidated statements of operations data and our unaudited statements of operations data as a percentage of revenues for each of the nine quarters in the period ended March 31, 2009. We have prepared the quarterly data on a consistent basis with the audited consolidated financial statements included in this prospectus, and the financial information reflects all necessary adjustments, consisting only of normal recurring adjustments, necessary for a fair presentation of this data and assumes a 1-for-12.5 reverse stock split of our common stock and preferred stock to be effected immediately prior to the effectiveness of our initial public offering registration statement. The results of historical periods are not necessarily indicative of the results of operations for a full year or any future period.

| | For the Three Months Ended | | | | | | | | |
	Mar 31, 2007	Jun 30, 2007	Sep 30, 2007	Dec 31, 2007	Mar 31, 2008	Jun 30, 2008	Sep 30, 2008	Dec 31, 2008	Mar 31, 2009
	(In thousands, except per share amounts)								
REVENUES	$ 9,133	$ 9,743	$10,484	$11,788	$13,263	$13,858	$14,181	$14,542	$15,995
COSTS AND EXPENSES:									
Operations and support(1)	2,776	3,080	3,194	3,553	4,012	4,333	4,580	4,835	5,106
Sales and marketing(1)	2,465	2,620	2,892	3,349	3,591	3,719	3,755	3,765	3,798
Technology(1)	1,238	1,368	1,414	1,843	2,175	2,404	2,467	2,465	2,712
General and administrative(1)	2,165	2,299	4,549	3,199	3,144	3,412	3,449	3,112	3,547
Total costs and expenses	8,644	9,367	12,049	11,944	12,922	13,868	14,251	14,177	15,163
Income (loss) from operations	489	376	(1,565)	(156)	341	(10)	(70)	365	832
Other income, net	144	222	332	253	180	143	117	28	55
Income (loss) before taxes	633	598	(1,233)	97	521	133	47	393	887
Income tax expense (benefit)	61	63	63	(9,308)	608	(95)	337	1,268	521
NET INCOME (LOSS)	$ 572	$ 535	$(1,296)	$ 9,405	$ (87)	$ 228	$ (290)	$ (875)	$ 366
Net income (loss) per share:									
Basic	$ 0.06	$ 0.06	$ (0.14)	$ 0.97	$ (0.01)	$ 0.02	$ (0.03)	$ (0.09)	$ 0.04
Diluted	$ 0.03	$ 0.03	$ (0.14)	$ 0.46	$ (0.01)	$ 0.01	$ (0.03)	$ (0.09)	$ 0.02
Weighted average shares outstanding:									
Basic	9,286	9,478	9,589	9,728	9,850	9,963	10,071	10,178	10,276
Diluted	19,706	19,953	9,589	20,578	9,850	21,000	10,071	10,178	21,017

(1) Stock-based compensation is included in above line items:

Operations and support	$ 74	$ 80	$ 69	$ 67	$ 77	$ 96	$ 89	$ 77	$ 86
Sales and marketing	192	199	149	169	228	238	215	197	223
Technology	66	74	69	79	132	229	188	145	174
General and administrative	198	188	857	573	547	584	492	436	476
Total	$ 530	$ 541	$1,144	$ 888	$ 984	$1,147	$ 984	$ 855	$ 959

51

	Mar 31, 2007	Jun 30, 2007	Sep 30, 2007	Dec 31, 2007	Mar 31, 2008	Jun 30, 2008	Sep 30, 2008	Dec 31, 2008	Mar 31, 2009
				For the Three Months Ended					
Other Operational Data:									
Installed restaurants (at period end):									
North America	5,956	6,426	6,819	7,391	7,823	8,350	8,788	9,295	9,548
International	243	314	384	470	581	764	921	1,040	1,097
Total	6,199	6,740	7,203	7,861	8,404	9,114	9,709	10,335	10,645
Seated diners (in thousands):									
North America	5,545	5,733	6,185	7,151	8,395	8,454	8,272	8,515	9,922
International	42	50	61	91	123	130	120	169	186
Total	5,587	5,783	6,246	7,242	8,518	8,584	8,392	8,684	10,108
Headcount (at period end):									
North America	159	166	176	192	206	219	234	238	245
International	20	21	28	34	42	49	58	59	55
Total	179	187	204	226	248	268	292	297	300

(In thousands)

	Mar 31, 2007	Jun 30, 2007	Sep 30, 2007	Dec 31, 2007	Mar 31, 2008	Jun 30, 2008	Sep 30, 2008	Dec 31, 2008	Mar 31, 2009
Additional Financial Data:									
Revenues by location:									
North America	$ 8,876	$ 9,417	$10,047	$11,261	$12,667	$13,156	$13,431	$13,811	$15,189
International	257	326	437	527	596	702	750	731	806
Total	$ 9,133	$ 9,743	$10,484	$11,788	$13,263	$13,858	$14,181	$14,542	$15,995
Revenues by type:									
Subscription	$ 4,887	$ 5,348	$ 5,824	$ 6,375	$ 6,887	$ 7,417	$ 7,854	$ 8,135	$ 8,389
Reservation	3,904	4,002	4,218	4,886	5,830	5,836	5,669	5,800	6,904
Installation and other	342	393	442	527	546	605	658	607	702
Total	$ 9,133	$ 9,743	$10,484	$11,788	$13,263	$13,858	$14,181	$14,542	$15,995
Income (loss) from operations:									
North America	$ 1,506	$ 1,690	$ (359)	$ 2,137	$ 2,409	$ 2,171	$ 2,187	$ 2,321	$ 2,326
International	(1,017)	(1,314)	(1,208)	(2,291)	(2,068)	(2,181)	(2,257)	(1,956)	(1,494)
Total	$ 489	$ 376	$(1,567)	$ (154)	$ 341	$ (10)	$ (70)	$ 365	$ 832
Depreciation and amortization:									
North America	$ 604	$ 671	$ 733	$ 809	$ 877	$ 959	$ 1,060	$ 1,130	$ 1,159
International	40	35	44	65	74	86	92	98	104
Total	$ 644	$ 706	$ 777	$ 874	$ 951	$ 1,045	$ 1,152	$ 1,228	$ 1,263
Stock-based compensation expense:									
North America	$ 439	$ 461	$ 1,061	$ 801	$ 872	$ 1,035	$ 892	$ 764	$ 834
International	91	80	83	87	112	112	92	91	125
Total	$ 530	$ 541	$ 1,144	$ 888	$ 984	$ 1,147	$ 984	$ 855	$ 959

52

	For the Three Months Ended								
	Mar 31, 2007	Jun 30, 2007	Sep 30, 2007	Dec 31, 2007	Mar 31, 2008	Jun 30, 2008	Sep 30, 2008	Dec 31, 2008	Mar 31, 2009
	(as a percentage of revenues)								
REVENUES	100%	100%	100%	100%	100%	100%	100%	100%	100%
COSTS AND EXPENSES:									
Operations and support	30	32	31	30	30	31	32	33	32
Sales and marketing	27	27	28	28	28	27	27	27	24
Technology	14	14	13	16	16	17	17	17	17
General and administrative	24	23	43	27	24	25	24	21	22
Total costs and expenses	95	96	115	101	98	100	100	97	95
Income (loss) from operations	5	4	(15)	(1)	2	0	0	3	5
Other income, net	2	2	3	2	2	1	0	0	0
Income (loss) before taxes	7	6	(12)	1	4	1	0	3	5
Income tax expense (benefit)	1	1	0	(79)	5	(1)	2	9	3
NET INCOME (LOSS)	6%	5%	(12)%	80%	(1)%	2%	(2)%	(6)%	2%

Revenue has increased sequentially as a result of adding more installed restaurants each quarter. As the number of installed restaurants increases, subscription revenues increase. As the number of restaurants on our network increases, the number of diners using our services generally increases, and reservation revenues tend to increase. While we generally experience some seasonality in our reservation revenues, typically peaking during the holiday season from November through February (Valentine's Day), we have historically been able to consistently increase our revenues in each quarter. We expect that reservation revenues, as a percentage of total revenues, will continue to increase as our installed base of restaurants and seated diners increases over time.

Our operations and support expenses have increased sequentially in absolute dollars, and have remained generally consistent as a percentage of revenues over time. We expect operations and support expenses to continue to increase in absolute dollars as we add more restaurant customers to our network.

Our sales and marketing expenses have increased sequentially in absolute dollars, and have remained generally consistent as a percentage of revenues over time. We expect sales and marketing expenses to increase in absolute dollars as we increase our headcount to support further growth in North American and international markets.

Our technology expenses have increased sequentially in absolute dollars, and increased as a percentage of revenues beginning in the fourth quarter of 2007 when we significantly increased technology headcount focused on projects related to website and ERB enhancements, internationalization and system control enhancements. We expect technology expenses to modestly increase in absolute dollars as we slow our recent rate of headcount growth in the future.

Excluding a one-time legal settlement for $1.6 million in the third quarter of 2007, our general and administrative expenses have increased sequentially in absolute dollars, and have remained generally consistent as a percentage of revenues over time, as we increased our financial and accounting resources and headcount focused on our international efforts. We expect general and administrative expenses to modestly increase in absolute dollars in the future.

In the fourth quarter of 2007, we determined that it would be more likely than not that our cumulative net operating losses and other deferred tax benefits would be realizable by us, creating a $9.4 million income tax benefit due to the deferred tax asset recorded on our balance sheet at the end

53

of 2007. In the short term, we will experience high effective tax rates as a result of stock-based compensation amounts not being deductible as an expense for tax purposes and being sizable compared to our overall income (loss) before taxes.

Liquidity and Capital Resources

	Years Ended December 31,			Three Months Ended March 31,	
	2006	2007	2008	2008	2009
			(In thousands)		
Consolidated Statements of Cash Flows Data:					
Purchases of property and equipment	$ 3,606	$ 5,449	$ 7,203	$ 1,616	$1,368
Depreciation and amortization					
North America	2,029	2,817	4,026	877	1,159
International	89	184	350	74	104
Total depreciation and amortization	2,118	3,001	4,376	951	1,263
Cash flows provided by operating activities	$ 5,903	$11,158	$ 8,544	$ 780	$3,694
Cash flows provided by (used in) investing activities	(3,039)	(5,025)	(24,330)	(1,616)	2,632
Cash flows provided by (used in) financing activities	(618)	5,269	(80)	35	16

As of March 31, 2009, we had cash and cash equivalents of $12.0 million and short-term investments of $13.2 million. Cash and cash equivalents consist of cash, money market accounts, certificates of deposit and commercial paper. Short-term investments consist of U.S. government agency securities, commercial paper and certificates of deposit. To date, we have experienced no loss or lack of access to our invested cash, cash equivalents or short-term investments; however, we can provide no assurances that access to our invested cash, cash equivalents and short-term investments will not be impacted by adverse conditions in the financial markets.

Amounts deposited with third party financial institutions exceed the Federal Deposit Insurance Corporation, or FDIC, and Securities Investor Protection Corporation, or SIPC, insurance limits, as applicable. These cash, cash equivalents and short-term investment balances could be impacted if the underlying financial institutions fail or are subjected to other adverse conditions in the financial markets. To date we have experienced no loss or lack of access to our cash, cash equivalents or short-term investments.

We have a $3.0 million line of credit to fund working capital under which we have no amounts drawn down as of March 31, 2009. This line of credit expires in July 2009.

Prior to 2005, we financed our operations and capital expenditures through private sales of preferred stock, lease financing, the use of a bank-provided line of credit and operations. Since 2005, we have been able to finance our operations, including international expansion, through cash from operating activities and proceeds from the exercise of vested and unvested employee stock options. We had cash and cash equivalents of $12.0 million at March 31, 2009, which is up $6.5 million from December 31, 2008, primarily due to the sale of $4.7 million of short-term investments. We believe we will have sufficient cash and cash equivalents and short-term investments to support our operating activities for at least the next twelve months.

Operating Activities

For the three months ended March 31, 2009, operating activities provided $3.7 million in cash, as a result of net income of $0.4 million, depreciation and amortization of $1.3 million and stock-based compensation of $1.0 million.

In 2008, operating activities provided $8.5 million in cash, as a result of a net loss of $1.0 million, offset by $4.4 million in depreciation and amortization and $4.0 million in stock-based

54

compensation. These amounts were offset by a cash usage of $2.2 million as a result of an increase in accounts receivable.

In 2007, operating activities provided $11.2 million in cash as a result of net income of $9.2 million, depreciation and amortization amounts of $3.0 million and stock-based compensation amounts of $3.1 million, combined with sources of cash from a $2.8 million increase in accounts payable and accrued expenses, a $2.3 million increase in the Dining Points payable, and a $1.1 million increase from deferred revenues. These amounts were offset by deferred taxes of $9.4 million and a cash usage of $1.8 million resulting from the increase in accounts receivable.

In 2006, operating activities provided $5.9 million in cash as a result of $0.2 million net income, $2.1 million in depreciation and amortization, increases in the Dining Points payable of $1.5 million, increases in deferred revenues of $1.0 million and $0.7 million in stock-based compensation.

Investing Activities

Our primary investing activities have consisted of purchases and sales of short-term investments and purchases of property and equipment. We expect to have ongoing capital expenditure requirements to support our growing restaurant installed base and other infrastructure needs. We expect to fund this investment with our existing cash, cash equivalents and short-term investments.

Financing Activities

Our financing activities have consisted primarily of net proceeds from the issuance and repurchase of common stock in each of the periods presented. During 2006, we repurchased 207,047 common shares from a common stockholder for total proceeds of $0.6 million, which resulted in net cash used of $0.6 million for the year. In 2007, proceeds from the issuance of common stock were $5.4 million, resulting from the exercise of employee stock options. In 2008, financing activities included the payment of $0.2 million in offering costs associated with the proposed initial public offering.

Quantitative and Qualitative Disclosure About Market Risk

We are exposed to market risks in the ordinary course of our business. These risks include primarily interest rate, foreign exchange risks and inflation.

Interest Rate Fluctuation Risk

We do not have any long-term borrowings.

Our investments include cash, cash equivalents and short-term investments. Cash and cash equivalents consist of cash, money market accounts, certificates of deposit and commercial paper. Short-term investments consist of U.S. government agency securities, commercial paper and certificates of deposit. The primary objective of our investment activities is to preserve principal while maximizing income without significantly increasing risk. We do not enter into investments for trading or speculative purposes. Our investments are exposed to market risk due to a fluctuation in interest rates, which may affect our interest income and the fair market value of our investments. Due to the short-term nature of our investment portfolio, we do not believe an immediate 10% increase in interest rates would have a material effect on the fair market value of our portfolio, and therefore we do not expect our operating results or cash flows to be materially affected to any degree by a sudden change in market interest rates.

Foreign Currency Exchange Risk

We have foreign currency risks related to our revenues and operating expenses denominated in currencies other than the U.S. dollar, principally the British pound sterling, the euro, the Japanese yen, the Canadian dollar and the Mexican peso. We do not believe movements in the foreign currencies in

55

which we transact will significantly affect future net earnings. Foreign currency risk can be quantified by estimating the change in cash flows resulting from a hypothetical 10% adverse change in foreign exchange rates. We believe such a change would not have a material impact on our results of operations.

Inflation Risk

We do not believe that inflation has had a material effect on our business, financial condition or results of operations. If our costs were to become subject to significant inflationary pressures, we may not be able to fully offset such higher costs through price increases. Our inability or failure to do so could harm our business, financial condition and results of operations.

Off Balance Sheet Arrangements

As of March 31, 2009, we did not have any off balance sheet arrangements.

Contractual Obligations

We lease our primary office space in San Francisco, California and other locations under various non-cancelable operating leases that expire between 2009 and 2013. We have no debt obligations, other than a $3.0 million line of credit for working capital, which to date has not had any borrowings under it. This credit facility expires in July 2009. Additionally, all property and equipment have been purchased for cash, and accordingly we have no capital lease obligations. Finally, we have no material long-term purchase obligations outstanding with any vendors or third parties.

	Payments Under Operating Leases (In thousands)
Year ending December 31:	
2009	$ 1,326
2010	1,348
2011	1,322
2012	1,344
2013	454
Total	$ 5,794

Recent Accounting Pronouncements

Effective January 1, 2008, we adopted SFAS No. 157, *Fair Value Measurements* (SFAS No. 157). In February 2008, the FASB issued a staff position, FSP No. 157-2, that delays the effective date of SFAS No. 157 for all non-financial assets and liabilities except for those recognized or disclosed in the financial statements at fair value at least annually. Therefore, we have adopted the provision of SFAS No. 157 with respect to our financial assets and liabilities only. SFAS No. 157 defines fair value, establishes a framework for measuring fair value and expands disclosures about fair value measurements. Fair value is defined under SFAS No. 157 as the exchange price that would be received for an asset or paid to transfer a liability (an exit price) in the principal or most advantageous market for the asset or liability in an orderly transaction between market participants on the measurement date. Valuation techniques used to measure fair value under SFAS No. 157 must maximize the use of observable inputs and minimize the use of unobservable inputs. The standard describes a fair value hierarchy based on three levels of inputs, of which the first two are considered observable and the last unobservable, that may be used to measure fair value which are the following:

Level 1—Quoted prices in active markets for identical assets or liabilities.

56

Level 2—Inputs other than Level 1 that are observable, either directly or indirectly, such as quoted prices for similar assets or liabilities; quoted prices in markets that are not active; or other inputs that are observable or can be corroborated by observable market data for substantially the full term of the assets or liabilities.

Level 3—Unobservable inputs that are supported by little or no market activity and that are significant to the fair value of the assets or liabilities.

The adoption of this statement required additional disclosures of assets and liabilities measured at fair value; it did not have a material impact on our consolidated results of operations and financial condition.

Effective January 1, 2008, we adopted SFAS No. 159, *The Fair Value Option for Financial Assets and Financial Liabilities* (SFAS No. 159) which permits entities to choose to measure many financial instruments and certain other items at fair value that are not currently required to be measured at fair value. We did not elect to adopt the fair value option under SFAS No. 159 as this Statement is not expected to have a material impact on our consolidated results of operations and financial condition.

In December 2007, the FASB issued SFAS No. 141(Revised 2007), *Business Combinations* (SFAS No. 141(R)). SFAS No. 141(R) establishes principles and requirements for how the acquirer of a business recognizes and measures in its financial statements the identifiable assets acquired, the liabilities assumed, and any noncontrolling interest in the acquiree. SFAS No. 141(R) also provides guidance for recognizing and measuring the goodwill acquired in the business combination and determines what information to disclose to enable users of the financial statements to evaluate the nature and financial effects of the business combination. We were required to adopt SFAS No. 141(R) for the fiscal year beginning January 1, 2009. The adoption of SFAS No. 141(R) did not have a material impact on our financial position or results of operations at the time of adoption.

In December 2007, the FASB issued SFAS No. 160, *Non-controlling Interests in Consolidated Financial Statements* (SFAS No. 160) which amends Accounting Research Bulletin No. 51, *Consolidated Financial Statements* (ARB No. 51), to establish accounting and reporting standards for the non-controlling interest in a subsidiary and for the deconsolidation of a subsidiary. It clarifies that a non-controlling interest in a subsidiary is an ownership interest in the consolidated entity that should be reported as equity separate and apart from the parent's equity in the consolidated financial statements. In addition to the amendments to ARB No. 51, this statement amends SFAS No. 128, *Earnings Per Share*, so that earnings per share data will continue to be calculated the same way those data were calculated before this statements was issued. SFAS No. 160 is effective for fiscal years, and interim periods within those fiscal years, beginning on or after December 15, 2008. The adoption of SFAS No. 160 did not have a material impact on our financial position or results of operations at the time of adoption.

In May 2008, the FASB issued SFAS No. 162, *The Hierarchy of General Accepted Accounting Principles* (SFAS No. 162). This statement documents the hierarchy of the various sources of accounting principles and the framework for selecting the principles used in preparing financial statements. This statement shall be effective 60 days following the SEC's approval of the Public Company Accounting Oversight Board amendments to AU Section 411, *The Meaning of Present Fairly in Conformity With Generally Accepted Accounting Principles*. We do not expect the adoption of SFAS No. 162 to have a material impact on our results of operations and financial position.

57

BUSINESS

Overview

We provide solutions that form an online network connecting reservation-taking restaurants and people who dine at those restaurants. Our solutions include our proprietary Electronic Reservation Book, or ERB, for restaurant customers and www.opentable.com, a popular restaurant reservation website for diners. The OpenTable network includes approximately 10,000 OpenTable restaurant customers spanning all 50 states as well as select markets outside of the United States. Since our inception in 1998, we have seated approximately 100 million diners through OpenTable reservations, and during the three months ended March 31, 2009, we seated an average of approximately three million diners per month. Restaurants pay us a one-time installation fee for onsite installation and training, a monthly subscription fee for the use of our software and hardware and a fee for each restaurant guest seated through online reservations. Our online restaurant reservation service is free to diners. For the twelve months ended December 31, 2007 and 2008, our net revenues were $41.1 million and $55.8 million, respectively. For the twelve months ended December 31, 2007 and 2008, our subscription revenues accounted for 55% and 54% of our total revenues, respectively, our reservation revenues accounted for 41% and 41% of our total revenues, respectively, and our installation and other revenues accounted for 4% and 5% of our total revenues, respectively. For the three months ended March 31, 2008 and 2009, our subscription revenues accounted for 52% and 52% of our total revenues, respectively, our reservation revenues accounted for 44% and 43% of our total revenues, respectively, and our installation and other revenues accounted for 4% and 5% of our total revenues, respectively.

The OpenTable ERB combines proprietary software and computer hardware to deliver a solution that computerizes restaurant host-stand operations and replaces traditional pen-and-paper reservation books. Our ERB streamlines and enhances a number of business-critical functions and processes for restaurants, including reservation management, table management, guest recognition and email marketing. This enables restaurants to manage all of their reservations—those booked by phone or online as well as walk-in diners—in one unified system. The ERB also automatically accepts online reservations in real time directly from the OpenTable website as well as from websites of our partners and restaurant customers. The ERBs at our restaurant customers connect via the Internet to form an online network of restaurant reservation books. We also operate the OpenTable website, which enables diners to quickly and conveniently find, choose and book tables at restaurants on the OpenTable network, overcoming the inefficiencies associated with the traditional process of reserving by phone. Diners appreciate the convenience of being able to secure a reservation at any time, even when the restaurant is closed, and the time savings of being able to instantly find and reserve available tables without having to call restaurants one by one until they find an available reservation that suits their needs. Online visitors come to the OpenTable website directly, via natural search engine results and via our partners' and restaurant customers' websites. During the twelve months ended December 31, 2008, less than 1% of reservations made through our website were attributable to paid-search advertising.

We initially focused on acquiring a critical mass of local restaurant customers in four metropolitan areas: Chicago, New York, San Francisco and Washington, D.C. These markets have since developed into active, local networks of restaurants and diners that continue to grow. We have applied and continue to apply the same fundamental strategy in developing and penetrating our other markets in the United States, Canada and Mexico. In 2004, we began to selectively expand into countries outside of North America that are characterized by large numbers of online consumer transactions and reservation-taking restaurants. To date, we have concentrated our international efforts in Germany, Japan and the United Kingdom. Our revenues outside of North America for the twelve months ended December 31, 2007 and 2008, were $1.5 million and $2.8 million, respectively, or 4% and 5% of our total revenues, respectively. Our revenues outside of North America for the three months ended March 31, 2009, were $0.8 million, or 5% of our total revenues.

58

Restaurant Industry Background

The commercial restaurant industry is broadly divided into "quick-service" and "full-service" segments. We target our offerings to full-service restaurants that accept reservations. We believe based on our internal estimates that there are approximately 30,000 reservation-taking restaurants in North America that seat approximately 600 million diners through reservations annually, though this number fluctuates with economic and other conditions.

The ability of the restaurant industry to leverage the power of the Internet for reservation transactions has been inhibited by two key characteristics. First, the reservation-taking restaurant industry has been slow to computerize host-stand operations. During the last decade, other reservation-taking industries, such as airlines and hotels, have experienced a dramatic shift in consumer behavior as reservations have migrated from the phone to the Internet. In contrast, given the restaurant industry's relatively basic transaction needs, generally requiring only the diner's name and phone number and no advance payment, restaurant reservations historically have been largely handled by the traditional pen-and-paper reservation book, despite the inherent operational inefficiencies and potential for error. Second, the reservation-taking restaurant industry is highly fragmented, with independent restaurants and small, local restaurant groups comprising a significant majority of restaurant locations. Unlike other industries in which suppliers can deliver goods and services to customers around the world, the restaurant industry is inherently local. These conditions make it time-consuming and costly to aggregate the breadth of local restaurant table inventory required to attract a critical mass of diners to make reservations online and to create an online restaurant reservation network.

In addition, reservation-taking restaurants generally share the following operational challenges:

- *Profitability is dependent on filling seats.* Because restaurants typically have a high fixed cost structure, restaurant profitability is heavily dependent on filling as many seats as possible. Similar to hotel rooms and airplane seats, restaurant table inventory is highly perishable, with unfilled seats representing a significant lost revenue opportunity.

- *Prospective business is lost due to the inefficiencies of reserving by phone.* Most restaurants are not staffed to answer the phone until late morning or early afternoon, and many are only open six days per week. As a result, they lose potential business when prospective guests are not able to secure reservations by phone at their convenience. Additionally, restaurants experience costly "no-shows" when guests fail to cancel their reservations because of the inconvenience of doing so over the phone.

- *Managing and preserving guest information is difficult.* One of the ways in which restaurants compete is by providing exceptional, personalized service, for example, by recognizing repeat diners and recalling their preferences or special occasions. Guest histories and preferences are typically stored in the memories of the maitre d' or host, and therefore the implications of losing a staff member who is familiar with a restaurant's best and most frequent guests are considerable. In an industry characterized by a high rate of employee turnover, the ability to preserve and transfer this information is critical.

- *Information technology resources to install and support computer-based systems are limited.* Few restaurants have the technical knowledge, resources or time to install computer systems and troubleshoot problems with computer systems or Internet connectivity. At the same time, the fast pace of business operations means that restaurants cannot tolerate service interruptions from an equipment or networking failure.

- *Marketing opportunities with measurable results are limited.* Typically, restaurants promote themselves through magazines and newspapers as well as online dining guides and directories. However, restaurants generally do not have the ability to track the number of people who ultimately dine in response to their advertisements, nor are the costs of these advertisements tied to the number of diners they attract. Therefore, restaurants usually are unable to measure or compare the effectiveness of these marketing channels.

59

Table of Contents

Diner Behavior and Trends

For many diners, part of the appeal of dining out is experiencing a variety of restaurants. Therefore, diners value sources that help them discover new restaurants and provide information about these restaurants. Historically, diners learned about restaurants through word of mouth and local print media, such as dining guides, newspapers and magazines. While diners continue to value personal recommendations, the Internet now puts a wealth of restaurant information at their fingertips. However, arguably the most important piece of information—what restaurants can accommodate a dining party—has been missing from online dining sources. As a result, when it comes to booking a restaurant reservation, diners have had to use the phone instead of the Internet.

Reserving by phone can be a highly inefficient and inconvenient process, requiring diners to call one restaurant at a time until they find an available reservation that meets their needs, and then make a reservation without knowing the full range of available choices. Phone reservations can only be secured during the restaurant's business hours. Diners who call when a restaurant is closed or during peak service hours oftentimes must leave a voicemail message and wait for the restaurant to call back. Diners who do get through to a reservationist may be put on hold or informed that there are no available tables at the desired time, requiring them to call another restaurant and repeat the process until they find a suitable reservation. Diners who need to change or cancel an existing reservation experience similar difficulties in doing so by phone.

The Internet has the potential to redefine the reservation experience for diners and streamline the operations and increase the return on marketing spend for reservation-taking restaurants. In order for diners to fully embrace online restaurant reservations, they need real-time access to table inventory across a broad selection of local restaurants and the ability to instantly book confirmed reservations around-the-clock.

Our Solution

Reservation-taking restaurants and diners have interconnected needs. Restaurants require cost-effective ways to attract guests and manage their reservations, while diners seek convenient ways to find available restaurants, choose among them and secure reservations. By creating an online network of restaurants and diners that transact with each other through real-time reservations, we have developed a specialized platform for addressing the needs of both.

Essential to this network is building a critical mass of local, computerized restaurant reservation books. We achieve this by offering software that provides important operational benefits for the restaurant, bundling it with computer hardware and installing this solution at the restaurant host stand, thereby creating a compelling solution for restaurants. We sell our solutions to individual restaurants within a market, typically one by one, via a direct sales force. We believe that we deliver a strong return on investment for our restaurant customers by streamlining their operations, filling additional seats and improving their quality of service. As a result, we have historically enjoyed high customer satisfaction and retention rates.

The OpenTable website gives diners real-time access to tables at restaurants on the OpenTable network. As more local restaurants are added to the network, the utility provided to diners increases and more diners discover the benefits of researching restaurants and making reservations on our website. The more diners who use our website to make their dining decisions, the more value we deliver to our restaurant customers and the more restaurants are attracted to our network.

Benefits of OpenTable to Reservation-Taking Restaurants

In response to the needs of reservation-taking restaurants, we offer the OpenTable ERB, an integrated solution consisting of proprietary OpenTable software which is installed on a touch-screen computer system and supported by various asset-protection and security tools. Additionally, we provide

60

restaurants with access to diners via our website as well as through our partners' websites. Participation in the OpenTable network helps restaurants:

- *Fill seats that might otherwise remain empty.* We help restaurants fill their seats and minimize "no-shows" by offering the convenience of online reservations directly through the OpenTable website as well as indirectly through the websites of our partners and restaurant customers, all of which are stored in the ERB. In addition, restaurants may elect to be featured in OpenTable marketing programs, which drive incremental business to participating restaurants through enhanced listings on the OpenTable website. Participating restaurants pay OpenTable a premium per-seated diner fee for diners seated in response to these special listings.

- *Create operational efficiencies by automating reservations and table management.* The reservation module of the ERB replaces the restaurant's pen-and-paper system with a computerized reservation book that records and tracks all reservations (online, phone and walk-in) in the same system, thereby improving accuracy and efficiency. Floor management capabilities improve operational efficiencies by helping restaurants maximize seat utilization, facilitate server rotations and improve table turns.

- *Boost guest recognition and overall guest service.* The integrated guest-management database included in the ERB enables restaurant staff to record diner preferences and histories in order to recognize repeat diners and provide them with personalized service. The ERB also includes email capabilities which provide restaurants with a cost-effective channel to reach and attract repeat diners. Additionally, we help restaurants monitor customer satisfaction by collecting and delivering guest feedback from OpenTable diners.

- *Computerize host-stand operations with customized, on-site installation and training and technical support.* We install our ERB, which combines proprietary software and computer hardware, at the restaurant, verifying Internet connectivity, configuring the system for the restaurant's unique needs and training staff members on its use. We monitor Internet connectivity and assist the restaurant in resolving connectivity issues. Additionally, we perform nightly data backups that enable us to restore the reservation book if necessary, and we provide around-the-clock technical support.

- *Market to a targeted audience with measurable results.* Our website enables diners to find restaurants that can accommodate them, giving restaurants valuable marketing exposure during the diners' decision-making process. Moreover, restaurants pay OpenTable only for those diners whom they ultimately serve, unlike other marketing channels such as magazines, newspapers and online dining guides and directories. Consequently, restaurants know the number of diners acquired through OpenTable and the costs of acquiring each of these diners.

Benefits of OpenTable to Diners

In response to the needs of diners, we offer the OpenTable website, a destination website for those seeking a convenient way to research restaurants and make reservations. Our website enables diners to:

- *Find available tables.* Diners can search for reservations by location, date, time and party size and view table availability across a variety of restaurants. Because our website connects directly to the thousands of ERBs residing at OpenTable restaurants, reservation search results reflect real-time availability.

- *Choose a restaurant.* In response to their searches on our website, diners are presented with a list of restaurants with available reservations at their desired dining times. Diners may also click on a restaurant listing to view additional information, including restaurant descriptions,

61

photos and menus. While making their restaurant choices, diners may also consult the OpenTable Diners' Choice lists that highlight restaurants that are most highly rated by OpenTable diners, for example, Best Overall, Best Italian, Most Romantic or Good for Groups.

- *Book instantly confirmed reservations for free.* When a diner reserves through the OpenTable website, the reservation is instantly recorded in the ERB located at the restaurant—the same system in which the host would record a phone reservation. Diners can also change or cancel reservations online as well as invite guests via email. Diners receive on-screen and email messages confirming their reservation details. Additionally, registered diners can earn Dining Reward Points when they make and honor OpenTable reservations. Points can be redeemed for Dining Cheques that are accepted at OpenTable restaurant customers.

Our Strategy

As our network of reservation-taking restaurants and diners grows, the value we deliver grows as well. Because the foundation of our network is building a critical mass of computerized reservation books, we enhance our offering to diners by adding new restaurant customers. In turn, as more diners use the OpenTable website to make their dining decisions and book their reservations, we deliver more value to our restaurant customers by helping them fill more of their seats. In this process, we grow the value of our business. The key elements of this strategy include:

Continue to Build the OpenTable Network in North America

The value of the OpenTable network grows as participation among restaurants and diners grows. Experience in our earliest markets provides a successful model that we have implemented while entering new markets, and, as a result, our newer markets in North America have grown relatively predictably over time. We intend to continue to build our North American network by employing this proven model.

- *Produce and maintain superior solutions.* We continue to evolve our ERB based on nearly a decade of in-field experience as well as feedback from our installed base of approximately 10,000 restaurant customers. Additionally, we will continue to optimize our website through insights gained from the experience of seating approximately 100 million diners through online reservations.

- *Leverage our direct sales force.* Over the last ten years, we have expended considerable resources to build a direct sales force skilled at selling the benefits of OpenTable to reservation-taking restaurants, which operate in an industry that is highly fragmented. We will continue to leverage our skilled direct sales force to add more restaurants to the network.

- *Provide excellent customer service and support.* We believe that our superior customer service is an integral component of high satisfaction rates among our restaurant customers and provides us with a deep understanding of restaurant needs and general industry trends. We will continue to employ highly trained operational teams to provide installation and training services for our restaurant customers and augment our in-house support staff with contract support services to deliver superior customer assistance.

- *Continue to attract diners to our website by offering the best reservation experience.* We believe that providing the best diner reservation experience increases market adoption of our services, builds our brand awareness and drives word-of-mouth referrals to our website. We continue to enhance our website for ease of use and augment it with unique, helpful restaurant content. For example, we have begun to leverage the collective feedback of OpenTable diners to publish user-generated content that diners use while making restaurant

62

choices. We will continue to evolve the diner reservation experience on our website through usability testing and website analytics.

Expand Internationally

We intend to augment our growing North American business by selectively expanding into countries outside of North America that are characterized by large numbers of online consumer transactions and reservation-taking restaurants. We currently have operations in Germany, Japan and the United Kingdom, each supported with a direct sales force and operational staff. We have approximately 1,000 restaurant customers in these markets. In general, our strategy internationally is to replicate the model we have successfully employed in North America. In particular, our initial focus in new international markets is to increase our restaurant customer base, and we believe the localized versions of our software solution will compete favorably against competitive software offerings, enabling us to expand our network of computerized reservation books across a broad selection of local restaurants.

Our Products

We have created a proprietary technology system comprised of stand-alone client-server applications located at each restaurant that connect via the Internet to our central servers which host our website. The distributed nature of this system design enables us to provide real-time solutions to our restaurant customers and to diners.

Restaurant Software and Hardware and Related Solutions

The ERB is an integrated solution consisting of proprietary OpenTable software that is installed on a dedicated, touch-screen computer system at the restaurant's host stand and supported by various asset-protection and security tools. The ERB supports reservation management, table and floor management, guest management, marketing and a number of other business processes. This functionality has evolved through seven major software releases over nine years based on feedback from and experience with thousands of restaurant customers. The software is built on a foundation that supports rapid translation into local languages.

We provide on-site installation, training and round-the-clock customer support for the ERB as part of our monthly subscription fee. We monitor Internet connectivity to the ERB, alerting restaurants when they are offline and working with them to resolve any problems we detect. We also provide data protection services, including managing firewalls and virus scanning software on all computers on our network to protect restaurants from harmful intrusions and performing nightly backups of each restaurant's database to prevent data loss in the event of a hardware failure. Our restaurant customers also receive a hardware replacement, populated with the restaurant's backed-up data, in the event of a computer failure, and software upgrades and updates, which are deployed automatically via the Internet to each ERB, requiring minimal interference with the restaurant's operations.

OpenTable Website

We design, build and operate the OpenTable website in North America and the United Kingdom as well as websites localized for Germany and Japan. Our system is a real-time reservation system with a patent pending on our high-speed inventory tracking and search technology. The OpenTable website maintains around-the-clock communications with restaurants on our online reservation network. As a result, any change made at the restaurant to the table inventory that affects the OpenTable website is updated on the website in real time, and diners using the website get current inventory information on every search request, typically in a few seconds.

In addition to the OpenTable website, we offer versions of the OpenTable website optimized for use on mobile devices.

63

OTRestaurant Website

We design, build and operate the OTRestaurant website, which serves as an information and services portal for our restaurant customers. The website provides restaurant customers with secure access to client-specific materials including detailed online reservation reports, online invoicing and feedback forms from recent diners. In addition, a restaurant can visit the OTRestaurant website to learn about upcoming OpenTable promotions, submit date-specific information such as Valentine's Day menus and update the profile information displayed on the OpenTable website, for example, restaurant description and hours of operation. The OTRestaurant website serves as a two-way communication channel between us and our restaurant customers, which ultimately improves the support we provide and drives increased operational efficiencies.

Sales and Marketing

Sales and Marketing to Restaurants

We employ a direct sales force of regional account executives. Our sales and marketing efforts focus on identifying qualified sales leads, communicating the benefits of computerizing the restaurant reservation book and filling seats through online reservations. Our marketing activities include lead generation, direct marketing, public relations and participation in trade shows and conferences.

Marketing to Diners

We enjoy significant word-of-mouth referrals and natural-search traffic to our website. We encourage repeat usage through our points-based loyalty program, OpenTable Dining Rewards, which allows diners to earn Dining Points when they make and honor OpenTable reservations. We also optimize our website to improve our positioning in natural search engine results. To date, we have found limited value in print, broadcast, online or paid-search advertising, and, as a result, we do not purchase a material amount of marketing from those channels.

In addition to operating our own destination website, we work with hundreds of partners to enhance their restaurant listings with OpenTable online reservation capabilities. We also encourage our restaurant customers to incorporate OpenTable reservation capabilities into their own websites, which not only introduces diners to the convenience of online reservations but also helps restaurants fill more seats by providing around-the-clock reservation capabilities.

Customer Support

One of the reasons we enjoy high satisfaction among our restaurant customers is the quality of the solutions we provide. These solutions include the following:

Implementation Services for Restaurants

Once the customer agreement is signed, an OpenTable Project Coordinator, or PC, contacts the restaurant to begin the implementation process. The PC works with a contact at the restaurant to schedule and plan for successful system installation and training. This includes the completion of a site survey to gather restaurant-specific information such as table layouts, reservation timeslot configuration, network and Internet connectivity setup, and other information necessary to properly set up the OpenTable system. Armed with a completed site survey, a Field Operations Specialist, or FOS, configures the OpenTable system for the restaurant prior to the on-site installation.

During a typical installation, the FOS loads the software onto the computer system provided by OpenTable, establishes proper network connectivity and checks the system by entering a test reservation from the OpenTable website. Working with the restaurant manager, the FOS then uses the administrative functionality of the ERB software to configure and optimize the restaurant's

64

computerized reservation book. The FOS also provides training to restaurant staff on using the various modules in the ERB.

Ongoing Restaurant Relationship Management

Each of our restaurant customers is assigned to an OpenTable Client Relations Manager, or CRM, who is the primary contact for that restaurant and owns the post-implementation restaurant relationship. CRMs encourage maximum utilization of the ERB to ensure that the restaurant realizes the full value of the system. For example, the CRM assists restaurants in adjusting their reservation books to maximize capacity utilization, reservation-enabling their websites, tracking guest preferences and marketing to their diners.

Restaurant Telephone Support

After the initial installation and training, restaurants may contact OpenTable via a toll-free number to receive technical support and follow-up training as part of our monthly service fee. Live telephone support is available 14 hours per day, seven days a week, with emergency support available around-the-clock.

All customer contacts are tracked in our proprietary Restaurant Operations Management System, or ROMS, to ensure cases are resolved quickly and completely. Cases are categorized by reason and sub-reason codes to identify trends and support root-cause analyses. These analyses provide important feedback to drive future process improvements and solutions enhancements.

Most routine support cases are handled by a U.S.-based third-party customer support partner. When necessary, the support partner escalates calls to our in-house support team located at our headquarters in San Francisco. Our support partner receives equivalent training and access to the same tools as the San Francisco support team.

Consumer Support for Website Users

Diners with questions about the OpenTable reservation network or the OpenTable website can access an online list of dynamically ordered frequently asked questions, or FAQs. If none of the FAQs address the concern, a diner can email our support team via a web-based form. We use a third-party email management system to queue, assign, track, categorize and report on these email inquiries. Emails are categorized to support analysis for website enhancement and continuous process improvement.

Technology

Our technology infrastructure supports the network of restaurants and diners critical to our business.

Data Centers and Network Access

Our primary data center is hosted by a leading provider of hosting services in Santa Clara, California. Backup systems in our corporate headquarters in San Francisco can be brought online in the event of a failure at the primary data center. We are in the process of bringing up a second data center site at a facility outside of California. The site will enable additional fault tolerance and will support our continued growth.

The data center hosts the OpenTable website, the OTRestaurant website and intranet applications that are used to manage the website content. The websites are designed to be fault-tolerant, with a collection of identical web servers connecting to an enterprise database. The design also includes load balancers, firewalls and routers that connect the components and provide connections to

65

the Internet. The failure of any individual component is not expected to affect the overall availability of our website.

Our system also includes a proprietary method of accessing website-relevant, real-time restaurant inventory from the data center, providing very fast response times. The system is designed to scale to accommodate the foreseeable growth in the number of restaurants and diners on our network.

Network Security

The data center and restaurant systems maintain real-time communication with proprietary, encrypted message protocols. We also use leading commercial antivirus, firewall and patch-management technology to protect and maintain the systems located at the data center and at each restaurant.

Internal Management Systems

We have developed proprietary systems to ensure rapid, high-quality customer service, software development and website updates. ROMS is a system-integrated customer support application that gives us unique customer resource management tools designed specifically for the restaurant industry. It houses detailed restaurant customer information encompassing the entire customer lifecycle, including initiating a contract, installing the OpenTable system, issuing monthly bills, tracking restaurant inventory and providing ongoing support. In addition, ROMS leverages system-integrated tools allowing for remote technical diagnosis and repair, while operating under multi-tiered security protocols to ensure restaurant customer information is protected. The Customer Help and Restaurant Management system, or CHARM, is a proprietary web content management and consumer support tool that enables rapid website customization. Restaurant profiles, descriptions, maps, partner reviews, restaurant messaging and reservation parameter configurations are all driven out of CHARM.

Development

We devote a substantial portion of our resources to developing new solutions and enhancing existing solutions, conducting product testing and quality assurance testing, improving core technology and strengthening our technological expertise in the restaurant table management and reservation market. As of March 31, 2009, our technical group consisted of 69 employees, who are focused on new feature development for existing solutions and the design of new solutions. We also outsource a portion of our software development to a third-party service provider located in India. For the twelve months ended December 31, 2007 and 2008 and the three months ended March 31, 2009, technology expenses totaled $5.9 million, $9.5 million and $2.7 million, respectively.

Intellectual Property

Our success depends upon our ability to protect our core technology and intellectual property. To accomplish this, we rely on a combination of intellectual property rights, including trade secrets, patents, copyrights and trademarks, as well as contractual restrictions. We enter into confidentiality and proprietary rights agreements with our employees, consultants and business partners, and we control access to and distribution of our proprietary information.

We have one issued patent which expires in 2020 and four patent applications pending in the United States. We have one patent application pending in India. We intend to pursue corresponding patent coverage in additional countries to the extent we believe such coverage is appropriate and cost effective.

Our registered trademarks in the United States and Japan include "OpenTable" and the OpenTable logo. "OpenTable" is also registered in Canada, Mexico, Australia and the European Union. "OpenTable.com" is also registered in the European Union. We have filed other trademark applications in the United States and certain other countries.

66

We are the registrant of the Internet domain name for our websites, www.opentable.com, www.otrestaurant.com and our international websites.

In addition to the foregoing protections, we generally control access to and use of our proprietary software and other confidential information through the use of internal and external controls, including contractual protections with employees, contractors, customers and partners. Our software is protected by United States and international copyright laws.

Competition

Competition for Reservation-Taking Restaurants

The primary competitor for the OpenTable ERB is the traditional pen-and-paper reservation book. Paper-based reservation books enjoy the advantage of being extremely familiar and simple; however, they are also time-consuming, error-prone, manual and not easily reproduced in case of loss or damage. Through our sales efforts, we explain the benefits of automation to restaurants including greater operational efficiency, superior guest recognition and service and the ability to fill additional seats by offering reservations over the Internet. Other companies attempt to address restaurant needs for computerized reservation management with a variety of technologies.

We believe the principal competitive factors in the market for computerized restaurant reservation management solutions include:

- comprehensive reservation, table and guest management functionality;

- ability to fill incremental seats for the restaurant;

- ability to deliver strong return on investment for restaurant customers;

- system responsiveness and ease-of-use;

- on-site, custom system installation and training;

- robust support; and

- security, reliability and data protection.

In international markets that we entered more recently and where we have not yet achieved a high degree of penetration, we face more intense competition from local software-development and application service provider, or ASP, vendors. We believe that, over time, the advantages that have established us as a leading provider in North America will help us as we compete in international markets.

Competition for Diners

Our primary competitor for diners making reservations is the phone. The phone enjoys two inherent advantages over online reservations. First, every restaurant and diner has a phone. Second, making reservations by phone is a familiar, ingrained experience for diners.

In order to compete effectively with the phone, the OpenTable website must offer diners a critical mass of restaurants from which to choose and access to reservation inventory comparable to that available by phone. When combined with the growing number of restaurant customers, the OpenTable online reservation network achieves these requirements by communicating directly and in real time with the ERB maintained at each restaurant. Additionally, we offer diners all the conveniences and time savings associated with booking reservations online, including the ability to: book reservations around-the-clock, even when restaurants are closed; find available tables in real time across a selection of local restaurants; receive immediate confirmation of the reservation via email;

67

change or cancel reservations online; and earn Dining Reward Points, redeemable for Dining Cheques accepted by our restaurant customers.

Secondary competition comes from allocation-based reservation-taking websites that offer diners the ability to book reservations for a limited selection of restaurant table inventory. Participating restaurants identify specific reservations, generally at non-peak and unpopular times, which can be offered for booking via these allocation sites. Unlike OpenTable reservations which are immediately recorded in the ERB residing at the restaurant host stand, these allocation reservations are communicated to the restaurant by traditional phone and fax systems, email or web-based accounts that restaurants can check to access reservation requests. These methods are prone to errors, such as lost or double-booked reservations, and require additional effort on the part of restaurants. We believe the limited reservation inventory and unreliable reservation processing methods associated with these allocation-based websites limit their value proposition for diners.

Employees

As of March 31, 2009, we had 300 full-time employees including 100 in operations and support, 81 in sales and marketing, 69 in technology and 50 in general and administrative functions. None of our employees are covered by collective bargaining agreements. In addition, as of March 31, 2009, we had four contractors who are full-time equivalents, including three in operations and support and one in technology functions.

Facilities

Our principal executive offices are located in San Francisco, California, in a 34,236-square-foot facility, under a lease expiring on April 30, 2013. We also have regional offices in Chicago, Illinois; Frankfurt, Germany; New York, New York; London, England; Mexico City, Mexico; and Tokyo, Japan.

Legal Proceedings

On May 12, 2009, Mount Hamilton Partners, LLC, or Mount Hamilton, filed a patent infringement lawsuit against us in the United States District Court for the Northern District of California, seeking, among other things, a judgment that OpenTable has infringed a certain patent held by Mount Hamilton, an injunctive order against the alleged infringing activities and an award for damages. If an injunction is granted, it could force us to stop or alter certain of our business activities, such as certain aspects of our points-based loyalty program, OpenTable Dining Rewards. Although we plan to deny Mount Hamilton's allegations and defend the claims vigorously, and we believe that we have substantial and meritorious defenses to the claims, neither the outcome of the litigation nor the amount and range of potential damages or exposure associated with the litigation can be assessed with certainty.

In addition to the Mount Hamilton lawsuit, from time to time, we may become involved in legal proceedings arising in the ordinary course of our business. We are not presently involved in any legal proceeding in which the outcome, if determined adversely to us, would be expected to have a material adverse effect on our business, operating results or financial condition.

68

MANAGEMENT

The following table provides information regarding our executive officers and directors as of March 31, 2009:

Name	Age	Position(s)
Jeffrey Jordan	50	Chief Executive Officer, Director
Matthew Roberts	40	Chief Financial Officer
Joel Brown	48	Senior Vice President, Operations
Michael Dodson	50	Senior Vice President, Sales
Charlie McCullough	57	Senior Vice President, Engineering
A. George "Skip" Battle(1)(2)	65	Director
Adam R. Dell	39	Director
J. William Gurley(2)	42	Director
Thomas H. Layton	46	Director
Danny Meyer(2)	51	Director
Michelle Peluso(1)	37	Director
Paul Pressler(1)	52	Director

(1)   Member of the audit committee

(2)   Member of the compensation committee

Executive Officers

Jeffrey Jordan has served as our chief executive officer since June 2007 and as a member of our board of directors since July 2007. From October 2004 to September 2006, Mr. Jordan served as the president of PayPal, the Internet-based payment system owned by eBay, Inc. For five years prior to that, Mr. Jordan served as senior vice president and general manager for eBay North America. From September 1998 to September 1999, Mr. Jordan served as chief financial officer for Hollywood Entertainment Corporation, a video rental company, and then president of its subsidiary, Reel.com. Previously, Mr. Jordan served in various capacities at The Walt Disney Corporation for eight years, most recently as senior vice president and chief financial officer of The Disney Store Worldwide. Before that, he worked for The Boston Consulting Group. Mr. Jordan holds a Master of Business Administration degree from the Stanford Graduate School of Business and a Bachelor of Arts degree from Amherst College.

Matthew Roberts has served as our chief financial officer since June 2005. Mr. Roberts was chief financial officer of E-LOAN, Inc., a provider of loans, from December 2000 to May 2005 and vice president of finance of E-LOAN, Inc. from January 1999 to November 2000. Mr. Roberts previously served as corporate controller of NetDynamics, Inc., an enterprise software company, and held a general manager position with Berkeley Systems, Inc., a consumer entertainment software company. Mr. Roberts is a Certified Public Accountant and holds a Bachelor of Science degree in Accounting from Santa Clara University.

Joel Brown has served as our senior vice president of operations since November 2001. From March 2000 to May 2001, Mr. Brown served as executive vice president of Charitableway, Inc., an application service provider linking businesses and the nonprofit sector. From April 1992 to March 2000, Mr. Brown served as vice president and general manager of the financial supplies group and the employer services group at Intuit, Inc., a provider of Internet and desktop finance solutions for consumers and small businesses. Mr. Brown holds a Master of Business Administration degree from the Harvard Business School and a Bachelor of Science degree in Industrial Engineering and Operations Research from the University of Michigan.

69

Michael Dodson has served as our senior vice president of sales since March 2002. From June 2000 to December 2001, Mr. Dodson served as a principal at The Destination Group, a private equity firm. From September 1997 to June 2000, Mr. Dodson served as vice president/general manager in the establishment services division of American Express, Inc. Mr. Dodson holds a Master of Business Administration degree from New York University's Stern School and a Bachelor of Science degree in Finance from Florida State University.

Charlie McCullough has served as our senior vice president, engineering since October 2003. From August 1998 to November 2002, Mr. McCullough served as executive vice president of engineering and operations of Wink Communications, Inc., an interactive television technology company. Mr. McCullough holds a Bachelor of Science degree in Software Engineering from the University of the State of New York, Regents College.

Board of Directors

A. George "Skip" Battle has served on our board of directors since December 2006. From January 2004 to July 2005, Mr. Battle served as executive chairman of Ask Jeeves, Inc., an Internet search engine company, and from December 2000 to January 2004 he served as chief executive officer of Ask Jeeves, Inc. From December 1995 to January 2006, Mr. Battle served as a member of the board of directors for PeopleSoft, Inc., an enterprise software company, and from August 1996 to June 2002 he served as a member of the board of directors for Barra, Inc., a software company. From 1968 until his retirement in 1995, Mr. Battle served in management roles at Arthur Andersen LLP and then Andersen Consulting LLP (now Accenture), where he became worldwide managing partner of market development and a member of the firm's executive committee. Mr. Battle is currently the chairman of the board of directors for Fair Isaac Corporation, an analytic products company, and is also a member of the board of directors for Netflix, Inc., an online DVD rental company, Expedia, Inc., an online travel reservations provider, and Advent Software, Inc., a software and consulting company, and a member of the board of the Masters Select family of mutual funds. Mr. Battle is also a member of the board of directors of Workday, Inc., a private company, and Berkeley Community Fund, a not-for-profit organization, and a member of the board of trustees of the United States Olympic Cycling Development Foundation. Mr. Battle holds a Master of Business Administration from the Stanford Graduate School of Business and a Bachelor of Arts degree in Economics from Dartmouth College.

Adam R. Dell has served on our board of directors since January 2000. Since January 2000, Mr. Dell has been the managing general partner of Impact Venture Partners, a venture capital firm focused on information technology investments. Prior to this time, Mr. Dell was a partner with Crosspoint Venture Partners in Northern California and a senior associate with Enterprise Partners in Southern California. Prior to becoming a venture capitalist, Mr. Dell worked as a corporate attorney in Austin, Texas, with the law firm of Winstead, Sechrest & Minick. Mr. Dell also founded and served as chairman of the board of MessageOne, which was acquired by Dell, Inc. in 2008. He currently serves on the board of directors of XO Communications and BagBorrowOrSteal and is a member of the Board of Trustees of the Santa Fe Institute. Mr. Dell holds a law degree from the University of Texas School of Law and a Bachelor of Arts degree in Political Economy from Tulane University.

J. William Gurley has served on our board of directors since October 2000. Mr. Gurley is a general partner of Benchmark Capital, a venture capital firm, which he joined in March 1999. Prior to joining Benchmark Capital, Mr. Gurley was a partner with Hummer Winblad Venture Partners, a venture capital firm, and a research analyst for Credit Suisse First Boston, an investment bank. Mr. Gurley is currently a member of the boards of directors of Fanbase, Linden Lab, Red5, Modern Feed, Nanosolar, Inc., Ruba, Tropos Networks Inc., Vudu and Zillow.com, all private companies. Mr. Gurley holds a Master of Business Administration degree from the University of Texas and a Bachelor of Science degree in Computer Science from the University of Florida.

70

Thomas H. Layton has served on our board of directors since May 1999. From September 2001 to June 2007, Mr. Layton served as our chief executive officer. Mr. Layton is currently the chief executive officer of Metaweb Technologies, Inc., an Internet technology company. From November 1995 to June 1999, Mr. Layton served as president and chief operating officer and was co-founder of CitySearch, Inc., a company that provided online city guides, which later merged with Ticketmaster, Inc., an event ticketing agency. Prior to his experience at CitySearch, Mr. Layton served as chief financial officer of Score Learning Corporation, an educational services company, from April 1994 to October 1995, and as president and chief operating officer from March 1995 to October 1995. From January 1989 to August 1992, Mr. Layton served as vice president and general manager of MicroFinancial Corporation, an equipment leasing company. From 1986 to 1988, Mr. Layton was an associate consultant with The Boston Consulting Group. Mr. Layton is a member of the board of directors of oDesk Corporation, a private company, and a co-founder and member of the board of directors of MAPLight.org, a non-profit organization. Mr. Layton holds a Master of Business Administration degree from the Stanford Graduate School of Business and a Bachelor of Science degree from the University of North Carolina at Chapel Hill.

Danny Meyer has served on our board of directors since February 2000. Mr. Meyer has been the president of Union Square Hospitality Group, or USHG, since 1996. USHG owns and operates a number of restaurants including Union Square Café, Eleven Madison Park, Gramercy Tavern, Tabla and The Modern, which have been featured in the *Michelin Guide, The New York Times* and Zagat Surveys. Mr. Meyer is currently a member of the board of directors of the following not-for-profit organizations: Share Our Strength, City Harvest, Irving Harris Foundation and New Yorkers for Parks. Mr. Meyer is also a member of the executive committees of the Madison Square Park Conservancy, Union Square Partnership and NYC & Co. Mr. Meyer holds a Bachelor degree in Political Science from Trinity College.

Michelle Peluso has served on our board of directors since March 2008. From December 2003 to February 2009, Ms. Peluso served as chief executive officer of Travelocity Global, an Internet travel company. From April 2002 to November 2003, Ms. Peluso served as Travelocity's chief operating officer and as senior vice president of product strategy and distribution. Prior to Travelocity, Ms. Peluso served as chief executive officer and founder of Site59, an Internet travel site purchased by Travelocity, from November 1999 to March 2002. Ms. Peluso is currently a member of the board of directors of the following non-profit organizations: Pembroke College NA Foundation, Christa House and TechnoServe. Ms. Peluso holds a Master's degree in Economics, Politics and Philosophy from Pembroke College at Oxford University and a Bachelor of Science degree from the Wharton School of Business at the University of Pennsylvania.

Paul Pressler has served on our board of directors since March 2008. Mr. Pressler was president and chief executive officer of Gap, Inc. from September 2002 to January 2007. Mr. Pressler also served on Gap, Inc.'s board of directors from October 2002 until January 2007. Prior to joining Gap, Inc., Mr. Pressler was with The Walt Disney Company where he was chairman of the company's global theme park and resorts division from January 1999 to September 2002, president of Disneyland from January 1995 to January 1999, president of The Disney Stores from September 1992 to January 1995, and senior vice president of consumer products from January 1987 to September 1992. Mr. Pressler is currently a member of the board of directors for Avon Products, Inc., a beauty products company, and Overture Acquisition Corporation, a blank check company formed for the purpose of completing a business combination transaction. Mr. Pressler holds a Bachelor of Science degree in Business Economics from the State University of New York at Oneonta.

71

Board Composition

Upon completion of this offering, our board of directors will consist of eight members, six of whom will qualify as "independent" according to the rules and regulations of The Nasdaq Stock Market.

In accordance with our amended and restated certificate of incorporation, immediately after this offering, our board of directors will be divided into three classes with staggered three-year terms. At each annual general meeting of stockholders, the successors to directors whose terms then expire will be elected to serve from the time of election and qualification until the third annual meeting following election. Our directors will be divided among the three classes as follows:

- The Class I directors will be Messrs. Dell and Layton and their terms will expire at the annual general meeting of stockholders to be held in 2010;

- The Class II directors will be Messrs. Gurley, Jordan and Meyer and their terms will expire at the annual general meeting of stockholders to be held in 2011; and

- The Class III directors will be Messrs. Battle and Pressler and Ms. Peluso and their terms will expire at the annual general meeting of stockholders to be held in 2012.

Any additional directorships resulting from an increase in the number of directors will be distributed among the three classes so that, as nearly as possible, each class will consist of one-third of the directors.

The division of our board of directors into three classes with staggered three-year terms may delay or prevent a change of our management or a change in control.

Board Committees

Our board of directors has or plans to establish the following committees: an audit committee, a compensation committee and a nominating and corporate governance committee. The composition and responsibilities of each committee are described below. Members serve on these committees until their resignation or until otherwise determined by our board.

Audit Committee

Our audit committee oversees our corporate accounting and financial reporting process. Among other matters, the audit committee evaluates the independent auditors' qualifications, independence and performance; determines the engagement of the independent auditors; reviews and approves the scope of the annual audit and the audit fee; discusses with management and the independent auditors the results of the annual audit and the review of our quarterly consolidated financial statements; approves the retention of the independent auditors to perform any proposed permissible non-audit services; monitors the rotation of partners of the independent auditors on the OpenTable engagement team as required by law; reviews our critical accounting policies and estimates; oversees our internal audit function and annually reviews the audit committee charter and the committee's performance. The current members of our audit committee are A. George "Skip" Battle, who is the chair of the committee, Michelle Peluso and Paul Pressler. All members of our audit committee meet the requirements for financial literacy under the applicable rules and regulations of the SEC and The Nasdaq Stock Market. Our board has determined that Mr. Battle is an audit committee financial expert as defined under the applicable rules of the SEC and has the requisite financial sophistication as defined under the applicable rules and regulations of The Nasdaq Stock Market. Mr. Battle, Ms. Peluso and Mr. Pressler are independent directors as defined under the applicable rules and regulations of the SEC and The Nasdaq Stock Market. The audit committee will operate under a written charter that will satisfy the applicable standards of the SEC and The Nasdaq Stock Market.

72

Compensation Committee

Our compensation committee reviews and recommends policies relating to compensation and benefits of our officers and employees. The compensation committee reviews and approves corporate goals and objectives relevant to compensation of our chief executive officer and other executive officers, evaluates the performance of these officers in light of those goals and objectives, and sets the compensation of these officers based on such evaluations. The compensation committee will also administer the issuance of stock options and other awards under our stock plans. The compensation committee will review and evaluate, at least annually, the performance of the compensation committee and its members, including compliance of the compensation committee with its charter. The current members of our compensation committee are J. William Gurley, A. George "Skip" Battle and Danny Meyer, with Mr. Gurley serving as the chair of the committee. All of the members of our compensation committee are independent under the applicable rules and regulations of the SEC, The Nasdaq Stock Market and the Internal Revenue Code.

Nominating and Corporate Governance Committee

The nominating and corporate governance committee will be responsible for making recommendations regarding candidates for directorships and the size and composition of our board. In addition, the nominating and corporate governance committee will be responsible for overseeing our corporate governance guidelines and reporting and making recommendations concerning governance matters. The nominating and corporate governance committee is comprised of all of the members of our board of directors. Potential candidates will be discussed by the entire board, and director nominees will be subject to the approval of the independent members of the board.

There are no family relationships among any of our directors or executive officers.

Compensation Committee Interlocks and Insider Participation

None of the members of our compensation committee is or has at any time during the past year been an officer or employee of ours. None of our executive officers currently serves or in the past year has served as a member of the board of directors or compensation committee of any entity that has one or more executive officers serving on our board or compensation committee.

Code of Business Conduct and Ethics

We have adopted a code of business conduct and ethics that applies to all of our employees, officers and directors, including those officers responsible for financial reporting. The code of business conduct and ethics will be available on our website at www.opentable.com. We expect that any amendments to the code, or any waivers of its requirements, will be disclosed on our website.

Director Compensation

We do not currently provide any cash compensation to our non-employee directors. From time to time, we have granted stock options to our non-employee directors as compensation for their services, but prior to this offering we did not have a formal policy in place with respect to such awards. Our directors who are also employees are compensated for their service as employees and do not receive any additional compensation for their service on our board.

Following the completion of this offering, under our 2009 Equity Incentive Award Plan, each non-employee director shall receive an initial stock option grant to purchase 32,000 shares of our common stock when he or she joins our board of directors, and thereafter an annual stock option grant to purchase 10,800 shares of our common stock on the date of each annual meeting of stockholders (provided that such non-employee director shall have served on our board of directors for at least six

73

months prior to the date of such annual meeting). The shares subject to the initial stock option grants shall vest as to 25% of the underlying shares on each anniversary of the date of grant, and subsequent annual stock option grants will vest on the first anniversary of the date of grant. The shares subject to the initial stock option grants and subsequent annual stock option grants shall automatically vest in full and become exercisable immediately prior to a change in control of the company. Members of our board of directors who are employees of our company and who subsequently terminate employment with our company and remain members of the board of directors shall not receive an initial stock option grant, but, to the extent that they are otherwise eligible, such persons shall receive, after termination of employment with our company, annual stock option grants as described above in this paragraph. Notwithstanding the foregoing, Messrs. Dell, Gurley and Layton will not receive the annual stock option grant described above until the 2011 annual meeting of stockholders.

The following table sets forth information regarding compensation earned by our directors who are not named executive officers during the fiscal year ended December 31, 2008.

Name	Option Awards(1)	All Other Compensation	Total
A. George Battle(2)	$ 46,703	$ —	$ 46,703
Adam Dell	—	—	—
J. William Gurley	—	—	—
Thomas H. Layton	—	—	—
Danny Meyer(3)	100,092	—	100,092
Michelle Peluso(4)	96,346	—	96,346
Paul Pressler(4)	96,346	—	96,346

(1)   Amount reflects the total compensation expense for the year ended December 31, 2008 calculated in accordance with SFAS No. 123R. The valuation assumptions used in determining such amounts are described in Note 2 to our financial statements included in this prospectus.

(2)   As of December 31, 2008, Mr. Battle held 26,562 shares of our common stock subject to repurchase by us at the original purchase price, all of which were acquired upon the exercise of stock options prior to vesting. The shares of common stock held by Mr. Battle vest as to 1/48th of the shares subject to the option on each monthly anniversary of the vesting commencement date, subject to his continued service as a member of our board of directors.

(3)   On March 27, 2008, we granted Mr. Meyer an option to purchase 32,000 shares of our common stock having an exercise price per share equal to $7.75 and a grant date fair value of $209,880. This option vests as to 1/48th of the shares subject to the option on each monthly anniversary of February 12, 2008, subject to Mr. Meyer's continued service as a member of our board of directors. This option remained outstanding as of December 31, 2008. The grant date fair value of this option was computed in accordance with SFAS No. 123R using the valuation assumptions set forth in Note 2 to our consolidated financial statements included in this prospectus.

(4)   In connection with the appointment of Ms. Peluso and Mr. Pressler to our board of directors, on March 27, 2008, we granted each an option to purchase 32,000 shares of our common stock having an exercise price per share equal to $7.75 and a grant date fair value of $209,880. Each option vests as to 1/48th of the shares subject to the option on each monthly anniversary of the date of grant, subject to the director's continued service as a member of our board of directors. Each of these options remained outstanding as of December 31, 2008. The grant date fair value of each

74

option was computed in accordance with SFAS No. 123R using the valuation assumptions set forth in Note 2 to our consolidated financial statements included in this prospectus.

Executive Compensation

Compensation Discussion and Analysis

This section discusses the principles underlying our policies and decisions with respect to the compensation of our executive officers who are named in the "2008 Summary Compensation Table" and the most important factors relevant to an analysis of these policies and decisions. These "named executive officers" for 2008 include Jeffrey Jordan, president and chief executive officer; Matthew Roberts, chief financial officer; Joel Brown, senior vice president, operations; Michael Dodson, senior vice president, sales; and Charlie McCullough, senior vice president, engineering.

Overview

We recognize that the ability to excel depends on the integrity, knowledge, imagination, skill, diversity and teamwork of our employees. To this end, we strive to create an environment of mutual respect, encouragement and teamwork that rewards commitment and performance and that is responsive to the needs of our employees. The principles and objectives of our compensation and benefits programs for our employees generally, and for our named executive officers specifically, are to:

- attract, engage and retain individuals of superior ability, experience and managerial talent enabling us to be an employer of choice in the highly-competitive and dynamic information technology industry;

- ensure compensation is closely aligned with our corporate strategies, business and financial objectives and the long-term interests of our stockholders;

- motivate and reward executives whose knowledge, skills and performance ensure our continued success; and

- ensure that total compensation is fair, reasonable and competitive.

Most of our compensation components simultaneously fulfill one or more of these principles and objectives. These components consist of (1) base salary, (2) performance bonuses, (3) equity incentives, (4) retirement savings opportunity, (5) perquisites and health and welfare benefits and (6) post-termination benefits. We view each component of executive compensation as related but distinct, and we also review total compensation of our executive officers to ensure that our overall compensation objectives are met. Not all elements are provided to all named executive officers. Instead, we determine the appropriate level for each compensation component based in part, but not exclusively, on our understanding of the market based on the experience of members of our board of directors and consistent with our recruiting and retention goals, our view of internal equity and consistency, the length of service of our executives, our overall performance and other considerations we deem relevant.

Our philosophy is to make a greater percentage of an executive officer's compensation tied to stockholder returns and to keep cash compensation to a nominally competitive level while providing the opportunity to be well-rewarded through equity if we perform well over time. We believe that because the achievement of our business and financial objectives will be reflected in the value of our equity, our executive officers will be incentivized to achieve these objectives when a portion of their compensation is tied to the value of our equity. To this end, we use stock options as a significant component of compensation because we believe that this best ties individual compensation to the creation of stockholder value. While we offer competitive base salaries, we believe stock-based compensation is a

75

significant motivator in attracting employees for Internet-related and other technology companies. Except as described below, we have not adopted any formal or informal policies or guidelines for allocating compensation between long-term and currently paid out compensation, between cash and non-cash compensation or among different forms of non-cash compensation.

Each of the primary elements of our executive compensation program is discussed in more detail below. While we have identified particular compensation objectives that each element of executive compensation serves, our compensation programs are designed to be flexible and complementary and to collectively serve all of the executive compensation objectives described above. Accordingly, whether or not specifically mentioned below, we believe that, as a part of our overall executive compensation policy, each individual element, to a greater or lesser extent, serves each of our objectives.

Compensation Determination Process

Compensation for our named executive officers historically has been highly individualized, resulted from arm's-length negotiations and has been based on a variety of informal factors including, in addition to the factors listed above, our financial condition and available resources, our need for that particular position to be filled, our board of directors' evaluation of the competitive market based on the experience of the members of our board of directors with other companies and their review of anonymous private company compensation surveys, the length of service of an executive and the compensation levels of our other executive officers, each as of the time of the applicable compensation decision. In years past, our president and chief executive officer, and, with respect to our president and chief executive officer, our board of directors, reviewed the performance of each named executive officer, generally on an annual basis, and based on this review and the factors described above, set the executive compensation package for him or her for the coming year. However, there was no predetermined time of year for such review. In 2008, there were no increases in compensation for our named executive officers. Upon consummation of this offering, the compensation committee will take on the responsibility for this annual review and decision-making process.

Historically, our board of directors has reviewed anonymous private company compensation surveys in setting the compensation of our named executive officers. In 2008, however, neither our president and chief executive officer nor our board of directors reviewed market compensation data in setting named executive officer compensation. In 2009, our compensation committee intends to engage Radford, a management consulting firm providing executive compensation advisory services, as a compensation consultant to help evaluate our compensation philosophy and provide guidance in administering our compensation program in the future. Following the completion of this offering, we anticipate that our compensation committee will determine executive compensation, at least in part, by reference to the compensation information for the executives of a peer group of comparable companies, although no such peer group has yet been determined. Our compensation committee plans to have our compensation consultant provide market data on a peer group of companies in the technology sector on an annual basis, and we intend to review this information and other information obtained by the members of our compensation committee in light of the compensation we offer to help ensure that our compensation program is competitive. We anticipate that our compensation committee may make adjustments in executive compensation levels in the future as a result of this more formal market comparison process.

We strive to achieve an appropriate mix between equity incentive awards and cash payments in order to meet our objectives. Any apportionment goal is not applied rigidly and does not control our compensation decisions, and our compensation committee does not have any policies for allocating compensation between long-term and short-term compensation or cash and non-cash compensation. Our mix of compensation elements is designed to reward recent results and motivate long-term performance through a combination of cash and equity incentive awards. We believe the most

76

important indicator of whether our compensation objectives are being met is our ability to motivate our named executive officers to deliver superior performance and retain them to continue their careers with us on a cost-effective basis.

The compensation levels of the named executive officers reflect to a significant degree the varying roles and responsibilities of such executives, as well as the length of time those executives have served our company. As a result of our board of directors' assessment of our president and chief executive officer's roles and responsibilities within our company, there is a significant compensation differential between his compensation levels and those of our other named executive officers.

Base Salaries

In general, base salaries for our named executive officers are initially established through arm's-length negotiation at the time the executive is hired, taking into account such executive's qualifications, experience and prior salary. Base salaries of our named executive officers are approved and reviewed periodically by our president and chief executive officer, and in the case of our president and chief executive officer's base salary, by our board of directors, and adjustments to base salaries are based on the scope of an executive's responsibilities, individual contribution, prior experience and sustained performance. Decisions regarding salary increases may take into account the executive officer's current salary, equity ownership and the amounts paid to an executive officer's peers inside our company by conducting an internal analysis, which compares the pay of each executive officer to other members of the management team. In making decisions regarding salary increases, we may also draw upon the experience of members of our board of directors with other companies and have historically reviewed anonymous private company compensation surveys when setting base salaries. Base salaries are also reviewed in the case of promotions or other significant changes in responsibility. No formulaic base salary increases are provided to our named executive officers. This strategy is consistent with our intent of offering base salaries that are cost-effective while remaining competitive.

None of our named executive officers received an increase in base salary during 2008, as our president and chief executive officer and our board of directors determined that prior increases in equity compensation better aligned the interests of our executives with our stockholders for 2008.

The actual base salaries paid to all of our named executive officers are set forth in the "2008 Summary Compensation Table."

Annual Cash Bonuses

In addition to base salaries, annual cash bonus opportunities have been awarded to our named executive officers when our board of directors or our president and chief executive officer has determined that such an incentive is necessary to align our corporate goals with the cash compensation payable to an executive. Historically, such annual cash bonus opportunities have been awarded to two of our named executive officers, namely Mr. Dodson, our senior vice president, sales and Mr. McCullough, our senior vice president, engineering.

In 2008, Mr. Dodson was eligible to receive an incentive bonus under a sales commission plan based on the number of new restaurant customers acquired during 2008. The target incentive bonus for Mr. Dodson was set at $200,000, which we determined was necessary to align his individual incentives with corporate sales objectives and to maintain competitive total compensation for his position in light of his lower base salary as compared to other senior vice presidents in our company. Mr. Dodson achieved new restaurant customer sales in 2008 that were 106% of the objective under his sales commission plan. As such, Mr. Dodson was awarded $212,787, or 106% of his target incentive. There is currently a similar 2009 incentive arrangement in place for Mr. Dodson. For both 2008 and 2009, Mr. Dodson's sales objectives were set at levels we determined to be challenging and requiring substantial effort on the part of Mr. Dodson to achieve. The objectives will not be achieved by average

77

or below average performance by Mr. Dodson. For example, in order to achieve these objectives, Mr. Dodson must manage sales in a manner that increases the number of new restaurant customers at a rate that exceeds current projections.

During 2008, Mr. McCullough was eligible to receive an annual cash incentive bonus of up to $30,000, based upon his individual performance, as measured using qualitative goals related to network reliability and product deliverables. Mr. McCullough received his full bonus of $30,000 for 2008. Under a similar bonus arrangement established for Mr. McCullough for 2009, the qualitative goals have been mutually agreed upon between Mr. McCullough and our president and chief executive officer. These goals were set in a manner to challenge Mr. McCullough and require him to achieve system performance improvements and new product developments at higher than historic levels.

The foregoing bonuses paid to our named executive officers are set forth in the "2008 Summary Compensation Table."

Long-Term Equity Incentives

The goals of our long-term, equity-based incentive awards are to align the interests of our named executive officers with the interests of our stockholders. Because vesting is based on continued employment, our equity-based incentives also encourage the retention of our named executive officers through the vesting period of the awards. In determining the size of the long-term equity incentives to be awarded to our named executive officers, we take into account a number of internal factors, such as the relative job scope, the value of existing long-term incentive awards, individual performance history, prior contributions to us and the size of prior grants. Although our board of directors did not refer to any competitive market data during 2008, historically, our board of directors has reviewed anonymous private company compensation surveys and drawn upon the experience of its members in determining long-term equity incentive awards. Based upon these factors, our board of directors determines the size of the long-term equity incentives at levels it considers appropriate to create a meaningful opportunity for reward predicated on the creation of long-term stockholder value. In addition, our board of directors has historically allowed our named executive officers to exercise their awards prior to vesting, with any shares issued upon such exercise subject to repurchase by us at the exercise price in the event the executive terminates his or her employment with us. We have not granted any equity awards other than stock options to our named executive officers to date. Following the completion of this offering, we expect our compensation committee to oversee our long-term equity incentive program.

To reward and retain our named executive officers in a manner that best aligns employees' interests with stockholders' interests, we use stock options as the primary incentive vehicles for long-term compensation. We believe that stock options are an effective tool for meeting our compensation goal of increasing long-term stockholder value by tying the value of the stock options to our future performance. Because employees are able to profit from stock options only if our stock price increases relative to the stock option's exercise price, we believe stock options provide meaningful incentives to employees to achieve increases in the value of our stock over time.

We use stock options to compensate our named executive officers both in the form of initial grants in connection with the commencement of employment and additional or "refresher" grants. To date there has been no set program for the award of refresher grants, and our board of directors retains discretion to make stock option awards to employees at any time, including in connection with the promotion of an employee, to reward an employee, for retention purposes or for other circumstances recommended by management.

The exercise price of each stock option grant is the fair market value of our common stock on the grant date. For 2008, the determination of the appropriate fair market value was made by the board of directors. In the absence of a public trading market, the board considered numerous objective and subjective factors to determine its best estimate of the fair market value of our common stock as

78

of the date of each option grant, including but not limited to, the following factors: (i) the rights, preferences and privileges of our preferred stock relative to our common stock; (ii) our performance and stage of development; (iii) valuations of our common stock; and (iv) the likelihood of achieving a liquidity event for the shares of common stock underlying these stock options, such as an initial public offering or sale of our company, given prevailing market conditions. Initial stock option awards to our named executive officers typically vest over a four-year period as follows: 25% of the shares underlying the option vest on the first anniversary of the date of the vesting commencement date, which is typically the date of hire, and the remainder of the shares underlying the option vest in equal monthly installments over the remaining 36 months thereafter. Other than as described below for February 5, 2007 stock option grants, refresher grants vest in equal monthly installments over four years from the vesting commencement date, typically the date of grant or the date the employee was promoted. We believe these vesting schedules appropriately encourage long-term employment with our company while allowing our executives to realize compensation in line with the value they have created for our stockholders. We do not have any security ownership requirements for our named executive officers.

Our board of directors typically provides for the acceleration of vesting of stock options in the event of a change in control of our company. In the event of a change in control, if our stock options are not assumed or substituted for by a successor, the vesting of the options fully accelerates. In the event stock options are assumed or substituted for, then typically the options immediately vest with respect to that percentage of the shares of the option, up to 100%, that equals (A)(i) six months plus (ii) the number of complete months the named executive officer has provided continuous service to us; divided by (B) the total number of months of the original vesting schedule for the shares, with any remaining unvested shares continuing to vest in accordance with the original vesting schedule. With respect to options granted to Mr. Roberts in 2005 and Mr. McCullough in 2004, vesting acceleration for options assumed or substituted for in a change in control is limited to 25% of the unvested shares subject to the option as of the date of the change in control and an additional 25% in the event Mr. Roberts or Mr. McCullough is terminated without cause or otherwise constructively terminated following the change in control. We believe that these acceleration opportunities further align the interests of our executives with those of our stockholders by providing our executives an opportunity to benefit alongside our stockholders in a corporate transaction.

On February 5, 2007, our board of directors granted each of our named executive officers, other than Mr. Jordan who was not yet employed by us, an option to purchase shares of our common stock that is subject to vesting terms different from that described above and not subject to accelerated vesting. These option grants were provided as a special incentive to our named executive officers to encourage further short-term and long-term growth of our company. The vesting schedule of each option is detailed in the section entitled "—Outstanding Equity Awards at 2008 Fiscal Year-End."

As a privately owned company, there has been no market for our common stock. Accordingly, in 2008, we had no program, plan or practice pertaining to the timing of stock option grants to executive officers coinciding with the release of material non-public information. The compensation committee intends to adopt a formal policy regarding the timing of grants in connection with this offering.

Retirement Savings

All of our full-time employees in the United States, including our named executive officers, are eligible to participate in our 401(k) plan. Pursuant to our 401(k) plan, employees may elect to reduce their current compensation by up to the statutorily prescribed annual limit, which was $15,500 in 2008, and to have the amount of this reduction contributed to our 401(k) plan. We currently match up to the first $500 of employee contributions under our 401(k) plan.

79

Perquisites

Historically, from time to time, our board of directors has provided certain of our named executive officers with perquisites that we believe are reasonable. We do not view perquisites as a significant element of our comprehensive compensation structure, but do believe they can be useful in attracting, motivating and retaining the executive talent for which we compete. We believe that these additional benefits may assist our executive officers in performing their duties and provide time efficiencies for our executive officers in appropriate circumstances, and we may consider providing additional perquisites in the future.

As the result of arm's-length negotiations in connection with the offer letter we entered into with Mr. Jordan in June 2007, Mr. Jordan is entitled to payment of, or reimbursement for, all expenses reasonably incurred by him in connection with his option to use a third party car service for his commute, along with the payment of any taxes incurred by him related to that car service. As the result of the same arm's-length negotiation, we have also agreed to reimburse Mr. Jordan for any taxes he might incur in connection with Section 409A of the Internal Revenue Code as the result of the options we have granted to him.

In the future, we may provide additional perquisites to our executive officers as an element of their overall compensation structure. We do not expect these perquisites to be a significant element of our compensation structure. All future practices regarding perquisites will be approved and subject to periodic review by our compensation committee.

Termination-Based Compensation

As the result of arm's-length negotiations in connection with the offer letter we entered into with Mr. Jordan, we have agreed to provide Mr. Jordan severance benefits if his employment is terminated by our company without cause at any time or if he is constructively terminated by us within twelve months following a change in control of our company. In such an event, Mr. Jordan is entitled to continued payment of his base salary for twelve months, continued health benefits coverage for twelve months, and six months', or in the case of a termination within twelve months following a change in control, twelve months', vesting acceleration with respect to the options granted to him in connection with his commencement of employment with us. Mr. Jordan must execute and not revoke a general release of all claims against us and our affiliates in order to receive any severance benefits. For a further description of Mr. Jordan's offer letter, see "—Offer Letter Agreements" below.

We have routinely granted and will continue to grant our named executive officers stock options under our equity incentive plans. For a description of the change in control provisions in such equity incentive plans applicable to these stock options, see "—Employee Benefit and Stock Plans—2009 Equity Incentive Award Plan" and "—Amended and Restated 1999 Stock Plan" below. The estimated value of these benefits, along with the benefits payable to Mr. Jordan upon a termination of his employment, is set forth below in the section entitled "Potential Payments Upon Change in Control and Upon Termination Following Change in Control."

Tax Considerations

Our board of directors has considered the potential future effects of Section 162(m) of the Internal Revenue Code on the compensation paid to our executive officers. Section 162(m) disallows a tax deduction for any publicly held corporation for individual compensation exceeding $1.0 million in any taxable year for our president and chief executive officer and each of the other named executive officers (other than our chief financial officer), unless compensation is performance based. As we are not currently publicly-traded, our board of directors has not previously taken the deductibility limit imposed by Section 162(m) into consideration in setting compensation. We expect that our compensation committee, however, will adopt a policy that, where reasonably practicable, we will seek to qualify the variable compensation paid to our executive officers for an exemption from the deductibility limitations of Section 162(m). As such, in approving the amount and form of compensation for our executive officers in the future, our compensation committee will consider all elements of the cost to our company of providing such compensation, including the potential impact of Section 162(m). However, our compensation committee may, in its judgment, authorize compensation payments that do not comply with the exemptions in Section 162(m) when it believes that such payments are appropriate to attract and retain executive talent.

2008 Summary Compensation Table

The following table summarizes the compensation that we paid to our chief executive officer, chief financial officer and each of our three other most highly compensated executive officers during the year ended December 31, 2008. We refer to these officers in this prospectus as our named executive officers.

Name and Principal Position	Year	Salary ($)	Option Awards ($)(1)	Non-Equity Incentive Plan Compensation ($)	All Other Compensation ($)(2)	Total ($)
Jeffrey Jordan, President and Chief Executive Officer	2008	$360,000	$1,146,592	$ —	$ 19,578	$1,526,170
Matthew Roberts, Chief Financial Officer	2008	225,000	124,828	—	500	350,328
Joel Brown, Senior Vice President, Operations	2008	225,000	93,627	—	500	319,127
Michael Dodson, Senior Vice President, Sales	2008	175,000	84,305	212,787	500	472,592
Charlie McCullough, Senior Vice President, Engineering	2008	235,000	100,764	30,000	500	366,264

(1)   The amounts included in the "Option Awards" column represent the compensation cost that was recognized by us in the year ended December 31, 2008, determined in accordance with SFAS No. 123R. The valuation assumptions used in determining such amounts are described in Note 2 to our consolidated financial statements included in this prospectus.

(2)   Represents a $500 401(k) matching contribution made by us for each of our named executive officers. Mr. Jordan's amount includes $12,887 for the provision of a car and driver and $6,191 for the reimbursement of taxes incurred by him for the provision of such benefit.

Grants of Plan-Based Awards in 2008 Table

The following table provides information regarding grants of non-equity incentive plan-based awards made during the year ended December 31, 2008, to each of our named executive officers.

Name	Estimated Future Payouts Under Non-Equity Incentive Plan Awards Target ($)(1)
Michael Dodson	$ 200,000
Charlie McCullough	30,000

(1)   Represents the annual cash bonus opportunity for 2008 for Mr. Dodson and Mr. McCullough.

81

Outstanding Equity Awards at 2008 Fiscal Year-End

The following table shows grants of stock options outstanding on December 31, 2008, the last day of our fiscal year, to each of our named executive officers. The unvested stock awards listed below reflect options exercised by our named executive officers prior to vesting.

			Option Awards				Stock Awards	
Name	Date of Grant	Vesting Commencement Date	Number of Securities Underlying Unexercised Options (#) Exercisable	Number of Securities Underlying Unexercised Options (#) Unexercisable	Option Exercise Price ($)	Option Expiration Date	Number of Shares of Stock That Have Not Vested (#)	Market Value of Shares of Stock That Have Not Vested ($)
Jeffrey Jordan	7/9/2007(1)	6/1/2007	—	—	—	—	479,810	$ 5,097,983
	7/9/2007(1)	6/1/2007	123,379	205,633	23.38	7/8/2017	—	—
Matthew Roberts	8/9/2005(2)	6/16/2005	68,266	—	1.50	8/8/2015	8,333	88,542
	2/5/2007(3)	6/16/2009	—	72,000	4.88	2/4/2017	—	—
Joel Brown	2/19/2004(4)	8/20/2007	—	—	—		13,333	141,667
	2/5/2007(5)	2/20/2007	23,334	64,666	4.88	2/4/2017	—	—
Michael Dodson	2/19/2004(4)	8/20/2007	—	—	—		33,333	354,167
	2/5/2007(6)	2/20/2007	39,334	80,666	4.88	2/4/2017	—	—
Charlie McCullough	2/19/2004(4)	8/20/07	—	—	—		20,000	212,500
	2/5/2007(7)	11/1/2007	4,000	82,000	4.88	2/4/2017	—	—

(1) These options and these shares, which were acquired upon exercise of options prior to vesting, vest as to 1/48th of the shares subject to the option on each monthly anniversary of the vesting commencement date until all shares are vested.

(2) These options and these shares, which were acquired upon exercise of options prior to vesting, vest as to 25% of the shares subject to the option on the first anniversary of the vesting commencement date and 1/48th of the shares subject to the option on each monthly anniversary of the vesting commencement date thereafter until all shares are vested.

(3) These options vest as to 1/24th of the total number of shares subject to the option on each monthly anniversary of the vesting commencement date until all shares are vested.

(4) These shares, which were acquired upon exercise of options prior to vesting, vest as to 1/36th of the total number of shares subject to the option on each monthly anniversary of the vesting commencement date until all shares are vested.

(5) On each monthly anniversary of the vesting commencement date, this option and these shares, which were acquired upon exercise of the option prior to vesting, vest as to 3,000 shares subject to the option for the first six months, 2,333 shares subject to the option for the next 36 months and 3,000 shares subject to the option for the following six months.

(6) On each monthly anniversary of the vesting commencement date, this option vests as to 3,000 shares subject to the option for the first six months, 1,333 shares subject to the option for the next 36 months and 3,000 shares subject to the option for the following 18 months.

(7) On each monthly anniversary of the vesting commencement date, this option and these shares vest as to 2,000 shares subject to the option for the first 26 months, 3,000 shares subject to the option for the next 12 months and 2,000 shares subject to the option for the following ten months.

82

Option Exercises and Stock Vested in 2008 Table

The following table shows information regarding the vesting of stock awards during the year ended December 31, 2008. The amounts listed below for stock awards reflect the vesting of options that were exercised by our named executive officers prior to vesting.

	Stock Awards	
Name	Number of Shares Acquired on Vesting (#)	Value Realized on Vesting ($)
Jeffrey Jordan	191,924	$1,055,582
Matthew Roberts	16,666	152,083
Joel Brown	12,666	133,782
Michael Dodson	20,000	210,500
Charlie McCullough	26,000	275,650

Pension Benefits

We do not maintain any defined benefit pension plans.

Nonqualified Deferred Compensation

We do not maintain any nonqualified deferred compensation plans.

Offer Letter Agreements

On June 5, 2007, we entered into an offer letter agreement with Mr. Jordan, setting forth the terms and conditions of his employment as our president and chief executive officer, effective as of June 1, 2007. We amended and restated the offer letter agreement on October 15, 2008. The offer letter agreement provides for an annual base salary of $360,000. The offer letter agreement, as amended and restated, provides for the payment of any taxes Mr. Jordan incurs solely as a result of Section 409A of the Internal Revenue Code with respect to the grant or vesting of the options granted to him in connection with his offer letter agreement. Mr. Jordan is also entitled to payment of, or reimbursement for, all expenses reasonably incurred by him in connection with the use of a third party car service, along with the payment of any taxes incurred by him related to the car service.

Mr. Jordan is also entitled to receive severance benefits if his employment is terminated by us without cause at any time or if he is constructively terminated by us within twelve months following a change in control of our company. In such an event, Mr. Jordan is entitled to continued payment of his base salary for twelve months and continued health benefits coverage for twelve months. Mr. Jordan is also entitled to six months', or in the case of a termination within twelve months following a change in control, twelve months', vesting acceleration with respect to the options granted to him in connection with his commencement of employment with us. Mr. Jordan must execute and not revoke a general release of all claims against us and our affiliates in order to receive any severance benefits.

We have also entered into offer letter agreements with each of our other named executive officers in connection with their commencement of employment with us. These offer letter agreements typically include the executive officer's initial base salary and stock option grant along with any vesting acceleration provisions with respect to that initial stock option grant. We no longer have any executory obligations under these agreements.

83

Potential Payments Upon Change in Control and Upon Termination Following Change in Control

Potential Payments Upon a Change in Control

The following table sets forth quantitative estimates of the benefits that would have accrued to each of our named executive officers upon a change in control of our company on December 31, 2008. Amounts below reflect potential payments pursuant to stock options granted under our 1999 Stock Plan.

Name of Executive Officer	Value of Accelerated Options if Not Assumed or Substituted(1)
Jeffrey Jordan	$ 2,638,956
Matthew Roberts	229,951
Joel Brown	140,334
Michael Dodson	350,834
Charlie McCullough	210,500

(1)   Amounts calculated based on the aggregate amount by which the fair market value of the common stock subject to unvested equity awards exceeded the aggregate exercise price of the awards as of December 31, 2008, using a per share fair market value equal to $10.63.

Potential Payments Upon Termination Apart From a Change in Control

The following table sets forth quantitative estimates of the benefits that would have accrued to Mr. Jordan if his employment had been terminated by us without cause on December 31, 2008, in the event such termination occurred prior to or more than twelve months following a change in control of our company, pursuant to Mr. Jordan's offer letter agreement described above under "—Offer Letter Agreements." No other named executive officer was eligible for benefits in the event of termination of employment during 2008.

Name of Executive Officer	Salary Continuation	Value of Accelerated Equity Awards(1)	Value of Continued Health Care Coverage Premiums	Total
Jeffrey Jordan	$ 360,000	$527,791	$ 15,085	$902,876

(1)   Amounts calculated based on the aggregate amount by which the fair market value of the common stock subject to unvested equity awards exceeded the aggregate exercise price of the awards as of December 31, 2008, using a per share fair market value equal to $10.63.

Potential Payments Upon Termination Following a Change in Control

The following table sets forth quantitative estimates of the benefits that would have accrued to Mr. Jordan pursuant to Mr. Jordan's offer letter agreement described above under "—Offer Letter Agreements" and to Mr. Roberts and Mr. McCullough pursuant to their option agreements if their employment had been terminated by us without cause or if they experienced a constructive termination

84

upon a change in control consummating on December 31, 2008. No other named executive officer was eligible for benefits in the event of termination of employment during 2008.

Name of Executive Officer	Salary Continuation	Value of Accelerated Equity Awards(1)	Value of Continued Health Care Coverage Premiums	Total
Jeffrey Jordan	$ 360,000	$1,055,582	$ 15,085	$1,430,667
Matthew Roberts	—	57,488	—	57,488
Charlie McCullough	—	52,625	—	52,625

(1)   Amounts calculated based on the aggregate amount by which the fair market value of the common stock subject to unvested equity awards exceeded the aggregate exercise price of the awards as of December 31, 2008, using a per share fair market value equal to $10.63.

Proprietary Information and Inventions Agreements

Each of our named executive officers has entered into a standard form agreement with respect to proprietary information and inventions. Among other things, this agreement obligates each named executive officer to refrain from disclosing any of our proprietary information received during the course of employment and, with some exceptions, to assign to us any inventions conceived or developed during the course of employment.

Employee Benefit and Stock Plans

2009 Equity Incentive Award Plan

Our board of directors has adopted and we expect our stockholders to adopt a 2009 Equity Incentive Award Plan, or the 2009 Plan. The principal purpose of the 2009 Plan is to attract, retain and motivate selected employees, consultants and directors through the granting of stock-based compensation awards and cash-based performance bonus awards. The 2009 Plan is also designed to permit us to make cash-based awards and equity-based awards intended to qualify as "performance-based compensation" under Section 162(m) of the Internal Revenue Code.

The principal features of the 2009 Plan are summarized below. This summary is qualified in its entirety by reference to the text of the 2009 Plan, which is filed as an exhibit to the registration statement of which this prospectus is a part.

Share reserve. Under the 2009 Plan, 1,240,104 shares of our common stock will be initially reserved for issuance pursuant to a variety of stock-based compensation awards, including stock options, stock appreciation rights, or SARs, restricted stock awards, restricted stock unit awards, deferred stock awards, dividend equivalent awards, performance share awards, performance stock unit awards, stock payment awards, performance-based awards and other stock-based awards, plus the number of shares remaining available for future awards under our 1999 Stock Plan as of the completion of this offering, which will also be the effective date of the 2009 Plan. The number of shares initially reserved for issuance or transfer pursuant to awards under the 2009 Plan will be increased by (i) the number of shares represented by awards outstanding under our 1999 Stock Plan that are forfeited or lapse unexercised and which following the effective date are not issued under the 1999 Stock Plan and (ii) an annual increase on the first day of each calendar year beginning in 2010 and ending in 2019, equal to the least of (A) 744,063 shares, (B) three percent (3%) of the shares of stock outstanding (on an as converted basis) on the last day of the immediately preceding calendar year and (C) such smaller number of shares of stock as determined by our board of directors; provided,

85

however, no more than 8,680,734 shares of stock may be issued upon the exercise of incentive stock options.

The following counting provisions will be in effect for the share reserve under the 2009 Plan:

- To the extent that an award terminates, expires or lapses for any reason, any shares subject to the award at such time will be available for future grants under the 2009 Plan;

- To the extent shares are tendered or withheld to satisfy the grant, exercise price or tax withholding obligation with respect to any award under the 2009 Plan, such tendered or withheld shares will be available for future grants under the 2009 Plan;

- The payment of dividend equivalents in cash in conjunction with any outstanding awards will not be counted against the shares available for issuance under the 2009 Plan; and

- To the extent permitted by applicable law or any exchange rule, shares issued in assumption of, or in substitution for, any outstanding awards of any entity acquired in any form of combination by us or any of our subsidiaries will not be counted against the shares available for issuance under the 2009 Plan.

Initially, there will be no limit on the number of shares that may be covered by stock-based awards or the maximum aggregate dollar amount subject to cash-based performance awards granted to any individual during any calendar year. However, after a limited transition period, no individual may be granted stock-based awards under the 2009 Plan covering more than 620,052 shares in any calendar year. The limited transition period will expire on the earliest of:

- the first material modification of the 2009 Plan;

- the issuance of all of the shares of our common stock reserved for issuance under the 2009 Plan;

- the expiration of the 2009 Plan;

- the first meeting of our stockholders at which members of our board of directors are to be elected that occurs after the close of the third calendar year following the calendar year in which our initial public offering occurs; or

- such earlier date as may be required by Section 162(m) of the Internal Revenue Code.

Administration. The compensation committee of our board of directors will administer the 2009 Plan unless our board of directors assumes authority for administration. The compensation committee must consist of at least two members of our board of directors, each of whom is intended to qualify as an "outside director," within the meaning of Section 162(m) of the Internal Revenue Code, a "non-employee director" for purposes of Rule 16b-3 under the Securities Exchange Act of 1934, as amended, or the Exchange Act, and an "independent director" within the meaning of the rules of The Nasdaq Stock Market, or other principal securities market on which shares of our common stock are traded. Our compensation committee currently meets these requirements. The 2009 Plan provides that the compensation committee may delegate its authority to grant awards to employees other than executive officers and certain senior executives of our company to a committee consisting of one or more members of our board of directors or one or more of our officers.

Subject to the terms and conditions of the 2009 Plan, the administrator has the authority to select the persons to whom awards are to be made, to determine the number of shares to be subject to awards and the terms and conditions of awards, and to make all other determinations and to take all other actions necessary or advisable for the administration of the 2009 Plan. The administrator is also authorized to adopt, amend or rescind rules relating to administration of the 2009 Plan. Our board of directors may at any time remove the compensation committee as the administrator and revest in itself

86

the authority to administer the 2009 Plan. The full board of directors will administer the 2009 Plan with respect to awards to non-employee directors.

Eligibility. Options, SARs, restricted stock and all other stock-based and cash-based awards under the 2009 Plan may be granted to individuals who are then our officers, employees or consultants or are the officers, employees or consultants of certain of our subsidiaries. Such awards also may be granted to our directors. Only employees may be granted incentive stock options, or ISOs.

Awards. The 2009 Plan provides that the administrator may grant or issue stock options, SARs, restricted stock, restricted stock units, deferred stock, dividend equivalents, performance awards, stock payments and other stock-based and cash-based awards, or any combination thereof. Each award will be set forth in a separate agreement with the person receiving the award and will indicate the type, terms and conditions of the award.

- *Nonqualified stock options*, or NQSOs, will provide for the right to purchase shares of our common stock at a specified price which may not be less than fair market value on the date of grant, and usually will become exercisable (at the discretion of the administrator) in one or more installments after the grant date, subject to the participant's continued employment or service with us and/or subject to the satisfaction of corporate performance targets and individual performance targets established by the administrator. NQSOs may be granted for any term specified by the administrator, but may not exceed ten years.

- *Incentive stock options* will be designed in a manner intended to comply with the provisions of Section 422 of the Internal Revenue Code and will be subject to specified restrictions contained in the Internal Revenue Code. Among such restrictions, ISOs must have an exercise price of not less than the fair market value of a share of common stock on the date of grant, may only be granted to employees, and must not be exercisable after a period of ten years measured from the date of grant. In the case of an ISO granted to an individual who owns (or is deemed to own) at least 10% of the total combined voting power of all classes of our capital stock, the 2009 Plan provides that the exercise price must be at least 110% of the fair market value of a share of common stock on the date of grant and the ISO must not be exercisable after a period of five years measured from the date of grant.

- *Restricted stock* may be granted to any eligible individual and made subject to such restrictions as may be determined by the administrator. Restricted stock, typically, may be forfeited for no consideration or repurchased by us at the original purchase price if the conditions or restrictions on vesting are not met. In general, restricted stock may not be sold, or otherwise transferred, until restrictions are removed or expire. Purchasers of restricted stock, unlike recipients of options, will have voting rights and will have the right to receive dividends, if any, prior to the time when the restrictions lapse; however, extraordinary dividends will generally be placed in escrow, and will not be released until restrictions are removed or expire.

- *Restricted stock units* may be awarded to any eligible individual, typically without payment of consideration, but subject to vesting conditions based on continued employment or service or on performance criteria established by the administrator. Like restricted stock, restricted stock units may not be sold, or otherwise transferred or hypothecated, until vesting conditions are removed or expire. Unlike restricted stock, stock underlying restricted stock units will not be issued until the restricted stock units have vested, and recipients of restricted stock units generally will have no voting or dividend rights prior to the time when vesting conditions are satisfied.

- *Deferred stock awards* represent the right to receive shares of our common stock on a future date. Deferred stock may not be sold or otherwise hypothecated or transferred until issued.

87

Deferred stock will not be issued until the deferred stock award has vested, and recipients of deferred stock generally will have no voting or dividend rights prior to the time when the vesting conditions are satisfied and the shares are issued. Deferred stock awards generally will be forfeited, and the underlying shares of deferred stock will not be issued, if the applicable vesting conditions and other restrictions are not met.

- *Stock appreciation rights* may be granted in connection with stock options or other awards, or separately. SARs granted in connection with stock options or other awards typically will provide for payments to the holder based upon increases in the price of our common stock over a set exercise price. The exercise price of any SAR granted under the 2009 Plan must be at least 100% of the fair market value of a share of our common stock on the date of grant. Except as required by Section 162(m) of the Internal Revenue Code with respect to a SAR intended to qualify as performance-based compensation as described in Section 162(m) of the Internal Revenue Code, there are no restrictions specified in the 2009 Plan on the exercise of SARs or the amount of gain realizable therefrom, although restrictions may be imposed by the administrator in the SAR agreements. SARs under the 2009 Plan will be settled in cash or shares of our common stock, or in a combination of both, at the election of the administrator.

- *Dividend equivalents* represent the value of the dividends, if any, per share paid by us, calculated with reference to the number of shares covered by the stock options, SARs or other awards held by the participant. Dividend equivalents may be settled in cash or shares and at such times as determined by the compensation committee or board of directors, as applicable.

- *Performance awards* may be granted by the administrator on an individual or group basis. Generally, these awards will be based upon specific performance targets and may be paid in cash or in common stock or in a combination of both. Performance awards may include "phantom" stock awards that provide for payments based upon the value of our common stock. Performance awards may also include bonuses that may be granted by the administrator on an individual or group basis and which may be payable in cash or in common stock or in a combination of both.

- *Stock payments* may be authorized by the administrator in the form of common stock or an option or other right to purchase common stock as part of a deferred compensation arrangement in lieu of all or any part of compensation, including bonuses, that would otherwise be payable in cash to the employee, consultant or non-employee director.

Change in control. In the event of a change in control where the acquiror does not assume or replace awards granted under the 2009 Plan, awards issued under the 2009 Plan will be subject to accelerated vesting such that 100% of such award will become vested and exercisable or payable, as applicable. In addition, the administrator will also have complete discretion to structure one or more awards under the 2009 Plan to provide that such awards will become vested and exercisable or payable on an accelerated basis. The administrator may also make appropriate adjustments to awards under the 2009 Plan and is authorized to provide for the acceleration, cash-out, termination, assumption, substitution or conversion of such awards in the event of a change in control or certain other unusual or nonrecurring events or transactions. Under the 2009 Plan, a change in control is generally defined as:

- the transfer or exchange in a single or series of related transactions by our stockholders of more than 50% of our voting stock to a person or group;

- a change in the composition of our board of directors over a two-year period such that 50% or more of the members of the board were elected through one or more contested elections;

88

- a merger, consolidation, reorganization or business combination in which we are involved, directly or indirectly, other than a merger, consolidation, reorganization or business combination which results in our outstanding voting securities immediately before the transaction continuing to represent a majority of the voting power of the acquiring company's outstanding voting securities and after which no person or group beneficially owns 50% or more of the outstanding voting securities of the surviving entity immediately after the transaction;

- the sale, exchange, or transfer of all or substantially all of our assets; or

- stockholder approval of our liquidation or dissolution.

Adjustments of awards. In the event of any stock dividend, stock split, combination or exchange of shares, merger, consolidation, spin-off, recapitalization, distribution of our assets to stockholders (other than normal cash dividends) or any other corporate event affecting the number of outstanding shares of our common stock or the share price of our common stock that would require adjustments to the 2009 Plan or any awards under the 2009 Plan in order to prevent the dilution or enlargement of the potential benefits intended to be made available thereunder, the administrator will make appropriate, proportionate adjustments to:

- the aggregate number and type of shares subject to the 2009 Plan;

- the terms and conditions of outstanding awards (including, without limitation, any applicable performance targets or criteria with respect to such awards); and

- the grant or exercise price per share of any outstanding awards under the 2009 Plan.

Amendment and termination. Our board of directors or the committee (with board approval) may terminate, amend or modify the 2009 Plan at any time and from time to time. However, we must generally obtain stockholder approval:

- to increase the number of shares available under the 2009 Plan (other than in connection with certain corporate events, as described above);

- to grant options with an exercise price that is below 100% of the fair market value of shares of our common stock on the grant date;

- to extend the exercise period for an option beyond ten years from the date of grant; or

- to the extent required by applicable law, rule or regulation (including any applicable stock exchange rule).

Notwithstanding the foregoing, an option may be amended to reduce the per share exercise price below the per share exercise price of such option on the grant date and no options may be granted in exchange for, or in connection with, the cancellation or surrender of options having a higher per share exercise price without receiving additional stockholder approval.

Expiration date. The 2009 Plan will expire on, and no option or other award may be granted pursuant to the 2009 Plan after ten years after the effective date of the 2009 Plan. Any award that is outstanding on the expiration date of the 2009 Plan will remain in force according to the terms of the 2009 Plan and the applicable award agreement.

Securities laws and federal income taxes. The 2009 Plan is designed to comply with various securities and federal tax laws as follows:

- *Securities laws.* The 2009 Plan is intended to conform to all provisions of the Securities Act and the Exchange Act and any and all regulations and rules promulgated by the SEC thereunder, including, without limitation, Rule 16b-3. The 2009 Plan will be administered,

89

and options will be granted and may be exercised, only in such a manner as to conform to such laws, rules and regulations.

- *Section 409A of the Internal Revenue Code.* Certain awards under the 2009 Plan may be considered "nonqualified deferred compensation" for purposes of Section 409A of the Internal Revenue Code, which imposes certain additional requirements regarding the payment of deferred compensation. Generally, if at any time during a taxable year a nonqualified deferred compensation plan fails to meet the requirements of Section 409A, or is not operated in accordance with those requirements, all amounts deferred under the 2009 Plan and all other equity incentive plans for the taxable year and all preceding taxable years, by any participant with respect to whom the failure relates, are includible in gross income for the taxable year to the extent not subject to a substantial risk of forfeiture and not previously included in gross income. If a deferred amount is required to be included in income under Section 409A, the amount also is subject to interest and an additional income tax. The interest imposed is equal to the interest at the underpayment rate plus one percentage point, imposed on the underpayments that would have occurred had the compensation been includible in income for the taxable year when first deferred, or if later, when not subject to a substantial risk of forfeiture. The additional federal income tax is equal to 20% of the compensation required to be included in gross income. In addition, certain states, including California, have laws similar to Section 409A, which impose additional state penalty taxes on such compensation.

- *Section 162(m) of the Internal Revenue Code.* In general, under Section 162(m) of the Internal Revenue Code, income tax deductions of publicly held corporations may be limited to the extent total compensation (including, but not limited to, base salary, annual bonus, and income attributable to stock option exercises and other non-qualified benefits) for certain executive officers exceeds $1,000,000 (less the amount of any "excess parachute payments" as defined in Section 280G of the Internal Revenue Code) in any taxable year of the corporation. However, under Section 162(m), the deduction limit does not apply to certain "performance-based compensation" established by an independent compensation committee that is adequately disclosed to, and approved by, stockholders. In particular, stock options and SARs will satisfy the "performance-based compensation" exception if the awards are made by a qualifying compensation committee, the 2009 Plan sets the maximum number of shares that can be granted to any person within a specified period and the compensation is based solely on an increase in the stock price after the grant date. Specifically, the option exercise price must be equal to or greater than the fair market value of the stock subject to the award on the grant date. Under a Section 162(m) transition rule for compensation plans of corporations which are privately held and which become publicly held in an initial public offering, the 2009 Plan will not be subject to Section 162(m) until a specified transition date, which is the earlier of:

  - the material modification of the 2009 Plan;

  - the issuance of all of the shares of our common stock reserved for issuance under the 2009 Plan;

  - the expiration of the 2009 Plan; or

  - the first meeting of our stockholders at which members of our board of directors are to be elected that occurs after the close of the third calendar year following the calendar year in which our initial public offering occurs.

After the transition date, rights or awards granted under the 2009 Plan, other than options and SARs, will not qualify as "performance-based compensation" for purposes of Section 162(m) unless

90

such rights or awards are granted or vest upon pre-established objective performance goals, the material terms of which are disclosed to and approved by our stockholders. Thus, we expect that such other rights or awards under the plan will not constitute performance-based compensation for purposes of Section 162(m).

We have attempted to structure the 2009 Plan in such a manner that, after the transition date the compensation attributable to stock options, SARs and other performance-based awards which meet the other requirements of Section 162(m) will not be subject to the $1,000,000 limitation. We have not, however, requested a ruling from the IRS or an opinion of counsel regarding this issue.

We intend to file with the SEC a registration statement on Form S-8 covering the shares of our common stock issuable under the 2009 Plan.

Amended and Restated 1999 Stock Plan

Our board of directors adopted, and our stockholders approved, the 1999 Stock Plan in March 1999, which was amended and restated in March 2008. An aggregate of 7,806,401 shares of our common stock is reserved for issuance under the 1999 Stock Plan. The 1999 Stock Plan provides for the grant of ISOs, NQSOs and restricted stock. As of March 31, 2009, options to purchase 2,402,605 shares of our common stock at a weighted average exercise price per share of $7.33 remained outstanding under the 1999 Stock Plan. As of March 31, 2009, options to purchase 162,836 shares of our common stock remained available for future issuance pursuant to awards granted under the 1999 Stock Plan.

Our board of directors, or a committee thereof appointed by our board of directors, has the authority to administer the 1999 Stock Plan and the awards granted under it. Following the completion of this offering, no further awards will be granted under the 1999 Stock Plan; all outstanding awards will continue to be governed by their existing terms.

Stock options. The 1999 Stock Plan provides for the grant of ISOs under the federal tax laws or NQSOs. ISOs may be granted only to employees. NQSOs and stock purchase rights may be granted to employees, directors or consultants. The exercise price of ISOs granted to employees who at the time of grant own stock representing more than 10% of the voting power of all classes of our common stock may not be less than 110% of the fair market value of our common stock on the date of grant, and the exercise price of ISOs granted to any other employees may not be less than 100% of the fair market value of our common stock on the date of grant. The exercise price of NQSOs to employees, directors or consultants who at the time of grant own stock representing more than 10% of the voting power of all classes of our common stock may not be less than 110% of the fair market value of our common stock on the date of grant, and the exercise price of nonstatutory stock options to all other employees, directors or consultants may not be less than 85% of the fair market value of our common stock on the date of grant. Shares subject to options under the 1999 Stock Plan generally vest in a series of installments over an optionee's period of service. Except with respect to options granted to officers, outside directors (as defined in the 1999 Stock Plan) and consultants, a grant of an option to purchase shares shall become exercisable at least as rapidly as 20% per year over the five-year period commencing on the date of grant.

In general, the maximum term of options granted is ten years. The maximum term of ISOs granted to an optionee who owns stock representing more than 10% of the voting power of all classes of our common stock is five years. If an optionee's service relationship with us terminates other than by death or disability, the optionee may exercise the vested portion of any option in such period of time as specified in the optionee's option agreement, but in no event will such period be less than three months following the termination of service. If an optionee's service relationship with us terminates by disability, the optionee may exercise the vested portion of any option in such period of time as specified in the optionee's option agreement, but in no event will such period be less than six months

91

following the termination of service. If an optionee's service relationship with us terminates as a result of the optionee's death, the optionee's designee may exercise the vested portion of any option in such period of time as specified in the optionee's option agreement, but in no event will such period be less then twelve months following the optionee's death. Shares of common stock representing any unvested portion of the option on the date of termination shall immediately cease to be issuable and shall become available for issuance under the 1999 Stock Plan. No option shall continue to be exercisable after the optionee's termination of service after the ten-year anniversary of the date of grant. If, after termination, the optionee does not exercise the option within the time period specified, the option shall terminate and the shares of common stock covered by such option will become available for issuance under the 1999 Stock Plan.

Restricted stock. Under the 1999 Stock Plan, restricted stock may be granted or sold to employees, directors or consultants, and made subject to such restrictions as may be determined by the administrator. The right to acquire restricted stock under the 1999 Stock Plan automatically expires if not exercised by the purchaser within 30 days after the grant of such right was communicated to the purchaser. The right to purchase restricted stock shall not be transferable and shall be exercisable only by the purchaser to whom such right was granted. The purchase price of restricted stock offered under the 1999 Stock Plan shall not be less than 85% of the fair market value of such shares, or in the case of purchase by an individual who owns more than 10% of the total combined voting power of all classes of outstanding stock of our company, it parent or any of our subsidiaries, the purchase price shall be at least 100% of the fair market value. For restricted stock subject to a repurchase right that is awarded to or purchased by an individual who is not an officer, outside director (as defined in the 1999 Plan) or consultant, the 1999 Stock Plan provides that such repurchase price shall lapse at least as rapidly as 20% per year over the five-year period beginning on the date of the award or sale. The repurchase right may be exercised only within 90 days after the termination of the purchaser's service with our company. Purchasers of restricted stock, unlike recipients of options, will have voting rights and will have the right to receive dividends, if any, prior to the time when the restrictions lapse, however, extraordinary dividends will generally be placed in escrow, and will not be released until restrictions are removed or expire.

Corporate transactions. In the event of a sale, transfer or other disposition of all or substantially all of our company's assets, or the consummation of certain mergers or consolidations of our company with or into another entity or any other corporate reorganization, the administrator of the 1999 Stock Plan has the discretion to take one or more of the following actions: (a) provide that any option shall immediately vest if such option is not assumed or substituted for by the surviving corporation or its parent and the surviving corporation; or (b) provide that the repurchase right of any restricted stock or option that is not assigned to the entity, or its parent or subsidiary, that employs the holder immediately after such corporate transaction shall lapse and all such shares shall become vested. In addition, in the event of such corporate transaction, the restricted stock repurchase right shall lapse with respect to that percentage of shares equal to (a)(i) six months plus (ii) the number of complete months the optionee has provided continuous service to our company, divided by (b) the total number of months of the original vesting schedule for the shares underlying the award.

We intend to file with the SEC a registration statement on Form S-8 covering the shares of our common stock issuable under the 1999 Stock Plan.

401(k) Plan

Currently, all of our employees over the age of 18 are eligible to participate in our 401(k) Plan. Under the 401(k) Plan, eligible employees may elect to reduce their current compensation by up to the lesser of 100% of their base salary and cash compensation or the prescribed annual limit and contribute these amounts to the 401(k) Plan. The annual limit in 2008 was $15,500. We may make matching or other contributions to the 401(k) Plan on behalf of eligible employees. In 2008, we

92

matched up to $500 in employee contributions to the 401(k) Plan. The 401(k) Plan is intended to qualify under Section 401 of the Internal Revenue Code so that contributions by employees to the 401(k) Plan, and income earned on the 401(k) Plan contributions, are not taxable to employees until withdrawn from the 401(k) Plan. The trustees under the 401(k) Plan, at the direction of each participant, invest the 401(k) Plan employee salary deferrals in selected investment options.

Limitation on Liability and Indemnification Matters

Our amended and restated certificate of incorporation and amended and restated bylaws, each to be effective upon the completion of this offering, will provide that we will indemnify our directors and officers, and may indemnify our employees and other agents, to the fullest extent permitted by the Delaware General Corporation Law, which prohibits our amended and restated certificate of incorporation from limiting the liability of our directors for the following:

- any breach of the director's duty of loyalty to us or to our stockholders;

- acts or omissions not in good faith or that involve intentional misconduct or a knowing violation of law;

- unlawful payment of dividends or unlawful stock repurchases or redemptions; and

- any transaction from which the director derived an improper personal benefit.

If Delaware law is amended to authorize corporate action further eliminating or limiting the personal liability of a director, then the liability of our directors will be eliminated or limited to the fullest extent permitted by Delaware law, as so amended. Our amended and restated certificate of incorporation does not eliminate a director's duty of care and, in appropriate circumstances, equitable remedies, such as injunctive or other forms of non-monetary relief, remain available under Delaware law. This provision also does not affect a director's responsibilities under any other laws, such as the federal securities laws or other state or federal laws. Under our amended and restated bylaws, we will also be empowered to purchase insurance on behalf of any person whom we are required or permitted to indemnify.

In addition to the indemnification required in our amended and restated certificate of incorporation and amended and restated bylaws, we plan to enter into indemnification agreements with each of our current directors, officers and some employees before the completion of this offering. These agreements will provide for the indemnification of our directors, officers and some employees for certain expenses and liabilities incurred in connection with any action, suit, proceeding or alternative dispute resolution mechanism, or hearing, inquiry or investigation that may lead to the foregoing, to which they are a party, or are threatened to be made a party, by reason of the fact that they are or were a director, officer, employee, agent or fiduciary of our company, or any of our subsidiaries, by reason of any action or inaction by them while serving as an officer, director, agent or fiduciary, or by reason of the fact that they were serving at our request as a director, officer, employee, agent or fiduciary of another entity. In the case of an action or proceeding by or in the right of our company or any of our subsidiaries, no indemnification will be provided for any claim where a court determines that the indemnified party is prohibited from receiving indemnification. We believe that these bylaw provisions and indemnification agreements are necessary to attract and retain qualified persons as directors and officers. We also maintain directors' and officers' liability insurance.

The limitation of liability and indemnification provisions in our amended and restated certificate of incorporation and amended and restated bylaws may discourage stockholders from bringing a lawsuit against directors for breach of their fiduciary duties. They may also reduce the likelihood of derivative litigation against directors and officers, even though an action, if successful, might benefit us and our stockholders. A stockholder's investment may be harmed to the extent we pay the costs of settlement and damage awards against directors and officers pursuant to these

93

indemnification provisions. Insofar as indemnification for liabilities arising under the Securities Act may be permitted to our directors, officers and controlling persons pursuant to the foregoing provisions, or otherwise, we have been advised that, in the opinion of the SEC, such indemnification is against public policy as expressed in the Securities Act, and is, therefore, unenforceable. There is no pending litigation or proceeding naming any of our directors or officers as to which indemnification is being sought, nor are we aware of any pending or threatened litigation that may result in claims for indemnification by any director or officer.

Rule 10b5-1 Sales Plans

Our directors and executive officers may adopt written plans, known as Rule 10b5-1 plans, in which they will contract with a broker to buy or sell shares of our common stock on a periodic basis. Under a Rule 10b5-1 plan, a broker executes trades pursuant to parameters established by the director or officer when entering into the plan, without further direction from them. The director or officer may amend or terminate the plan in some circumstances. Our directors and executive officers may also buy or sell additional shares outside of a Rule 10b5-1 plan when they are not in possession of material, nonpublic information.

94

CERTAIN RELATIONSHIPS AND RELATED TRANSACTIONS

We describe below transactions and series of similar transactions, during our last three fiscal years, to which we were a party or will be a party, in which:

- the amounts involved exceeded or will exceed $120,000; and

- any of our directors, executive officers, holders of more than 5% of our common stock or any member of their immediate family had or will have a direct or indirect material interest.

Participation in Initial Public Offering

Directors A. George "Skip" Battle, Michelle Peluso and Paul Pressler have indicated an interest in purchasing up to an aggregate of 58,822 shares of common stock in this offering, based on an assumed initial public offering price of $17.00 per share. However, because indications of interest are not binding agreements or commitments to purchase, these directors may elect not to purchase any shares in this offering.

Investors' Rights Agreement

We are party to an investors' rights agreement which provides that holders of our convertible preferred stock have the right to demand that we file a registration statement or request that their shares be covered by a registration statement that we are otherwise filing. For a more detailed description of these registration rights, see "Description of Capital Stock—Registration Rights."

Other Transactions

Director Danny Meyer is the founder and president of Union Square Hospitality Group, or USHG. USHG is a restaurant customer of ours, and during the twelve-month periods ended December 31, 2006, 2007 and 2008, USHG made aggregate payments to us of approximately $153,000, $163,000 and $175,000, respectively. Since January 1, 2009, USHG has made aggregate payments to us of approximately $72,000, and we currently expect that USHG may make aggregate payments to us that exceed $120,000 during 2009.

We have entered into an offer letter agreement with our chief executive officer that, among other things, provides for certain severance and change of control benefits. For a description of this agreement, see "Management—Executive Compensation—Compensation Discussion and Analysis—Offer Letter Agreements."

We have granted stock options to our executive officers and certain of our directors. For a description of these options, see "Management—Executive Compensation—Grants of Plan-Based Awards in 2008 Table."

We will enter into indemnification agreements with each of our current directors, officers and some employees before the completion of this offering. See "Management—Limitation on Liability and Indemnification Matters."

Other than as described above under this section "Certain Relationships and Related Transactions," since the beginning of our last fiscal year, we have not entered into any transactions, nor are there any currently proposed transactions, between us and a related party where the amount involved exceeds, or would exceed, $120,000, and in which any related person had or will have a direct or indirect material interest. We believe the terms of the transactions described above were comparable to terms we could have obtained in arm's length dealings with unrelated third parties.

95

Policies and Procedures for Related Party Transactions

We do not currently have, and prior to the completion of this offering we will not have, a formal, written policy or procedure for the review and approval of related party transactions. However, all related party transactions are currently reviewed by our board of directors.

Our board of directors has adopted a written related person transaction policy, effective upon the completion of this offering, which sets forth the policies and procedures for the review and approval or ratification of related person transactions. This policy covers any transaction, arrangement or relationship, or any series of similar transactions, arrangements or relationships, in which we were or are to be a participant, the amount involved exceeds $50,000 and a related person had or will have a direct or indirect material interest. While the policy covers related party transactions in which the amount involved exceeds $50,000, the policy states that related party transactions in which the amount involved exceeds $120,000 are required to be disclosed in applicable filings as required by the Securities Act, Exchange Act and related rules. Our board of directors set the $50,000 threshold for approval of related party transactions in the policy at an amount lower than that which is required to be disclosed under the Securities Act, Exchange Act and related rules because we believe it is appropriate for our audit committee to review transactions or potential transactions in which the amount involved exceeds $50,000, as opposed to $120,000. Pursuant to this policy, our audit committee will (i) review the relevant facts and circumstances of each related party transaction, including if the transaction is on terms comparable to those that could be obtained in arm's length dealings with an unrelated third party and the extent of the related party's interest in the transaction, and (ii) take into account the conflicts of interest and corporate opportunity provisions of our code of business conduct and ethics. Management will present to our audit committee each proposed related party transaction, including all relevant facts and circumstances relating thereto, and will update the audit committee as to any material changes to any related party transaction. All related party transactions may only be consummated if our audit committee has approved or ratified such transaction in accordance with the guidelines set forth in the policy. Certain types of transactions have been pre-approved by our audit committee under the policy. These pre-approved transactions include: (i) certain compensation arrangements; (ii) transactions in the ordinary course of business where the related party's interest arises only (a) from his or her position as a director of another entity that is party to the transaction, and/or (b) from an equity interest of less than 5% in another entity that is party to the transaction, or (c) from a limited partnership interest of less than 5%, subject to certain limitations; and (iii) transactions in the ordinary course of business where the interest of the related party arises solely from the ownership of a class of equity securities in our company where all holders of such class of equity securities will receive the same benefit on a pro rata basis. No director may participate in the approval of a related party transaction for which he or she is a related party.

PRINCIPAL AND SELLING STOCKHOLDERS

The following table sets forth, as of March 31, 2009, information regarding beneficial ownership of our capital stock by:

- each person, or group of affiliated persons, known by us to beneficially own more than 5% of our voting securities;
- each of our named executive officers;
- each of our directors;
- all of our executive officers and directors as a group; and
- each of the selling stockholders.

Beneficial ownership is determined according to the rules of the SEC and generally means that a person has beneficial ownership of a security if he, she or it possesses sole or shared voting or investment power of that security, including options and warrants that are currently exercisable or

96

exercisable within 60 days. Except as indicated by the footnotes below, we believe, based on the information furnished to us, that the persons named in the table below have sole voting and investment power with respect to all shares of common stock shown that they beneficially own, subject to community property laws where applicable.

This table lists applicable percentage ownership based on 20,031,903 shares of common stock outstanding as of March 31, 2009, after giving effect to the conversion of our outstanding preferred stock into shares of common stock in connection with this offering and based on 21,604,587 shares of common stock outstanding upon completion of this offering.

Common stock subject to stock options and warrants currently exercisable or exercisable within 60 days of March 31, 2009, are deemed to be outstanding for computing the percentage ownership of the person holding these options and warrants and the percentage ownership of any group of which the holder is a member but are not deemed outstanding for computing the percentage of any other person.

We have based our calculation of the percentage of beneficial ownership prior to the offering on 20,031,903 shares of common stock outstanding on March 31, 2009 (as adjusted to reflect at that date the conversion of all shares of our preferred stock outstanding into 9,075,737 shares of common stock). We have based our calculation of the percentage of beneficial ownership after the offering on 21,604,587 shares of our common stock outstanding immediately after the completion of this offering (assuming no exercise of the underwriters' overallotment option).

Unless otherwise noted below, the address for each of the stockholders in the table below is c/o OpenTable, Inc., 799 Market Street, 4th Floor, San Francisco, California 94103.

	Beneficial Ownership Prior to the Offering(1)					Beneficial Ownership After the Offering	
Name and Address of Beneficial Owner	Common Stock	Options Exercisable within 60 Days	Number of Shares Beneficially Owned	Percent	Shares Being Offered	Number of Shares Beneficially Owned	Percent
5% Stockholders:							
Benchmark Capital Partners IV, L.P.(2) 2480 Sand Hill Road, Suite 200 Menlo Park, CA 94025	5,290,211	—	5,290,211	26.41%	—	5,290,211	24.49%
Funds affiliated with Impact Venture Partners(3) 2705 Westlake Drive Austin, TX 78746	3,503,853	—	3,503,853	17.49%	—	3,503,853	16.22%
IAC/InterActiveCorp(4) 555 West 18th Street New York, NY 10011	2,177,550	—	2,177,550	10.87%	—	2,177,550	10.08%
Funds affiliated with Integral Capital Partners V, L.P.(5) 3000 Sand Hill Road Building Three, Suite 240 Menlo Park, CA 94025	1,503,072	—	1,503,072	7.50%	—	1,503,072	6.96%

97

Name and Address of Beneficial Owner	Beneficial Ownership Prior to the Offering(1)					Beneficial Ownership After the Offering	
	Common Stock	Options Exercisable within 60 Days	Number of Shares Beneficially Owned	Percent	Shares Being Offered	Number of Shares Beneficially Owned	Percent
Executive Officers and Directors:							
Jeff Jordan(6)	767,693	157,651	925,344	4.58%	—	925,344	4.28%
Matthew Roberts(7)	133,332	68,266	201,598	1.00%	—	201,598	*
Joel Brown(8)	257,599	35,000	292,599	1.46%	36,000	256,599	1.19%
Michael Dodson(9)	261,600	46,000	307,600	1.53%	32,000	275,600	1.27%
Charlie McCullough(10)	251,200	14,000	265,200	1.32%	16,000	249,200	1.15%
A. George "Skip" Battle(11)	50,270	—	50,270	*	—	50,270	*
Adam R. Dell(3)	3,503,853	—	3,503,853	17.49%	—	3,503,853	16.22%
J. William Gurley(2)	5,290,211	—	5,290,211	26.41%	—	5,290,211	24.49%
Thomas H. Layton(12)	2,379,019	—	2,379,019	11.88%	139,020	2,239,999	10.30%
Danny Meyer(13)	161,777	32,000	193,777	*	69,314	124,463	*
Michelle Peluso(14)	—	32,000	32,000	*	—	32,000	*
Paul Pressler(15)	—	32,000	32,000	*	—	32,000	*
All executive officers and directors as a group (12 persons)	13,056,554	416,917	13,473,471	67.21%	292,334	13,181,137	60.94%
Other Selling Stockholders:							
Glenn Allen	40,258	—	40,258	*	40,258	—	*
Bisharat Family Trust(16)	126,040	—	126,040	*	32,000	94,040	*
Brainstorm Ventures, L.P.(17)	70,118	—	70,118	*	36,487	33,631	*
Bryce Catlin(18)	16,000	6,000	22,000	*	1,000	21,000	*
Comdisco Ventures Fund A, LLC(19)	103,522	—	103,522	*	52,000	51,522	*
Michael & Leslye Dellar trustees of the Michael D. Dellar & Leslye L. Dellar Revocable Trust dated 11/5/96(20)	19,068	—	19,068	*	1,600	17,468	*
Sidney Gorham	25,266	—	25,266	*	25,266	—	*
Lynda Kim Halprin	40,000	—	40,000	*	40,000	—	*
Melchart, L.L.C.(21)	25,880	—	25,880	*	25,880	—	*
Pacific Asset Partners, LP(22)	87,676	—	87,676	*	87,676	—	*
Davis Peterson	42,400	—	42,400	*	9,600	32,800	*
Randall Reeves(23)	12,800	6,000	18,800	*	2,400	16,400	*
Chuck Templeton	207,684	—	207,684	1.04%	100,000	107,684	*
The Charles Schwab Corporation(24)†	77,065	—	77,065	*	77,065	—	*
Venture Frogs Fund I, L.L.C.(25)	74,611	—	74,611	*	74,611	—	*
W Capital Partners I, L.P.(26)	155,285	—	155,285	*	155,285	—	*
Worldspan OpenTable Holdings LLC(27)†	98,347	—	98,347	*	98,347	—	*
Michael Xenakis(28)	158,400	67,001	225,401	1.12%	8,000	217,401	1.01%
Zagat Survey, LLC(29)	155,285	—	155,285	*	155,285	—	*
Scott Carl Kovalik††	16,084	—	16,084	*	16,084	—	*
Snyder Revocable Trust dated May 9, 2000(30)††	5,714	—	5,714	*	5,714	—	*
Robert Goddard, Trustee of the Robert Goddard Family Trust, dated December 3, 2004†	2,857	—	2,857	*	2,857	—	*
Jeff Handy†	13,869	—	13,869	*	6,800	7,069	*
All other selling stockholders(31)	106,371	19,700	126,071	*	80,767	45,304	*

* Represents beneficial ownership of less than one percent (1%) of the outstanding common stock.

(†) The selling stockholder is an affiliate of a registered broker-dealer. Such selling stockholder has certified that it has purchased the shares being offered by it in the ordinary course of business, and at the time of the purchase of such shares, had no agreements or understandings, directly or indirectly, with any person to distribute such shares.

98

(††)   The selling stockholder is a registered broker-dealer. Such selling stockholder has certified that it has purchased the shares being offered by it in the ordinary course of business, and at the time of the purchase of such shares, had no agreements or understandings, directly or indirectly, with any person to distribute such shares. Selling stockholders that are broker-dealers are deemed to be "underwriters" within the meaning of Section 2(11) of the Securities Act.

(1)   Shares shown in the table above include shares held in the beneficial owner's name or jointly with others, or in the name of a bank, nominee or trustee for the beneficial owner's account.

(2)   Consists of 5,290,211 shares held by Benchmark Capital Partners IV, L.P., or BCP IV, as nominee for Benchmark Capital Partners IV, L.P., Benchmark Founders' Fund IV, L.P., Benchmark Founders' Fund IV-A, L.P., Benchmark Founders' Fund IV-B, L.P., Benchmark Founders' Fund IV-X, L.P. and related individuals, or Benchmark Funds. Benchmark Capital Management Co. IV, L.L.C., or BCMC IV, is the general partner of BCP IV. BCMC IV's managing members of the general partner are Alexandre Balkanski, Bruce Dunlevie, J. William Gurley, Kevin Harvey, Robert Kagle, Andrew Rachleff and Steven Spurlock. These individuals may be deemed to have shared voting and investment power over the shares held by the Benchmark Funds. Each of these individuals disclaims beneficial ownership of such shares, except to the extent of his pecuniary interest therein.

(3)   Represents 3,262,439 shares held by Impact Venture Partners, L.P. and 241,414 shares held by Impact Entrepreneurs Fund, L.P. Impact Venture Advisors, LLC is the sole general partner of Impact Venture Partners, L.P. and Impact Entrepreneurs Fund, L.P. Adam Dell is the sole managing member of Impact Venture Advisors, LLC. Mr. Dell may be deemed to have sole voting and investment power over the shares held by Impact Venture Partners, L.P. and Impact Entrepreneurs Fund, L.P. Mr. Dell disclaims beneficial ownership of such shares, except to the extent of his pecuniary interest therein.

(4)   The members of the board of directors of IAC/InterActiveCorp are Barry Diller, Victor Kaufman, Donald R. Keough, Bryan Lourd, John C. Malone, Arthur C. Martinez, Steven Rattner, David Rosenblatt, Alan Spoon, Alexander von Furstenberg and Michael P. Zeisser. These individuals may be deemed to have shared voting and investment power over the shares held by IAC/InterActiveCorp. Each of these individuals disclaims beneficial ownership of such shares, except to the extent of his pecuniary interest therein.

(5)   Represents 1,480,725 shares held by Integral Capital Partners V, L.P., 19,568 shares held by Integral Capital Partners V Side Fund, L.P. and 2,779 shares held by Integral Capital Partners V SLP Side Fund, LLC. The sole general partner of Integral Capital Partners V, L.P. is Integral Capital Management V, LLC. The managers of Integral Capital Management V, LLC are Pamela Hagenah, Glen Kacher, Roger McNamee, Charles Morris, John Powell and Brian Stansky. The sole general partner of each of Integral Capital Partners V Side Fund, L.P. and Integral Capital Partners V SLP Side Fund, LLC is ICP Management V, LLC. The managers of ICP Management V, LLC are Pamela Hagenah, Glen Kacher, Roger McNamee and John Powell. These individuals may be deemed to have shared voting and investment power over the shares held by Integral Capital Partners V, L.P., Integral Capital Partners V Side Fund, L.P. and Integral Capital Partners V SLP Side Fund, LLC, as applicable. Each of these individuals disclaims beneficial ownership of such shares, except to the extent of his or her pecuniary interest therein.

(6)   Includes 431,829 shares held by the Jordan Family Revocable Trust U/A 8/25/95, 52,700 shares held by the Jeffrey D. Jordan Annuity Trust dated February 5, 2008, 63,974 shares held by the Jeffrey D. Jordan Annuity Trust II dated October 2, 2008, 51,258 shares held by the Jeffrey D. Jordan Annuity Trust-2009 dated March 30, 2009, 52,700 shares held by the Karen A. Jordan Annuity Trust dated February 5, 2008, 63,974 shares held by the Karen A. Jordan Annuity Trust II dated October 2, 2008 and 51,258 shares held by the Karen A. Jordan Annuity Trust-2009 dated March 30, 2009. Includes 431,829 shares subject to our right of repurchase, which right lapses as to 15,993 shares each succeeding month over the next 27 months, and 157,651 shares subject to options that are exercisable within 60 days of March 31, 2009.

(7)   Includes 109,332 shares held by the Roberts Family Trust, dated April 24, 2008, and 24,000 shares held by the Matthew Roberts Annuity Trust, dated April 24, 2008. Includes 4,167 shares subject to our right of repurchase, which right lapses as to 1,388 shares each succeeding month over the next three months. Includes 68,266 shares subject to options that are exercisable within 60 days of March 31, 2009, of which 2,811 shares, if these options were exercised in full, would be subject to vesting and a right of repurchase in our favor upon Mr. Roberts' cessation of service prior to vesting. Mr. Roberts disclaims beneficial ownership of the shares held by the Matthew Roberts Annuity Trust, dated April 24, 2008.

(8)   Includes 257,599 shares held by Joel T. Brown and Lorraine D. Brown, or their successor(s), Trustees UTA dated October 27, 1998. Includes 11,334 shares subject to our right of repurchase, which right lapses as to 666

99

shares each succeeding month over the next 17 months. Includes 35,000 shares subject to options that are exercisable within 60 days of March 31, 2009.

(9)   Includes 28,333 shares subject to our right of repurchase, which right lapses as to 1,666 shares each succeeding month over the next 17 months. Includes 46,000 shares subject to options that are exercisable within 60 days of March 31, 2009.

(10)   Includes 251,200 shares held by The Charles McCullough and Carol McCullough Joint Living Trust. Includes 17,000 shares subject to our right of repurchase, which right lapses as to 1,000 shares each succeeding month over the next 17 months. Includes 14,000 shares subject to options that are exercisable within 60 days of March 31, 2009.

(11)   Includes 13,313 shares subject to our right of repurchase, which right lapses as to 634 shares each succeeding month over the next 21 months. Also includes 10,249 shares subject to our right of repurchase, which right lapses as to 366 shares each succeeding month over the next 28 months. Mr. Battle has indicated an interest in purchasing up to 44,117 shares of common stock in this offering at the initial public offering price, based on an assumed initial public offering price of $17.00 per share. Because this indication of interest is not a binding agreement or commitment to purchase, Mr. Battle may elect not to purchase any shares in this offering. However, if any shares are purchased by Mr. Battle, the number of shares beneficially owned and the percentage of common stock beneficially owned after the offering will differ from that set forth in the table above. If Mr. Battle purchases all 44,117 shares, the number of shares beneficially owned by Mr. Battle will increase to 94,387. In addition, if Mr. Battle and other directors purchase an aggregate of 58,822 shares, the number of shares beneficially owned by all executive officers and directors as a group will increase to 13,239,959 and the percentage of common stock beneficially owned by all executive officers and directors as a group will increase to 61.24%.

(12)   Includes 1,872,625 shares held by the Layton Community Property Trust, dated November 29, 1999, as amended, 480,000 shares held by the Layton 2002 Childrens Trust and 26,394 shares held by the Thomas H. Layton Separate Property Revocable Trust of November 29, 1999, as amended. Mr. Layton disclaims beneficial ownership of the shares held by the Layton 2002 Childrens Trust.

(13)   Includes 121,777 shares held by Hospitality Investments, G.P. Daniel Meyer Revocable Trust is the managing general partner of Hospitality Investments, G.P. Danny Meyer and Jack Polsky are the trustees of the Daniel Meyer Revocable Trust. These individuals may be deemed to have shared voting and investment power over the shares held by Hospitality Investments, G.P. Each of these individuals disclaims beneficial ownership of such shares, except to the extent of his pecuniary interest therein. Includes 32,000 shares subject to options that are exercisable within 60 days of March 31, 2009, of which 22,000 shares, if these options were exercised in full, would be subject to vesting and a right of repurchase in our favor upon Mr. Meyer's cessation of service prior to vesting.

(14)   Includes 32,000 shares subject to options that are exercisable within 60 days of March 31, 2009, of which 22,667 shares, if these options were exercised in full, would be subject to vesting and a right of repurchase in our favor upon Ms. Peluso's cessation of service prior to vesting. Ms. Peluso has indicated an interest in purchasing up to 5,882 shares of common stock in this offering at the initial public offering price, based on an assumed initial public offering price of $17.00 per share. Because this indication of interest is not a binding agreement or commitment to purchase, Ms. Peluso may elect not to purchase any shares in this offering. However, if any shares are purchased by Ms. Peluso, the number of shares beneficially owned and the percentage of common stock beneficially owned after the offering will differ from that set forth in the table above. If Ms. Peluso purchases all 5,882 shares, the number of shares beneficially owned by Ms. Peluso will increase to 37,882. In addition, if Ms. Peluso and other directors purchase an aggregate of 58,822 shares, the number of shares beneficially owned by all executive officers and directors as a group will increase to 13,239,959 and the percentage of common stock beneficially owned by all executive officers and directors as a group will increase to 61.24%.

(15)   Includes 32,000 shares subject to options that are exercisable within 60 days of March 31, 2009, of which 22,667 shares, if these options were exercised in full, would be subject to vesting and a right of repurchase in our favor upon Mr. Pressler's cessation of service prior to vesting. Mr. Pressler has indicated an interest in purchasing up to 8,823 shares of common stock in this offering at the initial public offering price, based on an assumed initial public offering price of $17.00 per share. Because this indication of interest is not a binding agreement or commitment to purchase, Mr. Pressler may elect not to purchase any shares in this offering. However, if any shares are purchased by Mr. Pressler, the number of shares beneficially owned and the percentage of common stock beneficially owned after the offering will differ from that set forth in the table above. If Mr. Pressler purchases all 8,823 shares, the number of shares beneficially owned by Mr. Pressler will increase to 40,823. In

100

addition, if Mr. Pressler and other directors purchase an aggregate of 58,822 shares, the number of shares beneficially owned by all executive officers and directors as a group will increase to 13,239,959 and the percentage of common stock beneficially owned by all executive officers and directors as a group will increase to 61.24%.

(16) George and Jaleh Bisharat are the trustees of the Bisharat Family Trust. These individuals may be deemed to share dispositive and voting power over the shares owned by Bisharat Family Trust. Each of these individuals disclaims beneficial ownership of such shares, except to the extent of his or her pecuniary interest therein. Ms. Bisharat previously served as a member of our board of directors and vice president of marketing. Her roles in these positions ended in 2007.

(17) Includes 46,585 shares held by Brainstorm Ventures, L.P. and 23,533 shares held by Keith Cox. The general partner of Brainstorm Ventures, L.P. is Brainstorm General Partner, LLC. The managing members of Brainstorm General Partner, LLC are Keith Cox, Eduardo Ralla and Zev Zaidman. These individuals may be deemed to share dispositive and voting power over the shares owned by Brainstorm Ventures, L.P. Each of these individuals disclaims beneficial ownership of such shares, except to the extent of his pecuniary interest therein. The address of BrainStorm Ventures, L.P. and Keith Cox is 6 Laurel Avenue, Belvedere, CA 94920.

(18) Includes 4,000 shares held by Bryce Catlin and Kristin Nicole Bruebaker, as Community Property. Includes 333 shares subject to our right of repurchase, which right lapses as to 166 shares each succeeding month over the next two months, 458 shares subject to our right of repurchase, which right lapses as to 41 shares each succeeding month over the next 11 months and 958 shares subject to our right of repurchase, which right lapses as to 41 shares each succeeding month over the next 23 months. Includes 6,000 shares subject to options that are exercisable within 60 days of March 31, 2009, of which 6,000 shares, if these options were exercised in full, would be subject to vesting and a right of repurchase in our favor upon Mr. Catlin's cessation of service prior to vesting. Mr. Catlin is a current employee of our company.

(19) John Bullock, Dan Bathon and Steve Karlson are the managing partners of Comdisco Ventures Fund A, LLC. These individuals may be deemed to share dispositive and voting power over the shares owned by Comdisco Ventures Fund A, LLC. Each of these individuals disclaims beneficial ownership of such shares, except to the extent of his pecuniary interest therein. The address of Comdisco Ventures Fund A, LLC is 52 Waltham Street, Lexington, MA 02421.

(20) Includes 19,068 shares held by Michael & Leslye Dellar trustees of the Michael D. Dellar & Leslye L. Dellar Revocable Trust dated 11/5/96. Michael Dellar and Leslye Dellar may be deemed to share dispositive and voting power over the shares owned by Michael D. Dellar & Leslye L. Dellar Revocable Trust dated 11/5/96. Each of these individuals disclaims beneficial ownership of such shares, except to the extent of his or her pecuniary interest therein.

(21) Richard Melman, Kevin Brown and Jay Stieber are the managing members of Melchart, L.L.C. These individuals may be deemed to share dispositive and voting power over the shares owned by Melchart, L.L.C. Each of these individuals disclaims beneficial ownership of such shares, except to the extent of his pecuniary interest therein. The address of Melchart, L.L.C. is 5419 N. Sheridan Road, Chicago, IL 60640.

(22) Pacific Management Ltd. is the general partner of Pacific Asset Partners, LP. Robert M. Stafford, Brian E. Dombkowski and Craig A. Stephens are the managing partners of Pacific Management Ltd. These individuals may be deemed to share dispositive and voting power over the shares owned by Pacific Asset Partners, LP. Each of these individuals disclaims beneficial ownership of such shares, except to the extent of his pecuniary interest therein. The address of Pacific Asset Partners, LP is Two Embarcadero Center, Suite 1340, San Francisco, CA 94111.

(23) Includes 6,000 shares subject to options that are exercisable within 60 days of March 31, 2009, of which 4,667 shares, if these options were exercised in full, would be subject to vesting and a right of repurchase in our favor upon Mr. Reeve's cessation of service prior to vesting. Mr. Reeves is a current employee of our company.

(24) The members of the board of directors of The Charles Schwab Corporation are William F. Aldinger III, Nancy H. Bechtle, Walter W. Bettinger II, C. Preston Butcher, Donald G. Fisher, Frank C. Herringer, Stephen T. McLin, Charles R. Schwab, Paula A. Sneed, Roger O. Walther and Robert N. Wilson. These individuals may be deemed to have shared voting and investment power over the shares held by The Charles Schwab Corporation. Each of these individuals disclaims beneficial ownership of such shares, except to the extent of his or her pecuniary interest therein. The address of The Charles Schwab Corporation is 101 Montgomery Street, San Francisco, CA 94104.

101

(25)   Venture Frogs, L.L.C. is the management company for Venture Frogs Fund I, L.L.C. Alfred Lin is the general manager of Venture Frogs, L.L.C. Mr. Lin may be deemed to have sole dispositive and voting power over the shares owned by Venture Frogs Fund I, L.L.C. Mr. Lin disclaims beneficial ownership of such shares, except to the extent of his pecuniary interest therein. The address of Venture Frogs Fund I, L.L.C. is 2280 Corporate Circle, Suite 100, Henderson, NV 89074.

(26)   WCPI, LLC is the general partner of W Capital Partners I, L.P. David Wachter, Stephen Wertheimer and Robert Migliorino are the managing members of WCPI, LLC. These individuals may be deemed to share dispositive and voting power over the shares owned by W Capital Partners I, L.P. Each of these individuals disclaims beneficial ownership of such shares, except to the extent of his pecuniary interest therein. The address of W Capital Partners I, L.P. is One East 52nd Street, 5th Floor, New York, NY 10022.

(27)   Sole voting and investment control of the shares being offered by Worldspan OpenTable Holdings LLC is exercised by its sole member, Worldspan, L.P. ("WLP"), a limited partnership. The general partner of WLP is Worldspan Technologies Inc. ("WTI"). The directors of WTI are Jeff Clarke and Eric J. Bock. Each of these individuals disclaims beneficial ownership of such shares, except to the extent of his pecuniary interest therein. The address of Worldspan OpenTable Holdings LLC is 400 Interpace Parkway, Building A, Parsippany, NJ 07054.

(28)   Includes 134,400 shares held by Michael W. & Yianna L. Xenakis, trustees of the Xenakis Family 2007 Revocable Trust, dated February 26, 2007 and 24,000 shares held by Michael Xenakis, trustee of the Michael Xenakis Annuity Trust dated May 15, 2008. Includes 11,333 shares subject to our right of repurchase, which right lapses as to 667 shares each succeeding month over the next 17 months. Includes 67,001 shares subject to options that are exercisable within 60 days of March 31, 2009. Mr. Xenakis serves as our senior vice president of product management.

(29)   Eugene H. Zagat Jr. and Nina S. Zagat are the managing members of Zagat Survey, LLC. These individuals may be deemed to share dispositive and voting power over the shares owned by Zagat Survey, LLC. Each of these individuals disclaims beneficial ownership of such shares, except to the extent of his pecuniary interest therein. The address of Zagat Survey, LLC is 4 Columbus Circle, New York, NY 10019.

(30)   William C. Snyder and Mary Ann Snyder are the trustees of the Snyder Revocable Trust dated May 9, 2000.

(31)   Includes each other selling stockholder who in the aggregate beneficially owns less than 1.0% of our common stock.

102

DESCRIPTION OF CAPITAL STOCK

General

Upon the completion of this offering, our amended and restated certificate of incorporation will authorize us to issue up to 100,000,000 shares of common stock, $0.0001 par value per share, and 5,000,000 shares of preferred stock, $0.0001 par value per share. The following information reflects a 1-for-12.5 reverse stock split of our common stock and preferred stock to be effected immediately prior to the effectiveness of our initial public offering registration statement, the filing of our amended and restated certificate of incorporation and the conversion of all outstanding shares of our preferred stock into shares of common stock immediately prior to the completion of this offering.

As of March 31, 2009, there were outstanding:

- 20,031,903 shares of common stock held by approximately 335 stockholders; and

- 2,402,605 shares of common stock issuable upon exercise of outstanding stock options.

All of our issued and outstanding shares of common stock and preferred stock are duly authorized, validly issued, fully paid and non-assessable. Our shares of common stock are not redeemable and, following the closing of this offering, will not have preemptive rights.

As of March 31, 2009, there were warrants outstanding for the purchase of an aggregate of 182,059 shares of common stock at a weighted average exercise price of $3.85 per share.

The following description of our capital stock and provisions of our amended and restated certificate of incorporation and amended and restated bylaws are summaries and are qualified by reference to the amended and restated certificate of incorporation and the amended and restated bylaws that will be in effect upon completion of this offering. Copies of these documents will be filed with the SEC as exhibits to our registration statement, of which this prospectus forms a part. The descriptions of the common stock and preferred stock reflect changes to our capital structure that will occur upon the closing of this offering.

Common Stock

Dividend Rights

Subject to preferences that may be applicable to any then outstanding preferred stock, holders of our common stock are entitled to receive dividends, if any, as may be declared from time to time by our board of directors out of legally available funds.

Voting Rights

Each holder of our common stock is entitled to one vote for each share on all matters submitted to a vote of the stockholders, including the election of directors. Our stockholders do not have cumulative voting rights in the election of directors. Accordingly, holders of a majority of the voting shares are able to elect all of the directors.

Liquidation

In the event of our liquidation, dissolution or winding up, holders of our common stock will be entitled to share ratably in the net assets legally available for distribution to stockholders after the payment of all of our debts and other liabilities and the satisfaction of any liquidation preference granted to the holders of any then outstanding shares of preferred stock.

103

Rights and Preferences

Holders of our common stock have no preemptive, conversion, subscription or other rights, and there are no redemption or sinking fund provisions applicable to our common stock. The rights, preferences and privileges of the holders of our common stock are subject to and may be adversely affected by, the rights of the holders of shares of any series of our preferred stock that we may designate in the future.

Warrants

The following table shows the outstanding warrants to purchase shares of our common stock as of March 31, 2009. These warrants may be exercised at any time prior to their respective termination dates.

Name of Holder	Class of Stock Subject to Warrant	Date of Issuance	Shares Subject to Warrant	Exercise Price
Comdisco, Inc.	Common Stock	August 3, 1999	6,315	$ 9.63/share
Comdisco, Inc.	Common Stock	August 3, 1999	1,094	11.63/share
Comdisco, Inc.	Common Stock	April 25, 2000	41,056	3.00/share
Comdisco, Inc.	Common Stock	April 25, 2000	41,362	9.63/share
Comerica Bank—California	Series A Preferred Stock	June 6, 2003	88,691	1.00/share
Deborah Meredith	Common Stock	March 5, 2007	3,541	4.88/share

The warrants issued to Comdisco, Inc. terminate upon the earlier of ten years from date of issuance or five years from the effective date of our initial public offering. The warrant issued to Comerica Bank terminates on June 6, 2010. However, the expiration date of this warrant will be extended until the third anniversary of the effective date of our initial public offering if we complete this offering within the three-year period immediately prior to June 6, 2010. Finally, the warrant issued to Deborah Meredith terminates upon the earlier of March 4, 2017, the occurrence of certain liquidation events as defined in our amended and restated certificate of incorporation or the consummation of our initial public offering.

Preferred Stock

Upon the completion of this offering, our board of directors will have the authority, without further action by our stockholders, to issue up to 5,000,000 shares of preferred stock in one or more series and to fix the rights, preferences, privileges and restrictions thereof. These rights, preferences and privileges could include dividend rights, conversion rights, voting rights, terms of redemption, liquidation preferences, sinking fund terms and the number of shares constituting any series or the designation of such series, any or all of which may be greater than the rights of common stock. The issuance of our preferred stock could adversely affect the voting power of holders of common stock and the likelihood that such holders will receive dividend payments and payments upon liquidation. In addition, the issuance of preferred stock could have the effect of delaying, deferring or preventing a change of control of our company or other corporate action. Upon completion of this offering, no shares of preferred stock will be outstanding, and we have no present plan to issue any shares of preferred stock.

Registration Rights

Demand Registration Rights

After the completion of this offering, the holders of approximately 9,023,083 shares of our common stock will be entitled to certain demand registration rights. At any time beginning on the

104

earlier of October 28, 2009 or six months after the consummation of this offering, the holders of at least a majority of these shares can, on not more than two occasions, request that we register all or a portion of their shares. Such request for registration must cover at least 35% of the shares entitled to registration rights or that number of shares with an anticipated aggregate offering price, net of underwriting discounts and commissions, exceeding $15,000,000. Additionally, we will not be required to effect a demand registration during the period beginning 60 days prior to the filing and 180 days following the effectiveness of a registration statement relating to a public offering of our securities.

Piggyback Registration Rights

After the completion of this offering, in the event that we propose to register any of our securities under the Securities Act, either for our own account or for the account of other security holders, the holders of approximately 9,023,083 shares of our common stock will be entitled to certain "piggyback" registration rights allowing the holder to include their shares in such registration, subject to certain marketing and other limitations. As a result, whenever we propose to file a registration statement under the Securities Act, other than with respect to a registration related to employee benefit plans, debt securities or corporate reorganizations, the holders of these shares are entitled to notice of the registration and have the right, subject to limitations that the underwriters may impose on the number of shares included in the registration, to include their shares in the registration.

Form S-3 Registration Rights

After the completion of this offering, the holders of approximately 9,023,083 shares of our common stock will be entitled to certain Form S-3 registration rights. The holders of at least 35% of these shares can make a written request that we register their shares on Form S-3 if we are eligible to file a registration statement on Form S-3 and if the aggregate price to the public of the shares offered is at least $3 million. These stockholders may make an unlimited number of requests for registration on Form S-3. However, we will not be required to effect a registration on Form S-3 if we have effected one such registration in a given 12-month period.

We will pay the registration expenses of the holders of the shares registered pursuant to the demand, piggyback and Form S-3 registrations described above. In an underwritten offering, the managing underwriter, if any, has the right, subject to specified conditions, to limit the number of shares such holders may include.

The demand, piggyback and Form S-3 registration rights described above will expire, with respect to any particular stockholder, after our initial public offering, when that stockholder can sell all of its shares under Rule 144 of the Securities Act during any three-month period. In any event, all such registration rights shall expire upon the earlier of five years after the consummation of this offering or the consummation of certain events, including the sale of all of our assets, a change of control of our company or a liquidation, dissolution or winding up of our company.

Pursuant to the investors' rights agreement, each stockholder that has registration rights has agreed that to the extent requested by us and the underwriters, such stockholder will not sell or otherwise dispose of any securities for a period of up to 180 days. However, we have an agreement with Integral Capital Partners and its affiliates that we will not request and not engage an underwriter who requests enforcement of the 180-day period against securities that are purchased by Integral Capital Partners or its affiliates in a public offering of such securities by us or in the open market following this offering. See section entitled "Underwriting."

105

Anti-Takeover Provisions

Certificate of Incorporation and Bylaws to be in Effect Upon the Completion of this Offering

Our amended and restated certificate of incorporation to be in effect upon the completion of this offering will provide for our board of directors to be divided into three classes with staggered three-year terms. Only one class of directors will be elected at each annual meeting of our stockholders, with the other classes continuing for the remainder of their respective three-year terms. Because our stockholders do not have cumulative voting rights, our stockholders holding a majority of the shares of common stock outstanding will be able to elect all of our directors. Our amended and restated certificate of incorporation and amended and restated bylaws to be effective upon the completion of this offering will provide that all stockholder actions must be effected at a duly called meeting of stockholders and not by a consent in writing, and that only our board of directors, chairman of the board, chief executive officer or president (in the absence of a chief executive officer) may call a special meeting of stockholders.

Our amended and restated certificate of incorporation and amended and restated bylaws will require a $66^2/3\%$ stockholder vote for the removal of a director without cause or the rescission, alteration, amendment or repeal of the bylaws by stockholders. The combination of the classification of our board of directors, the lack of cumulative voting and the $66^2/3\%$ stockholder voting requirements will make it more difficult for our existing stockholders to replace our board of directors as well as for another party to obtain control of us by replacing our board of directors. Since our board of directors has the power to retain and discharge our officers, these provisions could also make it more difficult for existing stockholders or another party to effect a change in management. In addition, the authorization of undesignated preferred stock makes it possible for our board of directors to issue preferred stock with voting or other rights or preferences that could impede the success of any attempt to change our control.

These provisions may have the effect of deterring hostile takeovers or delaying changes in our control or management. These provisions are intended to enhance the likelihood of continued stability in the composition of our board of directors and its policies and to discourage certain types of transactions that may involve an actual or threatened acquisition of us. These provisions are designed to reduce our vulnerability to an unsolicited acquisition proposal. The provisions also are intended to discourage certain tactics that may be used in proxy fights. However, such provisions could have the effect of discouraging others from making tender offers for our shares and, as a consequence, they also may inhibit fluctuations in the market price of our stock that could result from actual or rumored takeover attempts. Such provisions may also have the effect of preventing changes in our management.

Section 203 of the Delaware General Corporation Law

We are subject to Section 203 of the Delaware General Corporation Law, which prohibits a Delaware corporation from engaging in any business combination with any interested stockholder for a period of three years after the date that such stockholder became an interested stockholder, with the following exceptions:

- before such date, the board of directors of the corporation approved either the business combination or the transaction that resulted in the stockholder becoming an interested stockholder;

- upon completion of the transaction that resulted in the stockholder becoming an interested stockholder, the interested stockholder owned at least 85% of the voting stock of the corporation outstanding at the time the transaction began, excluding for purposes of determining the voting stock outstanding (but not the outstanding voting stock owned by the interested stockholder) those shares owned (i) by persons who are directors and also officers

106

and (ii) employee stock plans in which employee participants do not have the right to determine confidentially whether shares held subject to the plan will be tendered in a tender or exchange offer; or

- on or after such date, the business combination is approved by the board of directors and authorized at an annual or special meeting of the stockholders, and not by written consent, by the affirmative vote of at least $66^2/3\%$ of the outstanding voting stock that is not owned by the interested stockholder.

In general, Section 203 defines business combination to include the following:

- any merger or consolidation involving the corporation and the interested stockholder;

- any sale, transfer, pledge or other disposition of 10% or more of the assets of the corporation involving the interested stockholder;

- subject to certain exceptions, any transaction that results in the issuance or transfer by the corporation of any stock of the corporation to the interested stockholder;

- any transaction involving the corporation that has the effect of increasing the proportionate share of the stock or any class or series of the corporation beneficially owned by the interested stockholder; or

- the receipt by the interested stockholder of the benefit of any loss, advances, guarantees, pledges or other financial benefits by or through the corporation.

In general, Section 203 defines an "interested stockholder" as an entity or person who, together with the person's affiliates and associates, beneficially owns, or within three years prior to the time of determination of interested stockholder status did own, 15% or more of the outstanding voting stock of the corporation.

Acceleration of Options Upon Change of Control

Generally, under our 1999 Stock Plan and 2009 Plan, in the event of certain mergers, a reorganization or consolidation of our company with or into another corporation or the sale of all or substantially all of our assets or all of our capital stock wherein the successor corporation does not assume outstanding options or issue equivalent options, our board of directors is required to accelerate vesting of options outstanding under such plans.

Limitations of Liability and Indemnification

See "Management—Limitation on Liability and Indemnification Matters."

The Nasdaq Global Market Listing

Our common stock has been approved for listing on The Nasdaq Global Market under the symbol "OPEN," subject to official notice of issuance.

Transfer Agent and Registrar

The transfer agent and registrar for our common stock is Mellon Investor Services LLC.

107

SHARES ELIGIBLE FOR FUTURE SALE

Prior to this offering, there has been no public market for our common stock. Future sales of our common stock in the public market, or the availability of such shares for sale in the public market, could adversely affect market prices prevailing from time to time. As described below, only a limited number of shares will be available for sale shortly after this offering due to contractual and legal restrictions on resale. Nevertheless, sales of our common stock in the public market after such restrictions lapse, or the perception that those sales may occur, could adversely affect the prevailing market price at such time and our ability to raise equity capital in the future.

Based on the number of shares outstanding as of March 31, 2009, upon the completion of this offering, 21,604,587 shares of common stock will be outstanding, assuming no exercise of the underwriters' overallotment option and no exercise of outstanding options or warrants. Of the outstanding shares, all of the shares sold in this market will be freely tradable, except that any shares held by our affiliates, as that term is defined in Rule 144 under the Securities Act, may only be sold in compliance with the limitations described below. In addition, if members of our board of directors purchase shares in this offering, the shares purchased by them in this offering will be further subject to lock-up agreements, as described below.

The remaining 18,604,587 shares of common stock outstanding after this offering will be restricted as a result of securities laws or lock-up agreements as described below. Following the expiration of the lock-up period, all shares will be eligible for resale in compliance with Rule 144 or Rule 701 to the extent such shares have been released from any repurchase option that we may hold. "Restricted securities" as defined under Rule 144 were issued and sold by us in reliance on exemptions from the registration requirements of the Securities Act. These shares may be sold in the public market only if registered pursuant to an exemption from registration, such as Rule 144 or Rule 701 under the Securities Act.

Rule 144

In general, a person who has beneficially owned restricted shares of our common stock for at least six months would be entitled to sell their securities provided that (i) such person is not deemed to have been one of our affiliates at the time of, or at any time during the 90 days preceding, a sale and (ii) we are subject to the Exchange Act periodic reporting requirements for at least 90 days before the sale. Persons who have beneficially owned restricted shares of our common stock for at least six months but who are our affiliates at the time of, or any time during the 90 days preceding, a sale, would be subject to additional restrictions, by which such person would be entitled to sell within any three-month period only a number of securities that does not exceed the greater of either of the following:

- 1% of the number of shares of our common stock then outstanding, which will equal approximately 216,046 shares immediately after this offering assuming no exercise of the underwriters' overallotment option, based on the number of shares of common stock outstanding as of March 31, 2009; or

- the average weekly trading volume of our common stock on The Nasdaq Global Market during the four calendar weeks preceding the filing of a notice on Form 144 with respect to the sale.

provided, in each case, that we are subject to the Exchange Act periodic reporting requirements for at least 90 days before the sale. Such sales both by affiliates and by non-affiliates must also comply with the manner of sale, current public information and notice provisions of Rule 144.

108

Rule 701

Rule 701 under the Securities Act, as in effect on the date of this prospectus, permits resales of shares in reliance upon Rule 144 but without compliance with certain restrictions of Rule 144, including the holding period requirement. Most of our employees, executive officers or directors who purchased shares under a written compensatory plan or contract may be entitled to rely on the resale provisions of Rule 701, but all holders of Rule 701 shares are required to wait until 90 days after the date of this prospectus before selling their shares. However, substantially all Rule 701 shares are subject to lock-up agreements as described below and under "Underwriting" included elsewhere in this prospectus and will become eligible for sale upon the expiration of the restrictions set forth in those agreements.

Lock-Up Agreements

All of our directors and officers and substantially all of our stockholders have signed lock-up agreements under which they have agreed not to sell, transfer or dispose of, directly or indirectly, any shares of our common stock or any securities into or exercisable or exchangeable for shares of our common stock without the prior written consent of Merrill Lynch, Pierce, Fenner & Smith Incorporated for a period of 180 days, subject to a possible extension under certain circumstances, after the date of this prospectus. The holders of approximately 96.9% of our outstanding shares of common stock have executed lock-up agreements. These agreements are described below under "Underwriting."

Registration Rights

On the date beginning 180 days after the date of this prospectus, the holders of approximately 9,023,083 shares of our common stock, or their transferees, will be entitled to certain rights with respect to the registration of those shares under the Securities Act. For a description of these registration rights, please see "Description of Capital Stock—Registration Rights." After these shares are registered, they will be freely tradable without restriction under the Securities Act.

Stock Options

As soon as practicable after the completion of this offering, we intend to file a Form S-8 registration statement under the Securities Act to register shares of our common stock subject to options outstanding or reserved for issuance under our 1999 Stock Plan and 2009 Plan. This registration statement will become effective immediately upon filing, and shares covered by this registration statement will thereupon be eligible for sale in the public markets, subject to vesting restrictions, the lock-up agreements described above and Rule 144 limitations applicable to affiliates. For a more complete discussion of our stock plans, see "Management—Employee Benefit and Stock Plans."

109

MATERIAL UNITED STATES FEDERAL INCOME TAX
CONSEQUENCES TO NON-U.S. HOLDERS OF OUR COMMON STOCK

The following is a summary of the material United States federal income tax consequences to non-U.S. holders (as defined below) of the acquisition, ownership and disposition of our common stock issued pursuant to this offering. This discussion is not a complete analysis of all the potential United States federal income tax consequences relating thereto, nor does it address any estate and gift tax consequences or any tax consequences arising under any state, local or foreign tax laws, or any other United States federal tax laws. This discussion is based on the Internal Revenue Code of 1986, as amended, or the Internal Revenue Code, Treasury Regulations promulgated thereunder, judicial decisions, and published rulings and administrative pronouncements of the Internal Revenue Service, or IRS, all as in effect as of the date of this offering. These authorities may change, possibly retroactively, resulting in United States federal income tax consequences different from those discussed below. No ruling has been or will be sought from the IRS with respect to the matters discussed below, and there can be no assurance that the IRS will not take a contrary position regarding the tax consequences of the acquisition, ownership or disposition of our common stock, or that any such contrary position would not be sustained by a court.

This discussion is limited to non-U.S. holders who purchase our common stock issued pursuant to this offering and who hold our common stock as a "capital asset" within the meaning of Section 1221 of the Internal Revenue Code (generally, property held for investment). This discussion does not address all of the United States federal income tax consequences that may be relevant to a particular holder in light of such holder's particular circumstances. This discussion also does not consider any specific facts or circumstances that may be relevant to holders subject to special rules under the United States federal income tax laws, including, without limitation, U.S. expatriates, partnerships or other pass-through entities, real estate investment trusts, regulated investment companies, "controlled foreign corporations," "passive foreign investment companies," corporations that accumulate earnings to avoid United States federal income tax, financial institutions, insurance companies, brokers, dealers or traders in securities, commodities or currencies, tax-exempt organizations, tax-qualified retirement plans, persons subject to the alternative minimum tax, persons that own, or have owned, actually or constructively, more than 5% of our common stock and persons holding our common stock as part of a hedging or conversion transaction or straddle, or a constructive sale, or other risk reduction strategy.

PROSPECTIVE INVESTORS SHOULD CONSULT THEIR TAX ADVISORS REGARDING THE PARTICULAR UNITED STATES FEDERAL INCOME TAX CONSEQUENCES TO THEM OF ACQUIRING, OWNING AND DISPOSING OF OUR COMMON STOCK, AS WELL AS ANY TAX CONSEQUENCES ARISING UNDER ANY STATE, LOCAL OR FOREIGN TAX LAWS AND ANY OTHER UNITED STATES FEDERAL TAX LAWS.

Definition of Non-U.S. Holder

For purposes of this discussion, a non-U.S. holder is any beneficial owner of our common stock that is not a "U.S. person" or a partnership (or other entity treated as a partnership) for United States federal income tax purposes. A U.S. person is any of the following:

- an individual citizen or resident of the United States;

- a corporation (or other entity treated as a corporation for United States federal income tax purposes) created or organized under the laws of the United States, any state thereof or the District of Columbia;

- an estate the income of which is subject to United States federal income tax regardless of its source; or

110

- a trust (1) whose administration is subject to the primary supervision of a United States court and which has one or more United States persons who have the authority to control all substantial decisions of the trust, or (2) that has a valid election in effect under applicable Treasury Regulations to be treated as a U.S. person.

Distributions on Our Common Stock

If we make cash or other property distributions on our common stock, such distributions will constitute dividends for United States federal income tax purposes to the extent paid from our current or accumulated earnings and profits, as determined under United States federal income tax principles. Amounts not treated as dividends for United States federal income tax purposes will constitute a return of capital and will first be applied against and reduce a holder's tax basis in the common stock, but not below zero. Any excess will be treated as gain realized on the sale or other disposition of the common stock and will be treated as described under "—Gain on Disposition of Our Common Stock" below.

Dividends paid to a non-U.S. holder of our common stock generally will be subject to United States federal withholding tax at a rate of 30% of the gross amount of the dividends, or such lower rate specified by an applicable income tax treaty. To receive the benefit of a reduced treaty rate, a non-U.S. holder must furnish to us or our paying agent a valid IRS Form W-8BEN (or applicable successor form) certifying such holder's qualification for the reduced rate. This certification must be provided to us or our paying agent prior to the payment of dividends and must be updated periodically. Non-U.S. holders that do not timely provide us or our paying agent with the required certification, but that qualify for a reduced treaty rate, may obtain a refund of any excess amounts withheld by timely filing an appropriate claim for refund with the IRS.

If a non-U.S. holder holds our common stock in connection with the conduct of a trade or business in the United States, and dividends paid on the common stock are effectively connected with such holder's United States trade or business, the non-U.S. holder will be exempt from United States federal withholding tax. To claim the exemption, the non-U.S. holder must generally furnish to us or our paying agent a properly executed IRS Form W-8ECI (or applicable successor form).

Any dividends paid on our common stock that are effectively connected with a non-U.S. holder's United States trade or business (and if required by an applicable income tax treaty, attributable to a permanent establishment maintained by the non-U.S. holder in the United States) generally will be subject to United States federal income tax on a net income basis at the regular graduated United States federal income tax rates in much the same manner as if such holder were a resident of the United States. A non-U.S. holder that is a foreign corporation also may be subject to an additional branch profits tax equal to 30% (or such lower rate specified by an applicable income tax treaty) of its effectively connected earnings and profits for the taxable year, as adjusted for certain items. Non-U.S. holders should consult any applicable income tax treaties that may provide for different rules.

A non-U.S. holder who claims the benefit of an applicable income tax treaty generally will be required to satisfy applicable certification and other requirements prior to the distribution date. Non-U.S. holders should consult their tax advisors regarding their entitlement to benefits under a relevant income tax treaty.

Gain on Disposition of Our Common Stock

Subject to the discussion below regarding backup withholding, a non-U.S. holder generally will not be subject to United States federal income tax on any gain realized upon the sale or other disposition of our common stock, unless:

- the gain is effectively connected with the non-U.S. holder's conduct of a trade or business in the United States, and if required by an applicable income tax treaty, attributable to a permanent establishment maintained by the non-U.S. holder in the United States;

111

- the non-U.S. holder is a nonresident alien individual present in the United States for 183 days or more during the taxable year of the disposition, and certain other requirements are met; or

- our common stock constitutes a "United States real property interest" by reason of our status as a United States real property holding corporation, or USRPHC, for United States federal income tax purposes at any time within the shorter of the five-year period preceding the disposition or the non-U.S. holder's holding period for our common stock and our common stock has ceased to be regularly traded on an established securities market prior to the beginning of the calendar year in which the sale or other disposition occurs. The determination of whether we are a USRPHC depends on the fair market value of our United States real property interests relative to the fair market value of our other trade or business assets and our foreign real property interests.

We believe we are not currently and do not anticipate becoming a USRPHC for United States federal income tax purposes.

Gain described in the first bullet point above will be subject to United States federal income tax on a net income basis at the regular graduated United States federal income tax rates in the same manner as if such holder were a resident of the United States. A non-U.S. holder that is a foreign corporation also may be subject to an additional branch profits tax equal to 30% (or such lower rate specified by an applicable income tax treaty) of its effectively connected earnings and profits for the taxable year, as adjusted for certain items. Non-U.S. holders should consult any applicable income tax treaties that may provide for different rules.

Gain described in the second bullet point above will be subject to United States federal income tax at a flat 30% rate (or such lower rate specified by an applicable income tax treaty), but may be offset by United States source capital losses (even though the individual is not considered a resident of the United States), provided that the non-U.S. holder has timely filed U.S. federal income tax returns with respect to such losses.

Information Reporting and Backup Withholding

We must report annually to the IRS and to each non-U.S. holder the amount of distributions on our common stock paid to such holder and the amount of any tax withheld with respect to those distributions. These information reporting requirements apply even if no withholding was required because the distributions were effectively connected with the holder's conduct of a United States trade or business, or withholding was reduced or eliminated by an applicable income tax treaty. This information also may be made available under a specific treaty or agreement with the tax authorities in the country in which the non-U.S. holder resides or is established. Backup withholding, currently at a 28% rate, however, generally will not apply to distributions to a non-U.S. holder of our common stock provided the non-U.S. holder furnishes to us or our paying agent the required certification as to its non-U.S. status, such as by providing a valid IRS Form W-8BEN or IRS Form W-8ECI, or certain other requirements are met. Notwithstanding the foregoing, backup withholding may apply if either we or our paying agent has actual knowledge, or reason to know, that the holder is a U.S. person that is not an exempt recipient.

Backup withholding is not an additional tax. Any amounts withheld under the backup withholding rules may be allowed as a refund or a credit against a non-U.S. holder's United States federal income tax liability, provided the required information is timely furnished to the IRS.

112

UNDERWRITING

Merrill Lynch, Pierce, Fenner & Smith Incorporated is acting as representative of each of the underwriters named below. Subject to the terms and conditions set forth in a purchase agreement among us, the selling stockholders and the underwriters, we and the selling stockholders have agreed to sell to the underwriters, and each of the underwriters has agreed, severally and not jointly, to purchase from us, the number of shares of common stock set forth opposite its name below.

Underwriter	Number of Shares
Merrill Lynch, Pierce, Fenner & Smith Incorporated	
Allen & Company LLC	
Stifel, Nicolaus & Company, Incorporated	
ThinkEquity LLC	
Total	3,000,000

Subject to the terms and conditions set forth in the purchase agreement, the underwriters have agreed, severally and not jointly, to purchase all of the shares sold under the purchase agreement if any of these shares are purchased. If an underwriter defaults, the purchase agreement provides that the purchase commitments of the nondefaulting underwriters may be increased or the purchase agreement may be terminated.

We and the selling stockholders have agreed to indemnify the underwriters against certain liabilities, including liabilities arising from any untrue statement of a material fact included in, or the omission of a material fact from, this prospectus, the registration statement of which this prospectus is a part or any free writing prospectus, as well as settlement payments or other expenses related to any litigation, investigation or proceeding by any governmental agency, or claim based upon any such untrue statement or omission. We and the selling stockholders have also agreed to contribute to payments the underwriters may be required to make in respect of such liabilities. The indemnification and contribution obligations of our company and the selling stockholders shall not apply to liabilities arising from any untrue statement or omission made in reliance upon written information furnished to us by the underwriters.

The underwriters are offering the shares, subject to prior sale, when, as and if issued to and accepted by them, subject to approval of legal matters by their counsel, including the validity of the shares, and other conditions contained in the purchase agreement, such as the receipt by the underwriters of officer's certificates and legal opinions. The underwriters reserve the right to withdraw, cancel or modify offers to the public and to reject orders in whole or in part.

Commissions and Discounts

The underwriters have advised us and the selling stockholders that they propose initially to offer the shares to the public, including members of our board of directors, if they purchase shares in the offering, at the public offering price on the cover page of this prospectus and to dealers at that price less a concession not in excess of $ per share. The underwriters may allow, and the dealers may allow, a discount not in excess of $ per share to other dealers. After the initial public offering, the public offering price, concession and discount may be changed.

113

The following table shows the public offering price, underwriting discount and proceeds before expenses to us and the selling stockholders. The information assumes either no exercise or full exercise by the underwriters of their overallotment option.

	Per Share	Without Option	With Option
Public offering price	$	$	$
Underwriting discount	$	$	$
Proceeds, before expenses, to us	$	$	$
Proceeds, before expenses, to the selling stockholders	$	$	$

The expenses of the offering, not including the underwriting discount, are estimated at approximately $3.0 million and are payable by us.

Overallotment Option

We have granted an option to the underwriters to purchase up to 450,000 additional shares at the public offering price, less the underwriting discount. The underwriters may exercise this option for 30 days from the date of this prospectus solely to cover any overallotments. If the underwriters exercise this option, each will be obligated, subject to conditions contained in the purchase agreement, to purchase from us a number of additional shares proportionate to that underwriter's initial amount reflected in the above table.

No Sales of Similar Securities

All of our directors and officers and substantially all of our stockholders have agreed, subject to certain exceptions, not to sell or transfer any common stock or securities convertible into, exchangeable for, exercisable for, or repayable with common stock, other than the shares which we and the selling stockholders may sell in this offering, for 180 days after the date of this prospectus without first obtaining the written consent of Merrill Lynch, Pierce, Fenner & Smith Incorporated. The holders of approximately 96.9% of our outstanding shares of common stock have executed lock-up agreements. Specifically, we and these other individuals have agreed not to directly or indirectly:

- offer, pledge, sell or contract to sell any common stock;

- sell any option or contract to purchase any common stock;

- purchase any option or contract to sell any common stock;

- grant any option, right or warrant for the sale of any common stock;

- lend or otherwise dispose of or transfer any common stock;

- request or demand that we file a registration statement related to the common stock; or

- enter into any swap or other agreement that transfers, in whole or in part, the economic consequence of ownership of any common stock, whether any such swap or transaction is to be settled by delivery of shares or other securities, in cash or otherwise.

This lock-up provision applies to common stock and to securities convertible into or exchangeable or exercisable for or repayable with common stock. It also applies to common stock owned now or acquired later by the person executing the agreement or for which the person executing the agreement later acquires the power of disposition. The 180-day restricted period will be automatically extended if (1) during the last 17 days of the 180-day restricted period we issue an earning release or material news or a material event relating to its business occurs or (2) prior to the expiration of the 180-day restricted period, we announce that we will release earnings results or we become aware that material news or a

114

material event will occur during the 16-day period beginning on the last day of the 180-day restricted period, in which case the restrictions described above will continue to apply until the expiration of the 18-day period beginning on the issuance of the earnings release or the occurrence of the material news or material event, unless such extension is waived in writing by Merrill Lynch, Pierce, Fenner & Smith Incorporated.

Nasdaq Global Market Listing

Our common stock has been approved for listing on The Nasdaq Global Market under the symbol "OPEN," subject to official notice of issuance.

Before this offering, there has been no public market for our common stock. The initial public offering price will be determined through negotiations among us, the selling stockholders and the representative. In addition to prevailing market conditions, the factors to be considered in determining the initial public offering price are:

- the valuation multiples of publicly traded companies that the representative believes to be comparable to us;

- our financial information;

- the history of, and the prospects for, our company and the industry in which we compete;

- an assessment of our management, its past and present operations, and the prospects for, and timing of, our future revenues;

- the present state of our development; and

- the above factors in relation to market values and various valuation measures of other companies engaged in activities similar to ours.

An active trading market for the shares may not develop. It is also possible that after the offering the shares will not trade in the public market at or above the initial public offering price.

Price Stabilization, Short Positions and Penalty Bids

Until the distribution of the shares is completed, SEC rules may limit underwriters and selling group members from bidding for and purchasing our common stock. However, the representative may engage in transactions that stabilize the price of the common stock, such as bids or purchases to peg, fix or maintain that price.

In connection with the offering, the underwriters may purchase and sell our common stock in the open market. These transactions may include short sales, purchases on the open market to cover positions created by short sales and stabilizing transactions. Short sales involve the sale by the underwriters of a greater number of shares than they are required to purchase in the offering. "Covered" short sales are sales made in an amount not greater than the underwriters' option to purchase additional shares in the offering. The underwriters may close out any covered short position by either exercising their overallotment option or purchasing shares in the open market. In determining the source of shares to close out the covered short position, the underwriters will consider, among other things, the price of shares available for purchase in the open market as compared to the price at which they may purchase shares through the overallotment option. "Naked" short sales are sales in excess of the overallotment option. The underwriters must close out any naked short position by purchasing shares in the open market. A naked short position is more likely to be created if the underwriters are concerned that there may be downward pressure on the price of our common stock in the open market after pricing that could adversely affect investors who purchase in the offering.

115

Stabilizing transactions consist of various bids for or purchases of shares of common stock made by the underwriters in the open market prior to the completion of the offering.

The underwriters may also impose a penalty bid. This occurs when a particular underwriter repays to the underwriters a portion of the underwriting discount received by it because the representative has repurchased shares sold by or for the account of such underwriter in stabilizing or short covering transactions.

Similar to other purchase transactions, the underwriters' purchases to cover the syndicate short sales may have the effect of raising or maintaining the market price of our common stock or preventing or retarding a decline in the market price of our common stock. As a result, the price of our common stock may be higher than the price that might otherwise exist in the open market.

Neither we nor any of the underwriters make any representation or prediction as to the direction or magnitude of any effect that the transactions described above may have on the price of our common stock. In addition, neither we nor any of the underwriters make any representation that the representative will engage in these transactions or that these transactions, once commenced, will not be discontinued without notice.

Passive Market Making

In connection with the offering, the underwriters and selling group members may engage in passive market-making transactions in the common stock on The Nasdaq Stock Market in accordance with Rule 103 of Regulation M under the Exchange Act during the period before the commencement of offers or sales of common stock and extending through the completion and distribution. A passive market-maker must display its bids at a price not in excess of the highest independent bid of the security. However, if all independent bids are lowered below the passive market-maker's bid, that bid must be lowered when specified purchase limits are exceeded.

Electronic Offer, Sale and Distribution of Shares

A prospectus in electronic format will be made available on the websites maintained by one or more of the underwriters of this offering. Other than the electronic prospectus, the information on the websites of the underwriters is not part of this prospectus. The underwriters may agree to allocate a number of shares to underwriters for sale to their online brokerage account holders. Internet distributions will be allocated to underwriters that may make Internet distributions on the same basis as other allocations.

Other than the prospectus in electronic format, the information on any underwriter's or selling group member's web site and any information contained in any other website maintained by an underwriter or selling group member is not part of this prospectus or the registration statement of which this prospectus forms a part.

Other Relationships

Some of the underwriters and their affiliates have engaged in, and may in the future engage in, investment banking and other commercial dealings in the ordinary course of business with us. They have received customary fees for these transactions.

116

LEGAL MATTERS

Certain legal matters with respect to the legality of the issuance of the shares of common stock offered by us and the selling stockholders by this prospectus will be passed upon for us and the selling stockholders by Latham & Watkins LLP, Menlo Park, California. The underwriters are being represented by Davis Polk & Wardwell, Menlo Park, California, in connection with the offering.

EXPERTS

The consolidated financial statements as of December 31, 2007 and 2008 and for each of the three years in the period ended December 31, 2008 included in this prospectus, have been audited by Deloitte & Touche LLP, an independent registered public accounting firm, as stated in their report appearing herein and elsewhere in the registration statement (which report expresses an unqualified opinion on the consolidated financial statements and includes an explanatory paragraph relating to the Company's adoption of Financial Accounting Standards Board Interpretation No. 48, *Accounting for Uncertainty in Income Taxes—An Interpretation of FASB No. 109*). Such consolidated financial statements have been so included in reliance upon the report of such firm given upon their authority as experts in accounting and auditing.

WHERE YOU CAN FIND MORE INFORMATION

We have filed with the SEC a registration statement on Form S-1 under the Securities Act with respect to this offering of our common stock. This prospectus, which constitutes a part of the registration statement, does not contain all of the information set forth in the registration statement, some items of which are contained in exhibits to the registration statement as permitted by the rules and regulations of the SEC. For further information with respect to us and our common stock, we refer you to the registration statement, including the exhibits and the financial statements and notes filed as a part of the registration statement. Statements contained in this prospectus concerning the contents of any contract or any other document are not necessarily complete. If a contract or document has been filed as an exhibit to the registration statement, please see the copy of the contract or document that has been filed. Each statement is this prospectus relating to a contract or document filed as an exhibit is qualified in all respects by the filed exhibit. The exhibits to the registration statement should be referenced for the complete contents of these contracts and documents. You may obtain copies of this information by mail from the Public Reference Section of the SEC, 100 F Street, N.E., Room 1580, Washington, D.C. 20549, at prescribed rates. You may obtain information on the operation of the public reference rooms by calling the SEC at 1-800-SEC-0330. The SEC also maintains an Internet website that contains reports, proxy statements and other information about issuers, like us, that file electronically with the SEC. The address of that website is www.sec.gov.

As a result of this offering, we will become subject to the information and reporting requirements of the Securities Exchange Act and, in accordance with this law, will file periodic reports, proxy statements and other information with the SEC. These periodic reports, proxy statements and other information will be available for inspection and copying at the SEC's public reference facilities and the website of the SEC referred to above.

Through and including   , 2009 (the 25th day after the date of this prospectus), U.S. federal securities laws may require all dealers that effect transactions in our common stock, whether or not participating in this offering, to deliver a prospectus. This is in addition to the dealers' obligation to deliver a prospectus when acting as underwriters and with respect to their unsold allotments or subscriptions.

117

OPENTABLE, INC.

INDEX TO CONSOLIDATED FINANCIAL STATEMENTS

F-1

REPORT OF INDEPENDENT REGISTERED PUBLIC ACCOUNTING FIRM

To the Board of Directors and Stockholders of
OpenTable, Inc.
San Francisco, California

We have audited the accompanying consolidated balance sheets of OpenTable, Inc. and subsidiaries (the "Company") as of December 31, 2007 and 2008, and the related consolidated statements of operations, stockholders' equity and comprehensive income (loss), and cash flows for each of the three years in the period ended December 31, 2008. These financial statements are the responsibility of the Company's management. Our responsibility is to express an opinion on the financial statements based on our audits.

We conducted our audits in accordance with the standards of the Public Company Accounting Oversight Board (United States). Those standards require that we plan and perform the audit to obtain reasonable assurance about whether the financial statements are free of material misstatement. The Company is not required to have, nor were we engaged to perform, an audit of its internal control over financial reporting. Our audits included consideration of internal control over financial reporting as a basis for designing audit procedures that are appropriate in the circumstances, but not for the purpose of expressing an opinion on the effectiveness of the Company's internal control over financial reporting. Accordingly, we express no such opinion. An audit also includes examining, on a test basis, evidence supporting the amounts and disclosures in the financial statements, assessing the accounting principles used and significant estimates made by management, as well as evaluating the overall financial statement presentation. We believe that our audits provide a reasonable basis for our opinion.

In our opinion, such consolidated financial statements present fairly, in all material respects, the financial position of the Company as of December 31, 2007 and 2008, and the results of its operations and its cash flows for each of the three years in the period ended December 31, 2008, in conformity with accounting principles generally accepted in the United States of America.

As discussed in Note 2 to the consolidated financial statements, effective January 1, 2007, the Company adopted the provisions of Financial Accounting Standards Board Interpretation No. 48, *Accounting for Uncertainty in Income Taxes—an Interpretation of FASB No. 109.*

/s/ DELOITTE & TOUCHE LLP
San Jose, California
March 12, 2009
(May 20, 2009 as to Note 13)

F-2

-224-

OPENTABLE, INC.

CONSOLIDATED BALANCE SHEETS

	Years Ended December 31,		March 31, 2009	Pro forma March 31, 2009
	2007	2008		
			(Unaudited)	
ASSETS				
CURRENT ASSETS:				
Cash and cash equivalents	$ 21,661,000	$ 5,528,000	$ 12,010,000	$ 12,010,000
Short-term investments	—	17,259,000	13,194,000	13,194,000
Accounts receivable, net of allowance for doubtful accounts of $248,000, $543,000 and $633,000 at December 31, 2007 and 2008 and March 31, 2009	5,225,000	6,331,000	7,010,000	7,010,000
Prepaid expenses and other current assets	676,000	942,000	1,097,000	1,097,000
Deferred tax asset	1,669,000	4,828,000	4,828,000	4,828,000
Restricted cash	206,000	156,000	153,000	153,000
Total current assets	29,437,000	35,044,000	38,292,000	38,292,000
Property and equipment, net	8,378,000	11,125,000	11,069,000	11,069,000
Deferred tax asset	7,786,000	3,343,000	3,070,000	3,070,000
Other assets	213,000	1,371,000	2,156,000	2,156,000
TOTAL ASSETS	$ 45,814,000	$ 50,883,000	$ 54,587,000	$ 54,587,000
LIABILITIES AND STOCKHOLDERS' EQUITY				
CURRENT LIABILITIES:				
Accounts payable and accrued expenses	$ 10,545,000	$ 7,855,000	$ 9,066,000	$ 9,066,000
Accrued compensation	2,310,000	2,772,000	2,777,000	2,777,000
Deferred revenue	987,000	1,210,000	1,393,000	1,393,000
Dining rewards payable	5,836,000	8,462,000	9,221,000	9,221,000
Total current liabilities	19,678,000	20,299,000	22,457,000	22,457,000
DEFERRED REVENUE—Less current portion	3,651,000	3,900,000	3,725,000	3,725,000
Total liabilities	23,329,000	24,199,000	26,182,000	26,182,000
COMMITMENTS AND CONTINGENCIES (Note 7)				
STOCKHOLDERS' EQUITY:				
Convertible preferred stock, Series A , $0.0001 par value—7,040,000 shares authorized; 6,898,187 shares issued and outstanding; aggregate liquidation preference of $7,000,000	6,925,000	6,925,000	6,925,000	—
Convertible preferred stock, Series B , $0.0001 par value—2,240,000 shares authorized; 2,177,550 shares issued and outstanding; aggregate liquidation preference of $15,000,000	14,984,000	14,984,000	14,984,000	—
Common stock, $0.0001 par value—24,000,000 shares authorized; 11,097,490, 11,154,668 and 11,166,413 shares issued, 10,887,243, 10,944,421 and 10,956,166 shares outstanding at December 31, 2007 and 2008 and March 31, 2009; 20,242,150 shares issued and 20,031,903 shares outstanding pro forma	1,000	1,000	1,000	2,000
Additional paid-in capital	58,592,000	64,060,000	65,361,000	87,269,000
Treasury stock, at cost (210,247 shares at December 31, 2007 and 2008 and March 31, 2009)	(647,000)	(647,000)	(647,000)	(647,000)
Accumulated other comprehensive loss	(51,000)	(296,000)	(242,000)	(242,000)
Accumulated deficit	(57,319,000)	(58,343,000)	(57,977,000)	(57,977,000)
Total stockholders' equity	22,485,000	26,684,000	28,405,000	28,405,000
TOTAL LIABILITIES AND STOCKHOLDERS' EQUITY	$ 45,814,000	$ 50,883,000	$ 54,587,000	$ 54,587,000

See notes to consolidated financial statements.

F-3

OPENTABLE, INC.

CONSOLIDATED STATEMENTS OF OPERATIONS

	Years Ended December 31,			Three Months Ended March 31,	
	2006	2007	2008	2008	2009
				(Unaudited)	
REVENUES	$27,168,000	$41,148,000	$55,844,000	$13,263,000	$15,995,000
COSTS AND EXPENSES:					
Operations and support	9,548,000	12,603,000	17,760,000	4,012,000	5,106,000
Sales and marketing	7,675,000	11,326,000	14,830,000	3,591,000	3,798,000
Technology	4,024,000	5,863,000	9,511,000	2,175,000	2,712,000
General and administrative	5,972,000	12,212,000	13,117,000	3,144,000	3,547,000
Total costs and expenses	27,219,000	42,004,000	55,218,000	12,922,000	15,163,000
Income (loss) from operations	(51,000)	(856,000)	626,000	341,000	832,000
Other income, net	421,000	951,000	468,000	180,000	55,000
Income before taxes	370,000	95,000	1,094,000	521,000	887,000
Income tax expense (benefit)	176,000	(9,121,000)	2,118,000	608,000	521,000
NET INCOME (LOSS)	$ 194,000	$ 9,216,000	$(1,024,000)	$ (87,000)	$ 366,000
Net income (loss) per share:					
Basic	$ 0.02	$ 0.97	$ (0.10)	$ (0.01)	$ 0.04
Diluted	$ 0.01	$ 0.46	$ (0.10)	$ (0.01)	$ 0.02
Weighted average shares outstanding:					
Basic	9,132,000	9,522,000	10,016,000	9,850,000	10,276,000
Diluted	19,523,000	20,019,000	10,016,000	9,850,000	21,017,000
Pro forma net income (loss) per share—basic and diluted (unaudited)			$ (0.05)		$ 0.02
Pro forma weighted average shares outstanding used in calculating net income (loss) per share (unaudited):					
Basic			19,092,000		19,352,000
Diluted			19,092,000		21,017,000

See notes to consolidated financial statements.

F-4

OPENTABLE, INC.

CONSOLIDATED STATEMENTS OF STOCKHOLDERS' EQUITY AND COMPREHENSIVE INCOME (LOSS) (Continued)

	Series A Convertible Preferred Stock		Series B Convertible Preferred Stock		Common Stock		Treasury Stock		Additional Paid-in Capital	Deferred Stock-Based Compensation	Accumulated Other Comprehensive Loss	Accumulated Deficit	Total	Compreh Income
	Shares	Amount	Shares	Amount	Shares	Amount	Shares	Amount						
Balance at January 1, 2006	6,898,187	$6,925,000	2,177,550	$14,984,000	9,910,804	$ 1,000	—	—	$54,077,000	$ (900,000)	$ (34,000)	$ (66,729,000)	$ 8,324,000	
Issuance of common stock upon exercise of employee stock options	—	—	—	—	51,534	—	—	—	325,000	—	—	—	325,000	
Reversal of deferred stock-based compensation due to adoption of SFAS No. 123R	—	—	—	—	—	—	—	—	(900,000)	900,000	—	—	—	
Stock-based compensation expense	—	—	—	—	—	—	—	—	709,000	—	—	—	709,000	
Repurchase of unvested common shares	—	—	—	—	(350)	—	—	—	—	—	—	—	—	
Repurchase of common shares	—	—	—	—	(207,047)	—	207,047	(647,000)	—	—	—	—	(647,000)	
Foreign currency translation	—	—	—	—	—	—	—	—	—	—	2,000	—	2,000	$
Net income	—	—	—	—	—	—	—	—	—	—	—	194,000	194,000	1
Comprehensive income	—	—	—	—	—	—	—	—	—	—	—	—	—	$ 1
Balance at December 31, 2006	6,898,187	6,925,000	2,177,550	14,984,000	9,754,941	1,000	207,047	(647,000)	54,211,000	—	(32,000)	(66,535,000)	8,907,000	
Issuance of common stock upon exercise of employee stock options	—	—	—	—	1,178,095	—	—	—	1,276,000	—	—	—	1,276,000	
Stock-based compensation expense	—	—	—	—	—	—	—	—	3,103,000	—	—	—	3,103,000	
Income tax benefit from employee stock option exercise	—	—	—	—	—	—	—	—	84,000	—	—	—	84,000	
Repurchase of unvested common shares	—	—	—	—	(42,593)	—	—	—	(82,000)	—	—	—	(82,000)	
Repurchase of common shares	—	—	—	—	(3,200)	—	3,200	—	—	—	—	—	—	
Foreign currency translation	—	—	—	—	—	—	—	—	—	—	(19,000)	—	(19,000)	$ (
Net income	—	—	—	—	—	—	—	—	—	—	—	9,216,000	9,216,000	9,2
Comprehensive income	—	—	—	—	—	—	—	—	—	—	—	—	—	$ 9,1
Balance at December 31, 2007	6,898,187	6,925,000	2,177,550	14,984,000	10,887,243	1,000	210,247	(647,000)	58,592,000	—	(51,000)	(57,319,000)	22,485,000	

F-5

OPENTABLE, INC.

CONSOLIDATED STATEMENTS OF STOCKHOLDERS' EQUITY AND COMPREHENSIVE INCOME (LOSS) (Concluded)

	Series A Convertible Preferred Stock		Series B Convertible Preferred Stock		Common Stock		Treasury Stock		Additional Paid-in Capital	Accumulated Other Comprehensive Loss	Accumulated Deficit	Total	Comprehensive Income (Loss)
	Shares	Amount	Shares	Amount	Shares	Amount	Shares	Amount					
Balance at December 31, 2007	6,898,187	$6,925,000	2,177,550	$14,984,000	10,887,243	$ 1,000	210,247	$(647,000)	$58,592,000	$ (51,000)	$ (57,319,000)	$22,485,000	$ —
Issuance of common stock upon exercise of employee stock options	—	—	—	—	57,178	—	—	—	1,453,000	—	—	1,453,000	—
Stock-based compensation expense	—	—	—	—	—	—	—	—	4,015,000	—	—	4,015,000	—
Foreign currency translation	—	—	—	—	—	—	—	—	—	(311,000)	—	(311,000)	$ (311,000)
Unrealized gain on investments	—	—	—	—	—	—	—	—	—	66,000	—	66,000	66,000
Net loss	—	—	—	—	—	—	—	—	—	—	(1,024,000)	(1,024,000)	(1,024,000)
Comprehensive loss	—	—	—	—	—	—	—	—	—	—	—	—	$ (1,269,000)
Balance at December 31, 2008	6,898,187	$6,925,000	2,177,550	$14,984,000	10,944,421	$ 1,000	210,247	$(647,000)	$64,060,000	$ (296,000)	$ (58,343,000)	$26,684,000	
Issuance of common stock upon exercise of employee stock options*	—	—	—	—	11,745	—	—	—	329,000	—	—	329,000	
Stock-based compensation expense*	—	—	—	—	—	—	—	—	972,000	—	—	972,000	
Foreign currency translation*	—	—	—	—	—	—	—	—	—	86,000	—	86,000	$ 86,000
Unrealized loss on investments*	—	—	—	—	—	—	—	—	—	(32,000)	—	(32,000)	(32,000)
Net income*	—	—	—	—	—	—	—	—	—	—	366,000	366,000	366,000
Comprehensive income*	—	—	—	—	—	—	—	—	—	—	—	—	$ 420,000
Balance at March 31, 2009*	6,898,187	$6,925,000	2,177,550	$14,984,000	10,956,166	$ 1,000	210,247	$(647,000)	$65,361,000	$ (242,000)	$ (57,977,000)	$28,405,000	

*   Unaudited

See notes to consolidated financial statements.

F-6

OPENTABLE, INC.

CONSOLIDATED STATEMENTS OF CASH FLOWS

	Years Ended December 31,			Three Months Ended March 31,	
	2006	2007	2008	2008	2009
				(Unaudited)	
OPERATING ACTIVITIES:					
Net income (loss)	$ 194,000	$ 9,216,000	$ (1,024,000)	$ (87,000)	$ 366,000
Adjustments to reconcile net income (loss) to net cash provided by operating activities:					
Depreciation and amortization	2,118,000	3,001,000	4,376,000	951,000	1,263,000
Provision for doubtful accounts	527,000	432,000	1,042,000	170,000	402,000
Stock-based compensation	709,000	3,103,000	3,970,000	984,000	959,000
Write-off of property, equipment and software	148,000	223,000	265,000	72,000	200,000
Deferred taxes	—	(9,455,000)	1,284,000	—	272,000
Changes in operating assets and liabilities:					
Accounts receivable	(1,252,000)	(1,877,000)	(2,211,000)	(760,000)	(1,104,000)
Prepaid expenses and other current assets	(112,000)	(435,000)	(305,000)	(160,000)	(129,000)
Accounts payable & accrued expenses	741,000	2,839,000	(2,472,000)	(1,488,000)	655,000
Accrued compensation	371,000	691,000	478,000	139,000	31,000
Deferred revenue	982,000	1,083,000	515,000	204,000	19,000
Dining rewards payable	1,477,000	2,337,000	2,626,000	755,000	760,000
Net cash provided by operating activities	5,903,000	11,158,000	8,544,000	780,000	3,694,000
INVESTING ACTIVITIES:					
Purchases of property, equipment and software	(3,606,000)	(5,449,000)	(7,203,000)	(1,616,000)	(1,368,000)
Purchases of investments	—	(787,000)	(18,818,000)	—	(700,000)
Sales of investments	757,000	787,000	1,700,000	—	4,700,000
Increase (decrease) in restricted cash	(190,000)	424,000	(9,000)	—	—
Net cash provided by (used in) investing activities	(3,039,000)	(5,025,000)	(24,330,000)	(1,616,000)	2,632,000
FINANCING ACTIVITIES:					
Proceeds from issuance of common stock	12,000	378,000	77,000	15,000	15,000
Repurchase of common stock	(647,000)	(82,000)	—	—	—
Proceeds from early exercise of common stock	17,000	4,973,000	28,000	20,000	1,000
Offering costs in connection with initial public offering	—	—	(185,000)	—	—
Net cash provided by (used in) financing activities	(618,000)	5,269,000	(80,000)	35,000	16,000
EFFECT OF EXCHANGE RATES ON CASH	(58,000)	(5,000)	(267,000)	21,000	140,000
NET INCREASE (DECREASE) IN CASH AND CASH EQUIVALENTS	2,188,000	11,397,000	(16,133,000)	(780,000)	6,482,000
CASH AND CASH EQUIVALENTS—Beginning of period	8,076,000	10,264,000	21,661,000	21,661,000	5,528,000
CASH AND CASH EQUIVALENTS—End of period	$10,264,000	$21,661,000	$ 5,528,000	$20,881,000	$12,010,000
SUPPLEMENTAL DISCLOSURE OF OTHER CASH FLOW INFORMATION:					
Cash paid for income taxes	$ —	$ 382,000	$ 387,000	$ 64,000	$ 411,000
SUPPLEMENTAL DISCLOSURE OF NONCASH INVESTING AND FINANCING ACTIVITIES:					
Purchase of property and equipment recorded in accounts payable	$ 42,000	$ 114,000	$ 232,000	$ 189,000	$ 334,000
Vesting of early exercised stock options	$ 313,000	$ 898,000	$ 1,375,000	$ 373,000	$ 313,000
Accrued offering costs	$ —	$ —	$ 998,000	$ 187,000	$ 792,000

See notes to consolidated financial statements.

F-7

OPENTABLE, INC.

NOTES TO CONSOLIDATED FINANCIAL STATEMENTS

YEARS ENDED DECEMBER 31, 2006, 2007 AND 2008, AND THE THREE MONTHS
ENDED MARCH 31, 2008 AND 2009 (UNAUDITED)

1. Organization and Description of Business

OpenTable, Inc. and subsidiaries (collectively, the "Company"), a Delaware corporation, was formed on October 13, 1998. The Company provides solutions that form an online network connecting reservation-taking restaurants and people who dine at those restaurants. For restaurant customers, the Company provides a proprietary Electronic Reservation Book, or ERB, which combines proprietary software and computer hardware to deliver a solution that computerizes restaurant host-stand operations and replaces traditional pen-and-paper reservation books. The OpenTable ERB streamlines and enhances a number of business-critical functions and processes for restaurants, including reservation management, table management, guest recognition and email marketing. For diners, the Company operates www.opentable.com, a popular restaurant reservation website. The OpenTable website enables diners to find, choose and book tables at restaurants on the OpenTable network in real time, overcoming the inefficiencies associated with the traditional process of reserving by phone.

Certain Significant Risks and Uncertainties

The Company operates in a dynamic industry, and accordingly, can be affected by a variety of factors. For example, management of the Company believes that changes in any of the following areas could have a significant negative effect on the Company in terms of its future financial position, results of operations or cash flows: the ability to maintain an adequate rate of growth; the impact of the current economic climate on its business; the ability to effectively manage its growth; the ability to attract new restaurant customers; the ability to increase the number of visitors to its website and convert those visitors into diners; and the ability to retain existing restaurant customers and diners or encourage repeat reservations.

2. Summary of Significant Accounting Policies

Principles of Consolidation

These consolidated financial statements include the accounts of OpenTable, Inc. and its wholly-owned subsidiaries. All intercompany accounts and transactions have been eliminated in consolidation.

Use of Estimates

The preparation of the Company's financial statements in conformity with accounting principles generally accepted in the United States of America requires management to make estimates and assumptions that affect the reported amounts of assets and liabilities and disclosure of contingent assets and liabilities at the date of the financial statements and the reported amounts of income and expenses during the reporting period. These estimates are based on information available as of the date of the financial statements; therefore, actual results could differ from those estimates.

Unaudited Interim Financial Information

The accompanying consolidated balance sheet as of March 31, 2009, the consolidated statements of operations and of cash flows for the three months ended March 31, 2008 and 2009 and the consolidated statement of stockholders' equity and comprehensive income (loss) for the three months ended March 31, 2009 are unaudited. The unaudited interim financial statements have been

F-8

OPENTABLE, INC.

NOTES TO CONSOLIDATED FINANCIAL STATEMENTS (Continued)

YEARS ENDED DECEMBER 31, 2006, 2007 AND 2008, AND THE THREE MONTHS
ENDED MARCH 31, 2008 AND 2009 (UNAUDITED)

2. Summary of Significant Accounting Policies (Continued)

prepared on the same basis as the annual consolidated financial statements and, in the opinion of management, reflect all adjustments, which include only normal recurring adjustments, necessary to present fairly the Company's financial position and results of operations and cash flows for the three months ended March 31, 2008 and 2009. The financial data and other information disclosed in these notes to the consolidated financial statements related to the three-month periods are unaudited. The results of the three months ended March 31, 2009 are not necessarily indicative of the results to be expected for the year ending December 31, 2009 or for any other interim period of for any other future year.

Unaudited Pro Forma Consolidated Balance Sheet

Upon the consummation of the initial public offering contemplated herein, all of the outstanding shares of convertible preferred stock automatically convert into shares of common stock, and the warrant to purchase Series A convertible preferred stock converts to a warrant to purchase common stock. The March 31, 2009 unaudited pro forma consolidated balance sheet data has been prepared assuming the conversion of the convertible preferred stock outstanding into 9,075,737 shares of common stock.

Foreign Currency Translation

The Company's operations are conducted in various countries around the world and the financial statements of its foreign subsidiaries are reported in the applicable foreign currencies (functional currencies). Financial information is translated from the applicable functional currency to the U.S. dollar, the reporting currency, for inclusion in the Company's consolidated financial statements. Income, expenses, and cash flows are translated at average exchange rates prevailing during the fiscal year, and assets and liabilities are translated at fiscal year-end exchange rates. Resulting translation adjustments are included as a component of accumulated other comprehensive income (loss), net, in stockholders' equity. Foreign exchange transaction gains and losses are included in Other Income, net in the accompanying consolidated statements of operations. Exchange gains and losses on intercompany balances that are considered permanently invested are also included as a component of accumulated other comprehensive loss, in stockholders' equity.

Cash and Cash Equivalents

The Company considers all highly liquid short-term investments with original maturities of three months or less at the time of purchase to be cash equivalents. At December 31, 2007 and 2008, and March 31, 2009, cash and cash equivalents consist of cash, money market accounts and commercial paper.

Restricted Cash

Restricted cash represents money market accounts and a certificate of deposit held at a financial institution principally as security for deposits maintained in connection with the Company's credit card processors.

F-9

OPENTABLE, INC.

NOTES TO CONSOLIDATED FINANCIAL STATEMENTS (Continued)

YEARS ENDED DECEMBER 31, 2006, 2007 AND 2008, AND THE THREE MONTHS
ENDED MARCH 31, 2008 AND 2009 (UNAUDITED)

2. Summary of Significant Accounting Policies (Continued)

Short-term Investments

Short-term investments consist mainly of U.S. government agency securities, commercial paper and certificates of deposit. The Company classifies its investments as available-for-sale securities. Available-for-sale securities are carried at fair value with unrealized gains and losses reported as a component of accumulated other comprehensive income (loss), net, in stockholders' equity. For the periods ended December 31, 2007 and 2008, and March 31, 2009, realized and unrealized gains and losses on investments were not material. An impairment charge is recorded in the consolidated statements of operations for declines in fair value below the cost of an individual investment that are deemed to be other than temporary. Management judges whether a decline in value is temporary based on the length of time that the fair market value has been below cost combined with the severity of the decline.

Concentrations of Credit Risk

Financial instruments which potentially subject the Company to concentration of credit risk consist primarily of cash and cash equivalents, restricted cash, short-term investments and accounts receivable. The Company places its cash and cash equivalents, short-term investments and restricted cash with major financial institutions throughout the world, which management assesses to be of high credit quality, in order to limit the exposure of each investment.

Credit risk with respect to accounts receivable is dispersed due to the large number of customers. In addition, the Company's credit risk is mitigated by the relatively short collection period. Collateral is not required for accounts receivable. The Company maintains an allowance for doubtful accounts receivable balances. The allowance is based upon historical loss patterns, the number of days that billings are past due and an evaluation of the potential risk of loss associated with problem accounts. Accounts receivable written-off against the allowance for doubtful accounts were $437,000, $457,000, and $747,000 for the years ended December 31, 2006, 2007 and 2008, respectively, and $101,000 and $313,000 for the three months ended March 31, 2008 and 2009, respectively.

Deferred Offering Costs

Deferred offering costs of $1,183,000 and $1,975,000 are included in other assets on the Company's consolidated balance sheet at December 31, 2008 and March 31, 2009. Upon the consummation of the initial public offering contemplated herein, these amounts will be offset against the proceeds of the offering. There were no amounts capitalized as of December 31, 2007.

Property and Equipment, net

Property and equipment, net is stated at cost less accumulated depreciation and amortization. Depreciation is computed using the straight-line method over the estimated useful lives of the assets, which is four years for restaurant hardware and three years for all other asset categories except leasehold improvement, which are amortized over the shorter of the lease term or expected useful life of the improvements.

F-10

OPENTABLE, INC.

NOTES TO CONSOLIDATED FINANCIAL STATEMENTS (Continued)

YEARS ENDED DECEMBER 31, 2006, 2007 AND 2008, AND THE THREE MONTHS
ENDED MARCH 31, 2008 AND 2009 (UNAUDITED)

2. Summary of Significant Accounting Policies (Continued)

Website and Software Development Costs

Costs related to website and internal-use software development are accounted for in accordance with American Institute of Certified Public Accountants Statement of Position 98-1, *Accounting for the Costs of Computer Software Developed or Obtained for Internal Use* (SOP 98-1) and Emerging Issues Task Force Issue No. 00-2, *Accounting for Website Development Costs* (EITF 00-2). Such software is primarily related to the Company's website, including support systems. In accordance with SOP 98-1 and EITF 00-2, the Company begins to capitalize its costs to develop software when preliminary development efforts are successfully completed, management has authorized and committed project funding, and it is probable that the project will be completed and the software will be used as intended. Such costs are amortized on a straight-line basis over the estimated useful life of the related asset, generally estimated between two to four years. Costs incurred prior to meeting these criteria are expensed as incurred and recorded within Technology expenses within the accompanying consolidated statements of operations. Costs incurred for enhancements that are expected to result in additional features or functionality are capitalized and expensed over the estimated useful life of the enhancements, generally between two and three years.

The Company capitalized $150,000, $419,000, and $1,003,000 in website and internal-use software development costs during the years ended December 31, 2006, 2007 and 2008, respectively. The amounts capitalized for the three months ended March 31, 2008 and 2009, were $213,000 and $148,000, respectively. Amortization expense totaled $103,000, $175,000 and $431,000 during the fiscal years ended December 31, 2006, 2007 and 2008, respectively, and $75,000 and $149,000 for the three months ended March 31, 2008 and 2009, respectively. Such costs are recorded in Operations and Support within the accompanying consolidated statements of operations.

The Company follows the guidance in Statement of Financial Accounting Standard No. 86, *Accounting for the Costs of Computer Software to Be Sold, Leased, or Otherwise Marketed* (SFAS 86) in accounting for costs incurred in connection with development of the software contained in the ERB used by all restaurant customers, and in a limited number of certain transactions the Company sells reservation systems which do not include the Company's ongoing service. All costs incurred to establish the technological feasibility of a computer product to be sold, leased or otherwise marketed are expensed as incurred. Costs incurred subsequent to establishing technological feasibility and through general product release are capitalized and amortized over the estimated product life. The period between technological feasibility and general product release is extremely short and the costs incurred during this stage are not material for the fiscal years ended December 31, 2006, 2007 and 2008, and the three months ended March 31, 2008 and 2009, and are expensed as incurred.

Impairment of Long-Lived Assets and Long-Lived Assets to be Disposed of

The Company evaluates its long-lived assets for impairment whenever events or changes in circumstances indicate that the carrying amount of such assets may not be recoverable. Recoverability of assets to be held and used is measured by a comparison of the carrying amount of an asset group to future undiscounted net cash flows expected to be generated by the asset group. If such assets are considered to be impaired, the impairment to be recognized is measured by the amount by which the

F-11

OPENTABLE, INC.

NOTES TO CONSOLIDATED FINANCIAL STATEMENTS (Continued)

**YEARS ENDED DECEMBER 31, 2006, 2007 AND 2008, AND THE THREE MONTHS
ENDED MARCH 31, 2008 AND 2009 (UNAUDITED)**

2. Summary of Significant Accounting Policies (Continued)

carrying amount of the assets exceeds the fair value of the assets. Assets to be disposed of are reported at the lower of the carrying amount or fair value less costs to sell.

Revenue Recognition

The Company's revenues include installation fees for the Company's ERB (including training), monthly subscription fees and a per-seated diner fee for each diner seated through the Company's online reservation system. As the Company provides its application as a service, the Company follows the provisions of Securities and Exchange Commission Staff Accounting Bulletin No. 104, *Revenue Recognition* (SAB 104) and Emerging Issues Task Force Issue No. 00-21, *Revenue Arrangements with Multiple Deliverables* (EITF 00-21). The Company recognizes revenue when all of the following conditions are met: there is persuasive evidence of an arrangement; the service has been provided to the customer; the collection of the fees is reasonably assured; and the amount of fees to be paid by the customer is fixed or determinable. Amounts paid by the customer include the right to use Company hardware during the service period. Proportionate revenue related to the right to use Company hardware accounts for less than 10% of revenue for all periods presented.

Revenue from the installation of the ERB is recognized on a straight-line basis over the estimated customer life, commencing with customer acceptance. The estimated customer life is approximately six years, based on historical restaurant customer termination activity. To date, the impact of changes in the estimated customer life has not been material to the Company's results of operations or financial position. Subscription revenues are recognized on a straight-line basis during the contractual period over which the service is delivered. Reservation revenues (or per-seated diner fees) are recognized on a transaction-by-transaction basis, as diners are seated by restaurant customers. Amounts that have been invoiced are recorded in accounts receivable and in deferred revenue or revenues, depending on whether the revenue recognition criteria have been met. Revenues are shown net of $2,490,000, $4,032,000 and $5,184,000 for the fiscal years ended December 31, 2006, 2007 and 2008, respectively, and $1,316,000 and $1,630,000 for the three months ended March 31, 2008 and 2009, respectively, related to redeemable Dining Points issued to diners during the respective periods.

Installation Costs

The incremental direct customer acquisition costs associated with on-site system installations, including direct compensation costs of technicians providing installation services, are expensed as incurred.

Dining Point Loyalty Program

The Company provides a points-based loyalty program, "OpenTable Dining Rewards", to registered diners who book and honor reservations through the OpenTable website. OpenTable Dining Rewards involves the issuance of "Dining Points" which can be accumulated and redeemed for "Dining Cheques". When a diner accumulates a defined minimum number of points, he/she may redeem them for a Dining Cheque. Diners may present Dining Cheques at any OpenTable restaurant and their bill is reduced by the cheque amount. If a diner does not make a seated reservation within any 12 month

F-12

OPENTABLE, INC.

NOTES TO CONSOLIDATED FINANCIAL STATEMENTS (Continued)

YEARS ENDED DECEMBER 31, 2006, 2007 AND 2008, AND THE THREE MONTHS
ENDED MARCH 31, 2008 AND 2009 (UNAUDITED)

2. Summary of Significant Accounting Policies (Continued)

period, then his or her account is considered inactive and the accumulated Dining Points for the diner are reset to zero.

The recorded contra-revenue is an estimate of the eventual cash outlay related to the issued Dining Points and is booked at the time the points are earned by the diner (when the diner is "seated" by the restaurants). The Company estimates the expense for the issued Dining Points by analyzing the historical patterns of redemption and cheque cashing activity.

The Company recognizes the cost associated with Dining Points as contra-revenue in accordance with EITF No. 01-09, *Accounting for Consideration Given by a Vendor to a Customer (Including a Reseller of the Vendor's Products)*, and EITF No. 00-22, *Accounting for "Points" and Certain Other Time- or Volume- Based Sales Incentive Offers, and Offers for Free Products or Services to be Delivered in the Future*.

Technology

In the consolidated statement of operations, technology expense includes employee compensation associated with the development of new technologies.

Operations and Support

In the consolidated statements of operations, operations and support expense includes employee compensation associated with the installation, support and maintenance of restaurant customers, as well as costs associated with restaurant equipment and connectivity, referral payments and shipping costs associated with restaurant equipment. Operations and Support expenses also include amortization of capitalized website and development costs.

Advertising Expense

Advertising costs are expensed when incurred and are included in sales and marketing expense in the accompanying consolidated statements of operations. Advertising costs include direct-marketing costs such as email marketing, market research, printing, public relations and tradeshow expenses. The Company incurred $906,000, $1,072,000 and $1,355,000 of advertising costs during the fiscal years ended December 31, 2006, 2007 and 2008, respectively, and $263,000 and $274,000 for the three months ended March 31, 2008 and 2009, respectively.

Stock-Based Compensation

Prior to January 1, 2006, the Company accounted for stock-based employee compensation arrangements using the intrinsic value method of Accounting Principles Board Opinion No. 25, *Accounting for Stock Issued to Employees* (APB No. 25) and related interpretations, and complied with the disclosure-only provisions of SFAS No. 123, *Accounting for Stock-Based Compensation*, (SFAS No. 123) as amended by SFAS No. 148, *Accounting for Stock-Based Compensation, Transition and Disclosure, an amendment to SFAS Statement No. 123* (SFAS No. 148). Under APB No. 25 compensation expense for employees is based on the excess, if any, of the fair value of the Company's common stock over the exercise price of the option on the date of grant.

F-13

OPENTABLE, INC.

NOTES TO CONSOLIDATED FINANCIAL STATEMENTS (Continued)

YEARS ENDED DECEMBER 31, 2006, 2007 AND 2008, AND THE THREE MONTHS
ENDED MARCH 31, 2008 AND 2009 (UNAUDITED)

2. Summary of Significant Accounting Policies (Continued)

Effective January 1, 2006, the Company adopted SFAS No. 123R, *Share-Based Payment* (SFAS No. 123R), which requires compensation expense related to share-based transactions, including employee stock options, to be measured and recognized in the financial statements based on fair value. SFAS No. 123R revises SFAS No. 123, as amended, and supersedes APB No. 25. The Company adopted SFAS No. 123R using the modified prospective method. Under modified prospective application, SFAS No. 123R applies to new awards and to awards modified, repurchased, or cancelled after the required effective date. Additionally, compensation cost for the portion of awards for which the requisite service has not been rendered that are outstanding as of the required effective date are recognized as the requisite service is rendered on or after the required effective date. The compensation expense for that portion of awards is based on the grant-date fair value of those awards. The compensation expense for awards with grant dates prior to January 1, 2006, are attributed to periods beginning on or after the effective date using the attribution method that was used under SFAS No. 123, except that the method of recognizing forfeitures only as they occur is not continued.

The Company is using the graded vesting attribution method prescribed by SFAS 123R over the option vesting period, for all options granted on or after January 1, 2006. All options granted prior to January 1, 2006 are being amortized using a straight-line method.

Net Income (Loss) Per Share

Basic net income (loss) per share attributed to common shares is computed by dividing the net income (loss) for the period by the weighted average number of common shares outstanding during the period as reduced by the weighted average unvested common shares subject to repurchase by the Company. Diluted net income (loss) per share is computed by dividing the net income (loss) for the period by the weighted average number of common and potential dilutive shares outstanding during the period, to the extent such potential dilutive shares are dilutive. Potential dilutive shares are composed of incremental common shares issuable upon the exercise of stock options and warrants, unvested common shares subject to repurchase and convertible preferred stock. Nonvested performance-based awards are included in the diluted shares outstanding each period if established performance criteria have been met at the end of the respective periods. 343,000 shares were excluded from the dilutive shares outstanding for the years ended December 31, 2006, 2007 and 2008, and the three months ended March 31, 2008 and 2009, as the performance criteria had not been met as of the respective dates. Anti-dilutive shares in the amounts of 768,000, 667,000 and 11,669,000 were excluded from the dilutive shares outstanding for the fiscal years ended December 31, 2006, 2007 and 2008. Anti-dilutive shares in the amounts of 11,747,000 and 821,000 were excluded from the dilutive shares outstanding for the three months ended March 31,

F-14

OPENTABLE, INC.

NOTES TO CONSOLIDATED FINANCIAL STATEMENTS (Continued)

**YEARS ENDED DECEMBER 31, 2006, 2007 AND 2008, AND THE THREE MONTHS
ENDED MARCH 31, 2008 AND 2009 (UNAUDITED)**

2. Summary of Significant Accounting Policies (Continued)

2008 and 2009. The following table sets forth the computation of basic and diluted net income (loss) per share for the periods indicated:

	Years Ended December 31,			Three Months Ended March 31,	
	2006	2007	2008	2008	2009
				(Unaudited)	
Net income (loss)	$ 194,000	$ 9,216,000	$ (1,024,000)	$ (87,000)	$ 366,000
Basic shares:					
Weighted average common shares outstanding	9,132,000	9,522,000	10,016,000	9,850,000	10,276,000
Diluted shares:					
Weighted average shares used to compute basic net income (loss) per share	9,132,000	9,522,000	10,016,000	9,850,000	10,276,000
Effect of potentially dilutive securities:					
Unvested common shares subject to repurchase	788,000	659,000	—	—	583,000
Warrants to purchase common stock	7,000	24,000	—	—	36,000
Warrants to purchase convertible preferred stock	64,000	76,000	—	—	80,000
Employee stock options	456,000	662,000	—	—	966,000
Convertible preferred stock	9,076,000	9,076,000	—	—	9,076,000
Weighted average shares used to compute diluted net income (loss) per share	19,523,000	20,019,000	10,016,000	9,850,000	21,017,000
Net income (loss) per share:					
Basic	$ 0.02	$ 0.97	$ (0.10)	$ (0.01)	$ 0.04
Diluted	$ 0.01	$ 0.46	$ (0.10)	$ (0.01)	$ 0.02

F-15

OPENTABLE, INC.

NOTES TO CONSOLIDATED FINANCIAL STATEMENTS (Continued)

YEARS ENDED DECEMBER 31, 2006, 2007 AND 2008, AND THE THREE MONTHS
ENDED MARCH 31, 2008 AND 2009 (UNAUDITED)

2. Summary of Significant Accounting Policies (Continued)

Unaudited Pro Forma Net Income (Loss) per Share

Pro forma basic and diluted net income (loss) per share have been computed to give effect to the conversion of the Company's preferred stock (using the if converted method) into common stock as though the conversion had occurred on the original dates of issuance.

	Year Ended December 31, 2008	Three Months Ended March 31, 2009
	(Unaudited)	
Net income (loss)	$ (1,024,000)	$ 366,000
Basic shares:		
Weighted average shares used to compute basic net income (loss) per share	10,016,000	10,276,000
Pro forma adjustments to reflect assumed weighted effect of conversion of convertible preferred stock	9,076,000	9,076,000
Weighted average shares used to compute basic pro forma net income (loss) per share	19,092,000	19,352,000
Diluted shares:		
Weighted average shares used to compute diluted net income (loss) per share	10,016,000	21,017,000
Pro forma adjustments to reflect assumed weighted effect of conversion of convertible preferred stock	9,076,000	—
Weighted average shares used to compute diluted pro forma net income (loss) per share	19,092,000	21,017,000
Pro forma net income (loss) per share:		
Basic	$ (0.05)	$ 0.02
Diluted	$ (0.05)	$ 0.02

Comprehensive Income (Loss)

In accordance with SFAS No. 130, *Reporting Comprehensive Income* (SFAS No. 130), the Company reports by major components and as a single total, the change in its net assets during the period from nonowner sources. Comprehensive income (loss) consists of net income (loss) and accumulated other comprehensive income (loss), which includes certain changes in equity that are excluded from net income (loss). Specifically, it includes cumulative foreign currency translation and the unrealized gain (loss) from investments. Comprehensive income (loss) for the fiscal years ended December 31, 2006, 2007 and 2008, and the three months ended March 31, 2008 and 2009, is included within the Consolidated Statement of Stockholders' Equity and Comprehensive Income (Loss).

Accumulated other comprehensive loss of $242,000 as of March 31, 2009 was comprised of $34,000 of unrealized gain on investments and $276,000 of foreign currency translation losses.

F-16

OPENTABLE, INC.

NOTES TO CONSOLIDATED FINANCIAL STATEMENTS (Continued)

YEARS ENDED DECEMBER 31, 2006, 2007 AND 2008, AND THE THREE MONTHS
ENDED MARCH 31, 2008 AND 2009 (UNAUDITED)

2. Summary of Significant Accounting Policies (Continued)

Income Taxes

The Company records income taxes using the asset and liability method which requires the recognition of deferred tax assets and liabilities for the expected future tax consequences of events that have been recognized in the Company's financial statements or tax returns. In estimating future tax consequences, generally all expected future events other than enactments or changes in the tax law or rates are considered. Valuation allowances are provided when necessary to reduce deferred tax assets to the amount expected to be realized.

The Company operates in various tax jurisdictions and is subject to audit by various tax authorities. The Company provides for tax contingencies whenever it is deemed probable that a tax asset has been impaired or a tax liability has been incurred for events such as tax claims or changes in tax laws. Tax contingencies are based upon their technical merits, relative tax law, and the specific facts and circumstances as of each reporting period. Changes in facts and circumstances could result in material changes to the amounts recorded for such tax contingencies.

On January 1, 2007, the Company adopted Financial Accounting Standards Board ("FASB") Interpretation No. 48, *Accounting for Uncertainty in Income Taxes—an interpretation of FASB Statement No. 109* (FIN No. 48), which supplements SFAS No. 109, *Accounting for Income Taxes*, by defining the confidence level that a tax position must meet in order to be recognized in the financial statements. FIN No. 48 requires that the tax effects of a position be recognized only if it is "more-likely-than-not" to be sustained based solely on its technical merits as of the reporting date. The Company considers many factors when evaluating and estimating its tax positions and tax benefits, which may require periodic adjustments and which may not accurately anticipate actual outcomes.

With the adoption of FIN No. 48, companies are required to adjust their financial statements to reflect only those tax positions that are more-likely-than-not to be sustained. Any necessary adjustment would be recorded directly to retained earnings and reported as a change in accounting principle as of the date of adoption. FIN No. 48 prescribes a comprehensive model for the financial statement recognition, measurement, presentation and disclosure of uncertain tax positions taken or expected to be taken in income tax returns. The total amount of unrecognized tax benefits as of the adoption date was $14,879,000. The Company's policy is to recognize interest and penalties related to unrecognized tax benefits in income tax expense. See Note 9 for additional information, including the effects of adoption on the Company's consolidated financial position, results of operations and cash flows.

Recently Issued Accounting Standards

Effective January 1, 2008, the Company adopted SFAS No. 157, *Fair Value Measurements* (SFAS No. 157). In February 2008, the FASB issued a staff position, FSP No. 157-2, that delays the effective date of SFAS No. 157 for all non-financial assets and liabilities except for those recognized or disclosed in the financial statements at fair value at least annually. Therefore, the Company has adopted the provision of SFAS No. 157 with respect to its financial assets and liabilities only. SFAS No. 157 defines fair value, establishes a framework for measuring fair value and expands disclosures about fair value measurements. Fair value is defined under SFAS No. 157 as the exchange price that would be received

F-17

OPENTABLE, INC.

NOTES TO CONSOLIDATED FINANCIAL STATEMENTS (Continued)

YEARS ENDED DECEMBER 31, 2006, 2007 AND 2008, AND THE THREE MONTHS
ENDED MARCH 31, 2008 AND 2009 (UNAUDITED)

2. Summary of Significant Accounting Policies (Continued)

for an asset or paid to transfer a liability (an exit price) in the principal or most advantageous market for the asset or liability in an orderly transaction between market participants on the measure date. Valuation techniques used to measure fair value under SFAS No. 157 must maximize the use of observable inputs and minimize the use of unobservable inputs. The standard describes a fair value hierarchy based on three levels of inputs, of which the first two are considered observable and the last unobservable, that may be used to measure fair value which are the following:

> Level 1—Quoted prices in active markets for identical assets or liabilities

> Level 2—Inputs other than Level 1 that are observable, either directly or indirectly, such as quoted prices for similar assets or liabilities; quoted prices in markets that are not active; or other inputs that are observable or can be corroborated by observable market data for substantially the full term of the assets or liabilities.

> Level 3—Unobservable inputs that are supported by little or no market activity and that are significant to the fair value of the assets or liabilities.

The adoption of this statement required additional disclosures of assets and liabilities measured at fair value (see Note 3); it did not have a material impact on the Company's consolidated results of operations and financial condition.

Effective January 1, 2008, the Company adopted SFAS No. 159, *The Fair Value Option for Financial Assets and Financial Liabilities* (SFAS No. 159) which permits entities to choose to measure many financial instruments and certain other items at fair value that are not currently required to be measured at fair value. The Company did not elect to adopt the fair value option under SFAS No. 159 as this Statement is not expected to have a material impact on the Company's consolidated results of operations and financial condition.

In December 2007, the FASB issued SFAS No. 141 (Revised 2007), *Business Combinations* (SFAS No. 141 (R)). SFAS No. 141(R) establishes principles and requirements for how the acquirer of a business recognizes and measures in its financial statements the identifiable assets acquired, the liabilities assumed, and any noncontrolling interest in the acquiree. SFAS No. 141(R) also provides guidance for recognizing and measuring the goodwill acquired in the business combination and determines what information to disclose to enable users of the financial statements to evaluate the nature and financial effects of the business combination. The Company is required to adopt SFAS No. 141(R) for the fiscal year beginning January 1, 2009. The adoption of SFAS No. 141(R) did not have a material impact on the Company's financial position or results of operations at the time of adoption.

In December 2007, the FASB issued SFAS No. 160, *Non-controlling Interests in Consolidated Financial Statements* (SFAS No. 160) which amends Accounting Research Bulletin No. 51, *Consolidated Financial Statements* (ARB No. 51), to establish accounting and reporting standards for the non-controlling interest in a subsidiary and for the deconsolidation of a subsidiary. It clarifies that a non-controlling interest in a subsidiary is an ownership interest in the consolidated entity that should be reported as equity separate and apart from the parent's equity in the consolidated financial statements. In addition to the amendments to ARB No. 51, this statement amends SFAS No. 128, *Earnings Per*

F-18

OPENTABLE, INC.

NOTES TO CONSOLIDATED FINANCIAL STATEMENTS (Continued)

YEARS ENDED DECEMBER 31, 2006, 2007 AND 2008, AND THE THREE MONTHS
ENDED MARCH 31, 2008 AND 2009 (UNAUDITED)

2. Summary of Significant Accounting Policies (Continued)

Share, so that earnings per share data will continue to be calculated the same way those data were calculated before this statements was issued. SFAS No. 160 is effective for fiscal years, and interim periods within those fiscal years beginning on or after December 15, 2008. The adoption of SFAS No. 160 did not have a material impact on the Company's financial position or results of operations at the time of adoption.

In May 2008, the FASB issued SFAS No. 162, *The Hierarchy of Generally Accepted Accounting Principles* (SFAS No. 162). This statement documents the hierarchy of the various sources of accounting principles and the framework for selecting the principles used in preparing financial statements. This statement shall be effective 60 days following the SEC's approval of the Public Company Accounting Oversight Board amendments to AU Section 411, *The Meaning of Present Fairly in Conformity With Generally Accepted Accounting Principles*. SFAS No. 162 will not have a material impact to the Company's consolidated financial statements.

3. Short-Term Investments and Fair Value Measurements

Short-term investments, all of which have a term of less than one year, are summarized as follows:

	Amortized Cost	Unrealized Gains	Estimated Fair Market Value
At December 31, 2008:			
Commercial paper	$ 898,000	$ 1,000	899,000
U.S. government and agency securities	10,595,000	65,000	10,660,000
Certificates of deposit	5,700,000	—	5,700,000
Total	$17,193,000	$ 66,000	$17,259,000
	Amortized Cost	Unrealized Gains	Estimated Fair Market Value
At March 31, 2009 (unaudited):			
U.S. government and agency securities	$ 7,460,000	$ 34,000	7,494,000
Certificates of deposit	5,700,000	—	5,700,000
Total	$13,160,000	$ 34,000	$13,194,000

SFAS No. 157 clarifies that fair value is an exit price, representing the amount that would be received to sell an asset or paid to transfer a liability in an orderly transaction between market participants. As such, fair value is a market-based measurement that should be determined based on assumptions that market participants would use in pricing an asset or liability. As a basis for considering such assumptions, SFAS No. 157 establishes a three-tier value hierarchy, which prioritizes the inputs used in measuring fair value as follows: (Level 1) observable inputs such as quoted prices in active markets; (Level 2) inputs other than the quoted prices in active markets that are observable either directly or indirectly; and (Level 3) significant unobservable inputs in which there is little or no market data, which requires the Company to develop its own assumptions. This hierarchy requires the Company to use observable market data, when available, and to minimize the use of unobservable

F-19

OPENTABLE, INC.

NOTES TO CONSOLIDATED FINANCIAL STATEMENTS (Continued)

YEARS ENDED DECEMBER 31, 2006, 2007 AND 2008, AND THE THREE MONTHS
ENDED MARCH 31, 2008 AND 2009 (UNAUDITED)

3. Short-Term Investments and Fair Value Measurements (Continued)

inputs when determining fair value. On a recurring basis, the Company measures its marketable securities at fair value.

Investment instruments are classified within Level 1 or Level 2 of the fair value hierarchy because they are valued using quoted market prices, broker or dealer quotations, or alternative pricing sources with reasonable levels of price transparency. The types of instruments that are generally classified within Level 1 of the fair value hierarchy include money market securities and U.S. government and agency securities. The types of investments that are generally classified within Level 2 of the fair value hierarchy include, corporate securities and certificates of deposit.

In accordance with SFAS No. 157, the following table represents the Company's fair value hierarchy for its financial assets as follows:

	December 31, 2008			March 31, 2009		
	Aggregate Fair Value	Level 1	Level 2	Aggregate Fair Value	Level 1	Level 2
Commercial paper	$ 899,000	$ 899,000	$ —	$ —	$ —	$ —
U.S. government and agency securities	10,660,000	10,660,000	—	7,494,000	7,494,000	—
Certificates of deposit	5,700,000	—	5,700,000	5,700,000	—	5,700,000
Total short-term investments	$17,259,000	$11,559,000	$5,700,000	$13,194,000	$7,494,000	$5,700,000

The Company chose not to elect the fair value option as prescribed by SFAS No. 159 for its financial assets and liabilities that had not been previously carried at fair value. Therefore, financial assets and liabilities not carried at fair value, such as accounts payable, are still reported at their carrying values.

4. Property and Equipment

Property and equipment consists of the following:

	Years Ended December 31,		March 31, 2009
	2007	2008	(Unaudited)
Restaurant hardware	$11,838,000	$16,049,000	$ 15,825,000
Computer equipment	1,544,000	2,140,000	2,205,000
Software	657,000	824,000	860,000
Capitalized development	806,000	1,809,000	1,957,000
Furniture and fixtures	161,000	168,000	258,000
Total	15,006,000	20,990,000	21,105,000
Accumulated depreciation	(6,628,000)	(9,865,000)	(10,036,000)
Property and equipment, net	$ 8,378,000	$11,125,000	$ 11,069,000

F-20

OPENTABLE, INC.

NOTES TO CONSOLIDATED FINANCIAL STATEMENTS (Continued)

YEARS ENDED DECEMBER 31, 2006, 2007 AND 2008, AND THE THREE MONTHS
ENDED MARCH 31, 2008 AND 2009 (UNAUDITED)

5. Line of Credit

In August 2007, the Company entered into a $2,000,000 line of credit for working capital needs. In September 2008, the Company increased the line of credit to $3,000,000. This line of credit is available through July 2009 and no amounts were outstanding under this line of credit as of December 31, 2007 and 2008 or March 31, 2009. This line of credit agreement requires the Company to comply with various financial and non-financial covenants, including a minimum revenue requirement, and precludes the payment of dividends to shareholders without the permission of the lender. The Company was in compliance with all financial covenants for all periods and at December 31, 2007 and 2008, and March 31, 2009.

6. Other Income, Net

Other income, net, consists of the following:

	Years Ended December 31,			Three Months Ended March 31,	
	2006	2007	2008	2008	2009
				(Unaudited)	
Interest income	$426,000	$785,000	$ 545,000	$186,000	$ 86,000
Interest expense	(2,000)	(1,000)	—	—	—
Foreign exchange transaction gain (loss), net	(22,000)	120,000	(130,000)	(17,000)	(38,000)
Other non-operating income, net	19,000	47,000	53,000	11,000	7,000
Total	$421,000	$951,000	$ 468,000	$180,000	$ 55,000

7. Commitments and Contingencies

Office Facility Leases

The Company leases its office facilities under operating lease agreements that expire at various dates through 2013. The terms of the lease agreements provide for rental payments on a graduated basis. The Company recognizes rent expense on a straight-line basis over the lease period.

Rental expense, principally for leased office space under operating lease commitments, was $620,000, $710,000 and $1,420,000 for the years ended December 31, 2006, 2007 and 2008, respectively, and $318,000 and $373,000 for the three months ended March 31, 2008 and 2009, respectively.

F-21

OPENTABLE, INC.

NOTES TO CONSOLIDATED FINANCIAL STATEMENTS (Continued)

YEARS ENDED DECEMBER 31, 2006, 2007 AND 2008, AND THE THREE MONTHS
ENDED MARCH 31, 2008 AND 2009 (UNAUDITED)

7. Commitments and Contingencies (Continued)

Aggregate Future Lease Commitments

The Company minimum payments under non-cancelable operating leases for office space having initial terms in excess of one year are as follows at December 31, 2008:

Years ending December 31:	Operating Leases
2009	$1,458,000
2010	1,305,000
2011	1,312,000
2012	1,347,000
2013	456,000
Total minimum lease payments	$5,878,000

Litigation

In July 2007, a complaint was filed against the Company by Online Reservations LLC ("Online Reservations") alleging intellectual property rights infringement. Online Reservations sought damages and injunctive relief. On March 19, 2008 the Company reached a settlement with Online Reservations in the amount of $1,600,000. The settlement was recorded as general and administrative expense in the third quarter of fiscal year 2007.

The Company is also subject to various other legal proceedings and claims arising in the ordinary course of business. Although occasional adverse decisions or settlements may occur, management believes that the final disposition of such matters will not have a material adverse effect on the Company's business, financial position, results of operations or cash flows.

8. Stockholders' Equity

Common Stock

At December 31, 2008, there were 24,000,000 shares of common stock authorized, 11,154,668 shares issued and 10,944,421 shares outstanding. Holders of common stock are entitled to dividends if and when declared by the board of directors.

Common Stock Subject To Repurchase

Historically, the Company typically allowed employees to exercise options prior to vesting. However, beginning with May 2008, options granted did not contain an early exercise provision. The Company has the right to repurchase at the original purchase price any unvested (but issued) common shares upon termination of service of an employee. The consideration received for an exercise of an option is considered to be a deposit of the exercise price and the related dollar amount is recorded as a liability. The shares and liability are reclassified into equity on a ratable basis as the award vests. The Company recorded a liability in accounts payable and accrued expenses of $4,331,000, $2,984,000, and

F-22

-245-

OPENTABLE, INC.

NOTES TO CONSOLIDATED FINANCIAL STATEMENTS (Continued)

YEARS ENDED DECEMBER 31, 2006, 2007 AND 2008, AND THE THREE MONTHS
ENDED MARCH 31, 2008 AND 2009 (UNAUDITED)

8. Stockholders' Equity (Continued)

$2,672,000 relating to 1,110,030, 728,028, and 638,001 options that were exercised and are unvested at December 31, 2007 and 2008, and March 31, 2009 respectively. These shares which are subject to a repurchase right held by the Company are included in issued and outstanding shares as of December 31, 2007 and 2008, and March 31, 2009.

Treasury Stock

In November 2006, the Company repurchased 207,047 common shares at $3.13 per share, for $647,000.

In May 2007, in connection with litigation against a former employee, 3,200 shares of common stock were transferred back to the Company. As part of the settlement, the Company was not required to pay any consideration in return for the shares. These shares have been accounted for as treasury stock.

Common Stock Reserved For Future Issuance

At December 31, 2008, the Company has reserved the following shares of common stock for future issuances in connection with:

Series A convertible preferred stock	6,898,187
Series B convertible preferred stock	2,177,550
Warrants to purchase common stock	93,368
Warrants to purchase Series A convertible preferred stock	88,691
Stock option plan:	
Options outstanding	2,417,850
Options available for future grants	162,836
Total	11,838,482

Preferred Stock

On February 7, 2003, the Company issued 6,898,187 shares of the Company's Series A convertible preferred stock at $1.01 per share, resulting in gross proceeds of $7,000,000.

The Company is authorized to issue 7,040,000 shares of Series A convertible preferred stock ("Series A preferred stock") of which 6,898,187 shares are issued and outstanding at December 31, 2008.

The rights, preferences and privileges of the holders of Series A convertible preferred stock are as follows:

Dividends—The holders of the Series A convertible preferred stock shall be entitled to receive, prior and in preference to the shares of common stock, non-cumulative dividends at a rate of $0.10 per share per annum, payable when and if declared by the board of directors. For any other dividends or similar distributions, the Series A convertible preferred stock will participate with Series B convertible preferred stock and common stock on an as-converted basis. To date, no dividends have been declared.

F-23

OPENTABLE, INC.

NOTES TO CONSOLIDATED FINANCIAL STATEMENTS (Continued)

YEARS ENDED DECEMBER 31, 2006, 2007 AND 2008 AND THE THREE MONTHS ENDED MARCH 31, 2008 AND 2009
(UNAUDITED)

8. Stockholders' Equity (Continued)

Liquidation Rights—In the event of any liquidation, dissolution or winding up of the Company, holders of Series A convertible preferred stock shall be entitled to receive $1.01 per share, plus all declared but unpaid dividends, before any distributions of payments are made to the holders of common stock. All remaining assets of the Company available for distribution to its stockholders will be distributed among the holders of the common stock on a pro rata basis.

Conversion—Each share of Series A convertible preferred stock is convertible into common stock at the option of the holder on a one-for-one basis, subject to certain adjustments. Shares of Series A convertible preferred stock will be converted automatically, on the same terms upon (i) the approval of holders of at least a majority of then outstanding shares of Series A of convertible preferred stock and Series B convertible preferred stock voting as a single class, or (ii) closing of the Company's first underwritten public offering with gross proceeds equal to or exceeding $30,000,000.

Voting—The holders of Series A convertible preferred stock are entitled to the number of votes equal to the number of shares of common stock into which the preferred stock is convertible, subject to certain limitations.

On October 28, 2004, the Company issued 2,177,550 shares of the Company's Series B convertible preferred stock at $6.89 per share, resulting in gross proceeds of $15,000,000. The Company is authorized to issue 2,240,000 shares of Series B convertible preferred stock ("Series B preferred stock") of which 2,177,550 shares are issued and outstanding. The rights, preferences and privileges of the holders of Series B convertible preferred stock are as follows:

Dividends—The holders of the Series B convertible preferred stock shall be entitled to receive, prior and in preference to the shares of common stock, non-cumulative dividends at a rate of $0.69 per share per annum, payable when and if declared by the board of directors. For any other dividends or similar distributions, the Series B convertible preferred stock will participate with Series A convertible preferred stock and common stock on an as-converted basis. To date, no dividends have been declared.

Liquidation Rights—In the event of any liquidation, dissolution or winding up of the Company, holders of Series B convertible preferred stock shall be entitled to receive $6.89 per share, plus all declared but unpaid dividends, before any distributions of payments are made to the holders of any common stock. All remaining assets of the Company available for distribution to its stockholders will be distributed among the holders of the common stock on a pro rata basis.

Conversion—Each share of Series B convertible preferred stock is convertible into common stock at the option of the holder on a one-for-one basis, subject to certain adjustments. Shares of Series B convertible preferred stock will be converted automatically, on the same terms upon (i) the approval of holders of at least a majority of then outstanding shares of Series A convertible preferred stock and Series B of convertible preferred stock voting as a single class, or (ii) closing of the Company's first underwritten public offering with gross proceeds equal to or exceeding $30,000,000.

Voting—The holders of Series B convertible preferred stock are entitled to the number of votes equal to the number of shares of common stock into which the preferred stock is convertible, subject to certain limitations.

F-24

OPENTABLE, INC.

NOTES TO CONSOLIDATED FINANCIAL STATEMENTS (Continued)

YEARS ENDED DECEMBER 31, 2006, 2007 AND 2008 AND THE THREE MONTHS ENDED MARCH 31, 2008 AND 2009 (UNAUDITED)

8. Stockholders' Equity (Continued)

Stock Based Compensation under SFAS No. 123R

Effective January 1, 2006, the Company adopted SFAS No. 123R, which requires compensation costs related to share-based transactions, including employee stock options, to be recognized in the financial statements based on fair value.

Under SFAS No. 123R, the fair value of each option award is estimated on the date of grant using the Black-Scholes option pricing model. The Company determined weighted average valuation assumptions as follows:

- Volatility—As the Company does not have trading history for its common stock, the expected stock price volatility for the Company's common stock was estimated by taking the median historic price volatility for industry peers based on daily price observations over a period equivalent to the expected term of the stock option grants. Industry peers consist of several public companies in the technology industry similar in size, stage of life cycle and financial leverage. The Company did not rely on implied volatilities of traded options in its industry peers' common stock because the volume of activity was relatively low.

- Expected term—The expected term was estimated using the simplified method allowed under Securities and Exchange Commission Staff Accounting Bulletin No. 107, *Share-Based Payment.*

- Risk free rate—The risk free interest rate is based on the yields of U.S. Treasury securities with maturities similar to the expected term of the options for each option group.

- Forfeiture rate—The Company estimated the forfeiture rate based on our historical experience with forfeitures. The Company reviews the estimated forfeiture rates each period end and makes changes as factors affecting the forfeiture rate calculations and assumptions change.

- Dividend yield—The Company has never declared or paid any cash dividends and does not presently plan to pay cash dividends in the foreseeable future. Consequently, the Company used an expected dividend yield of zero.

The following table summarizes the assumptions relating to the Company's stock options for the years ended December 31, 2006, 2007 and 2008, as permitted under SFAS No. 123R:

	Years Ended December 31,		
	2006	2007	2008
Dividend yield	0%	0%	0%
Volatility	50%	48%-54%	55%
Risk free interest rate	4.56%-5.05%	3.61%-5.16%	1.54%-3.34%
Expected term, in years	5.50-7.00	5.27-6.65	5.92-6.53

No stock options were granted in the three months ended March 31, 2009.

As a result of adopting SFAS No. 123R, the Company recorded net stock-based compensation expense of $709,000, $3,103,000 and $3,970,000 for the years ended December 31, 2006, 2007 and 2008, respectively and $984,000 and $959,000 for the three months ended March 31, 2008 and 2009,

F-25

OPENTABLE, INC.

NOTES TO CONSOLIDATED FINANCIAL STATEMENTS (Continued)

YEARS ENDED DECEMBER 31, 2006, 2007 AND 2008 AND THE THREE MONTHS ENDED MARCH 31, 2008 AND 2009
(UNAUDITED)

8. Stockholders' Equity (Continued)

respectively. The Company capitalized $45,000 of stock-based compensation for the year ended December 31, 2008, and $13,000 for the three months ended March 31, 2009, in association with website and software development costs (see Note 2). No amounts were capitalized for the years ended December 31, 2006 and 2007.

Stock Options Plan

Under the 1999 Stock Plan (the "Plan"), 162,836 shares of common stock as of March 31, 2009 are reserved for the issuance of incentive stock options ("ISOs") or nonstatutory stock options ("NSOs") to eligible participants. During fiscal year 2006 and through March 31, 2009, the Board of Directors increased the number of shares of common stock authorized for issuance under the Plan by an additional 2,568,000. The ISOs may be granted at a price per share not less than the fair market value at the date of grant. The NSOs may be granted at a price per share not less than 85% of the fair market value at the date of grant. Options granted to date generally vest over a four-year period from the date of grant at a rate of 25% after one year, then monthly on a straight-line basis thereafter. Options granted generally are exercisable up to 10 years. Certain option holders are allowed to exercise unvested options to acquire restricted shares. Upon termination of service, the Company has the right to repurchase at the original purchase price any unvested (but issued) common shares. Common shares purchased under the Plan are subject to certain restrictions, including the right of first refusal by the Company for sale or transfer of these shares to outside parties. The Company's right of first refusal terminates upon completion of an initial public offering of common stock.

In January 2003, the Company initiated an option exchange program, under which plan participants could elect to cancel existing options. Participants electing cancellation were offered the opportunity to exchange such options for new options to be granted at least six months and one day following the cancellation, subject to the plan participant continuing to provide services to the Company through the grant date of the new options. The new options were subject to the same terms and conditions of the cancelled options with a modified vesting schedule under which employees received credit of 1/48th of the new grant for every four months of employment prior to February 2003. The remaining unvested options vest monthly over the 48 months beginning March 2003. Under the option exchange program, 242,491 options were canceled and replaced with 242,491 options with an exercise price of $0.10 per share. Through December 31, 2005, the replacement options were subject to variable plan accounting under APB No. 25. Stock-based compensation cost of $34,000 was recognized in the year ended December 31, 2005, related to these options for the difference between the option exercise price and the estimated fair value of the underlying common stock. On January 1, 2006, the Company adopted SFAS No. 123R, and the unamortized expense calculated under SFAS No. 123R was expensed in accordance with the remaining vesting period of these options.

Under the Plan, the Company granted 342,574 performance-based stock options to two executives. The first option was granted in November 2005 for 244,974 shares at an exercise price of $1.50 per share. The second option was granted in July 2006 for 97,600 shares at an exercise price of $1.50 per share. Beginning January 1, 2006, the Company accounted for this stock option as a fixed award in accordance with SFAS No. 123R. The grant-date fair value for this option, based on the Black-Scholes valuation model (using a 50% volatility factor, 6.11 years estimated life of the warrant, exercise price of $1.50, 0% dividend yield and 4.57% risk-free interest rate) was $380,000. The fair

F-26

OPENTABLE, INC.

NOTES TO CONSOLIDATED FINANCIAL STATEMENTS (Continued)

YEARS ENDED DECEMBER 31, 2006, 2007 AND 2008 AND THE THREE MONTHS ENDED MARCH 31, 2008 AND 2009
(UNAUDITED)

8. Stockholders' Equity (Continued)

value is to be amortized over the period during which management has estimated the performance metrics will be achieved. Stock-based compensation expense in the amount of $88,000, $88,000, and $71,000 was recognized in each of the years ended December 31, 2006, 2007 and 2008, respectively as well as $22,000 and $47,000 for the three months ended March 31, 2008 and 2009, respectively. The grant-date fair value for the second option, based on the Black-Scholes valuation model (using a 50% volatility factor, 6.26 estimated life of the warrant, exercise price of $1.50, 0% dividend yield and 5.05% risk-free interest rate) was $255,000. The fair value is to be amortized over the period during which management has estimated the performance metrics will be achieved by. Stock-based compensation expense, for the second option, in the amount of $46,000, $65,000 and $48,000 was recognized in the years ended December 31, 2006, 2007 and 2008, respectively as well as $16,000 and $10,000 for the three months ended March 31, 2008 and 2009, respectively.

A summary of the Company's stock option activity follows:

	Options Outstanding		Weighted Average Remaining Contractual Term (In Years)	Aggregate Intrinsic Value
	Number of Shares	Weighted Average Exercise Price		
Outstanding—January 1, 2006	994,676	$ 1.31		
Granted (weighted average fair value of $2.63)	345,280	1.50		
Exercised	(51,534)	0.56		
Canceled or expired	(33,684)	1.30		
Outstanding—December 31, 2006	1,254,738	$ 1.39		
Granted (weighted average fair value of $3.38)	2,260,644	7.78		
Exercised	(1,178,095)	4.47		
Canceled or expired	(340,048)	1.81		
Outstanding—December 31, 2007	1,997,239	$ 6.74		
Granted (weighted average fair value of $6.38)	561,848	8.59		
Exercised	(57,178)	1.85		
Canceled or expired	(84,059)	6.03		
Outstanding—December 31, 2008	2,417,850	$ 7.31		
Granted (unaudited)	0	—		
Exercised (unaudited)	(11,745)	$ 1.42		
Canceled or expired (unaudited)	(3,500)	$ 5.58		
Balance, March 31, 2009 (unaudited)	2,402,605	$ 7.33	7.92	$12,109,000
Available for grant—March 31, 2009 (unaudited)	162,836			
Options vested and expected to vest as of March 31, 2009 (unaudited)	2,208,282	$ 7.55	7.95	$10,841,000
Options exercisable as of March 31, 2009 (unaudited)	803,102	$ 7.31	7.61	$ 4,498,000

F-27

OPENTABLE, INC.

NOTES TO CONSOLIDATED FINANCIAL STATEMENTS (Continued)

YEARS ENDED DECEMBER 31, 2006, 2007 AND 2008 AND THE THREE MONTHS ENDED MARCH 31, 2008 AND 2009 (UNAUDITED)

8. Stockholders' Equity (Continued)

The Company has computed the aggregate intrinsic value amounts disclosed in the above table based on the difference between the original exercise price of the options and the fair value of the Company's common stock of $10.63 at March 31, 2009. The aggregate intrinsic value of awards exercised during the year ended December 31, 2006, 2007 and 2008 was $222,000, $6,220,000 and $502,000, respectively. As of December 31, 2008, the total stock options vested and expected to vest were 2,158,314 and had a weighted average exercise price of $7.63 per share, a weighted average contractual term of 8.16 years and a total intrinsic value of $10,584,000.

The options outstanding and exercisable as of December 31, 2008 have been segregated into ranges for additional disclosure as follows:

	Options Outstanding			Options Vested and Exercisable	
Exercise Price	Number Outstanding	Weighted Average Remaining Contractual Life (Years)	Weighted Average Exercise Price	Number Exercisable	Weighted Average Exercise Price
$0.10-$0.50	43,516	4.91	$ .22	43,516	$ .22
$1.50	669,060	7.04	1.50	224,709	1.50
$3.75-4.88	625,596	8.10	4.87	188,998	4.87
$4.88-$23.38	1,079,678	8.95	12.60	229,927	15.60
Total	2,417,850	8.13	$ 7.31	687,150	$ 7.06

As of March 31, 2009, total unrecognized compensation costs, adjusted for estimated forfeitures, related to non-vested stock options was $3,940,000, which is expected to be recognized over the next 2.52 years.

Warrants

In May 2000, the Company issued two warrants to purchase 14,455 fully paid and non-assessable shares of the Company's common stock at an exercise price of $3.75 per share in connection with executive recruitment. The warrants for 11,122 and 3,333, expired unexercised in May 2007 and October 2007, respectively.

In connection with an equipment lease agreement, during 2000 and 1999, the lessor received warrants from the Company to purchase shares of convertible preferred stock as follows:

- In 1999, the Company issued to the lessor warrants to purchase 6,940 shares of Series B convertible preferred stock at an exercise price of $8.75 per share and 1,202 shares of Series B preferred stock at an exercise price of $10.63 per share. The warrants are exercisable until August 2, 2009, or five years from an initial public offering by the Company, whichever is earlier.

- In 2000, the Company issued warrants to a lessor to purchase 11,764 shares of Series D redeemable convertible preferred stock at an exercise price of $10.63 per share and 11,851 shares of Series D redeemable convertible preferred stock at an exercise price of $33.75 per

F-28

OPENTABLE, INC.

NOTES TO CONSOLIDATED FINANCIAL STATEMENTS (Continued)

YEARS ENDED DECEMBER 31, 2006, 2007 AND 2008 AND THE THREE MONTHS ENDED MARCH 31, 2008 AND 2009
(UNAUDITED)

8. Stockholders' Equity (Continued)

share. The warrants are exercisable until April 25, 2010, or five years from an initial public offering by the Company, whichever is shorter.

During 2003, all outstanding Series B convertible preferred stock and Series D redeemable convertible preferred stock warrants related to the equipment lease line agreement were converted into common stock warrants to purchase 6,315, 1,094, 41,056 and 41,362 shares, respectively, of the Company's common stock, at prices of $9.63, $11.63, $3.00 and $9.63 per share, respectively. At December 31, 2007 and 2008 and March 31, 2009, all warrants remained outstanding.

During June 2003, in connection with a past financing agreement, the Company issued a warrant to purchase 88,691 shares of Series A convertible preferred stock with an exercise price of $1.00 per share. The warrant expires in June 2010. In the event that the Company completes its initial public offering prior to June 2010, the warrant will automatically be extended to expire on the third anniversary of the initial pubic offering. If the warrant reaches either of these expiration dates and has not been exercised, the warrant will automatically convert to preferred (or common as applicable) shares under a cashless exercise provision. At December 31, 2007 and 2008 and March 31, 2009, the warrant for 88,691 shares of Series A convertible preferred stock remains outstanding.

In March 2007, the Company issued a warrant to purchase 3,541 shares of common stock at an exercise price of $4.88 per share to a contractor. The warrant is exercisable through March 4, 2017, a liquidation event, or the consummation of an initial public offering by the Company, whichever is earlier. The fair value of the warrant based on the Black-Scholes valuation model (using a 50% volatility factor, 10 year expected life, exercise price of $4.88, 0% dividend yield and 4.51% risk-free interest rate) was $11,000 which was reflected as general and administrative expense in the year ended December 31, 2007. As of December 31, 2007 and 2008 and March 31, 2009, this warrant remained outstanding.

9. Income Taxes

The Company accounts for income taxes under the asset and liability method. Under this method, deferred tax assets and liabilities are determined based on differences between financial reporting and income tax bases of assets and liabilities, and are measured using the enacted tax rates and laws that will be in effect when the differences are expected to reverse.

F-29

OPENTABLE, INC.

NOTES TO CONSOLIDATED FINANCIAL STATEMENTS (Continued)

YEARS ENDED DECEMBER 31, 2006, 2007 AND 2008 AND THE THREE MONTHS ENDED MARCH 31, 2008 AND 2009
(UNAUDITED)

9. Income Taxes (Continued)

The Company's provisions for income taxes are as follows:

	Years Ended December 31,		
	2006	2007	2008
Current tax expense:			
Federal	$ 78,000	$ 94,000	$ 161,000
State	9,000	34,000	400,000
Foreign	89,000	121,000	273,000
Total current tax expense	176,000	249,000	834,000
Deferred tax expense:			
Federal	—	(7,876,000)	1,496,000
State	—	(1,494,000)	(212,000)
Foreign	—	—	—
Total deferred tax expense	—	(9,370,000)	1,284,000
Total income tax provision	$176,000	$(9,121,000)	$2,118,000

The difference between the actual rate and the federal statutory rate was as follows:

	Years Ended December 31,		
	2006	2007	2008
Tax at federal statutory rate	34.0%	34.0%	34.0%
State tax, net of federal benefit	26.2	145.7	11.2
Foreign rate differential	145.3	12.4	1.4
Stock-based compensation	59.0	1164.2	98.4
Other	27.7	28.4	32.2
Valuation allowance	(248.0)	(12,643.6)	16.7
Effective tax rate	44.2%	(11,259.0)	193.9%

As of December 31, 2007 and 2008 the Company had net deferred tax assets before valuation allowance of approximately $9,586,000 and $8,484,000, respectively. Realization of the deferred tax assets is dependent upon future taxable income, if any, the amount and timing of which are uncertain. Management evaluates the recoverability of deferred tax assets and the level of the valuation allowance in light of this uncertainty and had established a valuation allowance in an amount equal to the deferred tax assets at December 31, 2006. During the fourth quarter of 2007, management determined that it is more likely than not that the deferred tax assets will be realizable, based on the Company's earnings history and its projected future U.S. taxable income, and therefore the valuation allowance was substantially removed. A full valuation allowance for foreign tax credits in the amount of $131,000 and $313,000 was put in place at December 31, 2007 and 2008, respectively. The net valuation allowance decreased by approximately $10,326,000 during the year ended December 31, 2007 and increased $182,000 during the year ended December 31, 2008.

F-30

OPENTABLE, INC.

NOTES TO CONSOLIDATED FINANCIAL STATEMENTS (Continued)

YEARS ENDED DECEMBER 31, 2006, 2007 AND 2008 AND THE THREE MONTHS ENDED MARCH 31, 2008 AND 2009
(UNAUDITED)

9. Income Taxes (Continued)

The components of the Company's net deferred tax assets for federal and state income taxes at December 31 are as follows:

	2007	2008
Deferred tax assets:		
Net operating loss carryforwards	$ 6,606,000	$ 4,313,000
Deferred revenue	1,647,000	1,516,000
Dining rewards points	—	1,736,000
Accruals and reserves not currently deductible	1,565,000	1,715,000
Tax credits	348,000	628,000
Other	267,000	(1,000)
Total deferred tax assets	10,433,000	9,907,000
Deferred tax liabilities:		
Basis difference in fixed assets	(405,000)	(968,000)
State taxes	(442,000)	(455,000)
Total deferred tax liabilities	(847,000)	(1,423,000)
Net deferred tax assets before valuation allowance	9,586,000	8,484,000
Valuation allowance	(131,000)	(313,000)
Net deferred tax asset	$ 9,455,000	$ 8,171,000

At December 31, 2008, the Company had federal and state net operating loss carryforwards of approximately $10,373,000 and $9,818,000, respectively. The federal net operating losses will begin to expire in 2023. The state net operating losses will begin to expire in 2009. Utilization of the net operating loss carryforwards are subject to limitation due to the ownership change limitations provided by the Internal Revenue Code of 1986, as amended and similar state provisions. The Company has performed detailed analyses for purposes of Section 382 and determined an ownership change occurred in February 2003. Applicable limitations have been incorporated and some net operating losses will not be available. At December 31, 2008, the Company had federal minimum tax credits of $315,000 which have no expiration date. The Company also has foreign tax credits of approximately $313,000 which begin to expire in 2016.

The Company has deferred calculating U.S. income tax on certain foreign earnings that are deemed to be permanently reinvested overseas. Determination of the unrecognized deferred tax liability is not currently practical and the amount is not expected to be material.

Effective January 1, 2007, the Company adopted FIN No. 48. FIN No. 48 prescribes the minimum recognition threshold a tax position is required to meet before being recognized in the financial statements. The Company did not recognize any material net adjustment in its liability for unrecognized income tax benefits upon adoption of FIN No. 48, including any amounts for interest and penalties.

Unrecognized tax benefits on January 1, 2007 totaled $14,879,000. There was no change in unrecognized tax benefits during 2007. Unrecognized tax benefits on January 1, 2008 totaled $14,879,000. Additions based on tax positions related to the current year total $141,000. There were no

F-31

OPENTABLE, INC.

NOTES TO CONSOLIDATED FINANCIAL STATEMENTS (Continued)

YEARS ENDED DECEMBER 31, 2006, 2007 AND 2008 AND THE THREE MONTHS ENDED MARCH 31, 2008 AND 2009
(UNAUDITED)

9. Income Taxes (Continued)

reductions for tax positions related to prior years. Thus, unrecognized tax benefits at December 31, 2008 totaled $15,020,000.

In the event that any unrecognized tax benefits are recognized, the effective tax rate will be affected. Approximately $14,185,000 and $14,327,000 unrecognized tax benefit would impact the effective tax rate at December 31, 2007 and 2008, respectively, if recognized. The Company's policy is to classify interest accrued or penalties related to unrecognized tax benefits as a component of income tax expense. No such interest or penalties have been recorded to date for unrecognized tax benefits. The Company accrued approximately $15,000 and $39,000 for the payment of interest and penalties for other filings at December 31, 2007 and 2008, respectively.

All tax years remain open to examination by major taxing jurisdictions to which the Company is subject. The Company files a federal and many state returns. The Company does not anticipate significant changes to its uncertain tax positions through the next fiscal year.

10. Employee Benefit Plan

In 1999, the Company adopted a defined contribution plan that is intended to qualify under section 401(k) of the Internal Revenue Code. The 401(k) plan provides retirement benefits for eligible employees. The 401(k) plan stipulates that eligible employees may elect to contribute to it upon date of hire. The Company began matching employee contributions under the terms of the 401(k) plan in 2007. Matching contributions totaled $82,000, $99,000 and $72,000 for the years ended 2007 and 2008 and the three months ended March 31, 2009, respectively. No matching contributions were made during 2006.

11. Related Party Transactions

Compensation payments for contracting work were made to one of the members of the board of directors in the amount of $81,000, which the Company believes is the fair value of the services received for the year ended December 31, 2006. No amounts were paid in 2007 or 2008.

The Company paid a total of $5,000 to three members of the board of directors for reimbursable expenses incurred during the year ended December 31, 2008. There were no amounts incurred in 2006, 2007 or the three months ended March 31, 2009.

12. Segment Information

The Company has concluded that it operates in one industry—online reservations and guest management solutions. The Company has two reporting segments: North America and International, as defined by SFAS No. 131, *Disclosures about Segments of an Enterprise and Related Information*. Reportable segments have been identified based on how management makes operating decisions, assesses performance and allocates resources. The chief executive officer acts as the chief decision maker on behalf of both segments. Management reviews asset information on a global basis, not by segment.

F-32

OPENTABLE, INC.

NOTES TO CONSOLIDATED FINANCIAL STATEMENTS (Continued)

YEARS ENDED DECEMBER 31, 2006, 2007 AND 2008, AND THE THREE MONTHS
ENDED MARCH 31, 2008 AND 2009 (UNAUDITED)

12. Segment Information (Continued)

Summarized financial information concerning the reportable segments is as follows:

	North America Segment(1)	International Segment	Total Consolidated
Year ended December 31, 2006			
Revenues—subscription	$ 15,014,000	$ 440,000	$ 15,454,000
Revenues—reservations	10,605,000	59,000	10,664,000
Revenues—installation and other	1,035,000	15,000	1,050,000
Income (loss) from operations	3,106,000	(3,157,000)	(51,000)
Interest income	424,000	2,000	426,000
Depreciation and amortization expense	2,029,000	89,000	2,118,000
Purchases of property, equipment and software	3,296,000	310,000	3,606,000
Year ended December 31, 2007			
Revenues—subscription	$ 21,147,000	$ 1,287,000	$ 22,434,000
Revenues—reservations	16,820,000	190,000	17,010,000
Revenues—installation and other	1,634,000	70,000	1,704,000
Income (loss) from operations	4,974,000	(5,830,000)	(856,000)
Interest income	777,000	8,000	785,000
Depreciation and amortization expense	2,817,000	184,000	3,001,000
Purchases of property, equipment and software	4,885,000	564,000	5,449,000
Year ended December 31, 2008			
Revenues—subscription	$ 28,003,000	$ 2,290,000	$ 30,293,000
Revenues—reservations	22,745,000	390,000	23,135,000
Revenues—installation and other	2,317,000	99,000	2,416,000
Income (loss) from operations	9,088,000	(8,462,000)	626,000
Interest income	534,000	11,000	545,000
Depreciation and amortization expense	4,026,000	350,000	4,376,000
Purchases of property, equipment and software	6,301,000	902,000	7,203,000
Three Months ended March 31, 2008 (unaudited)			
Revenues—subscription	$ 6,407,000	$ 480,000	$ 6,887,000
Revenues—reservations	5,731,000	99,000	5,830,000
Revenues—installation and other	529,000	17,000	546,000
Income (loss) from operations	2,409,000	(2,068,000)	341,000
Interest income	185,000	1,000	186,000
Depreciation and amortization expense	877,000	74,000	951,000
Purchases of property, equipment and software	1,444,000	172,000	1,616,000
Three Months ended March 31, 2009 (unaudited)			
Revenues—subscription	$ 7,734,000	$ 655,000	$ 8,389,000
Revenues—reservations	6,790,000	114,000	6,904,000
Revenues—installation and other	665,000	37,000	702,000
Income (loss) from operations	2,326,000	(1,494,000)	832,000
Interest income	86,000	0	86,000
Depreciation and amortization expense	1,159,000	104,000	1,263,000
Purchases of property, equipment and software	1,318,000	50,000	1,368,000

(1) A significant majority of the Company's "Technology" costs are incurred in the United States and as such are allocated to the North America segment. There are no internal revenue transactions between the Company's reporting segments.

F-33

OPENTABLE, INC.

NOTES TO CONSOLIDATED FINANCIAL STATEMENTS (Continued)

YEARS ENDED DECEMBER 31, 2006, 2007 AND 2008, AND THE THREE MONTHS
ENDED MARCH 31, 2008 AND 2009 (UNAUDITED)

12. Segment Information (Continued)

Geographical Information

The Company is domiciled in the United States and has international operations in Canada, France, Germany, Japan, Mexico, Spain and the United Kingdom. Information regarding the Company's operations by geographic area is presented below:

	Years Ended December 31,			Three Months Ended March 31,	
	2006	2007	2008	2008	2009
				(Unaudited)	
Revenues:					
United States	$25,791,000	$37,864,000	$50,296,000	$11,972,000	$14,402,000
International—all other	1,377,000	3,284,000	5,548,000	1,291,000	1,593,000
Total revenues	$27,168,000	$41,148,000	$55,844,000	$13,263,000	$15,995,000
Long-lived assets(1):					
United States	$ 5,449,000	$ 7,319,000	$10,619,000	$ 8,108,000	$11,496,000
International—all others	708,000	1,272,000	1,877,000	1,360,000	1,729,000
Total long-lived assets	$ 6,157,000	$ 8,591,000	$12,496,000	$ 9,468,000	$13,225,000

(1)   Includes all non-current assets except deferred tax assets.

The Company has no customers that individually, or in the aggregate, which exceed 10% of revenues or accounts receivable as of and for any of the period presented above.

13. Subsequent Events (unaudited)

On January 21, 2009, the Board approved the filing of a registration statement with the Securities and Exchange Commission for an initial public offering of the Company's common stock.

On May 1, 2009, the Board approved a 1-for-12.5 reverse stock split of the Company's common stock and preferred stock to be effected immediately prior to the effectiveness of the Company's initial public offering. All shares and per share information referenced throughout the consolidated financial statements have been retroactively adjusted to reflect this stock split.

On May 1, 2009, the Board approved the 2009 Equity Incentive Award Plan. A total of 1,240,104 shares of common stock, subject to increase on an annual basis, were reserved for future issuance under the plan, which will become effective upon the completion of the Company's planned initial public offering.

On May 12, 2009, a patent infringement lawsuit was filed against the Company by Mount Hamilton Partners, LLC ("Mount Hamilton"). Mount Hamilton seeks damages and injunctive relief. If an injunction is granted, it could force the Company to stop or alter certain of its business activities, such as certain aspects of its points-based loyalty program. The Company believes it has substantial and meritorious defenses to these claims and intends to vigorously defend its position. The Company is not currently able to estimate the loss, if any, that may result from this claim.

* * * * * *

F-34

Through and including   , 2009 (the 25th day after the date of this prospectus), all dealers that effect transactions in these securities, whether or not participating in this offering, may be required to deliver a prospectus. This is in addition to the dealers' obligation to deliver a prospectus when acting as underwriters and with respect to their unsold allotments or subscriptions.

3,000,000 Shares

Common Stock

PROSPECTUS

Merrill Lynch & Co.

Allen & Company LLC

Stifel Nicolaus

ThinkEquity LLC

, 2009

PART II
INFORMATION NOT REQUIRED IN PROSPECTUS

Item 13.   Other Expenses of Issuance and Distribution

The following table sets forth the costs and expenses, other than underwriting discounts and commissions, payable in connection with the sale and distribution of the securities being registered. All amounts are estimated except the SEC registration fee and the FINRA filing fee. Except as otherwise noted, all the expenses below will be paid by OpenTable.

Item	Amount
SEC Registration fee	$ 2,807
FINRA filing fee	4,500
Initial Nasdaq Global Market listing fee	100,000
Legal fees and expenses	1,565,000(1)
Accounting fees and expenses	825,000
Printing and engraving expenses	160,000
Transfer Agent and Registrar fees	11,850(2)
Blue Sky fees and expenses	20,000
Directors and Officers Insurance	255,000
Miscellaneous Fees and expenses	55,843
Total	$3,000,000

(1)   Approximately $35,000 of this amount will be paid by certain selling stockholders.

(2)   Approximately $8,350 of this amount will be paid by the selling stockholders.

Item 14.   Indemnification of Directors and Officers

Section 145 of the Delaware General Corporation Law authorizes a court to award, or a corporation's board of directors to grant, indemnity to directors and officers in terms sufficiently broad to permit such indemnification under certain circumstances for liabilities, including reimbursement for expenses incurred, arising under the Securities Act of 1933, as amended. Our amended and restated certificate of incorporation to be in effect upon the completion of this offering provides for indemnification of our directors, officers, employees and other agents to the maximum extent permitted by the Delaware General Corporation Law, and our amended and restated bylaws to be in effect upon the completion of this offering provide for indemnification of our directors, officers, employees and other agents to the maximum extent permitted by the Delaware General Corporation Law. In addition, we will enter into indemnification agreements with our directors, officers and some employees containing provisions which are in some respects broader than the specific indemnification provisions contained in the Delaware General Corporation Law. The indemnification agreements may require us, among other things, to indemnify our directors against certain liabilities that may arise by reason of their status or service as directors and to advance their expenses incurred as a result of any proceeding against them as to which they could be indemnified. Reference is also made to Section 6 of the underwriting agreement to be filed as Exhibit 1.1 hereto, which provides for indemnification by the underwriter of our officers and directors against certain liabilities.

Item 15.   Recent Sales of Unregistered Securities

During the last three years, we made sales of the following unregistered securities:

    1.   On March 5, 2007, we issued a warrant to purchase an aggregate of 3,541 shares of our common stock at an exercise price of $4.88 per share to a consultant. The warrant

II-1

        may be exercised at any time prior to its termination date, which is the earlier of March 4, 2017, the occurrence of certain liquidation events as defined in our amended and restated certificate of incorporation or the consummation of our initial public offering.

2.   Since March 31, 2006, we have granted stock options to purchase an aggregate of 3,167,161 shares of our common stock at exercise prices ranging from $1.50 to $23.38 per share to a total of 325 employees, consultants and directors under our 1999 Stock Plan.

3.   Since March 31, 2006, we have issued and sold an aggregate of 1,287,133 shares of our common stock to employees, consultants and directors at prices ranging from $0.10 to $7.75 per share pursuant to exercises of options granted under our 1999 Stock Plan.

       Unless otherwise stated, the sales of the above securities were deemed to be exempt from registration under the Securities Act in reliance upon Section 4(2) of the Securities Act or Regulation D or Regulation S promulgated thereunder, or Rule 701 promulgated under Section 3(b) of the Securities Act as transactions by an issuer not involving any public offering or pursuant to benefit plans and contracts relating to compensation as provided under Rule 701. The recipients of the securities in each of these transactions represented their intentions to acquire the securities for investment only and not with a view to or for sale in connection with any distribution thereof, and appropriate legends were placed upon the stock certificates issued in these transactions. All recipients had adequate access, through their relationships with OpenTable, to information about OpenTable.

Item 16.   Exhibits and Financial Statements

    (a)   Exhibits

Exhibit No.	Description of Exhibit
1.1*	Form of Underwriting Agreement.
3.1*	Restated Certificate of Incorporation of OpenTable, Inc., as currently in effect.
3.2*	Form of Restated Certificate of Incorporation of OpenTable, Inc. (effecting a 1-for-12.5 reverse stock split of OpenTable, Inc. common stock and preferred stock).
3.3*	Form of Amended and Restated Certificate of Incorporation of OpenTable, Inc., to be in effect upon completion of the offering.
3.4**	Bylaws of OpenTable, Inc., as currently in effect.
3.5*	Form of Amended and Restated Bylaws of OpenTable, Inc., to be in effect upon completion of the offering.
4.1*	Form of OpenTable, Inc.'s Common Stock Certificate.
4.2*	Amended and Restated Investor Rights Agreement, by and between OpenTable, Inc. and the investors listed on Exhibit A thereto, dated October 28, 2004.
4.3*	Warrant Agreement to purchase shares of Common Stock issued to Comdisco, Inc., dated August 3, 1999.
4.4*	Warrant Agreement to purchase shares of Common Stock issued to Comdisco, Inc., dated April 25, 2000.
4.5*	Warrant To Purchase shares of Series A Preferred Stock issued to Comerica Bank, dated June 6, 2003.

Exhibit No.	Description of Exhibit
4.6*	Warrant to purchase shares of Common Stock issued to Deborah Meredith, dated March 5, 2007.
5.1*	Form of Opinion of Latham & Watkins LLP.
10.1*	OpenTable, Inc. 1999 Stock Plan.
10.2*	OpenTable, Inc. 2009 Equity Incentive Award Plan.
10.3*	Form of Indemnification Agreement made by and between OpenTable, Inc. and each of its directors, officers and some employees.
10.4*	Amended and Restated Offer Letter, between OpenTable, Inc. and Jeffrey Jordan, dated October 15, 2008.
10.5*	Offer Letter, between OpenTable, Inc. and Matthew Roberts, dated June 16, 2005.
10.6*	Offer Letter, between OpenTable, Inc. and Joel Brown, dated November 7, 2001.
10.7*	Offer Letter, between OpenTable, Inc. and Michael Dodson, dated March 2, 2002.
10.8*	Offer Letter, between OpenTable, Inc. and Charlie McCullough, dated September 8, 2003.
10.9*	Loan and Security Agreement, between Comerica Bank and OpenTable, Inc., dated July 30, 2007, as amended September 18, 2008.
10.10*	Office Lease, by and between OpenTable, Inc. and CFRI Market Street Corp., dated March 29, 2007, as amended May 22, 2008.
10.11*	OpenTable, Inc. Independent Director Equity Compensation Policy.
21.1	List of subsidiaries.
23.1*	Consent of Latham & Watkins LLP (included in Exhibit 5.1).
23.2	Consent of Deloitte & Touche LLP, independent registered public accounting firm.
24.1	Power of Attorney (see page II-5 of the original filing).

*   Previously filed.

**   Previously filed as Exhibit 3.3 to Registration Statement on Form S-1 (file no. 333-157034) filed with the SEC on January 30, 2009.

(b)   Financial Statement Schedules

Schedules have been omitted because the information required to be set forth therein is not applicable or is shown in the consolidated financial statements or notes thereto.

Item 17.   Undertakings

Insofar as indemnification for liabilities arising under the Securities Act may be permitted as to directors, officers and controlling persons of the registrant pursuant to the provisions described in Item 14, or otherwise, we have been advised that in the opinion of the SEC such indemnification is against public policy as expressed in the Securities Act and is, therefore, unenforceable. In the event that a claim for indemnification against such liabilities (other than the payment by the registrant of expenses incurred or paid by a director, officer or controlling person of the registrant in the successful defense of any action, suit or proceeding) is asserted by such director, officer or controlling person in connection with the securities being registered, we will, unless in the opinion of our counsel the matter has been settled by controlling precedent, submit to a court of appropriate jurisdiction the question whether such indemnification by it is against public policy as expressed in the Securities Act and will be governed by the final adjudication of such issue.

II-3

The undersigned registrant hereby undertakes that:

(1)   For purposes of determining any liability under the Securities Act, the information omitted from the form of prospectus as filed as part of this registration statement in reliance upon Rule 430A and contained in a form of prospectus filed by the registrant pursuant to Rule 424(b)(1) or (4) or 497(h) under the Securities Act shall be deemed to be part of this registration statement as of the time it was declared effective.

(2)   For the purpose of determining any liability under the Securities Act, each post-effective amendment that contains a form of prospectus shall be deemed to be a new registration statement relating to the securities offered therein, and the offering of such securities at that time shall be deemed to be the initial *bona fide* offering thereof.

(3)   That, for the purpose of determining liability of the registrant under the Securities Act to any purchaser in the initial distribution of the securities:

The undersigned registrant undertakes that in a primary offering of securities of the undersigned registrant pursuant to this registration statement, regardless of the underwriting method used to sell the securities to the purchaser, if the securities are offered or sold to such purchaser by means of any of the following communications, the undersigned registrant will be a seller to the purchaser and will be considered to offer or sell such securities to such purchaser:

(i) Any preliminary prospectus or prospectus of the undersigned registrant relating to the offering required to be filed pursuant to Rule 424;

(ii) Any free writing prospectus relating to the offering prepared by or on behalf of the undersigned registrant or used or referred to by the undersigned registrant;

(iii) The portion of any other free writing prospectus relating to the offering containing material information about the undersigned registrant or its securities provided by or on behalf of the undersigned registrant; and

(iv) Any other communication that is an offer in the offering made by the undersigned registrant to the purchaser.

The undersigned registrant hereby undertakes to provide to the underwriter at the closing specified in the underwriting agreements, certificates in such denominations and registered in such names as required by the underwriters to permit prompt delivery to each purchaser.

II-4

SIGNATURES

Pursuant to the requirements of the Securities Act of 1933, as amended, we have duly caused this Post-Effective Amendment No. 2 to the Registration Statement on Form S-1 to be signed on its behalf by the undersigned, thereunto duly authorized, in the City of San Francisco, State of California, on the 21st day of May, 2009.

OPENTABLE, INC.

By: /s/ JEFFREY JORDAN
_____

Jeffrey Jordan
Chief Executive Officer

Pursuant to the requirements of the Securities Act of 1933, as amended, this Post-Effective Amendment No. 2 to the Registration Statement has been signed by the following persons in the capacities and on the dates indicated.

Signature	Title	Date
/s/ JEFFREY JORDAN Jeffrey Jordan	Chief Executive Officer and Director (principal executive officer)	May 21, 2009
/s/ MATTHEW ROBERTS Matthew Roberts	Chief Financial Officer (principal financial and accounting officer)	May 21, 2009
* A. George "Skip" Battle	Director	May 21, 2009
* Adam R. Dell	Director	May 21, 2009
* J. William Gurley	Director	May 21, 2009
* Thomas H. Layton	Director	May 21, 2009
* Danny Meyer	Director	May 21, 2009
* Michelle Peluso	Director	May 21, 2009
* Paul Pressler	Director	May 21, 2009

*By: /s/ JEFFREY JORDAN
_____

Jeffrey Jordan
Attorney-in-fact

EXHIBIT INDEX

Exhibit No.	Description of Exhibit
1.1*	Form of Underwriting Agreement.
3.1*	Restated Certificate of Incorporation of OpenTable, Inc., as currently in effect.
3.2*	Form of Restated Certificate of Incorporation of OpenTable, Inc. (effecting a 1-for-12.5 reverse stock split of OpenTable, Inc. common stock and preferred stock).
3.3*	Form of Amended and Restated Certificate of Incorporation of OpenTable, Inc., to be in effect upon completion of the offering.
3.4**	Bylaws of OpenTable, Inc., as currently in effect.
3.5*	Form of Amended and Restated Bylaws of OpenTable, Inc., to be in effect upon completion of the offering.
4.1*	Form of OpenTable, Inc.'s Common Stock Certificate.
4.2*	Amended and Restated Investor Rights Agreement, by and between OpenTable, Inc. and the investors listed on Exhibit A thereto, dated October 28, 2004.
4.3*	Warrant Agreement to purchase shares of Common Stock issued to Comdisco, Inc., dated August 3, 1999.
4.4*	Warrant Agreement to purchase shares of Common Stock issued to Comdisco, Inc., dated April 25, 2000.
4.5*	Warrant To Purchase shares of Series A Preferred Stock issued to Comerica Bank, dated June 6, 2003.
4.6*	Warrant to purchase shares of Common Stock issued to Deborah Meredith, dated March 5, 2007.
5.1*	Form of Opinion of Latham & Watkins LLP.
10.1*	OpenTable, Inc. 1999 Stock Plan.
10.2*	OpenTable, Inc. 2009 Equity Incentive Award Plan.
10.3*	Form of Indemnification Agreement made by and between OpenTable, Inc. and each of its directors, officers and some employees.
10.4*	Amended and Restated Offer Letter, between OpenTable, Inc. and Jeffrey Jordan, dated October 15, 2008.
10.5*	Offer Letter, between OpenTable, Inc. and Matthew Roberts, dated June 16, 2005.
10.6*	Offer Letter, between OpenTable, Inc. and Joel Brown, dated November 7, 2001.
10.7*	Offer Letter, between OpenTable, Inc. and Michael Dodson, dated March 2, 2002.
10.8*	Offer Letter, between OpenTable, Inc. and Charlie McCullough, dated September 8, 2003.
10.9*	Loan and Security Agreement, between Comerica Bank and OpenTable, Inc., dated July 30, 2007, as amended September 18, 2008.
10.10*	Office Lease, by and between OpenTable, Inc. and CFRI Market Street Corp., dated March 29, 2007, as amended May 22, 2008.
10.11*	OpenTable, Inc. Independent Director Equity Compensation Policy.
21.1	List of subsidiaries.
23.1*	Consent of Latham & Watkins LLP (included in Exhibit 5.1).
23.2	Consent of Deloitte & Touche LLP, independent registered public accounting firm.
24.1	Power of Attorney (see page II-5 of original filing).

*   Previously filed.

**   Previously filed as Exhibit 3.3 to Registration Statement on Form S-1 (file no. 333-157034) filed with the SEC on January 30, 2009.

OPENTABLE, INC.
FREE WRITING PROSPECTUS,
MAY 11, 2009

FWP 1 a2193157zfwp.htm FWP

Filed Pursuant to Rule 433
Issuer Free Writing Prospectus
Relating to Preliminary Prospectus dated May 11, 2009
Registration No. 333-157034

This free writing prospectus relates only to the securities described below and should be read together with the preliminary prospectus dated May 11, 2009 relating to this offering (the "*Preliminary Prospectus*"), included in Amendment No. 5 to the Registration Statement on Form S-1 (File No. 333-157034) relating to these securities. The most recent amendment to such Registration Statement can be accessed through the following link: *http://www.sec.gov/Archives/edgar/data/1125914/ 000104746909005322/0001047469-09-005322-index.idea.htm.* The following information supplements and updates the information contained in the Preliminary Prospectus.

The disclosure set forth in the Preliminary Prospectus under "Risk Factors—Assertions by third parties of infringement by us of their intellectual property rights could result in significant costs and substantially harm our business and operating results." has been updated to read in substance as follows:

Other parties have asserted, and may in the future assert, that we have infringed their intellectual property rights. Such litigation may involve patent holding companies or other adverse patent owners who have no relevant product revenue, and therefore our own issued and pending patents may provide little or no deterrence. For example, on May 12, 2009, Mount Hamilton Partners, LLC, or Mount Hamilton, filed a patent infringement lawsuit against us in the United States District Court for the Northern District of California, seeking, among other things, a judgment that we have infringed a certain patent held by Mount Hamilton, an injunctive order against the alleged infringing activities and an award for damages. If an injunction is granted, it could force us to stop or alter certain of our business activities, such as certain aspects of our points-based loyalty program, OpenTable Dining Rewards. We could also be required to pay damages in an unspecified amount. Neither the outcome of the litigation nor the amount and range of potential damages or exposure associated with the litigation can be assessed with certainty.

Furthermore, we cannot predict whether assertions of third party intellectual property rights or claims arising from such assertions will substantially harm our business and operating results. If we are forced to defend against any infringement claims, including the alleged infringement claims of Mount Hamilton, whether they are with or without merit or are determined in our favor, we may face costly litigation and diversion of technical and management personnel. Furthermore, an adverse outcome of a dispute may require us to pay damages, potentially including treble damages and attorneys' fees, if we are found to have willfully infringed a party's patent or copyright rights; cease making, licensing or using solutions that are alleged to incorporate the intellectual property of others; expend additional development resources to redesign our solutions; and enter into potentially unfavorable royalty or license agreements in order to obtain the right to use necessary technologies. Royalty or licensing agreements, if required, may be unavailable on terms acceptable to us, or at all. In any event, we may need to license intellectual property which would require us to pay royalties or make one-time payments.

The disclosure set forth in the Preliminary Prospectus under "Business—Legal Proceedings" has been updated to read in substance as follows:

On May 12, 2009, Mount Hamilton filed a patent infringement lawsuit against us in the United States District Court for the Northern District of California, seeking, among other things, a judgment that OpenTable has infringed a certain patent held by Mount Hamilton, an injunctive order against the alleged infringing activities and an award for damages. If an injunction is granted, it could force us to stop or alter certain of our business activities, such as certain aspects of our points-based loyalty program, OpenTable Dining Rewards. Although we plan to deny Mount Hamilton's allegations and defend the claims vigorously, and we believe that we have substantial and meritorious defenses to the claims, neither the outcome of the litigation nor the amount and range of potential damages or exposure associated with the litigation can be assessed with certainty.

In addition to the Mount Hamilton lawsuit, from time to time, we may become involved in legal proceedings arising in the ordinary course of our business. We are not presently involved in any legal proceeding in which the outcome, if determined adversely to us, would be expected to have a material adverse effect on our business, operating results or financial condition.

The table and accompanying footnotes set forth in the Preliminary Prospectus under "Principal and Selling Stockholders" have been updated to read in substance as follows:

Name and Address of Beneficial Owner	Beneficial Ownership Prior to the Offering(1)				Shares Being Offered	Beneficial Ownership After the Offering	
	Common Stock	Options Exercisable within 60 Days	Number of Shares Beneficially Owned	Percent		Number of Shares Beneficially Owned	Percent
5% Stockholders:							
Benchmark Capital Partners IV, L.P.(2) 2480 Sand Hill Road, Suite 200 Menlo Park, CA 94025	5,290,211	—	5,290,211	26.41%	—	5,290,211	24.49%
Funds affiliated with Impact Venture Partners(3) 2705 Westlake Drive Austin, TX 78746	3,503,853	—	3,503,853	17.49%	—	3,503,853	16.22%
IAC/InterActiveCorp(4) 555 West 18th Street New York, NY 10011	2,177,550	—	2,177,550	10.87%	—	2,177,550	10.08%
Funds affiliated with Integral Capital Partners V, L.P.(5) 3000 Sand Hill Road Building Three, Suite 240 Menlo Park, CA 94025	1,503,072	—	1,503,072	7.50%	—	1,503,072	6.96%
Executive Officers and Directors:							
Jeff Jordan(6)	767,693	157,651	925,344	4.58%	—	925,344	4.28%
Matthew Roberts(7)	133,332	68,266	201,598	1.00%	—	201,598	*
Joel Brown(8)	257,599	35,000	292,599	1.46%	36,000	256,599	1.19%
Michael Dodson(9)	261,600	46,000	307,600	1.53%	32,000	275,600	1.27%
Charlie McCullough(10)	251,200	14,000	265,200	1.32%	16,000	249,200	1.15%
A. George "Skip" Battle(11)	50,270	—	50,270	*	—	50,270	*
Adam R. Dell(3)	3,503,853	—	3,503,853	17.49%	—	3,503,853	16.22%
J. William Gurley(2)	5,290,211	—	5,290,211	26.41%	—	5,290,211	24.49%
Thomas H. Layton(12)	2,379,019	—	2,379,019	11.88%	139,020	2,239,999	10.30%
Danny Meyer(13)	161,777	32,000	193,777	*	69,314	124,463	*
Michelle Peluso(14)	—	32,000	32,000	*	—	32,000	*
Paul Pressler(15)	—	32,000	32,000	*	—	32,000	*

2

| Name and Address of Beneficial Owner | Beneficial Ownership Prior to the Offering(1) | | | | Shares Being Offered | Beneficial Ownership After the Offering | |
	Common Stock	Options Exercisable within 60 Days	Number of Shares Beneficially Owned	Percent		Number of Shares Beneficially Owned	Percent
All executive officers and directors as a group (12 persons)	13,056,554	416,917	13,473,471	67.21%	292,334	13,181,137	60.94%
Other Selling Stockholders:							
Glenn Allen	40,258	—	40,258	*	40,258	—	*
Bisharat Family Trust(16)	126,040	—	126,040	*	32,000	94,040	*
Brainstorm Ventures, L.P.(17)	70,118	—	70,118	*	36,487	33,631	*
Bryce Catlin(18)	16,000	6,000	22,000	*	1,000	21,000	*
Comdisco Ventures Fund A, LLC (19)	103,522	—	103,522	*	52,000	51,522	*
Michael & Leslye Dellar trustees of the Michael D. Dellar & Leslye L. Dellar Revocable Trust dated 11/5/96(20)	19,068	—	19,068	*	1,600	17,468	*
Sidney Gorham	25,266	—	25,266	*	25,266	—	*
Lynda Kim Halprin	40,000	—	40,000	*	40,000	—	*
Melchart, L.L.C.(21)	25,880	—	25,880	*	25,880	—	*
Pacific Asset Partners, LP(22)	87,676	—	87,676	*	87,676	—	*
Davis Peterson	42,400	—	42,400	*	9,600	32,800	*
Randall Reeves(23)	12,800	6,000	18,800	*	2,400	16,400	*
Chuck Templeton	207,684	—	207,684	1.04%	100,000	107,684	*
The Charles Schwab Corporation (24)†	77,065	—	77,065	*	77,065	—	*
Venture Frogs Fund I, L.L.C.(25)	74,611	—	74,611	*	74,611	—	*
W Capital Partners I, L.P.(26)	155,285	—	155,285	*	155,285	—	*
Worldspan OpenTable Holdings LLC(27)†	98,347	—	98,347	*	98,347	—	*
Michael Xenakis(28)	158,400	67,001	225,401	1.12%	8,000	217,401	1.01%
Zagat Survey, LLC(29)	155,285	—	155,285	*	155,285	—	*
Scott Carl Kovalik††	16,084	—	16,084	*	16,084	—	*
Snyder Revocable Trust dated May 9, 2000(30)††	5,714	—	5,714	*	5,714	—	*
Robert Goddard, Trustee of the Robert Goddard Family Trust, dated December 3, 2004†	2,857	—	2,857	*	2,857	—	*
Jeff Handy†	13,869	—	13,869	*	6,800	7,069	*
All other selling stockholders(31)	106,371	19,700	126,071	*	80,767	45,304	*

* Represents beneficial ownership of less than one percent (1%) of the outstanding common stock.

(†) The selling stockholder is an affiliate of a registered broker-dealer. Such selling stockholder has certified that it has purchased the shares being offered by it in the ordinary course of business, and at the time of the purchase of such shares, had no agreements or understandings, directly or indirectly, with any person to distribute such shares.

(††) The selling stockholder is a registered broker-dealer. Such selling stockholder has certified that it has purchased the shares being offered by it in the ordinary course of business, and at the time of the purchase of such shares, had no agreements or understandings, directly or indirectly, with any person to distribute such shares. Selling stockholders that are broker-dealers are deemed to be "underwriters" within the meaning of Section 2(11) of the Securities Act.

(1) Shares shown in the table above include shares held in the beneficial owner's name or jointly with others, or in the name of a bank, nominee or trustee for the beneficial owner's account.

3

(2)   Consists of 5,290,211 shares held by Benchmark Capital Partners IV, L.P., or BCP IV, as nominee for Benchmark Capital Partners IV, L.P., Benchmark Founders' Fund IV, L.P., Benchmark Founders' Fund IV-A, L.P., Benchmark Founders' Fund IV-B, L.P., Benchmark Founders' Fund IV-X, L.P. and related individuals, or Benchmark Funds. Benchmark Capital Management Co. IV, L.L.C., or BCMC IV, is the general partner of BCP IV. BCMC IV's managing members of the general partner are Alexandre Balkanski, Bruce Dunlevie, J. William Gurley, Kevin Harvey, Robert Kagle, Andrew Rachleff and Steven Spurlock. These individuals may be deemed to have shared voting and investment power over the shares held by the Benchmark Funds. Each of these individuals disclaims beneficial ownership of such shares, except to the extent of his pecuniary interest therein.

(3)   Represents 3,262,439 shares held by Impact Venture Partners, L.P. and 241,414 shares held by Impact Entrepreneurs Fund, L.P. Impact Venture Advisors, LLC is the sole general partner of Impact Venture Partners, L.P. and Impact Entrepreneurs Fund, L.P. Adam Dell is the sole managing member of Impact Venture Advisors, LLC. Mr. Dell may be deemed to have sole voting and investment power over the shares held by Impact Venture Partners, L.P. and Impact Entrepreneurs Fund, L.P. Mr. Dell disclaims beneficial ownership of such shares, except to the extent of his pecuniary interest therein.

(4)   The members of the board of directors of IAC/InterActiveCorp are Barry Diller, Victor Kaufman, Donald R. Keough, Bryan Lourd, John C. Malone, Arthur C. Martinez, Steven Rattner, David Rosenblatt, Alan Spoon, Alexander von Furstenberg and Michael P. Zeisser. These individuals may be deemed to have shared voting and investment power over the shares held by IAC/InterActiveCorp. Each of these individuals disclaims beneficial ownership of such shares, except to the extent of his pecuniary interest therein.

(5)   Represents 1,480,725 shares held by Integral Capital Partners V, L.P., 19,568 shares held by Integral Capital Partners V Side Fund, L.P. and 2,779 shares held by Integral Capital Partners V SLP Side Fund, LLC. The sole general partner of Integral Capital Partners V, L.P. is Integral Capital Management V, LLC. The managers of Integral Capital Management V, LLC are Pamela Hagenah, Glen Kacher, Roger McNamee, Charles Morris, John Powell and Brian Stansky. The sole general partner of each of Integral Capital Partners V Side Fund, L.P. and Integral Capital Partners V SLP Side Fund, LLC is ICP Management V, LLC. The managers of ICP Management V, LLC are Pamela Hagenah, Glen Kacher, Roger McNamee and John Powell. These individuals may be deemed to have shared voting and investment power over the shares held by Integral Capital Partners V, L.P., Integral Capital Partners V Side Fund, L.P. and Integral Capital Partners V SLP Side Fund, LLC, as applicable. Each of these individuals disclaims beneficial ownership of such shares, except to the extent of his or her pecuniary interest therein.

(6)   Includes 431,829 shares held by the Jordan Family Revocable Trust U/A 8/25/95, 52,700 shares held by the Jeffrey D. Jordan Annuity Trust dated February 5, 2008, 63,974 shares held by the Jeffrey D. Jordan Annuity Trust II dated October 2, 2008, 51,258 shares held by the Jeffrey D. Jordan Annuity Trust-2009 dated March 30, 2009, 52,700 shares held by the Karen A. Jordan Annuity Trust dated February 5, 2008, 63,974 shares held by the Karen A. Jordan Annuity Trust II dated October 2, 2008 and 51,258 shares held by the Karen A. Jordan Annuity Trust-2009 dated March 30, 2009. Includes 431,829 shares subject to our right of repurchase, which right lapses as to 15,993 shares each succeeding month over the next 27 months, and 157,651 shares subject to options that are exercisable within 60 days of March 31, 2009.

(7)   Includes 109,332 shares held by the Roberts Family Trust, dated April 24, 2008, and 24,000 shares held by the Matthew Roberts Annuity Trust, dated April 24, 2008. Includes 4,167 shares subject to our right of repurchase, which right lapses as to 1,388 shares each succeeding month over the next three months. Includes 68,266 shares subject to options that are exercisable within 60 days of March 31, 2009, of which 2,811 shares, if these options were exercised in full, would be subject to vesting and a right of repurchase in our favor upon Mr. Roberts' cessation of service prior to vesting. Mr. Roberts disclaims beneficial ownership of the shares held by the Matthew Roberts Annuity Trust, dated April 24, 2008.

(8)   Includes 257,599 shares held by Joel T. Brown and Lorraine D. Brown, or their successor(s), Trustees UTA dated October 27, 1998. Includes 11,334 shares subject to our right of repurchase, which right lapses as to 666 shares each succeeding month over the next 17 months. Includes 35,000 shares subject to options that are exercisable within 60 days of March 31, 2009.

4

(9) Includes 28,333 shares subject to our right of repurchase, which right lapses as to 1,666 shares each succeeding month over the next 17 months. Includes 46,000 shares subject to options that are exercisable within 60 days of March 31, 2009.

(10) Includes 251,200 shares held by The Charles McCullough and Carol McCullough Joint Living Trust. Includes 17,000 shares subject to our right of repurchase, which right lapses as to 1,000 shares each succeeding month over the next 17 months. Includes 14,000 shares subject to options that are exercisable within 60 days of March 31, 2009.

(11) Includes 13,313 shares subject to our right of repurchase, which right lapses as to 634 shares each succeeding month over the next 21 months. Also includes 10,249 shares subject to our right of repurchase, which right lapses as to 366 shares each succeeding month over the next 28 months. Mr. Battle has indicated an interest in purchasing up to 57,693 shares of common stock in this offering at the initial public offering price, based on an assumed initial public offering price of $13.00 per share. Because this indication of interest is not a binding agreement or commitment to purchase, Mr. Battle may elect not to purchase any shares in this offering. However, if any shares are purchased by Mr. Battle, the number of shares beneficially owned and the percentage of common stock beneficially owned after the offering will differ from that set forth in the table above. If Mr. Battle purchases all 57,693 shares, the number of shares beneficially owned by Mr. Battle will increase to 107,963. In addition, if Mr. Battle and other directors purchase an aggregate of 76,925 shares, the number of shares beneficially owned by all executive officers and directors as a group will increase to 13,258,062 and the percentage of common stock beneficially owned by all executive officers and directors as a group will increase to 61.33%.

(12) Includes 1,872,625 shares held by the Layton Community Property Trust, dated November 29, 1999, as amended, 480,000 shares held by the Layton 2002 Childrens Trust and 26,394 shares held by the Thomas H. Layton Separate Property Revocable Trust of November 29, 1999, as amended. Mr. Layton disclaims beneficial ownership of the shares held by the Layton 2002 Childrens Trust.

(13) Includes 121,777 shares held by Hospitality Investments, G.P. Daniel Meyer Revocable Trust is the managing general partner of Hospitality Investments, G.P. Danny Meyer and Jack Polsky are the trustees of the Daniel Meyer Revocable Trust. These individuals may be deemed to have shared voting and investment power over the shares held by Hospitality Investments, G.P. Each of these individuals disclaims beneficial ownership of such shares, except to the extent of his pecuniary interest therein. Includes 32,000 shares subject to options that are exercisable within 60 days of March 31, 2009, of which 22,000 shares, if these options were exercised in full, would be subject to vesting and a right of repurchase in our favor upon Mr. Meyer's cessation of service prior to vesting.

(14) Includes 32,000 shares subject to options that are exercisable within 60 days of March 31, 2009, of which 22,667 shares, if these options were exercised in full, would be subject to vesting and a right of repurchase in our favor upon Ms. Peluso's cessation of service prior to vesting. Ms. Peluso has indicated an interest in purchasing up to 7,693 shares of common stock in this offering at the initial public offering price, based on an assumed initial public offering price of $13.00 per share. Because this indication of interest is not a binding agreement or commitment to purchase, Ms. Peluso may elect not to purchase any shares in this offering. However, if any shares are purchased by Ms. Peluso, the number of shares beneficially owned and the percentage of common stock beneficially owned after the offering will differ from that set forth in the table above. If Ms. Peluso purchases all 7,693 shares, the number of shares beneficially owned by Ms. Peluso will increase to 39,693. In addition, if Ms. Peluso and other directors purchase an aggregate of 76,925 shares, the number of shares beneficially owned by all executive officers and directors as a group will increase to 13,258,062 and the percentage of common stock beneficially owned by all executive officers and directors as a group will increase to 61.33%.

(15) Includes 32,000 shares subject to options that are exercisable within 60 days of March 31, 2009, of which 22,667 shares, if these options were exercised in full, would be subject to vesting and a right of repurchase in our favor upon Mr. Pressler's cessation of service prior to vesting. Mr. Pressler has indicated an interest in purchasing up to 11,539 shares of common stock in this offering at the initial public offering price, based on an assumed initial public offering price of $13.00 per share. Because this indication of interest is not a binding agreement or commitment to purchase, Mr. Pressler may elect not to purchase any shares in this offering. However, if any shares are purchased by Mr. Pressler, the number of shares beneficially owned and the

5

percentage of common stock beneficially owned after the offering will differ from that set forth in the table above. If Mr. Pressler purchases all 11,539 shares, the number of shares beneficially owned by Mr. Pressler will increase to 43,539. In addition, if Mr. Pressler and other directors purchase an aggregate of 76,925 shares, the number of shares beneficially owned by all executive officers and directors as a group will increase to 13,258,062 and the percentage of common stock beneficially owned by all executive officers and directors as a group will increase to 61.33%.

(16) George and Jaleh Bisharat are the trustees of the Bisharat Family Trust. These individuals may be deemed to share dispositive and voting power over the shares owned by Bisharat Family Trust. Each of these individuals disclaims beneficial ownership of such shares, except to the extent of his or her pecuniary interest therein. Ms. Bisharat previously served as a member of our board of directors and vice president of marketing. Her roles in these positions ended in 2007.

(17) Includes 46,585 shares held by Brainstorm Ventures, L.P. and 23,533 shares held by Keith Cox. The general partner of Brainstorm Ventures, L.P. is Brainstorm General Partner, LLC. The managing members of Brainstorm General Partner, LLC are Keith Cox, Eduardo Ralla and Zev Zaidman. These individuals may be deemed to share dispositive and voting power over the shares owned by Brainstorm Ventures, L.P. Each of these individuals disclaims beneficial ownership of such shares, except to the extent of his pecuniary interest therein. The address of BrainStorm Ventures, L.P. and Keith Cox is 6 Laurel Avenue, Belvedere, CA 94920.

(18) Includes 4,000 shares held by Bryce Catlin and Kristin Nicole Bruebaker, as Community Property. Includes 333 shares subject to our right of repurchase, which right lapses as to 166 shares each succeeding month over the next two months, 458 shares subject to our right of repurchase, which right lapses as to 41 shares each succeeding month over the next 11 months and 958 shares subject to our right of repurchase, which right lapses as to 41 shares each succeeding month over the next 23 months. Includes 6,000 shares subject to options that are exercisable within 60 days of March 31, 2009, of which 6,000 shares, if these options were exercised in full, would be subject to vesting and a right of repurchase in our favor upon Mr. Catlin's cessation of service prior to vesting. Mr. Catlin is a current employee of our company.

(19) John Bullock, Dan Bathon and Steve Karlson are the managing partners of Comdisco Ventures Fund A, LLC. These individuals may be deemed to share dispositive and voting power over the shares owned by Comdisco Ventures Fund A, LLC. Each of these individuals disclaims beneficial ownership of such shares, except to the extent of his pecuniary interest therein. The address of Comdisco Ventures Fund A, LLC is 52 Waltham Street, Lexington, MA 02421.

(20) Includes 19,068 shares held by Michael & Leslye Dellar trustees of the Michael D. Dellar & Leslye L. Dellar Revocable Trust dated 11/5/96. Michael Dellar and Leslye Dellar may be deemed to share dispositive and voting power over the shares owned by Michael D. Dellar & Leslye L. Dellar Revocable Trust dated 11/5/96. Each of these individuals disclaims beneficial ownership of such shares, except to the extent of his or her pecuniary interest therein.

(21) Richard Melman, Kevin Brown and Jay Stieber are the managing members of Melchart, L.L.C. These individuals may be deemed to share dispositive and voting power over the shares owned by Melchart, L.L.C. Each of these individuals disclaims beneficial ownership of such shares, except to the extent of his pecuniary interest therein. The address of Melchart, L.L.C. is 5419 N. Sheridan Road, Chicago, IL 60640.

(22) Pacific Management Ltd. is the general partner of Pacific Asset Partners, LP. Robert M. Stafford, Brian E. Dombkowski and Craig A. Stephens are the managing partners of Pacific Management Ltd. These individuals may be deemed to share dispositive and voting power over the shares owned by Pacific Asset Partners, LP. Each of these individuals disclaims beneficial ownership of such shares, except to the extent of his pecuniary interest therein. The address of Pacific Asset Partners, LP is Two Embarcadero Center, Suite 1340, San Francisco, CA 94111.

(23) Includes 6,000 shares subject to options that are exercisable within 60 days of March 31, 2009, of which 4,667 shares, if these options were exercised in full, would be subject to vesting and a right of repurchase in our favor upon Mr. Reeve's cessation of service prior to vesting. Mr. Reeves is a current employee of our company.

(24) The members of the board of directors of The Charles Schwab Corporation are William F. Aldinger III, Nancy H. Bechtle, Walter W. Bettinger II, C. Preston Butcher, Donald G. Fisher, Frank C. Herringer, Stephen

6

T. McLin, Charles R. Schwab, Paula A. Sneed, Roger O. Walther and Robert N. Wilson. These individuals may be deemed to have shared voting and investment power over the shares held by The Charles Schwab Corporation. Each of these individuals disclaims beneficial ownership of such shares, except to the extent of his or her pecuniary interest therein. The address of The Charles Schwab Corporation is 101 Montgomery Street, San Francisco, CA 94104.

(25) Venture Frogs, L.L.C. is the management company for Venture Frogs Fund I, L.L.C. Alfred Lin is the general manager of Venture Frogs, L.L.C. Mr. Lin may be deemed to have sole dispositive and voting power over the shares owned by Venture Frogs Fund I, L.L.C. Mr. Lin disclaims beneficial ownership of such shares, except to the extent of his pecuniary interest therein. The address of Venture Frogs Fund I, L.L.C. is 2280 Corporate Circle, Suite 100, Henderson, NV 89074.

(26) WCPI, LLC is the general partner of W Capital Partners I, L.P. David Wachter, Stephen Wertheimer and Robert Migliorino are the managing members of WCPI, LLC. These individuals may be deemed to share dispositive and voting power over the shares owned by W Capital Partners I, L.P. Each of these individuals disclaims beneficial ownership of such shares, except to the extent of his pecuniary interest therein. The address of W Capital Partners I, L.P. is One East 52nd Street, 5th Floor, New York, NY 10022.

(27) Sole voting and investment control of the shares being offered by Worldspan OpenTable Holdings LLC is exercised by its sole member, Worldspan, L.P. ("WLP"), a limited partnership. The general partner of WLP is Worldspan Technologies Inc. ("WTI"). The directors of WTI are Jeff Clarke and Eric J. Bock. Each of these individuals disclaims beneficial ownership of such shares, except to the extent of his pecuniary interest therein. The address of Worldspan OpenTable Holdings LLC is 400 Interpace Parkway, Building A, Parsippany, NJ 07054.

(28) Includes 134,400 shares held by Michael W. & Yianna L. Xenakis, trustees of the Xenakis Family 2007 Revocable Trust, dated February 26, 2007 and 24,000 shares held by Michael Xenakis, trustee of the Michael Xenakis Annuity Trust dated May 15, 2008. Includes 11,333 shares subject to our right of repurchase, which right lapses as to 667 shares each succeeding month over the next 17 months. Includes 67,001 shares subject to options that are exercisable within 60 days of March 31, 2009. Mr. Xenakis serves as our senior vice president of product management.

(29) Eugene H. Zagat Jr. and Nina S. Zagat are the managing members of Zagat Survey, LLC. These individuals may be deemed to share dispositive and voting power over the shares owned by Zagat Survey, LLC. Each of these individuals disclaims beneficial ownership of such shares, except to the extent of his pecuniary interest therein. The address of Zagat Survey, LLC is 4 Columbus Circle, New York, NY 10019.

(30) William C. Snyder and Mary Ann Snyder are the trustees of the Snyder Revocable Trust dated May 9, 2000.

(31) Includes each other selling stockholder who in the aggregate beneficially owns less than 1.0% of our common stock.

OpenTable has filed a registration statement (including a prospectus) with the SEC for the offering to which this communication relates. Before you invest, you should read the prospectus in that registration statement and other documents OpenTable has filed with the SEC for more complete information about OpenTable and this offering. You may get these documents for free by visiting EDGAR on the SEC website at *www.sec.gov*. Alternatively, OpenTable, any underwriter or any dealer participating in the offering will arrange to send you the prospectus if you request it by calling toll-free 1-866-500-5408.

7

COVER PAGE TO OPENTABLE, INC. RULE 424(b)(1) PROSPECTUS

[NOTE: THIS IS THE ONLY DOCUMENT THAT SHOWS THE ACTUAL OFFERING PRICE]

424B1 1 a2193211z424b1.htm 424B1

Use these links to rapidly review the document

Filed pursuant to Rule 424(b)(1)
Registration No. 333-157034

PROSPECTUS

3,000,000 Shares

Common Stock

This is the initial public offering of our common stock. We are offering 1,572,684 shares of the common stock offered by this prospectus, and the selling stockholders are offering 1,427,316 shares. We will not receive any proceeds from the sale of shares to be offered by the selling stockholders. Our common stock has been approved for listing on The Nasdaq Global Market under the symbol "OPEN."

Investing in our common stock involves a high degree of risk. See "Risk Factors" on page 10 of this prospectus.

	Per Share	Total
Public offering price	$20.00	$60,000,000
Underwriting discount	$1.40	$4,200,000
Proceeds, before expenses, to OpenTable, Inc.	$18.60	$29,251,922
Proceeds, before expenses, to the selling stockholders	$18.60	$26,548,078

The underwriters have a 30-day option to purchase up to an additional 450,000 shares of common stock from us to cover overallotments, if any.

Neither the Securities and Exchange Commission nor any state securities commission nor any other regulatory body has approved or disapproved of these securities or determined if this prospectus is truthful or complete. Any representation to the contrary is a criminal offense.

The shares will be ready for delivery on or about May 27, 2009.

Merrill Lynch & Co.

Allen & Company LLC

OpenTable, Inc. Purchase Agreement (Exhibit 1.1 to the Registration Statement)

EX-1.1 2 a2192796zex-1_1.htm EXHIBIT 1.1

Exhibit 1.1

OPENTABLE, INC.

(a Delaware corporation)

[•] Shares of Common Stock

(Par Value $0.0001 Per Share)

PURCHASE AGREEMENT

MERRILL LYNCH & CO.
Merrill Lynch, Pierce, Fenner & Smith
 Incorporated
as Representative of the several Underwriters
4 World Financial Center
New York, New York 10080

Ladies and Gentlemen:

OpenTable, Inc., a Delaware corporation (the "Company"), and the persons listed in Schedule B hereto (the "Selling Stockholders"), confirm their respective agreements with Merrill Lynch & Co., Merrill Lynch, Pierce, Fenner & Smith Incorporated ("Merrill Lynch") and each of the other Underwriters named in Schedule A hereto (collectively, the "Underwriters," which term shall also include any underwriter substituted as hereinafter provided in Section 10 hereof), for whom Merrill Lynch is acting as representative (in such capacity, the "Representative"), with respect to (i) the sale by the Company and the Selling Stockholders, acting severally and not jointly, and the purchase by the Underwriters, acting severally and not jointly, of the respective numbers of shares of Common Stock, par value $0.0001 per share, of the Company ("Common Stock") set forth in Schedules A and B hereto and (ii) the grant by the Company to the Underwriters, acting severally and not jointly, of the option described in Section 2(b) hereof to purchase all or any part of [•] additional shares of Common Stock to cover overallotments, if any. The aforesaid [•] shares of Common Stock (the "Initial Securities") to be purchased by the Underwriters and all or any part of the [•] shares of Common Stock subject to the option described in Section 2(b) hereof (the "Option Securities") are hereinafter called, collectively, the "Securities."

The Company and the Selling Stockholders understand that the Underwriters propose to make a public offering of the Securities as soon as the Representative deems advisable after this Agreement has been executed and delivered.

The Company has filed with the Securities and Exchange Commission (the "Commission") a registration statement on Form S-1 (No. 333-•), including the related preliminary prospectus or prospectuses, covering the registration of the Securities under the Securities Act of 1933, as amended (the "1933 Act"). Promptly after execution and delivery of this Agreement, the Company will prepare and file a prospectus in accordance with the provisions of Rule 430A ("Rule 430A") of the rules and regulations of the Commission under the 1933 Act (the "1933 Act Regulations") and paragraph (b) of Rule 424 ("Rule 424(b)") of the 1933 Act Regulations. The information included in such prospectus that was omitted from such registration statement at the time it became effective but that is deemed to be part of such registration statement at the time it became effective pursuant to paragraph (b) of Rule 430A is referred to as "Rule 430A Information." Each prospectus used before such registration statement became effective, and any prospectus that omitted the Rule 430A Information, that was used after such effectiveness and prior to the execution and delivery of this Agreement, is herein called a "preliminary prospectus." Such registration statement, including the amendments thereto, the exhibits and any schedules thereto, at the time it became effective, and including the Rule 430A Information, is herein called the "Registration Statement." Any registration statement filed pursuant to Rule 462(b) of the 1933 Act Regulations is herein referred to as the "Rule 462(b) Registration Statement," and after such filing the term "Registration Statement" shall include the Rule 462(b) Registration Statement. The final prospectus in the form first furnished to the Underwriters for use in connection with the offering of the Securities is herein called the "Prospectus." For purposes of this Agreement, all references to the Registration Statement, any preliminary prospectus, the Prospectus or any amendment or supplement to any of the foregoing shall be deemed to include the copy filed with the Commission pursuant to its Electronic Data Gathering, Analysis and Retrieval system ("EDGAR").

SECTION 1.   Representations and Warranties.

(a)   *Representations and Warranties by the Company*. The Company represents and warrants to each Underwriter as of the date hereof, as of the Applicable Time referred to in Section 1(a)(i) hereof, as of the Closing Time referred to in Section 2(c) hereof, and as of each Date of Delivery (if any) referred to in Section 2(b) hereof, and agrees with each Underwriter, as follows:

(i)   Compliance with Registration Requirements. Each of the Registration Statement, any Rule 462(b) Registration Statement and any post-effective amendment thereto has become effective under the 1933 Act and no stop order suspending the effectiveness of the Registration Statement, any Rule 462(b) Registration Statement or any post-effective amendment thereto has been issued under the 1933 Act and no proceedings for that purpose have been instituted or are pending or, to the knowledge of the Company, are threatened by the Commission, and any request on the part of the Commission for additional information has been complied with.

At the respective times the Registration Statement, any Rule 462(b) Registration Statement and any post-effective amendments thereto became effective and at the Closing Time (and, if any Option Securities are purchased, at the Date of Delivery), the Registration Statement, the Rule 462(b) Registration Statement and any amendments and supplements thereto complied and will comply in all material respects with the requirements of the 1933 Act and the 1933 Act Regulations and did not and will not contain an untrue statement of a material fact or omit to state a material fact required to be stated therein or necessary to make the statements therein not misleading. Neither the Prospectus nor any amendments or supplements thereto (including any prospectus wrapper), at the time the Prospectus or any such amendment or supplement was issued and at the Closing Time (and, if any Option Securities are purchased, at the Date of Delivery), included or will include an untrue statement of a material fact or omitted or will omit to state a material fact necessary in order to make the statements therein, in the light of the circumstances under which they were made, not misleading.

As of the Applicable Time (as defined below), neither (x) the Issuer General Use Free Writing Prospectus(es) (as defined below) issued at or prior to the Applicable Time and the Statutory Prospectus (as defined below) and the information included on Schedule C hereto, all considered together (collectively, the "General Disclosure Package"), nor (y) any individual Issuer Limited Use Free Writing Prospectus, when considered together with the General Disclosure Package, included any untrue statement of a material fact or omitted to state any material fact necessary in order to make the statements therein, in the light of the circumstances under which they were made, not misleading.

2

As used in this subsection and elsewhere in this Agreement:

"Applicable Time" means ●:00 [a/p]m (Eastern time) on [DATE] or such other time as agreed by the Company and Merrill Lynch.

"Statutory Prospectus" as of any time means the prospectus relating to the Securities that is included in the Registration Statement immediately prior to the Applicable Time.

"Issuer Free Writing Prospectus" means any "issuer free writing prospectus," as defined in Rule 433 of the 1933 Act Regulations ("Rule 433"), relating to the Securities that (i) is required to be filed with the Commission by the Company, (ii) is a "road show that is a written communication" within the meaning of Rule 433(d)(8)(i) whether or not required to be filed with the Commission or (iii) is exempt from filing pursuant to Rule 433(d)(5)(i) because it contains a description of the Securities or of the offering that does not reflect the final terms, in each case in the form filed or required to be filed with the Commission or, if not required to be filed, in the form retained in the Company's records pursuant to Rule 433(g).

"Issuer General Use Free Writing Prospectus" means any Issuer Free Writing Prospectus that is intended for general distribution to prospective investors (other than a Bona Fide Electronic Road Show (as defined below)), as evidenced by its being specified in Schedule E hereto.

"Issuer Limited Use Free Writing Prospectus" means any Issuer Free Writing Prospectus that is not an Issuer General Use Free Writing Prospectus.

The Company has made available a "*bona fide* electronic road show," as defined in Rule 433, in compliance with Rule 433 (d)(8)(ii) (the "Bona Fide Electronic Road Show") such that no filing of any "road show" (as defined in Rule 433(h)) is required in connection with the offering of the Securities.

Each Issuer Free Writing Prospectus, as of its issue date and at all subsequent times through the completion of the public offer and sale of the Securities or until any earlier date that the issuer notified or notifies Merrill Lynch as described in the next sentence, did not, does not and will not include any information that conflicted, conflicts or will conflict with the information contained in the Registration Statement or the Prospectus, and any preliminary or other prospectus deemed to be a part thereof that has not been superseded or modified.

The representations and warranties in this subsection shall not apply to statements in or omissions from the Registration Statement, the Prospectus or any Issuer Free Writing Prospectus made in reliance upon and in conformity with written information furnished to the Company by any Underwriter through Merrill Lynch expressly for use therein.

Each preliminary prospectus (including the prospectus filed as part of the Registration Statement as originally filed or as part of any amendment thereto) complied when so filed in all material respects with the 1933 Act Regulations and each preliminary prospectus and the Prospectus delivered to the Underwriters for use in connection with this offering was identical to the electronically transmitted copies thereof filed with the Commission pursuant to EDGAR, except to the extent permitted by Regulation S-T.

At the time of filing the Registration Statement, any 462(b) Registration Statement and any post-effective amendments thereto, at the earliest time thereafter that the Company or another

3

offering participant made a *bona fide* offer (within the meaning of Rule 164(h)(2) of the 1933 Act Regulations) of the Securities and at the date hereof, the Company was not and is not an "ineligible issuer," as defined in Rule 405 of the 1933 Act Regulations.

(ii)   Independent Accountants. The accounting firm who certified the consolidated financial statements and supporting schedules included in the Registration Statement is an independent public registered accounting firm as required by the 1933 Act and the 1933 Act Regulations.

(iii)   Financial Statements. The consolidated financial statements included in the Registration Statement, the General Disclosure Package and the Prospectus, together with the related schedules and notes, present fairly in all material respects the financial position of the Company and its consolidated subsidiaries at the dates indicated and the consolidated statement of operations, stockholders' equity and cash flows of the Company and its consolidated subsidiaries for the periods specified, in each case on the basis stated in the Registration Statement; said consolidated financial statements have been prepared in conformity with generally accepted accounting principles ("GAAP") applied on a consistent basis throughout the periods involved. The supporting schedules, if any, present fairly in accordance with GAAP the information required to be stated therein. The selected financial data and the summary financial information included in the Prospectus present fairly the information shown therein and have been compiled on a basis consistent with that of the audited financial statements included in the Registration Statement. All disclosures contained in the Registration Statement, the General Disclosure Package or the Prospectus regarding "non-GAAP financial measures" (as such term is defined by the rules and regulations of the Commission) comply with Regulation G of the 1934 Act and Item 10 of Regulation S-K of the 1933 Act, to the extent applicable.

(iv)   No Material Adverse Change in Business. Since the respective dates as of which information is given in the Registration Statement, the General Disclosure Package or the Prospectus, except as otherwise stated therein, (A) there has been no material adverse change in the condition, financial or otherwise, or in the earnings, business affairs or business prospects of the Company and its subsidiaries considered as one enterprise (a "Material Adverse Effect"), (B) there have been no transactions entered into by the Company or any of its subsidiaries, other than those in the ordinary course of business, which are material with respect to the Company and its subsidiaries considered as one enterprise, and (C) there has been no dividend or distribution of any kind declared, paid or made by the Company on any class of its capital stock.

(v)   Good Standing of the Company. The Company has been duly organized and is validly existing as a corporation in good standing under the laws of the state of Delaware and has corporate power and authority to own, lease and operate its properties and to conduct its business as described in the Prospectus and to enter into and perform its obligations under this Agreement; and the Company is duly qualified as a foreign corporation to transact business and is in good standing in each other jurisdiction in which such qualification is required, whether by reason of the ownership or leasing of property or the conduct of business, except where the failure so to qualify or to be in good standing would not result in a Material Adverse Effect.

(vi)   Good Standing of Subsidiaries. Each "significant subsidiary" of the Company (as such term is defined in Rule 1-02 of Regulation S-X) (each a "Subsidiary" and, collectively, the "Subsidiaries") has been duly organized and is validly existing as a corporation, to the extent applicable, in good standing, to the extent such concept exists, under the laws of the jurisdiction of its organization, has corporate or organizational power and authority to own, lease and operate its properties and to conduct its business as described in the Prospectus and is duly qualified as a

4

foreign corporation, to the extent applicable, to transact business and is in good standing, to the extent such concept exists, in each jurisdiction in which such qualification is required, whether by reason of the ownership or leasing of property or the conduct of business, except where the failure so to qualify or to be in good standing would not result in a Material Adverse Effect; except as otherwise disclosed in the Registration Statement, all of the issued and outstanding capital stock and other ownership interests of each such Subsidiary has been duly authorized and validly issued, is fully paid and non-assessable and is owned by the Company, directly or through subsidiaries, free and clear of any security interest, mortgage, pledge, lien, encumbrance, claim or equity; none of the outstanding shares of capital stock or other ownership interests of any Subsidiary was issued in violation of the preemptive or similar rights of any securityholder of such Subsidiary. The only subsidiaries of the Company are the subsidiaries listed on Exhibit 21 to the Registration Statement.

(vii)   Capitalization. The authorized, issued and outstanding capital stock of the Company is as set forth in the Prospectus in the column entitled "Actual" under the caption "Capitalization" (except for subsequent issuances, if any, pursuant to this Agreement, pursuant to reservations, agreements or employee benefit plans referred to in the Prospectus or pursuant to the exercise of convertible securities or options referred to in the Prospectus). The shares of issued and outstanding capital stock, including the Securities to be purchased by the Underwriters from the Selling Stockholders, have been duly authorized and validly issued and are fully paid and non-assessable; none of the outstanding shares of capital stock, including the Securities to be purchased by the Underwriters from the Selling Stockholders, was issued in violation of the preemptive or other similar rights of any securityholder of the Company.

(viii)   Authorization of Agreement. This Agreement has been duly authorized, executed and delivered by the Company.

(ix)   Authorization and Description of Securities. The Securities to be purchased by the Underwriters from the Company have been duly authorized for issuance and sale to the Underwriters pursuant to this Agreement and, when issued and delivered by the Company pursuant to this Agreement against payment of the consideration set forth herein, will be validly issued and fully paid and non-assessable; the Common Stock conforms to all statements relating thereto contained in the Prospectus and such description conforms to the rights set forth in the instruments defining the same; no holder of the Securities will be subject to personal liability by reason of being such a holder; and the issuance of the Securities is not subject to the preemptive or other similar rights of any securityholder of the Company.

(x)   Absence of Defaults and Conflicts. Neither the Company nor any of its subsidiaries is in violation of its charter or by-laws or other organizational documents or in default in the performance or observance of any obligation, agreement, covenant or condition contained in any contract, indenture, mortgage, deed of trust, loan or credit agreement, note, lease or other agreement or instrument to which the Company or any of its subsidiaries is a party or by which it or any of them may be bound, or to which any of the property or assets of the Company or any subsidiary is subject (collectively, "Agreements and Instruments") except for such defaults that would not reasonably be expected to result in a Material Adverse Effect; and the execution, delivery and performance of this Agreement and the consummation of the transactions contemplated herein and in the Registration Statement (including the issuance and sale of the Securities and the use of the proceeds from the sale of the Securities as described in the Prospectus under the caption "Use of Proceeds") and compliance by the Company with its obligations hereunder have been duly authorized by all necessary corporate action and do not and will not, whether with or without the giving of notice or passage of time or both, conflict with or

5

constitute a breach of, or default or Repayment Event (as defined below) under, or result in the creation or imposition of any lien, charge or encumbrance upon any property or assets of the Company or any subsidiary pursuant to, the Agreements and Instruments (except for such conflicts, breaches, defaults or Repayment Events or liens, charges or encumbrances that would not reasonably be expected to result in a Material Adverse Effect), nor will such action result in any violation of the provisions of the charter or by-laws of the Company or any subsidiary or any applicable law, statute, rule, regulation, judgment, order, writ or decree of any government, government instrumentality or court, domestic or foreign, having jurisdiction over the Company or any subsidiary or any of their assets, properties or operations. As used herein, a "Repayment Event" means any event or condition which gives the holder of any note, debenture or other evidence of indebtedness (or any person acting on such holder's behalf) the right to require the repurchase, redemption or repayment of all or a portion of such indebtedness by the Company or any subsidiary.

(xi) Absence of Labor Dispute. No labor dispute with the employees of the Company or any subsidiary exists or, to the knowledge of the Company, is imminent, and the Company is not aware of any existing or imminent labor disturbance by the employees of any of its or any subsidiary's principal suppliers, customers or contractors, which, in either case, would result in a Material Adverse Effect.

(xii) Absence of Proceedings. There is no action, suit, proceeding, inquiry or investigation before or brought by any court or governmental agency or body, domestic or foreign, now pending, or, to the knowledge of the Company, threatened, against or affecting the Company or any subsidiary, which is required to be disclosed in the Registration Statement (other than as disclosed therein), or which would reasonably be expected to result in a Material Adverse Effect, or which would reasonably be expected to materially and adversely affect the properties or assets thereof or the consummation of the transactions contemplated in this Agreement or the performance by the Company of its obligations hereunder; the aggregate of all pending legal or governmental proceedings to which the Company or any subsidiary is a party or of which any of their respective property or assets is the subject which are not described in the Registration Statement, including ordinary routine litigation incidental to the business, could not result in a Material Adverse Effect.

(xiii) Accuracy of Exhibits. There are no contracts or documents which are required to be described in the Registration Statement or the Prospectus or to be filed as exhibits thereto which have not been so described and filed as required.

(xiv) Possession of Intellectual Property. The Company and its subsidiaries own or possess, or can acquire on reasonable terms, adequate patents, patent rights, licenses, inventions, copyrights, know-how (including trade secrets and other unpatented and/or unpatentable proprietary or confidential information, systems or procedures), trademarks, service marks, trade names or other intellectual property (collectively, "Intellectual Property") necessary to carry on the business now operated by them, and neither the Company nor any of its subsidiaries has received any notice of any infringement of or conflict with asserted rights of others with respect to any Intellectual Property or of any facts or circumstances which would render any Intellectual Property invalid or unenforceable and which infringement or conflict (if the subject of any unfavorable decision, ruling or finding) or invalidity or unenforceability, singly or in the aggregate, would reasonably be expected to result in a Material Adverse Effect.

(xv) Absence of Further Requirements. No filing with, or authorization, approval, consent, license, order, registration, qualification or decree of, any court or governmental

6

authority or agency is necessary or required for the performance by the Company of its obligations hereunder, in connection with the offering, issuance or sale of the Securities hereunder or the consummation of the transactions contemplated by this Agreement, except (i) such as have been already obtained or as may be required under the 1933 Act or the 1933 Act Regulations or state securities laws and (ii) filing with the Secretary of State of Delaware an amended and restated certificate of incorporation.

(xvi) <u>Absence of Manipulation</u>. Neither the Company nor any affiliate of the Company has taken, nor will the Company or any affiliate take, directly or indirectly, any action which is designed to or which has constituted or which would be expected to cause or result in stabilization or manipulation of the price of any security of the Company to facilitate the sale or resale of the Securities.

(xvii) <u>Possession of Licenses and Permits</u>. The Company and its subsidiaries possess such permits, licenses, approvals, consents and other authorizations (collectively, "Governmental Licenses") issued by the appropriate federal, state, local or foreign regulatory agencies or bodies necessary to conduct the business now operated by them, except where the failure so to possess would not reasonably be expected to, singly or in the aggregate, result in a Material Adverse Effect; the Company and its subsidiaries are in compliance with the terms and conditions of all such Governmental Licenses, except where the failure so to comply would not reasonably be expected to, singly or in the aggregate, result in a Material Adverse Effect; all of the Governmental Licenses are valid and in full force and effect, except when the invalidity of such Governmental Licenses or the failure of such Governmental Licenses to be in full force and effect would not reasonably be expected to, singly or in the aggregate, result in a Material Adverse Effect; and neither the Company nor any of its subsidiaries has received any notice of proceedings relating to the revocation or modification of any such Governmental Licenses which, singly or in the aggregate, if the subject of an unfavorable decision, ruling or finding, would reasonably be expected to result in a Material Adverse Effect.

(xviii) <u>Title to Property</u>. The Company and its subsidiaries have good and marketable title to all real property owned by the Company and its subsidiaries and good title to all other properties owned by them, in each case, free and clear of all mortgages, pledges, liens, security interests, claims, restrictions or encumbrances of any kind except such as (a) are described in the Prospectus or (b) do not, singly or in the aggregate, materially affect the value of such property and do not interfere with the use made and proposed to be made of such property by the Company or any of its subsidiaries; and all of the leases and subleases material to the business of the Company and its subsidiaries, considered as one enterprise, and under which the Company or any of its subsidiaries holds properties described in the Prospectus, are in full force and effect, and neither the Company nor any subsidiary has any notice of any material claim of any sort that has been asserted by anyone adverse to the rights of the Company or any subsidiary under any of the leases or subleases mentioned above, or affecting or questioning the rights of the Company or such subsidiary to the continued possession of the leased or subleased premises under any such lease or sublease.

(xix) <u>Investment Company Act</u>. The Company is not required, and upon the issuance and sale of the Securities as herein contemplated and the application of the net proceeds therefrom as described in the Prospectus will not be required, to register as an "investment company" under the Investment Company Act of 1940, as amended (the "1940 Act").

(xx) <u>Environmental Laws</u>. Except as described in the Registration Statement and except as would not reasonably be expected to, singly or in the aggregate, result in a Material

7

Adverse Effect, (A) neither the Company nor any of its subsidiaries is in violation of any applicable federal, state, local or foreign statute, law, rule, regulation, ordinance, code or rule of common law or any judicial or administrative interpretation thereof, including any judicial or administrative order, consent, decree or judgment, relating to the effect of the environment on human health, pollution or protection of the environment (including, without limitation, ambient air, surface water, groundwater, land surface or subsurface strata) or wildlife, including, without limitation, laws and regulations relating to the release into the environment or threatened release into the environment of chemicals, pollutants, contaminants, wastes, toxic substances, hazardous substances, petroleum or petroleum products, asbestos-containing materials or mold (collectively, "Hazardous Materials") or to the manufacture, processing, distribution, use, treatment, storage, disposal, transport or handling of Hazardous Materials (collectively, "Environmental Laws"), (B) the Company and its subsidiaries have all permits, authorizations and approvals required for their respective operations under any applicable Environmental Laws and are each in compliance with their requirements, (C) there are no pending or, to the knowledge of the Company threatened administrative, regulatory or judicial actions, suits, demands, demand letters, claims, liens, notices of noncompliance or violation, investigation or proceedings relating to any Environmental Law against the Company or any of its subsidiaries and (D) to the knowledge of the Company, there are no events or circumstances existing as of the date hereof that would reasonably be expected to (1) form the basis of an order for clean-up or remediation, (2) form the basis of an action, suit or proceeding by any private party or governmental body or agency, or (3) give rise to any liability, in each case, against or affecting the Company or any of its subsidiaries relating to Hazardous Materials or any Environmental Laws.

      (xxi)   <u>Registration Rights</u>. (i) There are no persons with registration rights or other similar rights to have any securities registered pursuant to the Registration Statement other than rights which have been waived or complied with and (ii) there are no persons with registration rights or other similar rights to have any securities registered by the Company under the 1933 Act other than as described in the Prospectus.

      (xxii)   <u>Accounting Controls and Disclosure Controls</u>. The Company and each of its subsidiaries maintain a system of internal accounting controls sufficient to provide reasonable assurances that (A) transactions are executed in accordance with management's general or specific authorization; (B) transactions are recorded as necessary to permit preparation of financial statements in conformity with GAAP and to maintain accountability for assets; (C) access to assets is permitted only in accordance with management's general or specific authorization; and (D) the recorded accountability for assets is compared with the existing assets at reasonable intervals and appropriate action is taken with respect to any differences. Except as described in the Prospectus, since the end of the Company's most recent audited fiscal year, there has been (1) no material weakness in the Company's internal control over financial reporting (whether or not remediated) and (2) no change in the Company's internal control over financial reporting that has materially affected, or is reasonably likely to materially affect, the Company's internal control over financial reporting.

      The Company and its consolidated subsidiaries employ disclosure controls and procedures that are designed to ensure that information required to be disclosed by the Company in the reports that it files or submits under the 1934 Act is recorded, processed, summarized and reported, within the time periods specified in the Commission's rules and forms, and is accumulated and communicated to the Company's management, including its principal executive officer or officers and principal financial officer or officers, as appropriate, to allow timely decisions regarding disclosure.

8

(xxiii)   Compliance with the Sarbanes-Oxley Act. The Company has taken all necessary actions to ensure that, upon the effectiveness of the Registration Statement, it will be in compliance with all provisions of the Sarbanes-Oxley Act of 2002 and all rules and regulations promulgated thereunder or implementing the provisions thereof (the "Sarbanes-Oxley Act") that are then in effect and which the Company is required to comply with as of the effectiveness of the Registration Statement, and is actively taking steps to ensure that it will be in compliance with other provisions of the Sarbanes-Oxley Act not currently in effect, upon the effectiveness of such provisions, or which will become applicable to the Company at all times after the effectiveness of the Registration Statement.

(xxiv)   Payment of Taxes. Except to the extent the failure or inadequacy would not result in a Material Adverse Effect, (A) all United States federal income tax returns of the Company and its subsidiaries required by law to be filed have been filed and all taxes shown by such returns or otherwise assessed, which are due and payable, have been paid, except assessments against which appeals have been or will be promptly taken and as to which adequate reserves have been provided, (B) the Company and its subsidiaries have filed all other tax returns that are required to have been filed by them pursuant to applicable foreign, state, local or other law and has paid all taxes due pursuant to such returns or pursuant to any assessment received by the Company and its subsidiaries, except for such taxes, if any, as are being contested in good faith and as to which adequate reserves have been provided and (C) the charges, accruals and reserves on the books of the Company in respect of any income and corporation tax liability for any years not finally determined are adequate to meet any assessments or re-assessments for additional income tax for any years not finally determined.

(xxv)   Insurance. The Company and its subsidiaries carry or are entitled to the benefits of insurance, with financially sound and reputable insurers, in such amounts and covering such risks as is generally maintained by companies engaged in the same or similar business of the same or similar size and/or otherwise similarly situated, and all such insurance is in full force and effect. The Company has no reason to believe that it or any subsidiary will not be able (A) to renew its existing insurance coverage as and when such policies expire or (B) to obtain comparable coverage from similar institutions as may be necessary or appropriate to conduct its business as now conducted and at a cost that would not result in a Material Adverse Effect.

(xxvi)   Statistical and Market-Related Data. Any statistical and market-related data included in the Registration Statement and the Prospectus are based on or derived from sources that the Company believes to be reliable and accurate, and, to the extent required, the Company has obtained the written consent to the use of such data from such sources.

(xxvii)   Foreign Corrupt Practices Act. Neither the Company nor, to the knowledge of the Company, any director, officer, agent, employee, affiliate or other person acting on behalf of the Company or any of its subsidiaries is aware of or has taken any action, directly or indirectly, that would result in a violation by such persons of the Foreign Corrupt Practices Act of 1977, as amended, and the rules and regulations thereunder (the "FCPA"), including, without limitation, making use of the mails or any means or instrumentality of interstate commerce corruptly in furtherance of an offer, payment, promise to pay or authorization of the payment of any money, or other property, gift, promise to give, or authorization of the giving of anything of value to any "foreign official" (as such term is defined in the FCPA) or any foreign political party or official thereof or any candidate for foreign political office, in contravention of the FCPA and the Company and, to the knowledge of the Company, its subsidiaries have conducted their businesses in compliance with the FCPA and have instituted and maintain policies and procedures designed to ensure continued compliance therewith.

9

(xxviii)   Money Laundering Laws. The operations of the Company are and have been conducted at all times in compliance with applicable financial recordkeeping and reporting requirements of the Currency and Foreign Transactions Reporting Act of 1970, as amended, the money laundering statutes of all jurisdictions, the rules and regulations thereunder and any related or similar rules, regulations or guidelines, issued, administered or enforced by any governmental agency (collectively, the "Money Laundering Laws") and no action, suit or proceeding by or before any court or governmental agency, authority or body or any arbitrator involving the Company with respect to the Money Laundering Laws is pending or, to the best knowledge of the Company, threatened.

(xxix)   OFAC. Neither the Company nor, to the knowledge of the Company, any director, officer, agent, employee, affiliate or person acting on behalf of the Company is currently subject to any U.S. sanctions administered by the Office of Foreign Assets Control of the U.S. Treasury Department ("OFAC"); and the Company will not directly or indirectly use the proceeds of the offering, or lend, contribute or otherwise make available such proceeds to any subsidiary, joint venture partner or other person or entity, for the purpose of financing the activities of any person currently subject to any U.S. sanctions administered by OFAC.

(b)   *Representations and Warranties by the Selling Stockholders.* Each Selling Stockholder, severally and not jointly, represents and warrants to each Underwriter as of the date hereof and as of the Closing Time, and agrees with each Underwriter, as follows:

(i)   Accurate Disclosure. Neither the General Disclosure Package nor the Prospectus or any amendments or supplements thereto includes any untrue statement of a material fact or omits to state a material fact necessary in order to make the statements therein, in the light of the circumstances under which they were made, not misleading, provided that such representations and warranties set forth in this Section 1(b)(i) apply only to statements or omissions made in reliance upon and in conformity with information relating to such Selling Stockholder furnished in writing by or on behalf of such Selling Stockholder expressly for use in the Registration Statement, any preliminary prospectus, the Time of Sale Prospectus, any issuer free writing prospectus as defined in Rule 433(h) under the Securities Act, or the Prospectus or any amendment or supplement thereto (the "Provided Information"); such Selling Stockholder is not prompted to sell the Securities to be sold by such Selling Stockholder hereunder by any information concerning the Company or any subsidiary of the Company which is not set forth in the General Disclosure Package or the Prospectus.

(ii)   Authorization of this Agreement. This Agreement has been duly authorized, executed and delivered by or on behalf of such Selling Stockholder.

(iii)   Authorization of Power of Attorney and Custody Agreement. The Power of Attorney and Custody Agreement, in the form heretofore furnished to the Representative (the "Power of Attorney and Custody Agreement"), has been duly authorized, executed and delivered by such Selling Stockholder and is the valid and binding agreement of such Selling Stockholder.

(iv)   Noncontravention. The execution and delivery of this Agreement and the Power of Attorney and Custody Agreement and the sale and delivery of the Securities to be sold by such Selling Stockholder and the consummation of the transactions contemplated herein and compliance by such Selling Stockholder with its obligations hereunder do not and will not, whether with or without the giving of notice or passage of time or both, (A) conflict with or constitute a breach of, or default under, or result in the creation or imposition of any tax, lien, charge or encumbrance upon the Securities to be sold by such Selling Stockholder or any

10

property or assets of such Selling Stockholder pursuant to any contract, indenture, mortgage, deed of trust, loan or credit agreement, note, license, lease or other agreement or instrument to which such Selling Stockholder is a party or by which such Selling Stockholder may be bound, or to which any of the property or assets of such Selling Stockholder is subject, or (B) result in any violation of (1) the provisions of the charter or by-laws or other organizational instrument of such Selling Stockholder, if applicable, or (2) any applicable treaty, law, statute, rule, regulation, judgment, order, writ or decree of any government, government instrumentality or court, domestic or foreign, having jurisdiction over such Selling Stockholder or any of its properties.

      (v)   <u>Certificates Suitable for Transfer</u>. The Securities to be sold by such Selling Stockholder pursuant to this Agreement are certificated securities in registered form. Certificates for all of the Securities to be sold by such Selling Stockholder pursuant to this Agreement, in suitable form for transfer by delivery or accompanied by duly executed instruments of transfer or assignment in blank with signatures guaranteed, have been placed in custody with Mellon Investor Services LLC ("Custodian") with irrevocable conditional instructions to deliver such Securities to the Underwriters pursuant to this Agreement.

      (vi)   <u>Valid Title</u>. Such Selling Stockholder has, and at the Closing Time will have, valid title to such Securities to be sold by such Selling Stockholder free and clear of all security interests, claims, liens, equities or other encumbrances and the legal right and power, and all authorization and approval required by law, to enter into this Agreement and the Power of Attorney and Custody Agreement and to sell, transfer and deliver the Securities to be sold by such Selling Stockholder.

      (vii)   <u>Delivery of Securities</u>. Upon payment of the purchase price for the Securities to be sold by such Selling Stockholder pursuant to this Agreement, delivery of such Securities, as directed by the Underwriters, to Cede & Co. ("Cede") or such other nominee as may be designated by The Depository Trust Company ("DTC"), registration of such Securities in the name of Cede or such other nominee, and the crediting of such Securities on the books of DTC to securities accounts (within the meaning of Section 8-501(a) of the UCC) of the Underwriters (assuming that neither DTC nor any such Underwriter has notice of any "adverse claim," within the meaning of Section 8-105 of the Uniform Commercial Code then in effect in the State of New York ("UCC"), to such Securities), (A) under Section 8-501 of the UCC, the Underwriters will acquire a valid "security entitlement" in respect of such Securities and (B) no action (whether framed in conversion, replevin, constructive trust, equitable lien, or other theory) based on any "adverse claim," within the meaning of Section 8-102 of the UCC, to such Securities may be asserted against the Underwriters with respect to such security entitlement; for purposes of this representation, such Selling Stockholder may assume that when such payment, delivery and crediting occur, (a) such Securities will have been registered in the name of Cede or another nominee designated by DTC, in each case on the Company's share registry in accordance with its certificate of incorporation, bylaws and applicable law, (b) DTC will be registered as a "clearing corporation," within the meaning of Section 8-102 of the UCC, (c) appropriate entries to the accounts of the several Underwriters on the records of DTC will have been made pursuant to the UCC, (d) to the extent DTC, or any other securities intermediary which acts as "clearing corporation" with respect to the Securities, maintains any "financial asset" (as defined in Section 8-102(a)(9)) of the UCC in a clearing corporation pursuant to Section 8-111 of the UCC, the rules of such clearing corporation may affect the rights of DTC or such securities intermediaries and the ownership interest of the Underwriters, (e) claims of creditors of DTC or any other securities intermediary or clearing corporation may be given priority to the extent set forth in Section 8-511(b) and 8-511(c) of the UCC and (f) if at any time DTC or other securities intermediary does not have sufficient Securities to satisfy claims of all of its entitlement holders with respect

11

thereto then all holders will share pro rata in the Securities then held by DTC or such securities intermediary.

(viii)   Absence of Manipulation. Such Selling Stockholder has not taken, and will not take, directly or indirectly, any action which is designed to or which has constituted or would reasonably be expected to cause or result in stabilization or manipulation of the price of any security of the Company to facilitate the sale or resale of the Securities.

(ix)   Absence of Further Requirements. No filing with, or consent, approval, authorization, order, registration, qualification or decree of, any court or governmental authority or agency, domestic or foreign, is necessary or required for the performance by each Selling Stockholder of its obligations hereunder or in the Power of Attorney and Custody Agreement, or in connection with the sale and delivery of the Securities hereunder or the consummation of the transactions contemplated by this Agreement, except such as may have previously been made or obtained or as may be required under the 1933 Act or the 1933 Act Regulations or state securities laws.

(x)   Restriction on Sale of Securities. Such Selling Stockholder shall have executed and delivered to the Representatives or to counsel for the Underwriters a lock-up agreement substantially in the form of Exhibit C.

(xi)   No Association with FINRA. Except as described in the completed FINRA Questionnaire provided by such Selling Stockholder to the Company on or before [•], 2009, neither such Selling Stockholder nor any of its affiliates directly, or indirectly through one or more intermediaries, controls, or is controlled by, or is under common control with, or is a person associated with (within the meaning of Article I (dd) of the By-laws of the National Association of Securities Dealers, Inc.), any member firm of the National Association of Securities Dealers, Inc.

(c)   Officer's Certificates. Any certificate signed by any officer of the Company or any of its subsidiaries delivered to the Representatives or to counsel for the Underwriters shall be deemed a representation and warranty by the Company to each Underwriter as to the matters covered thereby; and any certificate signed by or on behalf of the Selling Stockholders as such and delivered to the Representative or to counsel for the Underwriters pursuant to the terms of this Agreement shall be deemed a representation and warranty by such Selling Stockholder to the Underwriters as to the matters covered thereby.

SECTION 2.   Sale and Delivery to Underwriters; Closing.

(a)   Initial Securities. On the basis of the representations and warranties herein contained and subject to the terms and conditions herein set forth, the Company and each Selling Stockholder, severally and not jointly, agree to sell to each Underwriter, severally and not jointly, and each Underwriter, severally and not jointly, agrees to purchase from the Company and each Selling Stockholder, at the price per share set forth in Schedule C, that proportion of the number of Initial Securities set forth in Schedule B opposite the name of the Company or such Selling Stockholder, as the case may be, which the number of Initial Securities set forth in Schedule A opposite the name of such Underwriter, plus any additional number of Initial Securities which such Underwriter may become obligated to purchase pursuant to the provisions of Section 10 hereof, bears to the total number of Initial Securities, subject, in each case, to such adjustments among the Underwriters as the Representative in its sole discretion shall make to eliminate any sales or purchases of fractional securities.

12

(b)   *Option Securities.* In addition, on the basis of the representations and warranties herein contained and subject to the terms and conditions herein set forth, the Company hereby grants an option to the Underwriters, severally and not jointly, to purchase up to an additional [•] shares of Common Stock, as set forth in Schedule B, at the price per share set forth in Schedule C, less an amount per share equal to any dividends or distributions declared by the Company and payable on the Initial Securities but not payable on the Option Securities. The option hereby granted will expire 30 days after the date hereof and may be exercised in whole or in part from time to time only for the purpose of covering overallotments which may be made in connection with the offering and distribution of the Initial Securities upon notice by Merrill Lynch to the Company setting forth the number of Option Securities as to which the several Underwriters are then exercising the option and the time and date of payment and delivery for such Option Securities. Any such time and date of delivery (a "Date of Delivery") shall be determined by Merrill Lynch, but shall not be later than seven full business days after the exercise of said option, nor in any event prior to the Closing Time, as hereinafter defined. If the option is exercised as to all or any portion of the Option Securities, each of the Underwriters, acting severally and not jointly, will purchase that proportion of the total number of Option Securities then being purchased which the number of Initial Securities set forth in Schedule A opposite the name of such Underwriter bears to the total number of Initial Securities, subject in each case to such adjustments as Merrill Lynch in its discretion shall make to eliminate any sales or purchases of fractional shares.

(c)   *Payment.* Payment of the purchase price for, and delivery of certificates for, the Initial Securities shall be made at the offices of Davis Polk & Wardwell, 1600 El Camino Real, Menlo Park, California, or at such other place as shall be agreed upon by the Representative and the Company and the Selling Stockholders, at 9:00 A.M. (Eastern time) on the third (fourth, if the pricing occurs after 4:30 P.M. (Eastern time) on any given day) business day after the date hereof (unless postponed in accordance with the provisions of Section 10), or such other time not later than ten business days after such date as shall be agreed upon by the Representative and the Company and the Selling Stockholders (such time and date of payment and delivery being herein called "Closing Time").

In addition, in the event that any or all of the Option Securities are purchased by the Underwriters, payment of the purchase price for, and delivery of certificates for, such Option Securities shall be made at the above-mentioned offices, or at such other place as shall be agreed upon by the Representative and the Company, on each Date of Delivery as specified in the notice from the Representative to the Company.

Payment shall be made to the Company and the Selling Stockholders by wire transfer of immediately available funds to bank accounts designated by the Company and the Custodian pursuant to each Selling Stockholder's Power of Attorney and Custody Agreement, as the case may be, against delivery to the Representative for the respective accounts of the Underwriters of certificates for the Securities to be purchased by them. It is understood that each Underwriter has authorized the Representative, for its account, to accept delivery of, receipt for, and make payment of the purchase price for, the Initial Securities and the Option Securities, if any, which it has agreed to purchase. Merrill Lynch, individually and not as representative of the Underwriters, may (but shall not be obligated to) make payment of the purchase price for the Initial Securities or the Option Securities, if any, to be purchased by any Underwriter whose funds have not been received by the Closing Time or the relevant Date of Delivery, as the case may be, but such payment shall not relieve such Underwriter from its obligations hereunder.

(d)   *Denominations; Registration.* Certificates for the Initial Securities and the Option Securities, if any, shall be in such denominations and registered in such names as the Representative may request in writing at least one full business day before the Closing Time or the relevant Date of Delivery, as the case may be. The certificates for the Initial Securities and the Option Securities, if any, will be

13

made available for examination and packaging by the Representative in The City of New York not later than 10:00 A.M. (Eastern time) on the business day prior to the Closing Time or the relevant Date of Delivery, as the case may be.

SECTION 3.   Covenants of the Company and the Selling Stockholders. The Company covenants with each Underwriter as set forth in subsection (a) through (l) below, and each of the Selling Stockholders covenants with each Underwriter as set forth in subsection (l) below:

(a)   *Compliance with Securities Regulations and Commission Requests*. The Company, subject to Section 3(b), will comply with the requirements of Rule 430A, and will notify the Representative immediately, (i) when any post-effective amendment to the Registration Statement shall become effective, or any supplement to the Prospectus or any amended Prospectus shall have been filed, (ii) of the receipt of any comments from the Commission, (iii) of any request by the Commission for any amendment to the Registration Statement or any amendment or supplement to the Prospectus or for additional information, (iv) of the issuance by the Commission of any stop order suspending the effectiveness of the Registration Statement or of any order preventing or suspending the use of any preliminary prospectus, or of the suspension of the qualification of the Securities for offering or sale in any jurisdiction, or of the initiation or threatening of any proceedings for any of such purposes or of any examination pursuant to Section 8(e) of the 1933 Act concerning the Registration Statement and (v) if the Company becomes the subject of a proceeding under Section 8A of the 1933 Act in connection with the offering of the Securities. The Company will effect the filings required under Rule 424(b), in the manner and within the time period required by Rule 424(b) (without reliance on Rule 424(b)(8)), and will take such steps as it deems necessary to ascertain promptly whether the form of prospectus transmitted for filing under Rule 424(b) was received for filing by the Commission and, in the event that it was not, it will promptly file such prospectus. The Company will make every reasonable effort to prevent the issuance of any stop order and, if any stop order is issued, to obtain the lifting thereof as soon as practicable.

(b)   *Filing of Amendments and Exchange Act Documents*. The Company will give the Representative notice of its intention to file or prepare any amendment to the Registration Statement (including any filing under Rule 462(b)) or any amendment, supplement or revision to either the prospectus included in the Registration Statement at the time it became effective or to the Prospectus, and will furnish the Representative with copies of any such documents a reasonable amount of time prior to such proposed filing or use, as the case may be, and will not file or use any such document to which the Representative or counsel for the Underwriters shall object (other than a document which the Company believes, based on advice of legal counsel, it is required by law to file). The Company will give the Representative notice of its intention to make any such filing from the Applicable Time to the Closing Time and will furnish the Representative with copies of any such documents a reasonable amount of time prior to such proposed filing, as the case may be, and will not file or use any such document to which the Representative or counsel for the Underwriters shall object (other than a document which the Company believes, based on advice of legal counsel, it is required by law to file).

(c)   *Delivery of Registration Statements*. The Company has furnished or will deliver upon request to the Representative and counsel for the Underwriters, without charge, conformed copies of the Registration Statement as originally filed and of each amendment thereto (including exhibits filed therewith) and facsimile signed copies of all consents and certificates of experts. The copies of the Registration Statement and each amendment thereto furnished to the Underwriters will be identical to the electronically transmitted copies thereof filed with the Commission pursuant to EDGAR, except to the extent permitted by Regulation S-T.

14

(d)   *Delivery of Prospectuses.* The Company has delivered to each Underwriter, without charge, as many copies of each preliminary prospectus as such Underwriter reasonably requested, and the Company hereby consents to the use of such copies for purposes permitted by the 1933 Act. The Company will furnish to each Underwriter, without charge, during the period when the Prospectus is required to be delivered under the 1933 Act, such number of copies of the Prospectus (as amended or supplemented) as such Underwriter may reasonably request. The Prospectus and any amendments or supplements thereto furnished to the Underwriters will be identical to the electronically transmitted copies thereof filed with the Commission pursuant to EDGAR, except to the extent permitted by Regulation S-T.

(e)   *Continued Compliance with Securities Laws.* The Company will comply with the 1933 Act and the 1933 Act Regulations so as to permit the completion of the distribution of the Securities as contemplated in this Agreement and in the Prospectus. If at any time when a prospectus is required by the 1933 Act to be delivered in connection with sales of the Securities, any event shall occur or condition shall exist as a result of which it is necessary, in the opinion of counsel for the Underwriters or for the Company, to amend the Registration Statement or amend or supplement the Prospectus in order that the Prospectus will not include any untrue statements of a material fact or omit to state a material fact necessary in order to make the statements therein not misleading in the light of the circumstances existing at the time it is delivered to a purchaser, or if it shall be necessary, in the opinion of such counsel, at any such time to amend the Registration Statement or amend or supplement the Prospectus in order to comply with the requirements of the 1933 Act or the 1933 Act Regulations, the Company will promptly prepare and file with the Commission, subject to Section 3(b), such amendment or supplement as may be necessary to correct such statement or omission or to make the Registration Statement or the Prospectus comply with such requirements, and the Company will furnish to the Underwriters such number of copies of such amendment or supplement as the Underwriters may reasonably request. If at any time following issuance of an Issuer Free Writing Prospectus there occurred or occurs an event or development as a result of which such Issuer Free Writing Prospectus conflicted or would conflict with the information contained in the Registration Statement relating to the Securities or included or would include an untrue statement of a material fact or omitted or would omit to state a material fact necessary in order to make the statements therein, in the light of the circumstances, prevailing at that subsequent time, not misleading, the Company will promptly notify Merrill Lynch and will promptly amend or supplement, at its own expense, such Issuer Free Writing Prospectus to eliminate or correct such conflict, untrue statement or omission.

(f)   *Blue Sky Qualifications.* The Company will use its reasonable best efforts, in cooperation with the Underwriters, to qualify the Securities for offering and sale under the applicable securities laws of such states and other jurisdictions (domestic or foreign) as the Representative may designate and to maintain such qualifications in effect for a period of not less than one year from the later of the effective date of the Registration Statement and any Rule 462(b) Registration Statement; provided, however, that the Company shall not be obligated to file any general consent or otherwise subject itself to service of process or to qualify as a foreign corporation or as a dealer in securities in any jurisdiction in which it is not so qualified or to subject itself to taxation in respect of doing business in any jurisdiction in which it is not otherwise so subject.

(g)   *Rule 158.* The Company will timely file such reports pursuant to the Securities Exchange Act of 1934 (the "1934 Act") as are necessary in order to make generally available to its securityholders as soon as practicable an earnings statement for the purposes of, and to provide to the Underwriters the benefits contemplated by, the last paragraph of Section 11(a) of the 1933 Act.

(h)   *Use of Proceeds.* The Company will use the net proceeds received by it from the sale of the Securities in the manner specified in the Prospectus under "Use of Proceeds."

15

(i) *Listing*. The Company will use its reasonable best efforts to effect the listing of the Common Stock (including the Securities) on the Nasdaq Global Market.

(j) *Restriction on Sale of Securities*. During a period of 180 days from the date of the Prospectus, the Company will not, without the prior written consent of Merrill Lynch, (i) directly or indirectly, offer, pledge, sell, contract to sell, sell any option or contract to purchase, purchase any option or contract to sell, grant any option, right or warrant to purchase or otherwise transfer or dispose of any share of Common Stock or any securities convertible into or exercisable or exchangeable for Common Stock or file any registration statement under the 1933 Act with respect to any of the foregoing or (ii) enter into any swap or any other agreement or any transaction that transfers, in whole or in part, directly or indirectly, the economic consequence of ownership of the Common Stock, whether any such swap or transaction described in clause (i) or (ii) above is to be settled by delivery of Common Stock or such other securities, in cash or otherwise. The foregoing sentence shall not apply to (A) the Securities to be sold hereunder, (B) any shares of Common Stock issued by the Company upon the exercise of an option or warrant or the conversion of a security outstanding on the date hereof (including any preferred stock) and referred to in the Prospectus, (C) any shares of Common Stock issued or options to purchase Common Stock granted pursuant to existing employee benefit plans of the Company and equity incentive plans adopted by the Company in connection with the public offering referred to in the Prospectus or (D) any shares of Common Stock issued pursuant to any non-employee director stock plan or dividend reinvestment plan. Notwithstanding the foregoing, if (1) during the last 17 days of the 180-day restricted period the Company issues an earnings release or material news or a material event relating to the Company occurs or (2) prior to the expiration of the 180-day restricted period, the Company announces that it will release earnings results or becomes aware that material news or a material event will occur during the 16-day period beginning on the last day of the 180-day restricted period, the restrictions imposed in this clause (j) shall continue to apply until the expiration of the 18-day period beginning on the issuance of the earnings release or the occurrence of the material news or material event.

(k) *Reporting Requirements*. The Company, during the period when the Prospectus is required to be delivered under the 1933 Act, will file all documents required to be filed with the Commission pursuant to the 1934 Act within the time periods required by the 1934 Act and the rules and regulations of the Commission thereunder.

(l) *Issuer Free Writing Prospectuses*. Each of the Company and each Selling Stockholder represents and agrees that, unless it obtains the prior consent of the Representative, and each Underwriter represents and agrees that, unless it obtains the prior consent of the Company and the Representative, it has not made and will not make any offer relating to the Securities that would constitute an "issuer free writing prospectus," as defined in Rule 433, or that would otherwise constitute a "free writing prospectus," as defined in Rule 405, required to be filed with the Commission or, in the case of each Selling Stockholder, whether or not required to be filed with the Commission. Any such free writing prospectus consented to by the Company and the Representative is hereinafter referred to as a "Permitted Free Writing Prospectus." Each of the Company and each Selling Stockholder represents, severally and not jointly, that it has treated or agrees that it will treat each Permitted Free Writing Prospectus as an "issuer free writing prospectus," as defined in Rule 433, and has complied and will comply with the requirements of Rule 433 applicable to any Permitted Free Writing Prospectus, including timely filing with the Commission where required, legending and record keeping.

SECTION 4. Payment of Expenses.

(a) *Expenses*. The Company will pay or cause to be paid all expenses incident to the performance of its obligations under this Agreement, other than to the extent described in section (b) below, including (i) the preparation, printing and filing of the Registration Statement (including financial

16

statements and exhibits) as originally filed and of each amendment thereto, (ii) the preparation, printing and delivery to the Underwriters of this Agreement, any Agreement among Underwriters and such other documents as may be required in connection with the offering, purchase, sale, issuance or delivery of the Securities, (iii) the preparation, issuance and delivery of the certificates for the Securities to the Underwriters, including any stock or other transfer taxes and any stamp or other duties payable upon the sale, issuance or delivery of the Securities to the Underwriters, (iv) the fees and disbursements of the Company's counsel, accountants and other advisors, (v) the qualification of the Securities under securities laws in accordance with the provisions of Section 3(f) hereof, including filing fees and the reasonable fees and disbursements of counsel for the Underwriters in connection therewith and in connection with the preparation of the Blue Sky Survey and any supplement thereto, (vi) the printing and delivery to the Underwriters of copies of each preliminary prospectus, any Permitted Free Writing Prospectus and of the Prospectus and any amendments or supplements thereto and any costs associated with electronic delivery of any of the foregoing by the Underwriters to investors, (vii) the preparation, printing and delivery to the Underwriters of copies of the Blue Sky Survey and any supplement thereto, (viii) the fees and expenses of any transfer agent or registrar for the Securities, (ix) the costs and expenses of the Company relating to investor presentations on any "road show" undertaken in connection with the marketing of the Securities, including without limitation, expenses associated with the production of road show slides and graphics, fees and expenses of any consultants engaged in connection with the road show presentations, travel and lodging expenses of the representatives of the Company and officers of the Company and any such consultants, and the cost of aircraft and other transportation chartered in connection with the road show, provided, however, that the Underwriters and the Company agree to share equally the costs of any aircraft or other transportation so chartered, (x) the filing fees incident to, and the reasonable fees and disbursements of counsel to the Underwriters in connection with, the review by the Financial Industry Regulatory Authority, Inc. ("FINRA") of the terms of the sale of the Securities and (xi) the fees and expenses incurred in connection with the listing of the Securities on the Nasdaq Global Market.

(b)   *Expenses of the Selling Stockholders.* The Selling Stockholders, severally and not jointly, will pay all expenses incident to the performance of their respective obligations under, and the consummation of the transactions contemplated by this Agreement, including (i) any stamp duties, capital duties and stock transfer taxes, if any, payable upon the sale of the Securities by such Selling Stockholder to the Underwriters, and their transfer between the Underwriters pursuant to an agreement between such Underwriters, and (ii) the fees and disbursements of their respective counsel and other advisors.

(c)   *Termination of Agreement.* If this Agreement is terminated by the Representative in accordance with the provisions of Section 5, Section 9(a)(i) or Section 11 hereof, the Company and the Selling Stockholders, severally and not jointly, shall reimburse the Underwriters for all of their accountable out-of-pocket expenses actually incurred, including the reasonable fees and disbursements of counsel for the Underwriters.

(d)   *Allocation of Expenses.* The provisions of this Section shall not affect any agreement that the Company and the Selling Stockholders may make for the sharing of such costs and expenses.

SECTION 5.   Conditions of Underwriters' Obligations. The obligations of the several Underwriters hereunder are subject to the accuracy of the representations and warranties of the Company and the Selling Stockholders contained in Section 1 hereof or in certificates of any officer of the Company or any subsidiary of the Company or on behalf of any Selling Stockholder delivered pursuant to the provisions hereof, to the performance by the Company of its covenants and other obligations hereunder, and to the following further conditions:

(a)   *Effectiveness of Registration Statement.* The Registration Statement, including any Rule 462(b) Registration Statement, has become effective and at Closing Time no stop order suspending the

17

effectiveness of the Registration Statement shall have been issued under the 1933 Act or proceedings therefor initiated or threatened by the Commission, and any request on the part of the Commission for additional information shall have been complied with to the reasonable satisfaction of counsel to the Underwriters. A prospectus containing the Rule 430A Information shall have been filed with the Commission in the manner and within the time frame required by Rule 424(b) without reliance on Rule 424(b)(8) or a post-effective amendment providing such information shall have been filed and declared effective in accordance with the requirements of Rule 430A.

(b)   *Opinion of Counsel for Company.* At Closing Time, the Representative shall have received the favorable opinion, dated as of Closing Time, of Latham & Watkins LLP, counsel for the Company, in form and substance satisfactory to counsel for the Underwriters, together with signed or reproduced copies of such letter for each of the other Underwriters to the effect set forth in Exhibit A-1 hereto and to such further effect as counsel to the Underwriters may reasonably request.

(c)   *Opinion of Counsel for OpenTable Europe Ltd.* At Closing Time, the Representative shall have received the favorable opinion, dated as of Closing Time, of [•], counsel for OpenTable Europe Ltd., in form and substance satisfactory to counsel for the Underwriters, together with signed or reproduced copies of such letter for each of the other Underwriters to the effect set forth in Exhibit A-2 hereto and to such further effect as counsel to the Underwriters may reasonably request.

(d)   *Opinion of Counsel for the Selling Stockholders.* At Closing Time, the Representative shall have received the favorable opinion, dated as of Closing Time, of [•], counsel for the Selling Stockholders, in form and substance satisfactory to counsel for the Underwriters, together with signed or reproduced copies of such letter for each of the other Underwriters to the effect set forth in Exhibit B hereto and to such further effect as counsel to the Underwriters may reasonably request.

(e)   *Opinion of Counsel for Underwriters.* At Closing Time, the Representative shall have received the favorable opinion, dated as of Closing Time, of Davis Polk & Wardwell, counsel for the Underwriters, together with signed or reproduced copies of such letter for each of the other Underwriters with respect to the matters set forth in clauses (i), (ii), (v), (vi) (solely as to preemptive or other similar rights arising by operation of law or under the charter or by-laws of the Company), (viii) through (x), inclusive, (xi), (xiii) (solely as to the information in the Prospectus under "Description of Capital Stock—Common Stock") and the penultimate paragraph of Exhibit A hereto. In giving such opinion such counsel may rely, as to all matters governed by the laws of jurisdictions other than the law of the State of New York and the federal law of the United States and the General Corporation Law of the State of Delaware, upon the opinions of counsel satisfactory to the Representative. Such counsel may also state that, insofar as such opinion involves factual matters, they have relied, to the extent they deem proper, upon certificates of officers of the Company and its subsidiaries and certificates of public officials.

(f)   *Officers' Certificate.* At Closing Time, there shall not have been, since the date hereof or since the respective dates as of which information is given in the Prospectus or the General Disclosure Package, any material adverse change in the condition, financial or otherwise, or in the earnings, business affairs or business prospects of the Company and its subsidiaries considered as one enterprise, and the Representative shall have received a certificate of the President or a Vice President of the Company and of the chief financial or chief accounting officer of the Company, dated as of Closing Time, to the effect that (i) there has been no such material adverse change, (ii) the representations and warranties in Section 1(a) hereof are true and correct with the same force and effect as though expressly made at and as of Closing Time, (iii) the Company has complied with all agreements and satisfied all conditions on its part to be performed or satisfied at or prior to Closing Time, and (iv) no stop order suspending the effectiveness of the Registration Statement has been issued and no proceedings for that purpose have been instituted or are pending or, to their knowledge, threatened by the Commission.

18

(g)   *Certificate of Selling Stockholders.* At Closing Time, the Representative shall have received a certificate of an Attorney-in-Fact on behalf of each Selling Stockholder, dated as of Closing Time, to the effect that (i) the representations and warranties of each Selling Stockholder contained in Section 1(b) hereof are true and correct in all respects with the same force and effect as though expressly made at and as of Closing Time and (ii) each Selling Stockholder has complied in all material respects with all agreements and all conditions on its part to be performed under this Agreement at or prior to Closing Time.

(h)   *Accountant's Comfort Letter.* At the time of the execution of this Agreement, the Representative shall have received from Deloitte & Touche LLP a letter dated such date, in form and substance satisfactory to the Representative, together with signed or reproduced copies of such letter for each of the other Underwriters containing statements and information of the type ordinarily included in accountants' "comfort letters" to underwriters with respect to the financial statements and certain financial information contained in the Registration Statement and the Prospectus.

(i)   *Bring-down Comfort Letter.* At Closing Time, the Representative shall have received from Deloitte & Touche LLP a letter, dated as of Closing Time, to the effect that they reaffirm the statements made in the letter furnished pursuant to subsection (h) of this Section, except that the specified date referred to shall be a date not more than three business days prior to Closing Time.

(j)   *Approval of Listing.* At Closing Time, the Securities shall have been approved for listing in the Nasdaq Global Market, subject only to official notice of issuance.

(k)   *No Objection.* FINRA has confirmed that it has not raised any objection with respect to the fairness and reasonableness of the underwriting terms and arrangements.

(l)   *Lock-up Agreements.* At the date of this Agreement, the Representative shall have received an agreement substantially in the form of Exhibit C hereto signed by the persons listed on Schedule D hereto.

(m)   *Conditions to Purchase of Option Securities.* In the event that the Underwriters exercise their option provided in Section 2 (b) hereof to purchase all or any portion of the Option Securities, the representations and warranties of the Company contained herein and the statements in any certificates furnished by the Company and any subsidiary of the Company hereunder shall be true and correct as of each Date of Delivery and, at the relevant Date of Delivery, the Representative shall have received:

(i)   Officers' Certificate. A certificate, dated such Date of Delivery, of the President or a Vice President of the Company and of the chief financial or chief accounting officer of the Company confirming that the certificate delivered at the Closing Time pursuant to Section 5(f) hereof remains true and correct as of such Date of Delivery.

(ii)   Opinion of Counsel for Company. The favorable opinion of Latham & Watkins LLP, counsel for the Company, in form and substance satisfactory to counsel for the Underwriters, dated such Date of Delivery, relating to the Option Securities to be purchased on such Date of Delivery and otherwise to the same effect as the opinion required by Section 5(b) hereof.

(iii)   Opinion of Counsel for OpenTable Europe Ltd. The favorable opinion of [   ], counsel for OpenTable Europe Ltd., in form and substance satisfactory to counsel for the Underwriters, dated such Date of Delivery, relating to the Option Securities to be purchased on

19

such Date of Delivery and otherwise to the same effect as the opinion required by Section 5(c) hereof.

(iv)   Opinion of Counsel for Underwriters. The favorable opinion of Davis Polk & Wardwell, counsel for the Underwriters, dated such Date of Delivery, relating to the Option Securities to be purchased on such Date of Delivery and otherwise to the same effect as the opinion required by Section 5(e) hereof.

(v)   Bring-down Comfort Letter. A letter from Deloitte & Touche LLP, in form and substance satisfactory to the Representative and dated such Date of Delivery, substantially in the same form and substance as the letter furnished to the Representative pursuant to Section 5(h) hereof, except that the "specified date" in the letter furnished pursuant to this paragraph shall be a date not more than five days prior to such Date of Delivery.

(n)   Additional Documents. At Closing Time and at each Date of Delivery counsel for the Underwriters shall have been furnished with such documents and opinions as they may require for the purpose of enabling them to pass upon the issuance and sale of the Securities as herein contemplated, or in order to evidence the accuracy of any of the representations or warranties, or the fulfillment of any of the conditions, herein contained; and all proceedings taken by the Company and the Selling Stockholders in connection with the issuance and sale of the Securities as herein contemplated shall be satisfactory in form and substance to the Representative and counsel for the Underwriters.

(o)   Termination of Agreement. If any condition specified in this Section shall not have been fulfilled when and as required to be fulfilled, this Agreement, or, in the case of any condition to the purchase of Option Securities on a Date of Delivery which is after the Closing Time, the obligations of the several Underwriters to purchase the relevant Option Securities, may be terminated by the Representative by notice to the Company and the Selling Stockholders at any time at or prior to Closing Time or such Date of Delivery, as the case may be, and such termination shall be without liability of any party to any other party except as provided in Section 4 and except that Sections 1, 6, 7 and 8 shall survive any such termination and remain in full force and effect.

SECTION 6.   Indemnification.

(a)   Indemnification of Underwriters. The Company agrees to indemnify and hold harmless each Underwriter, its affiliates, as such term is defined in Rule 501(b) under the 1933 Act (each, an "Affiliate"), its selling agents and each person, if any, who controls any Underwriter within the meaning of Section 15 of the 1933 Act or Section 20 of the 1934 Act as follows:

(i)   against any and all loss, liability, claim, damage and expense whatsoever, as incurred, arising out of any untrue statement or alleged untrue statement of a material fact contained in the Registration Statement (or any amendment thereto), including the Rule 430A Information or the omission or alleged omission therefrom of a material fact required to be stated therein or necessary to make the statements therein not misleading or arising out of any untrue statement or alleged untrue statement of a material fact included in any preliminary prospectus, any Issuer Free Writing Prospectus or the Prospectus (or any amendment or supplement thereto), or the omission or alleged omission therefrom of a material fact necessary in order to make the statements therein, in the light of the circumstances under which they were made, not misleading;

(ii)   against any and all loss, liability, claim, damage and expense whatsoever, as incurred, to the extent of the aggregate amount paid in settlement of any litigation, or any investigation or proceeding by any governmental agency or body, commenced or threatened, or

20

of any claim whatsoever based upon any such untrue statement or omission, or any such alleged untrue statement or omission; provided that (subject to Section 6(e) below) any such settlement is effected with the written consent of the Company and the Selling Stockholders;

(iii)   against any and all expense whatsoever, as incurred (including the fees and disbursements of counsel chosen by Merrill Lynch), reasonably incurred in investigating, preparing or defending against any litigation, or any investigation or proceeding by any governmental agency or body, commenced or threatened, or any claim whatsoever based upon any such untrue statement or omission, or any such alleged untrue statement or omission, to the extent that any such expense is not paid under (i) or (ii) above;

provided, however, that this indemnity agreement shall not apply to any loss, liability, claim, damage or expense to the extent arising out of any untrue statement or omission or alleged untrue statement or omission made in reliance upon and in conformity with written information furnished to the Company by any Underwriter through Merrill Lynch expressly for use in the Registration Statement (or any amendment thereto), including the Rule 430A Information, or any preliminary prospectus, any Issuer Free Writing Prospectus or the Prospectus (or any amendment or supplement thereto).

(b)   Each Selling Stockholder, severally and not jointly, agrees to indemnify and hold harmless each Underwriter, its Affiliates and selling agents and each person, if any, who controls any Underwriter within the meaning of Section 15 of the 1933 Act or Section 20 of the 1934 Act to the extent and in the manner set forth in clauses (a)(i), (ii) and (iii) above in connection with the offering of the Securities by the Selling Stockholder; provided, however, that the aggregate indemnification liability of each Selling Stockholder shall not exceed the gross proceeds received by such person from the sale of the Securities sold by such person in the public offering pursuant to this Agreement; and provided, further that each Selling Stockholder shall be liable only to the extent that such untrue statement or alleged untrue statement or omission or alleged omission has been made in the Registration Statement, any preliminary prospectus, the Prospectus or such amendment or supplement in reliance upon and in conformity with Provided Information.

(c)   *Indemnification of Company, Directors and Officers and Selling Stockholders.* Each Underwriter severally agrees to indemnify and hold harmless the Company, its directors, each of its officers who signed the Registration Statement, and each person, if any, who controls the Company within the meaning of Section 15 of the 1933 Act or Section 20 of the 1934 Act, and each Selling Stockholder and each person, if any, who controls any Selling Stockholder within the meaning of Section 15 of the 1933 Act or Section 20 of the 1934 Act, against any and all loss, liability, claim, damage and expense described in the indemnity contained in subsection (a) of this Section, as incurred, but only with respect to untrue statements or omissions, or alleged untrue statements or omissions, made in the Registration Statement (or any amendment thereto), including the Rule 430A Information or any preliminary prospectus, any Issuer Free Writing Prospectus or the Prospectus (or any amendment or supplement thereto) in reliance upon and in conformity with written information furnished to the Company by such Underwriter through Merrill Lynch expressly for use therein.

(d)   *Actions against Parties; Notification.* Each indemnified party shall give notice as promptly as reasonably practicable to each indemnifying party of any action commenced against it in respect of which indemnity may be sought hereunder, but failure to so notify an indemnifying party shall not relieve such indemnifying party from any liability hereunder to the extent it is not materially prejudiced as a result thereof and in any event shall not relieve it from any liability which it may have otherwise than on account of this indemnity agreement. In the case of parties indemnified pursuant to Section 6(a) or 6(b) above, counsel to the indemnified parties shall be selected by Merrill Lynch, and, in the case of parties indemnified pursuant to Section 6(c) above, counsel to the indemnified parties shall be

21

selected by the Company. An indemnifying party may participate at its own expense in the defense of any such action; provided, however, that counsel to the indemnifying party shall not (except with the consent of the indemnified party) also be counsel to the indemnified party. In no event shall the indemnifying parties be liable for fees and expenses of more than one counsel (in addition to any local counsel) separate from their own counsel for all indemnified parties in connection with any one action or separate but similar or related actions in the same jurisdiction arising out of the same general allegations or circumstances. No indemnifying party shall, without the prior written consent of the indemnified parties, settle or compromise or consent to the entry of any judgment with respect to any litigation, or any investigation or proceeding by any governmental agency or body, commenced or threatened, or any claim whatsoever in respect of which indemnification or contribution could be sought under this Section 6 or Section 7 hereof (whether or not the indemnified parties are actual or potential parties thereto), unless such settlement, compromise or consent (i) includes an unconditional release of each indemnified party from all liability arising out of such litigation, investigation, proceeding or claim and (ii) does not include a statement as to or an admission of fault, culpability or a failure to act by or on behalf of any indemnified party.

(e) *Settlement without Consent if Failure to Reimburse.* If at any time an indemnified party shall have requested an indemnifying party to reimburse the indemnified party for fees and expenses of counsel, such indemnifying party agrees that it shall be liable for any settlement of the nature contemplated by Section 6(a)(ii) effected without its written consent if (i) such settlement is entered into more than 45 days after receipt by such indemnifying party of the aforesaid request, (ii) such indemnifying party shall have received notice of the terms of such settlement at least 30 days prior to such settlement being entered into and (iii) such indemnifying party shall not have reimbursed such indemnified party in accordance with such request prior to the date of such settlement.

(f) *Other Agreements with Respect to Indemnification.* The provisions of this Section shall not affect any agreement among the Company and the Selling Stockholders with respect to indemnification.

SECTION 7.   Contribution. If the indemnification provided for in Section 6 hereof is for any reason unavailable to or insufficient to hold harmless an indemnified party in respect of any losses, liabilities, claims, damages or expenses referred to therein, then each indemnifying party shall contribute to the aggregate amount of such losses, liabilities, claims, damages and expenses incurred by such indemnified party, as incurred, (i) in such proportion as is appropriate to reflect the relative benefits received by the Company and the Selling Stockholders on the one hand and the Underwriters on the other hand from the offering of the Securities pursuant to this Agreement or (ii) if the allocation provided by clause (i) is not permitted by applicable law, in such proportion as is appropriate to reflect not only the relative benefits referred to in clause (i) above but also the relative fault of the Company and the Selling Stockholders on the one hand and of the Underwriters on the other hand in connection with the statements or omissions which resulted in such losses, liabilities, claims, damages or expenses, as well as any other relevant equitable considerations.

The relative benefits received by the Company and the Selling Stockholders on the one hand and the Underwriters on the other hand in connection with the offering of the Securities pursuant to this Agreement shall be deemed to be in the same respective proportions as the total net proceeds from the offering of the Securities pursuant to this Agreement (before deducting expenses) received by the Company and the Selling Stockholders and the total underwriting discount received by the Underwriters, in each case as set forth on the cover of the Prospectus bear to the aggregate initial public offering price of the Securities as set forth on the cover of the Prospectus.

22

The relative fault of the Company and the Selling Stockholders on the one hand and the Underwriters on the other hand shall be determined by reference to, among other things, whether any such untrue or alleged untrue statement of a material fact or omission or alleged omission to state a material fact relates to information supplied by the Company or the Selling Stockholders or by the Underwriters and the parties' relative intent, knowledge, access to information and opportunity to correct or prevent such statement or omission.

The Company, the Selling Stockholders and the Underwriters agree that it would not be just and equitable if contribution pursuant to this Section 7 were determined by pro rata allocation (even if the Underwriters were treated as one entity for such purpose) or by any other method of allocation which does not take account of the equitable considerations referred to above in this Section 7. The aggregate amount of losses, liabilities, claims, damages and expenses incurred by an indemnified party and referred to above in this Section 7 shall be deemed to include any legal or other expenses reasonably incurred by such indemnified party in investigating, preparing or defending against any litigation, or any investigation or proceeding by any governmental agency or body, commenced or threatened, or any claim whatsoever based upon any such untrue or alleged untrue statement or omission or alleged omission.

Notwithstanding the provisions of this Section 7, no Underwriter shall be required to contribute any amount in excess of the amount by which the total price at which the Securities underwritten by it and distributed to the public were offered to the public exceeds the amount of any damages which such Underwriter has otherwise been required to pay by reason of any such untrue or alleged untrue statement or omission or alleged omission. Notwithstanding the provisions of this Section 7, no Selling Stockholder shall be required to contribute any amount in excess of the gross proceeds received by such Selling Stockholder from the sale of the Securities in the public offering exceeds the amount of any damages which such Selling Stockholder has otherwise been required to pay by reason of any such untrue or alleged untrue statement or omission or alleged omission.

No person guilty of fraudulent misrepresentation (within the meaning of Section 11(f) of the 1933 Act) shall be entitled to contribution from any person who was not guilty of such fraudulent misrepresentation.

For purposes of this Section 7, each person, if any, who controls an Underwriter within the meaning of Section 15 of the 1933 Act or Section 20 of the 1934 Act and each Underwriter's Affiliates and selling agents shall have the same rights to contribution as such Underwriter, and each director of the Company, each officer of the Company who signed the Registration Statement, and each person, if any, who controls the Company or any Selling Stockholder within the meaning of Section 15 of the 1933 Act or Section 20 of the 1934 Act shall have the same rights to contribution as the Company or such Selling Stockholder, as the case may be. The Underwriters' respective obligations to contribute pursuant to this Section 7 are several in proportion to the number of Initial Securities set forth opposite their respective names in Schedule A hereto and not joint.

The provisions of this Section shall not affect any agreement among the Company and the Selling Stockholders with respect to contribution.

SECTION 8.   Representations, Warranties and Agreements to Survive. All representations, warranties and agreements contained in this Agreement or in certificates of officers of the Company or any of its subsidiaries or the Selling Stockholders submitted pursuant hereto, shall remain operative and in full force and effect regardless of (i) any investigation made by or on behalf of any Underwriter or its Affiliates or selling agents, any person controlling any Underwriter, its officers or directors, any person controlling the Company or any person controlling any Selling Stockholder and (ii) delivery of and payment for the Securities.

23

SECTION 9.   Termination of Agreement.

(a)   *Termination; General.* The Representative may terminate this Agreement, by notice to the Company and the Selling Stockholders, at any time at or prior to Closing Time (i) if there has been, since the time of execution of this Agreement or since the respective dates as of which information is given in the Prospectus or General Disclosure Package, any material adverse change in the condition, financial or otherwise, or in the earnings, business affairs or business prospects of the Company and its subsidiaries considered as one enterprise, whether or not arising in the ordinary course of business, or (ii) if there has occurred any material adverse change in the financial markets in the United States or the international financial markets, any outbreak of hostilities or escalation thereof or other calamity or crisis or any change or development involving a prospective change in national or international political, financial or economic conditions, in each case the effect of which is such as to make it, in the judgment of the Representative, impracticable or inadvisable to market the Securities or to enforce contracts for the sale of the Securities, or (iii) if trading in any securities of the Company has been suspended or materially limited by the Commission or the Nasdaq Global Market, or if trading generally on the American Stock Exchange, the New York Stock Exchange or the Nasdaq Global Market has been suspended or materially limited, or minimum or maximum prices for trading have been fixed, or maximum ranges for prices have been required, by any of said exchanges or by such system or by order of the Commission, FINRA or any other governmental authority, or (iv) a material disruption has occurred in commercial banking or securities settlement or clearance services in the United States, or (v) if a banking moratorium has been declared by either Federal or New York authorities.

(b)   *Liabilities.* If this Agreement is terminated pursuant to this Section, such termination shall be without liability of any party to any other party except as provided in Section 4 hereof, and provided further that Sections 1, 6, 7 and 8 shall survive such termination and remain in full force and effect.

SECTION 10.   Default by One or More of the Underwriters. If one or more of the Underwriters shall fail at Closing Time or a Date of Delivery to purchase the Securities which it or they are obligated to purchase under this Agreement (the "Defaulted Securities"), the Representative shall have the right, within 24 hours thereafter, to make arrangements for one or more of the non-defaulting Underwriters, or any other underwriters, to purchase all, but not less than all, of the Defaulted Securities in such amounts as may be agreed upon and upon the terms herein set forth; if, however, the Representative shall not have completed such arrangements within such 24-hour period, then:

(i)   if the number of Defaulted Securities does not exceed 10% of the number of Securities to be purchased on such date, each of the non-defaulting Underwriters shall be obligated, severally and not jointly, to purchase the full amount thereof in the proportions that their respective underwriting obligations hereunder bear to the underwriting obligations of all non-defaulting Underwriters, or

(ii)   if the number of Defaulted Securities exceeds 10% of the number of Securities to be purchased on such date, this Agreement or, with respect to any Date of Delivery which occurs after the Closing Time, the obligation of the Underwriters to purchase and of the Company to sell the Option Securities to be purchased and sold on such Date of Delivery shall terminate without liability on the part of any non-defaulting Underwriter.

No action taken pursuant to this Section shall relieve any defaulting Underwriter from liability in respect of its default.

24

In the event of any such default which does not result in a termination of this Agreement or, in the case of a Date of Delivery which is after the Closing Time, which does not result in a termination of the obligation of the Underwriters to purchase and the Company to sell the relevant Option Securities, as the case may be, either the (i) Representative or (ii) the Company and any Selling Stockholder shall have the right to postpone Closing Time or the relevant Date of Delivery, as the case may be, for a period not exceeding seven days in order to effect any required changes in the Registration Statement or Prospectus or in any other documents or arrangements. As used herein, the term "Underwriter" includes any person substituted for an Underwriter under this Section 10.

SECTION 11.   Default by one or more of the Selling Stockholders or the Company. (a) If a Selling Stockholder shall fail at Closing Time to sell and deliver the number of Securities which such Selling Stockholder is obligated to sell hereunder, and the remaining Selling Stockholders do not exercise the right hereby granted to increase, pro rata or otherwise, the number of Securities to be sold by them hereunder to the total number to be sold by all Selling Stockholders as set forth in Schedule B hereto, then the Underwriters may, at option of the Representative, by notice from the Representative to the Company and the non-defaulting Selling Stockholders, either (i) terminate this Agreement without any liability on the fault of any non-defaulting party except that the provisions of Sections 1, 4, 6, 7 and 8 shall remain in full force and effect or (ii) elect to purchase the Securities which the non-defaulting Selling Stockholders and the Company have agreed to sell hereunder. No action taken pursuant to this Section 11 shall relieve any Selling Stockholder so defaulting from liability, if any, in respect of such default.

In the event of a default by any Selling Stockholder as referred to in this Section 11, each of the Representative, the Company and the non-defaulting Selling Stockholders shall have the right to postpone Closing Time for a period not exceeding seven days in order to effect any required change in the Registration Statement or Prospectus or in any other documents or arrangements.

(b) If the Company shall fail at Closing Time or at the Date of Delivery to sell the number of Securities that it is obligated to sell hereunder, then this Agreement shall terminate without any liability on the part of any nondefaulting party; provided, however, that the provisions of Sections 1, 4, 6, 7 and 8 shall remain in full force and effect. No action taken pursuant to this Section shall relieve the Company from liability, if any, in respect of such default.

SECTION 12.   Notices. All notices and other communications hereunder shall be in writing and shall be deemed to have been duly given if mailed or transmitted by any standard form of telecommunication. Notices to the Underwriters shall be directed to the Representative at 4 World Financial Center, New York, New York 10080, attention of •; notices to the Company shall be directed to it at 799 Market Street, 4th Floor, San Francisco, California 94103, attention of •; and notices to the Selling Stockholders shall be directed to •, attention of •.

SECTION 13.   No Advisory or Fiduciary Relationship. Each of the Company and each Selling Stockholder acknowledges and agrees that (a) the purchase and sale of the Securities pursuant to this Agreement, including the determination of the public offering price of the Securities and any related discounts and commissions, is an arm's-length commercial transaction between the Company and the Selling Stockholder, on the one hand, and the several Underwriters, on the other hand, (b) in connection with the offering contemplated hereby and the process leading to such transaction each Underwriter is and has been acting solely as a principal and is not the agent or fiduciary of the Company or any Selling Stockholder, or its respective stockholders, creditors, employees or any other party, (c) no Underwriter has assumed or will assume an advisory or fiduciary responsibility in favor of the Company or any Selling Stockholder with respect to the offering contemplated hereby or the process leading thereto (irrespective of whether such Underwriter has advised or is currently advising the Company or any Selling Stockholder on other matters) and no Underwriter has any obligation to the Company or any

25

Selling Stockholder with respect to the offering contemplated hereby except the obligations expressly set forth in this Agreement, (d) the Underwriters and their respective affiliates may be engaged in a broad range of transactions that involve interests that differ from those of each of the Company and each Selling Stockholder, and (e) the Underwriters have not provided any legal, accounting, regulatory or tax advice with respect to the offering contemplated hereby and the Company and each of the Selling Stockholders has consulted its own respective legal, accounting, regulatory and tax advisors to the extent it deemed appropriate.

SECTION 14.   Parties. This Agreement shall each inure to the benefit of and be binding upon the Underwriters, the Company and the Selling Stockholders and their respective successors. Nothing expressed or mentioned in this Agreement is intended or shall be construed to give any person, firm or corporation, other than the Underwriters, the Company and the Selling Stockholders and their respective successors and the controlling persons and officers and directors referred to in Sections 6 and 7 and their heirs and legal representatives, any legal or equitable right, remedy or claim under or in respect of this Agreement or any provision herein contained. This Agreement and all conditions and provisions hereof are intended to be for the sole and exclusive benefit of the Underwriters, the Company and the Selling Stockholders and their respective successors, and said controlling persons and officers and directors and their heirs and legal representatives, and for the benefit of no other person, firm or corporation. No purchaser of Securities from any Underwriter shall be deemed to be a successor by reason merely of such purchase.

SECTION 15.   GOVERNING LAW. THIS AGREEMENT SHALL BE GOVERNED BY AND CONSTRUED IN ACCORDANCE WITH THE LAWS OF THE STATE OF NEW YORK.

SECTION 16.   TIME. TIME SHALL BE OF THE ESSENCE OF THIS AGREEMENT. EXCEPT AS OTHERWISE SET FORTH HEREIN, SPECIFIED TIMES OF DAY REFER TO NEW YORK CITY TIME.

SECTION 17.   Counterparts. This Agreement may be executed in any number of counterparts, each of which shall be deemed to be an original, but all such counterparts shall together constitute one and the same Agreement.

SECTION 18.   Effect of Headings. The Section headings herein are for convenience only and shall not affect the construction hereof.

26

If the foregoing is in accordance with your understanding of our agreement, please sign and return to the Company and the Attorney-in-Fact for the Selling Stockholders a counterpart hereof, whereupon this instrument, along with all counterparts, will become a binding agreement among the Underwriters, the Company and the Selling Stockholders in accordance with its terms.

Very truly yours,

OPENTABLE, INC.

By _____
   Title:

[Attorney-in-Fact]

By _____
   As Attorney-in-Fact acting on behalf of the Selling Stockholders
   named in Schedule B hereto

CONFIRMED AND ACCEPTED,
      as of the date first above written:

MERRILL LYNCH & CO.

MERRILL LYNCH, PIERCE, FENNER & SMITH
      INCORPORATED

By _____
         Authorized Signatory

For itself and as Representative of the other Underwriters named in Schedule A hereto.

27